Rhetoric thoroughly infused the world and literature of Greco-Roman antiquity. This *Companion* provides a comprehensive overview of rhetorical theory and practice in that world, from Homer to early Christianity, accessible to students and non-specialists, whether within classics or from other periods and disciplines. Its basic premise is that rhetoric is less a discrete object to be grasped and mastered than a hotly contested set of practices that include disputes over the very definition of rhetoric itself. Standard treatments of ancient oratory tend to take it too much on its own terms and to isolate it unduly from other social and cultural concerns. This volume provides an overview of the shape and scope of the problems while also identifying core themes and propositions: for example, persuasion, virtue, and public life are virtual constants. But they mix and mingle differently, and the contents designated by each of these terms can also shift.

A complete list of books in the series is at the back of the book.

THE CAMBRIDGE
COMPANION TO
ANCIENT RHETORIC

EDITED BY
ERIK GUNDERSON

CAMBRIDGE UNIVERSITY PRESS
Cambridge, New York, Melbourne, Madrid, Cape Town, Singapore, São Paulo, Delhi

Cambridge University Press
The Edinburgh Building, Cambridge CB2 8RU, UK

Published in the United States of America by Cambridge University Press, New York

www.cambridge.org
Information on this title: www.cambridge.org/9780521677868

© Cambridge University Press 2009

First published 2009

Printed in the United Kingdom at the University Press, Cambridge

A catalogue record for this publication is available from the British Library

Library of Congress Cataloging-in-Publication Data
The Cambridge companion to ancient rhetoric / edited by Erik Gunderson.
p.   cm.
Includes bibliographical references and indexes.
ISBN 978-0-521-86054-3 – ISBN 978-0-521-67786-8 (paperback)
1. Rhetoric, Ancient.   I. Gunderson, Erik.   II. Title.

PA181.C36 2009
808′.0938–dc22

2009010979

ISBN 978-0-521-86054-3 hardback
ISBN 978-0-521-67786-8 paperback

CONTENTS

CONTENTS

NOTES ON CONTRIBUTORS

WILLIAM W. BATSTONE is Professor of Greek and Latin at The Ohio State University. His major interests concern the intersections between modern theories of culture, psychology, literature, history, and rhetoric and the ancient practice of literature and the performance of self. He especially studies the prose and poetry of the Roman Republic. He has written on Plautus, Sallust, Caesar, Catullus, Cicero, Vergil, Horace, and Propertius, including a book (with Cynthia Damon) on Julius Caesar's *Civil War.*

JOY CONNOLLY is Associate Professor of Classics at New York University. Her work includes *The State of Speech: Rhetoric and Political Thought in Ancient Rome* (2007) and articles on Latin poetry, Greek imperial culture, and the seventeenth- and eighteenth-century reception of classical texts. Currently she is writing *Talk about Virtue*, a book about Roman republicanism and its relevance for contemporary political theory, and essays on Vergil and the younger Pliny.

JOHN DUGAN is Associate Professor of Classics at the University at Buffalo and co-editor of the journal *Arethusa*. He is the author of *Making a New Man: Ciceronian Self-Fashioning in the Rhetorical Works* (2005). He has also published articles on the interaction between ancient medicine and literary theory and modern critical approaches to Roman rhetoric. He is currently working on a project related to Cicero's political and legal theory.

SIMON GOLDHILL is Professor of Greek at Cambridge University, and a Fellow of King's College. He has published widely on many aspects of Greek literature and its relation to Greek culture and to the classical tradition. His books include *Reading Greek Tragedy* (1986), *The Poet's Voice* (1989), *Foucault's Virginity* (1998), *Who Needs Greek?* (2000), and most recently *How to Stage Greek Tragedy Today* (2008) and *Jerusalem, City of Longing* (2008). Professor Goldhill has also taught at Paris, Princeton, Chicago, and lectured all over the world.

ERIK GUNDERSON is Associate Professor of Classics at the University of Toronto. He is the author of *Staging Masculinity: The Rhetoric of Performance in the Roman*

World (2000), *Declamation, Paternity and Roman Identity: Authority, and the Rhetorical Self* (2003), and Nox Philologiae: *Aulus Gellius and the Fantasy of the Ancient Library* (2009). His research interests include ancient rhetoric, Latin prose, and literary theory.

MALCOLM HEATH is Professor of Greek Language and Literature at the University of Leeds. His publications on ancient rhetoric include *Hermogenes on Issues: Strategies of Argument in Later Greek Rhetoric* (1995) and *Menander: A Rhetor in Context* (2004). He is also the author of *The Poetics of Greek Tragedy* (1987), *Political Comedy in Aristophanes* (1987), *Unity in Greek Poetics* (1989), and *Interpreting Classical Texts* (2002), and he has translated Aristotle's *Poetics* for Penguin Classics (1996). He is currently working on a study of Aristotle's anthropology of poetry, as a preliminary step towards the long-term goal of a theoretical commentary on the *Poetics*.

JOHN HENDERSON is Professor of Classics at the University of Cambridge and a Fellow of King's College. His books on Latin authors include monographs on Plautus, Phaedrus, Seneca, Statius, Pliny, Juvenal, and Isidore, besides general studies of epic, comedy, satire, history, art, culture, and the history of classics.

JON HESK is Senior Lecturer in Greek and Classical Studies at the University of St. Andrews. He is the author of *Deception and Democracy in Classical Athens* (2000) and *Sophocles' Ajax* (2003). He is currently working on a number of projects to do with Greek drama and Greek rhetoric.

PETER MACK is Professor of English and Comparative Literature at the University of Warwick. His books include *Renaissance Argument: Valla and Agricola in the Traditions of Rhetoric and Dialectic* (1993) and *Elizabethan Rhetoric: Theory and Practice* (2002). He edited the journal *Rhetorica* 1998–2002. He is currently working on studies of Montaigne and Shakespeare and a History of Renaissance rhetoric.

TODD PENNER is Associate Professor of Religious Studies and Director of the Gender Studies Program at Austin College (Texas). He is author of *In Praise of Christian Origins: Stephen and the Hellenists in Lukan Apologetic Historiography* (2004). Most recently, he has focused on the secular modern formations of biblical scholarship. Together with Caroline Vander Stichele, he has edited several collections of essays dealing with gender in ancient religious discourses, the early Christian book of Acts, feminist and post-colonial criticisms applied to biblical traditions, and method and theory in the study of religion. They have also co-authored a gender-critical introduction to early Christian literature.

JAMES I. PORTER is Professor of Classics and Comparative Literature at the University of California, Irvine. His research areas are in literature, aesthetics, and intellectual history. He is the author of *Nietzsche and the Philology of the Future* (2000) and *The Invention of Dionysus: An Essay on The Birth of Tragedy* (2000), and editor of *Constructions of the Classical Body* (1999) and *Classical Pasts: The Classical Traditions of Greece and Rome* (2006). His book *The Origins of Aesthetic Inquiry in Ancient Greece: Matter, Sensation and Experience*, is forthcoming from Cambridge University Press. His next projects include a study of the idea of Homer from antiquity to the present and a study of ancient literary aesthetics after Aristotle.

DAVID ROSENBLOOM is Senior Lecturer in Classics at Victoria University of Wellington, New Zealand and Visiting Associate Professor of Classics at Johns Hopkins University. In addition to a book on Aeschylus' *Persians* in the Duckworth Companions to Greek and Roman Tragedy series, he has published on tragedy, comedy, oratory, and fifth-century Athenian history.

CATHERINE STEEL is Professor of Classics at the University of Glasgow. She is the author of *Cicero, Rhetoric and Empire* (2001), *Reading Cicero* (2005), and *Roman Oratory* (2006).

CAROLINE VANDER STICHELE is Lecturer in Religious Studies at the University of Amsterdam. Her research focuses on the cultural reception of biblical characters and images, as well as the rhetoric of gender in early Christianity. Most recently she has been working on the reception of Salome in modern arts. Together with Todd Penner, she has co-authored numerous essays on gender constructions and ideology in the book of Acts, the writings of Paul, and other early Christian texts. They have also co-written several essays related to the reception of the Bible in film, and have just completed a co-authored gender-critical introduction to early Christian literature.

ROBERT WARDY teaches philosophy and classics at St. Catharine's College, the University of Cambridge. He is the author of *The Birth of Rhetoric: Gorgias, Plato and their Successors* (1996), *Aristotle in China: Language, Categories and Translation* (2000) and *Doing Greek Philosophy* (2006). His research interests include theories of rationality and motivation.

VICTORIA WOHL is Associate Professor of Classics at the University of Toronto. She is the author of *Intimate Commerce: Exchange, Gender, and Subjectivity in Greek Tragedy* (1998) and *Love among the Ruins: The Erotics of Democracy in Classical Athens* (2003). Her current project is a study of the legal discourse of classical Athens, *Law's Cosmos: Juridical Discourse in Athenian Forensic Oratory* (forthcoming).

NANCY WORMAN is Associate Professor of Classics and Comparative Literature at Barnard College, Columbia University. She works on Greek drama, Greek and Roman rhetoric, and ancient literary criticism. Her latest book, *Abusive Mouths in Classical Athens* (2008), looks at the imagery of insult and appetite in Greek drama, oratory, and rhetorical theory. She is currently at work on a new project that explores landscape imagery in ancient literary criticism.

ACKNOWLEDGMENTS

No extended voyage is ever without its difficulties. When imagining the far shore before even formally proposing the journey, I did not neglect to picture for myself in detail the horrors of the deep, horrors that are properly feared by all such as are brazen enough to set sail. Nevertheless I cannot but acknowledge that the whole voyage has been far more reminiscent of a lazy afternoon punting on the Cam than it has been akin to the saga of a sea-tossed Ulysses. Editors, though, like to swap stories of Storm and Strife such as might impress a pint-side audience of land lubbers and credulous graduate students. Mine will assuredly be fictions. Accordingly, if I should succumb to generic dictates and compose for such ears some lay rehearsing all the requisite sorrows, one wherein the narrative of my pleasure cruise is transformed into some yarn of a periplus off so far as monstrous Colchis and back again, then a goodly measure of the blame must accrue to my many companions of these several years: as a consequence of their hard work I have been given the tools with which to cause such bald lies to be mistaken for the truth. I gratefully declare myself to have been the first to receive an education in rhetoric from this volume.

Generosity, effort, dedication, and professionalism – all unglamorous, but each so very welcome – were evinced by everyone at Cambridge University Press. Michael Sharp and Elizabeth Noden can be named. But the anonymous did their part as well. And I owe them all a debt of gratitude.

Introduction

First and foremost: what is rhetoric?[1]
(Quintilian, *Institutes* 2.15.1)

Barring failures of reasoning, conclusions flow more or less inevitably from premises. The choice of a definition of rhetoric is accordingly a decisive moment for any account of rhetoric. Aristotle immediately follows his propositions concerning the role of definitions by enjoining a definition of his own: "Let rhetoric be the capacity to discover the possible means of persuasion concerning any subject."[2] However, the number of available definitions of rhetoric embarrasses in more than one sense. On the one hand it is clear that Aristotle's account of rhetoric is itself reacting to other contemporary competing accounts. And, on the other hand, Aristotle's definition is not the last one that will be offered. For example, Quintilian chooses, "Knowing how to speak well."[3] Quintilian's definition itself comes after a long and detailed discussion of the variety of other available definitions, including Aristotle's.[4]

Post-classical thought also offers its own modifications of these ancient positions as well as some novelties. Kant yokes rhetoric and poetry when describing the arts of speech: "The rhetorical arts are oratory and poetry." He goes on to define rhetoric as "the art of carrying on a serious business of the understanding as if it were a free play of the imagination" and poetry as "the art of conducting a free play of the imagination as if it were a serious

---

[1] *Ante omnia: quid sit rhetorice.* The attentive will observe both that we are well into the *Institutio* itself and that Quintilian has been using this term for a while now before he elects to declare the primacy of the task of defining it.

[2] Ἔστω δὴ ἡ ῥητορικὴ δύναμις περὶ ἕκαστον τοῦ θεωρῆσαι τὸ ἐνδεχόμενον πιθανόν; *Rhetoric* 1355b25–26.

[3] *Rhetoricen esse bene dicendi scientiam; Institutes* 2.15.38. *Scientia* implies more than mere knowing, though: it entails a solid understanding of the subject. The term corresponds to and often translates the Greek word *epistēmē*.

[4] Further discussion of Quintilian's history of definitions can be found in my chapter in this volume.

business of the understanding."[5] Nietzsche, who cites and modifies Kant's portrait of rhetoric, recognizes that defining rhetoric is a fundamental move that nevertheless routinely yields difficulties:

> Generally speaking, the moderns are inaccurate in their definitions, whereas the competition over the correct definition of rhetoric goes on throughout the whole of antiquity, and specifically among philosophers and orators ... Those who avoided giving a strict definition have at least sought to determine the orator's *telos* or *officium* [end or task]. This is the *peithein, dicendo persuadere* [persuade, persuade through speaking]: it was difficult to incorporate this into the *horismos* [definition] because the effect is not the essence of the thing, and furthermore, persuasion does not always take place even with the best orator.[6]

Nietzsche himself ultimately declares that "the rhetorical" is none other than "*a further development*, guided by the clear light of the understanding, of *the artistic means which are already found in language*."[7] For Nietzsche, then, language is always already rhetorical. Nietzsche's definition offers a useful point of departure for the present volume: it is post-classical, but both engaged with and influenced by the ancient accounts. The critic observes how the potential has passed into the actual. One seeks to explicate a genealogy of rhetoric.

It is possible to avoid overt engagement with later developments in the history of rhetoric, but it is hard to imagine that one can avoid taking a stand, either implicitly or explicitly, relative to the question of rhetoric when constituting a Companion to it. For what, after all, is the thing to which such a volume is addressing itself? Whose Companion is this?

I cannot answer this question of the essence of ancient rhetoric. At least I cannot answer it without doing the reader an injustice disguised as a benefaction. Let me step back, then, to explore how this difficulty is but one of many that have confronted me, and how this volume is of itself an attempt both to give a sensible form to such questions and to begin to answer them even as it regularly disputes the proposition that any simple answer could be available to us. My first difficulty: where are we to find a meta-discourse that can capture ancient rhetoric and deliver it up to us as a discrete object, a thing to be known, and known completely? Aristotle asks us to theorize, Quintilian promises us knowledge, but too many questions

---

[5] Kant 1951 §51.

[6] Nietzsche 1989: 5 (translation modified).

[7] Nietzsche 1989: 21 (original emphasis).

are begged if we proceed at once either to speculation or to memorizing our lessons.

So there are basic epistemological issues before us. Among them is the meaning of the very word "rhetoric" itself.[8] Scrupulous speakers of English could systematically use two discrete words when speaking about the science of speaking well and speaking well itself. The former is rhetoric, the latter is oratory.[9] One word is taken from the Greek, the other from Latin. The one term knows, the other does. However, a rigid distinction between the two terms "rhetoric" and "oratory" does not reflect standard English usage: the first entry (1.a.) for "oratory" in the *Oxford English Dictionary* ends by offering as a synonym the word "rhetoric," and the adjective "oratorical" (s.v.) is similarly glossed in its very first entry with the word "rhetorical."

A desire for rhetorical consistency when deploying the terms rhetoric and oratory is quite conducive to a number of admirable ends. The distinction will often be observed below in the name of neatly distinguishing theory ("proper") from practice ("proper"). However, such rigor potentially obscures any number of genealogical questions pertaining to the emergence of the (perhaps not entirely coherent) concept of rhetoric itself. We might attend, for example, to the debate at Rome over what, if anything, to do when it comes to translating the Greek term *rhētorikē* into Latin. Quintilian rejects *oratoria* and *oratrix* and decides merely to transliterate: *rhetorice*.[10] Quintilian divides *rhetorice*: it covers the art, the artist, and the work.[11] The first is "knowing how to speak well" (*bene dicendi scientia*), the second is "the orator" (*orator*), and the third is "good oratory" (*bona oratio*). Note in particular that the genus, *rhetorice*, becomes homonymous with one of the species into which it has been divided: the first of these, "knowing how to speak well," gives the very words of Quintilian's own gloss on the meaning of the term *rhetorice*.

---

[8] Connoisseurs of rhetorical theory will be able at once to categorize this dispute. This is the *stasis horikē* (Lat. *status finitionis*): "What is the proper terminology with which to describe what has happened?" See Hermogenes, *On Issues* 2.15. Compare Quintilian, *Institutes* 3.6.5 and 7.3.2–4. See also the first appendix to this volume.

[9] *OED*, 2nd edn., s.v. "Rhetoric (n.1) 1.a.": "The art of using language so as to persuade or influence others; the body of rules to be observed by a speaker or writer in order that he may express himself with eloquence." *OED*, 2nd edn., s.v., "Oratory (n.2) 1.b.": "The exercise of eloquence; the delivery of orations or speeches; rhetorical or eloquent language."

[10] Quintilian, *Institutes* 2.14.1.

[11] Quintilian, *Institutes* 2.14.5: *igitur rhetorice (iam enim sine metu cauillationis utemur hac appellatione) sic, ut opinor, optime diuidetur ut de arte, de artifice, de opere dicamus.*

The English word "rhetoric," despite a certain investment in the theoretical in contradistinction to the practical, itself entertains some of this same breadth found in Quintilian's *rhetorice*, a word that though allegedly explanatory itself nevertheless still requires further explanation. In English as well "rhetoric" is a governing category. "Rhetoric" is likewise regularly used not just to designate the art, but also its products, especially in such disparaging contemporary idioms as "that's all just so much rhetoric."[12] In fact "rhetoric" can also be very broad indeed and thus a synonym for technique or style.[13] And, though such has yet to appear in the *OED*, the Merriam–Webster Dictionary already has "discourse" as a synonym for rhetoric.[14] And in practice a good many contemporary scholarly uses of the word rhetoric are already juxtaposing the expansive sense of rhetoric to the even more expansive understanding of the term "discourse." One has the sense that the trajectory of the English word is sending it in the direction of the protean Greek term *logos*.

Such a trend entails the unwriting of a segment of the history of rhetoric itself. In Plato's *Gorgias* Socrates is keen on outmaneuvering his interlocutor Gorgias. First, he refuses to listen to a demonstration (*epideixis*) from Gorgias concerning the art of rhetoric.[15] As epideictic is itself one of the species of oratory, one can see here the philosopher's resistance to submitting himself to a rhetoric of rhetoric. Instead philosophical dialogue (*dialekhthēnai*) will elicit a definition: we are only interested in a philosophy of rhetoric. And Socrates is quick to commit Gorgias to a limited definition. The parties agree: rhetoric is a science (*epistēmē*) whose object is language/discourse/accounts (*peri logous*), but its object is not every sort of *logos*.[16] For example, medicine covers a specific discursive field: it is the science of that subset of *logoi* that pertain to illness (*tous ge peri ta nosēmata*).[17] At issue, then, will be exactly which *logoi* rhetoric is authorized to teach. One ought to note that in order to delimit the domain of rhetoric, we have to leave open the ambiguous question of *logos*, the word for words. Philosophy, for its own purposes, has made rhetoric into something smaller than what it might otherwise have been.[18]

[12] *OED*, 2nd edn., s.v. "Rhetoric (n.1) 2.b."
[13] *OED*, 2nd edn., s.v. "Rhetoric (n.1) 2.e."
[14] "Rhetoric"; www.merriam-webster.com/dictionary/rhetoric (accessed May 15, 2008).
[15] See Plato, *Gorgias* 447a–c.
[16] Plato, *Gorgias* 449d9–e4.
[17] Plato, *Gorgias* 450a4.
[18] See Wardy's chapter in this volume as well as Wardy 1996 for a much more detailed account of the negative relationship between rhetoric and philosophy, which yields the that and the not-that.

An "imprecise" deployment of the term rhetoric that straddles various lexical possibilities rather than committing itself to designating always and only the science of speaking well (*hē tekhnē rhētorikē*) need not be taken as mere slovenly use, a capitulation to the uneducated morass of idiom, and a falling away from theoretical precision. Instead it is potentially an intervention in the way one will approach the question of the "proper" domain of rhetoric itself. What is the origin of this propriety, of this theoretical specificity? To deny that there is a question or to depict it as a settled question, these are themselves rhetorical tropes. Conversely one can imagine a rejoinder (*cauillatio*) to my advocacy of the expansive use: I am assuming my own conclusion. Such a vice, though, is permitted in an introduction, provided that the arguments that follow ultimately support this initial claim.

But let us go back to enumerating some of the problems of constituting a Companion to ancient rhetoric. There are a variety of practical concerns to address as well. What sense does it make to speak of ancient rhetoric? When does "antiquity" begin? When does it end? Here one could argue at some length, or, eschewing explicit determinations, merely speak as one usually speaks and silently contribute to the established consensus of the scholarly community that precedes. In any case, there are at least one thousand years of material available to any who would wish to take it up. Centuries on either side can be given or taken according to one's pleasure – and not one's erudite certainty. And, naturally, endless controversy could erupt around which authors are given how much space once the preliminary determination of period has been made. Moreover, given the relatively expansive sense of rhetorical culture within which this volume operates, while some less familiar rhetorical authors – such as the comic poet Plautus – will be heard from, nevertheless some of the canonical ones will be given less space than that to which they are accustomed. Perhaps, like the worthy ____ they will never even be mentioned.

By "ancient" English idiom also frequently designates "ancient Greek and Latin." And so we make another major assumption. It would also be useful to explore the speech traditions of the ancient Mediterranean cultures in general before settling on Athens and Rome: the peoples of Asia Minor, other early Italic civilizations, and even various "barbarian" cultures such as those of North Africa or Northern Europe might offer useful points of comparison or even some vital and often neglected elements as we compose our portrait of rhetoric, a portrait that might otherwise be satisfied to depict a specifically fifth-century BCE Greek invention. Nevertheless, as Robert Wardy argues below, it is not at all inappropriate to think of rhetoric as the invention of a specific time and place. However, to find the moment of rhetoric's christening is not the same as to fully compass its genealogy. I am especially interested in these genealogical questions. And we ought to note in passing that inheritance law and disputed kinship produced a great deal of rhetorical theory and practice.

To continue with this theme of kinship, though: the question "What is rhetoric?" entails as a corollary knowing what it is not, what is like it, and what is dissimilar from it. One would wish to know its parents, its brothers and sisters, its cousins, its children as well as how it gets on with them. Of course, we could be very narrow and ignore the broader family tree: rhetoric would be anything that the teachers of rhetoric designated as such. The ancient rhetorical handbooks would be our guide here. There would be no shortage of explicit answers to our question if this were the path we opted to take. But such only brings us back to our first observation: there are too many handbook definitions even if we wanted to appreciate rhetoric only on those terms. And yet if we again look to ancient orations and take our lead from the practice of oratory when rethinking the question of the theory of rhetoric, we will find these orations to be obsessed with characterizing a man by his family, his friends, and his enemies. A specific issue is seldom argued, a whole life is regularly narrated. Narrow definitions are eschewed. Just about everything is fair play. One needs, one is told, to look at the big picture.

And yet this big picture is not at all a neutral image taken in harsh light by the crime-scene photographer. It is a landscape done in watercolors, a portrait drawn in charcoal, a study in oils. The media can be mixed. Perspective is always an issue. The question of context regularly falls back into a problem of text. In an ancient oration we are regularly either given plenty of context or (strategically) assumed to share certain key assumptions with the speaker. But such a context is, of course, a partisan context, a one-sided context, a context that inevitably leads us to a specific verdict. And the big picture can become very big indeed. Isocrates surveys for his fourth-century BCE audience events from the tenth century BCE and the era of the Trojan war.[19] Attacks on enemies regularly survey the whole of their lives as Aeschines does with Timarchus or Cicero with Antonius. It is possible for a speech to cover a great deal of ground even where seemingly narrow questions of law are at issue. Many speeches even consider such to be highly desirable.

[19] See Isocrates, *Panegyricus* 34–37 and *Panathenaicus* 42–48. Compare Tacitus, *Annals* 4.43, where claimants concerning a disputed shrine evoke poems, myths about the children of Heracles, and the dispensations of both Greek kings and Roman magistrates.

Lacking a clear sense of what, when, who, and how, it is hard to make an unambiguous case about rhetoric itself. And so, when I first pondered what it would mean to construct a Companion to ancient rhetoric, I smiled to recall the advice of Lucian's Professor of Rhetoric. The depraved master advises his would-be student as to the essential qualities needed if one wishes to take the easy road to rhetorical mastery: ignorance, insolence, recklessness, shamelessness.[20] It is not even immediately clear that those who undertake the hard road towards explicating rhetoric might not be evincing some of these paradoxical "virtues."

There you have it: a preliminary account of my own aporia.[21] Although oratory can speak exhaustively about anything, nobody can hope to give a comprehensive account of rhetoric.[22] Nevertheless, rhetorical handbooks are almost as old as oratory itself. Despite the difficulty of the task, there has been no shortage of those who have elected to attempt it. Presumably it is not just shamelessness that typifies these works. One might plead instead necessity. For how can one not speak of rhetoric?

As will become abundantly clear below, rhetoric continually argued for its own centrality to ancient culture. These arguments had a great deal of merit. For a substantial period, to be educated and to be trained in rhetoric were nearly identical propositions. The ancient curriculum began with elementary lessons and ended with advanced rhetorical exercises. Imagine an educational system today that presupposed that all children aspired to go to law school and prepared them for that eventuality. Some might diverge from this course; most would drop out somewhere along the way; but a precious few would become consummate barristers. The modern lawyer, though, tends to confine his or her work to the law itself. Conversely the trained speaker of yore was supposed to be skilled in court, listened to on matters of policy, and the spokesperson for the community at times of celebration or sorrow.

This is not, of course, to indicate that the orator did not have a number of important rivals. It is only to indicate that he is one of the leading players in the cultural game of antiquity and one of the ones who stand a substantial chance of "winning" any given contest. Philosophers and poets are also masters of language, and they too make a claim on our attention. They often

---

[20] Lucian, *Professor of Public Speaking* 15: κόμιζε τοίνυν τὸ μέγιστον μὲν τὴν ἀμαθίαν, εἶτα θράσος, ἐπὶ τούτοις δὲ τόλμαν καὶ ἀναισχυντίαν.

[21] Lysias 19.1: "This particular case puts me in quite a bind . . ." (πολλήν μοι ἀπορίαν παρέχει ὁ ἀγὼν οὑτοσί . . .).

[22] Lysias 12.1: "It does not seem hard, men of the jury, to start my accusation, but rather to stop once I get started" (Οὐκ ἄρξασθαί μοι δοκεῖ ἄπορον εἶναι, ὦ ἄνδρες δικασταί, τῆς κατηγορίας, ἀλλὰ παύσασθαι λέγοντι).

plead a case against rhetoric. The elite of birth and of wealth have their own expectations to be taken seriously irrespective of their scholarly credentials. On occasion priests are also capable of making their own pressing demands. There is the raw power of position: the king, the tyrant, and the emperor need not be eloquent in the least for the brute language of force can be all too readily understood by all.

Nevertheless, most of these competing authorities regularly avoid defining themselves against rhetorical authority. Instead they commonly opt to take it up for themselves in at least some measure. Plato uses the arts of speech even as he critiques the orators. Cicero and Seneca use their rhetorical craft to offer, they say, a superior articulation of philosophy. Euripides has listened attentively to the speakers of his day and offers us verse debates. Seneca the Elder shows us Ovid in the rhetoric schoolhouse, enjoying himself with rhetorical games that in some measure reproduce themselves in his witty verse. Herodotus strings together stories and has a sense of the profound rhetoricity of both history and culture. The most stirring passages in Livy are the orations, as are the darkest in Tacitus. Sallust was excerpted for his. The well-born sometimes take exclusive pride in station and find a threat in that upstart rhetoric and its self-siring authority, but others find in it a resource to add to their other advantages. Pericles' family was impeccable, but he is remembered as eloquent and sage, rather than well-born. Caesar had every advantage of birth, and yet his contemporaries would know him as perhaps Rome's second-best orator before they found in him a man who intended to command rather than to persuade. The elder Cato was a new man by birth, an old one by habit, a critic of novel and exotic oratory, and an avid albeit somewhat furtive student of the same. The end of monarchy marks the beginning of a community of speech and persuasion, so the story goes at both Greece and Rome. Conversely the rule of autocrats is measured both by their own speech and by the way they are spoken to. In the imperial age of Rome safe speech becomes its own sort of art.

It should be clear that when reading ancient literature it would be inadequate to set rhetoric off in its own corner, to segregate speeches from plays, for example. Drama has much that is rhetorical in it, and, conversely, oratory itself is regularly quite stagy in its relationship not just to performance but also to persona. A study of "rhetoric in Euripides" is potentially misleading if not at a minimum read in conjunction with something like "drama in Cicero." For it is not immediately clear that the one thing is really "inside" the other.[23]

---

[23] See especially Lycurgus' *Against Leocrates*, where a wealth of dramatic verse has been incorporated into his prose.

The major discourses of antiquity are in a constant and often agonistic dialogue. We should not be over-hasty in judging who has won the debate about debate and successfully subordinated one sort of language to another.

There are a number of introductory texts already available to readers who wish to explore ancient rhetoric. The basic orientation of such a volume can be historical and aim at outlining the evolution of rhetorical theory and oratorical practice over time. The work of George Kennedy exemplifies such an approach. Here the story of rhetoric unfolds as a relatively self-contained narrative obeying its own logic. Or, in a parallel gesture, an introduction to rhetoric can cover authors. The difficulty here is who is left off the list and whether or not some vital theme is thus omitted as well. Similarly such an approach can easily beg questions about the relationship between a life, a body of work, and a major mode of discourse. An overview of oratory can also be more structural and explore various aspects of oratory as outlined in technical discussions of the art from antiquity: deliberative oratory versus judicial oratory, word order, tropes, and so forth. Lausberg's *Handbook of Literary Rhetoric* represents the acme of this method.[24]

One should not underestimate the returns available to those who invest in appreciating ancient orations within the terms set forth by ancient rhetorical theory. It is important to appreciate the canonical structure of an ancient oration: introduction, narration, proofs, and peroration.[25] Divergences from this structure become immediate targets for further reflection: "What has provoked the shift?" Meanwhile knowing the ancient taxonomy of, for example, types of introduction itself gives ready access to useful critical questions: "This is an instance of the 'subtle' approach. Why this instead of a 'direct' introduction? To what extent and in what manner have the virtues of clarity, brevity, and plausibility been pursued or set to one side?" There are three major kinds of oration: legal speeches, deliberative political speeches, and display speeches. Cicero's First Verrine oration is technically a prosecution, but it is governed by a major opening gambit: Cicero assumes the obvious guilt of Verres and shifts over to a largely deliberative mode: "What will people think of you senators on the jury if you acquit such a man?" The speech as a whole is in fact rife with unusual technical features. The interaction between categories itself offers endless opportunities: in Lysias a simple style joined with direct narratives regularly

---

[24] Lausberg 1998.
[25] "The canonical structure": this notion is a (useful) fiction of the moment. See Heath, Hesk, and Steel in this volume for the debates about taxonomy and the efforts at canonizing one version over another.

yields an ethos for the speaker that can be leveraged in the course of the formal segment of the speech dedicated to proofs, especially when it comes to arguments from plausibility which ask the audience to consider the likelihood of a man such as this doing a thing like that.

This volume assumes that its readers will also be reading editions of Demosthenes, Lysias, and Cicero. It also assumes that the notes and introductory materials to such editions will include some degree of nitty-gritty technical analysis of the speech at hand. A "good" edition will note the architecture of the speech, the tropes used in the peroration will be catalogued, and so forth. Rather than reproduce such efforts, this *Companion* aims instead at offering further themes as well as further methodological issues to explore. In a similar vein there is an assumption throughout that one must move beyond the simple application of an ancient theoretical text to an ancient speech. That sort of agenda-setting on the part of a theorist should not be conceded. Nevertheless, the outlines of such theories really do need to be understood. One should keep a copy of something like the *Rhetoric to Herennius* to hand: it is exceptionally explicit, clear, and useful.[26] Cicero, while setting his own agenda for his own text, assumes that his readers already have access to the basic rule-books. He will offer something more: "I'll not rehearse some fixed curriculum drawn from the cradle of that antiquated and childish instruction of my youth ... It's not that I scorn those things that the Greek teachers of rhetoric have left behind, but these things are readily available and to hand for all. My version of them would not explicate them any more elegantly nor express them any more plainly..."[27] The rhetoric of Cicero's own rhetorical theory is patent: he is trying to persuade us to do things otherwise. Compare, then, the very text you are presently reading. We too claim to offer something more (authoritative).

Assuredly none of the aforementioned alternate approaches to rhetoric are by any means "false," but each does correspond to a vision of what

[26] A rough and ready surrogate for a rhetorical handbook is on offer in the first appendix to this volume.

[27] In full: *repetamque non ab incunabulis nostrae ueteris puerilisque doctrinae quendam ordinem praeceptorum, sed ea, quae quondam accepi in nostrorum hominum eloquentissimorum et omni dignitate principum disputatione esse uersata; non quo illa contemnam, quae Graeci dicendi artifices et doctores reliquerunt, sed cum illa pateant in promptuque sint omnibus, neque ea interpretatione mea aut ornatius explicari aut planius exprimi possint, dabis hanc ueniam, mi frater, ut opinor, ut eorum, quibus summa dicendi laus a nostris hominibus concessa est, auctoritatem Graecis anteponam;* Cicero, *On the Orator* 1.23. Compare Plato, *Phaedrus* 266d and Aristotle, *Rhetoric* 1.1–3 on "other theoretical works."

most defines rhetoric and hence properly shapes an account of rhetoric. Their various forms are thus an index of a variety of theories of rhetoric, theories that are being promulgated by modern as well as by ancient authors. This volume adopts and adapts these approaches while nevertheless recognizing that the very desire to specify the nature of our relationship to words is itself a rhetorical move. And this desire to define often bespeaks a desire to end the debate about the nature of language. It is useful to resist this impulse as it can efface the complexity of the debate itself.

Nevertheless, this Companion will in general take seriously Nietzsche's proposition: "rhetoric" is a latent possibility of language itself and rhetorical features such as metaphors and metonymies are not so much imposed upon it as inevitably emerge from within it. What is of interest, then, are the specific ways in which various latent capacities of language were harnessed, codified, and contested within the ancient world. The reader is offered a guide to the complex and variable social space in which questions of language and authority were negotiated in antiquity. The volume examines rhetoric's competitors and the compromises over territory, compromises that yield a sense of the field of rhetoric as a semi-discrete and autonomous cultural space. In this sense the many rhetorical handbooks can be seen less as umpires than as players on the field. The boundaries between philosophy, oratory, and literature emerge not as positive substances but as locations where a kind of debate about debate erupts and is adjudicated. A central conceit is that eloquence was a ubiquitous concern in antiquity. As a corollary, then, public oratory can be viewed as a special case of eloquence rather than its own proper and separate sphere. A technical discussion of oratory as per Quintilian is itself a still more special case: the *Institutes* argues that eloquence is its object and that it has a special privilege relative to that object. This is itself a rhetorical claim as well as a claim about rhetoric. This *Companion* offers a sustained effort to be faithful to the complexity of the debate over the nature of rhetoric itself. Accordingly chapters dedicated to individual authors have been avoided lest the discussion of a topic be turned into a seemingly authoritative monologue. Readers are themselves encouraged to participate in the difficult and important task of coming to terms with rhetoric in its complexity.

The first major division of the present volume offers an archaeology of rhetoric; it illustrates the sorts of raw materials that were available for use when the formal concept of rhetoric became codified as a distinct project in its own right. Then we examine this codification. This question of origins, though, must not be mistaken for finding a rhetoric before rhetoric, an essence that was already there, some unadulterated precipitate that remains after the inessential has been boiled off. Nor do we find a science that has raised itself up from a pre-scientific muddle of random practices. The birth of rhetoric is not nearly so tidy as all of that.

Nancy Worman explores the verbal practices of archaic Greek poetry. There are speeches in Homer, but looking here for explicit rhetorical instruction can be less revelatory than seeking out the implicit logic that gives coherence to this linguistic community. Of course, reading Homer and abstracting from his practice is a very old strategy indeed: the scholiasts on Homer offer a set of rhetorical glosses on the inset speeches. Choice details of the various strategies employed are regularly highlighted by his commentators who are keen to expose the poet's motives at every turn. Indeed "Homer's rhetoric" can be found throughout by those who are looking for it. For example, the scholiast detects a "rhetorical metalepsis" in the second line of the *Iliad*: the "philhellenic" poet shifts the blame for the myriad woes of the war from Achilles to his anger and thus avoids defaming the hero.[28] One can see in the scholiasts an anachronism: the ancient poet is read by a commentator who explicates him in a contemporary idiom that is informed by the history of rhetorical theory. Such comments can nevertheless offer perceptive interpretations, and it would be dangerous indeed for this volume to disclaim the possibilities of reading a text with fresh eyes. For her part, Worman attempts to outline a sociological version of the underpinnings of eloquence according to Homer and one that is more immanently tied to the archaic period itself. A highly competitive community of warrior elites struggles for prestige and influence. But non-verbal considerations are fundamentally a part of their rhetorical community: verbal style, bodily comportment, and moral content are all conflated. Oratory gives a language and a body to their social practice, and speech both participates in and shapes broader questions of community and conflict. Furthermore a sense of the community itself is always a key stake in these deadly serious games. We see how the "disorderly" are excluded from the idealized community presented to us in archaic verse more generally, and how the graciousness of orderly speech and the aristocracy of this well-ordered community each refer back to one another. Cruelty is a necessary attendant upon civility. What is surprising here is the manner in which the discursive strategies of the archaic elite are subsequently reproduced in democratic Athens. The social logic of who is to be given an ear, how, and why obeys rules first laid out in very different genres, periods, and places.

---

[28] ἢ <μυρία:> ῥητορικὴ ἡ μετάληψις· παρὸν γὰρ ἦν φάναι· "ὃς μυρί' Ἀχαιοῖς ἄλγε' ἔθηκεν"· ἀλλ' ὡς φιλέλλην οὐ τῷ ἥρωϊ ἐπάγει τὴν βλασφημίαν, ἀλλὰ τῷ πάθει; *Scholia Graeca in Homeri Iliadem* (*scholia vetera*) 1.2.b.

One can see in the praise poetry of Pindar a transitional form that stands between the poles of the elite warriors of the Homeric age and the democratic community of the Athenians. Pindar's odes, as Leslie Kurke puts it, fuse the realm of mythic heroes and the civic community, by "embedding the central mythic section within the ode performed by a chorus of the victor's fellow citizens. And rather than dramatize the conflict of *oikos* [i.e. the individual house] and *polis* [i.e. the city-state], epinikion skillfully assimilated the interests of these two spheres."[29] Epinician poetry is important for the later theoretical elaboration of display oratory more generally, but Pindar is already grappling with a question that affects other types of rhetoric as well. The rhetorical presentation of excellence within a civic context remains a live issue within democratic Athens. Rich citizens financed public works, outfitted ships for the fleet, and even, as in Pindar's world, paid for choruses of their fellow citizens. When such a citizen is accused of a crime or when he advises a course of action, the rhetorical problem of how to articulate and how to resolve questions of unequal contributions within a constitutional framework of equality under the law is keenly felt.[30] Such a transposition of epinician themes into a juridical or deliberative context can be seen in cases such as Demosthenes' *Against Meidias* and his *On the Crown*.

One probably should have been told the parallel story of the prehistory of rhetoric at Rome. Readers are encouraged to consult the works of Thomas Habinek on this topic, especially "Why was Latin Literature Invented?" and *The World of Roman Song* as well as his introduction to ancient rhetoric and oratory more generally.[31] One sees in Habinek's work as well the important relationship between the sociology of the archaic period, its protocols of speech and the eventual emergence of the rules of oratory in the Republican period at Rome. Song, ritual, and native Italic performance culture are vital precursors to Roman oratory.[32] Strategies that ensure aristocratic hegemony, social cohesion, and the distinctiveness of "good speech" as set against the baseness of everyday speech are core elements of the birth of Latin literature that profoundly shape the speeches of the Roman orators as well as other texts from other genres.

---

[29] Kurke 1991: 7.
[30] Ober 1989a remains, as will be noted in several of the chapters below, the seminal study of this issue.
[31] Habinek 1998: 34–68, Habinek 2005b, and Habinek 2005a.
[32] Although the argument of Fraenkel 2007 generally foregrounds Plautus' relationship to his Greek models, readers who approach this work via the index and its more rhetorical headings can learn a great deal about early speech and song.

Robert Wardy examines the problem of language itself. The debate over *logos*, and who will be able to give the authoritative account of the word for words, is a fundamental moment in the emergence of "rhetoric." The history of Greek philosophy is, significantly, a history of a debate over the status of *logos*. We first catch sight of a nascent philosophy competing with the authoritative language of Greek verse and wisdom literature more generally. The philosophers strive to articulate the relationship between listening to philosophical discourse and listening to reason itself. These narratological distinctions are vital philosophical issues. Gorgias arrives and puckishly hauls the *logos* of philosophy back down towards the worldly problems of everyday speech. Plato intervenes and raises it aloft again. And amidst the fracas a bastard is christened: rhetoric. Note the problem for those who have been attentive to rhetoric's family tree. Rhetoric is less born than it is named. And it is named as philosophy is working out the space of *logos*. Rhetoric emerges precisely as an exposed child, as something that has been cast out of the house of philosophy as one of the illegitimate children of *logos*. As a "family drama" this scenario is no mere moment of theater, it is a brand set upon rhetoric that is never again forgotten, a legacy of illegitimacy that is forever a part of the story of rhetoric itself. Rhetoric is hereafter condemned to plead its own case for its share of the patrimony of *logos*, and rhetoric must argue in terms most unfavorable to itself.

The archaeology of the emergence of rhetoric as an autonomous field ends with Malcolm Heath describing the various attempts by theorists to codify rhetoric. That is, even as the term "rhetoric" might ideally designate a determinate domain of speech and there might correspond to this domain a specific well-ordered theoretical overview, such a "scientism" of rhetoric is not to be found in antiquity despite the regular assertion that such is indeed on offer. Instead rhetorical theory is flexible, alive, and disputed throughout antiquity. Heath's diachronic view of rhetorical theory reveals proto-theoretical moments in Homer, Gorgias, and Antiphon. Rhetorical handbooks appear very early on: the philosophers both incorporate this material and distance themselves from it. Here we see the inverse of some of what Wardy has argued: it is Plato and Aristotle who can be described as belated. This tension that I am drawing out between the positions taken by Wardy and Heath is itself a product of the question of the "essence" of rhetoric. How (or even if) one asks and answers this question profoundly affects one's subsequent relationship to the field under investigation. On the one hand we have the ongoing practice of instruction in eloquence, and on the other we have philosophers who are keen to give both a name and a determinate place to a competing technology of language.

Heath presents rhetorical theory as a living tradition, and one that often forgets its own past in the name of the purportedly authoritative formulations of the present, a present that understands itself to be the culmination of prior efforts. Thus we see a variety of rhetorical handbooks, variously organized, and sometimes being misread between generations. Hot topics emerge, disappear, and then reappear. Some works are synthetic overviews, others are specialist monographs. The relationship to philosophy is negotiated and renegotiated even as philosophy and its various schools evolve. And in the case of Cicero we can see a specific author working through and refining his approach to rhetorical theory over the course of a lifetime.

On the one hand these three chapters are intended to offer a prologue to the study of rhetoric. But on the other hand they ought to instill a healthy sense of skepticism. Much of what one says in antiquity about rhetoric needs to be weighed with great care. There are any number of categorical or absolute formulations available, and yet these same utterances often hide their own disputed status, their place in history, or their relationship to the social order. There are many "last words" on the topic available to us, and yet none of them ever really succeed in being such.

Part II surveys "the field of language" and the various dimensions of rhetoric's role as an authoritative discourse concerning language. We now start to take rhetoric more on its own terms without, though, ever becoming too complacent or complicit. The first chapter is Catherine Steel's "Divisions of speech." As with Malcolm Heath's "Codifications of rhetoric" just before it, this chapter offers an overview of the ways in which practical oratory is mapped out by rhetorical theory. Here, though, the emphasis is on the taxonomy itself, and the perspective is relatively more synchronic rather than diachronic. Steel shows us the elaborated system of canonical theory. These divisions are the divisions within which one teaches the art. And as divisions they both reveal and conceal their subject matter. A sense of an organic whole can be lost. Other problems can arise: for example, invention can squeeze out arrangement. The handbooks can offer a sense that a recipe for good oratory is being communicated. And yet when one makes a critical reading of actual orations, the number of ingredients and their relationships does not always fit tidily within their teachings. Jon Hesk will follow up on this issue in more detail.

Steel's account of style within the handbooks and its broader cultural import feeds rather directly into Jim Porter's account of rhetoric and aesthetics. As above, one is asked to appreciate the connectedness of rhetoric with other domains of knowledge. However, in this instance we are generally looking at rhetoric once it has established itself as a major cultural center rather than in its emergence as an institution. Nevertheless, another visit to its origins reveals an ambiguous play between voice, body, and voice as body. The embodied voice becomes an object of analysis in its own right. And though it is never fully purified and abstracted, nevertheless when studied as pure and abstract the voice becomes a privileged object and the place where a sense of beauty and the sublime more generally are articulated. Thus the study of rhetoric and theories of art and music remain in constant and profound communication with one another in ancient thought. Meanwhile concepts of beauty and the invisible body of the elite male are likewise subtly conjoined such that the loftiness of the aesthetic sublime and the heights of social station never drift too far apart.

My own chapter examines the way in which rhetorical theory is itself rhetorical. In many ways it is a demonstration of the sort of work that can emerge within the context of the volume as a whole given that it engages with almost every other essay in the *Companion*. If one rereads Quintilian with an eye to his own status as a rhetorical performer, then a different text emerges from the one we usually see. The masterful textbook on oratory can be reread with an emphasis on the mastery itself: who is speaking to us? how? why? What doesn't he say? What sorts of cultural conflicts are revealed, and what concealed? The beauty and authority of the elite male performer once again become vital reference points as we take a critical look at how texts that might otherwise be taken for neutral accounts concerning oratory are themselves highly partisan examples of the practice which they preach.

Joy Connolly thinks through the politics of a rhetorical education. Education today is frequently presented as a rather neutral affair: knowledge is conveyed; skills are exercised. One perhaps emphasizes the economic or social opportunities it enables, but, excepting tactless sociologists, one also politely avoids pushing this too far. It was not ever thus. Ancient education has a much more explicit account of its relationship to questions of privilege and hierarchy. Connolly's chapter offers a careful exploration of everything that is entailed in a rhetorical education that promises both ethics and excellence. Rhetoric becomes a venue for symbolic domination, and education an education in mastery. The production and recognition of "good men" is at stake. Connolly evokes a theme we have already seen in Porter: there is something "beautiful" and "noble" about the whole process whereby the good, beneficial, and beautiful citizens make the good, beneficial, and beautiful arguments. Nevertheless, education does not present itself as the cynical art of conflating these three; instead it offers lessons in becoming who one wishes to be, in learning to champion the perspective of the law, and in negotiating and renegotiating one's place in a complex society. Rhetoric is, then, the sincere art of conflating the three.

Part III investigates practice. The first two parts should have provided a backdrop against which oratory proper can be fully appreciated as a special case of the polished use of language. The opening chapter is again both a technical survey and an introduction to Part III as a whole. Jon Hesk's "Types of Oratory" takes up the question of the three genres of speech in antiquity: deliberative, forensic, and display oratory. Once again the taxonomy itself is investigated, and Hesk is particularly sensitive to the question of the fit between theory and practice here. Many speeches seem to mix their messages and to straddle genres. And many authors use their speeches to pursue multiple ends simultaneously. Thus the basic divisions from our theoretical accounts are a necessary but nevertheless insufficient means of exploring speech as we find it. A more historically and sociologically sensitive approach to oratory brings clarity to elements of ancient practice that have been left opaque within the theoretical literature.

Victoria Wohl pursues in more detail questions of the relationship between oratory and society that Jon Hesk broaches. She is particularly interested in the psychic life of Athenian oratory. She examines the manner in which politics and psychology are sutured together such that the net result is a civic rhetoric that is profoundly connected with the structure of the Athenian self. On this reading, rhetoric is not the art of deception but rather a place where home truths are produced and disseminated. Metaphor and metonymy are not just figures of speech, they are also figures of thought, and figures that give shape to thought and experience more generally. Accordingly tropes are not mere tropes, and rhetoric is not mere rhetoric. One has to take seriously the politics of representation and of substitution: at stake is the community's sense of the structure of its internal relations. Oratory provides its audience with a theory of citizenship that articulates the legitimate vertical and horizontal ties between one and all.

John Dugan takes up the relation between public speech and civic society at Rome. Once again the approach is to examine both the implicit and the explicit politics of rhetorical practice. Roman orations delineate the contours of an imagined community and present to the audience a vision of itself as well as a portrait of legitimate authority in its relationship to that same community. There is, though, a theory of this practice that is never made explicit in ancient rhetorical theory. In fact fluidity and ambiguity are essential features of Roman oratory. The constitution is unwritten, and the Republic itself subject to competing strategic definitions and redefinitions. Thus even as the prized terms retain a certain fixity in this culture obsessed with heeding "tradition," there is a great deal of actual flexibility and improvisation when we watch the orators at work. Dugan's thesis fits well with Wohl's: rhetorical criticism and the analysis of ancient politics are interrelated projects.

David Rosenbloom analyzes the connections between oratory and drama at Athens. These two forms of public discourse are obviously related, but the details of this relationship can be difficult to appreciate. Rosenbloom finds a serious critique of public oratory in the dramatists despite their own profound engagement with many of the same discursive strategies. Conversely orators themselves emplot the discourse of public life according to theatrical tropes: tragic ironies and frank-spoken raillery are vital components of public speech outside the theater. Both drama and oratory wrestle with problems of persuasion, but drama is very wary indeed of oratory's sway: democratic oratory is staged as a species of violent usurpation, and the dramatists entertain a dangerous nostalgia for anti-democratic social orders. As ever we need to appreciate the politics of public discourse and to understand that "oratory proper" is only one version of that discourse, and a version that is in constant competition with other versions.

The exchanges between the dramaturgical and the rhetorical realms are pushed even further by William Batstone. Batsone argues for the thoroughly performative nature of the Roman self. Oratory is like drama, yes. But drama is itself just the most pointedly ironic and self-aware instantiation of the ubiquitous performance of Roman identity. If we attend to the drama of the Roman self we are able to see the whole of life as an earnest improvisational game filled with rhetorical competitions. Who will get to say who and what we all are? This is a question asked in genre after genre at Rome. And two figures, the good man and the wily slave keep on taking center stage. But it is not always easy to tell them apart. One can see here as well a clear progression from Dugan's argument where we find a wily and improvisational Cicero. We are moving out to a more general thesis that such performances are ubiquitous and that they are profoundly "Roman." For it is through such performances that debates over the very category of Romanness are articulated and adjudicated.

The Second Sophistic offered a radical reinvestment in ancient rhetorical culture. As Simon Goldhill shows us, rival claims to authority have largely been cast aside: rhetoric declares rhetoric to be all-important, and there are few detractors. Rhetoric has also unabashedly become an end in itself. However, as a cultural moment the Second Sophistic is itself paradoxical even as it delights in paradoxes: this return to the glories of the birth of rhetoric means that the "authentic" life of this highly self-conscious era is lived in borrowed clothes. Jim Porter has prepared us to appreciate what such a nostalgia surrounding the voice entails. Greek literature under the Roman Empire invests heavily in the tongue, in its transmissibility, in the power of education. But this education in the language of the Greece of yore is thoroughly contemporary in spirit: the *pax Romana* is the enabling condition of an international educated elite who speak old Attic Greek. There is a new politics to this rhetorical education that recalls without duplicating the old politics. And the deracinated tongue that terrified Attic drama is now championed as the triumph of rhetorical culture and culture as rhetoric. Achilles Tatius will even playfully convert Plato's fears about language and desire into positive virtues. This is a world where one does not even dismiss learning except in the most erudite and recondite terms. In short, we have seen it all before, but never quite like this. And that is the point.

Goldhill's chapter is a bridge to the concluding part of the volume, which comes in the form of two epilogues. The first examines another stream of language and authority in antiquity that eventually joins up with the current of rhetorical culture we have explored more fully in the volume. Todd Penner and Caroline Vander Stichele track the complex emergence of Christian rhetoric. On the one hand we find here a different "ancient oratory" from that investigated above. And a substantial portion of this difference can be attributed to different social organization and different social practices. Nevertheless we also see how two familiar themes are once again vital to an appreciation of Christian rhetoric: performance and authority. The theme of "frank speech" – something vital to rhetorical self-definition in old Athens and in the then-contemporary Second Sophistic – is reworked by these outsiders in such a way that early Christians can position themselves as figures whose distinctive message deserves to be given a hearing. In this they invoke a number of the tropes used by Socrates and the Cynics. The net result is a rhetorical practice that fuses Jewish and Greco-Roman traditions and that reworks the basic rhetorical resources imparted by the schools to forge a new performative style adapted for a new community. And it is oratory itself that helps to conjure and sustain this very community. In some ways we are looking at a parallel Second Sophistic: a birth-*cum*-rebirth of rhetoric but this time one that is self-conscious about questions of difference, exclusion, and marginalization within the world of the *pax Romana*. We have the opportunity to see the power of rhetoric to give birth to a new community from a complex agglomeration of traditions, not just to reproduce the long-standing dominant structures.

The second epilogue looks at the rediscovery of ancient rhetoric in the Renaissance. Peter Mack himself makes his major themes perfectly clear from the start: we are looking at recovery, addition, and change. We need to know what the Renaissance knew, and when they knew it. Their "ancient rhetoric" was a different collection of texts than the whole corpus now available, and these texts were studied with a different relative weight than one usually gives them today. But even as the recovery of antiquity advances we see concomitant addition and change. Ancient rhetoric is used and reused. It is worked over from a practical standpoint. Another community of discourse is giving birth to itself out of an encounter with this older one. Some repackage, some revolutionize. But all are engaged in a process with familiar outlines: what is the proper shape of a rhetorical handbook? How is rhetoric to be codified? What are the divisions and types of speech? As Heath, Steel, and Hesk showed for the classical period, so we find again in the Renaissance that questions of theory matter when it comes to appreciating shifts in the spirit of practice. Classical rhetorical teaching is significantly expanded and reworked in the Renaissance in order to suit a linguistic community that was much more one of readers and writers rather than listeners and speakers proper. A sustained engagement with old handbooks yields new tools: dialectical reading, elaborate epistolary theory, and techniques for generating verbal richness in general. Innovations emerging from a deep engagement with the rhetorical tradition give rise to the distinctiveness of Renaissance literature.

It would have been easy to multiply the chapters on reception. An obvious addition would be the relationship of the Byzantine era to the rhetorical culture of earlier Greek authors. There are several major, interlocking, and involuted strands to this topic. The Byzantine reception of classical Greece involves close and careful first-hand readings of early Greek orators and theorists. It also includes readings of the reception of the classical period by Greek authors working in the Roman imperial era such as Hermogenes' commentaries on Demosthenes.[33] And we cannot forget that there is also an excited reception of the Second Sophistic's rhetorical culture in its own right and that Byzantine rhetoric in many ways strikes the observer as a further elaboration of that same movement. Furthermore the Byzantines read the reception of classical Greece by the Church Fathers as well as the positive contributions of the Church Fathers themselves. Speaking well and speaking the truth, speaking clearly and speaking in a majestic manner: old rhetorical issues start to bear new theological weight as well. The raw ingredients of this heady mix of traditions to which the Byzantines both found and made themselves heir are already somewhat on offer in the present volume, but the details of their actual combination within Byzantine culture's long and complex history will need to be sought elsewhere.[34]

---

[33] In fact Hermogenes himself becomes the object of successive layers of commentary within the Byzantine era.

[34] Consider consulting Kustas 1973 (especially chapters 1 and 2); Kennedy 1980: 161–72; Kennedy 1983 (chapters 4 through 6); and Constantinides 2003.

The reception of classical rhetoric and oratory in Europe from the eighteenth through the twenty-first centuries would also offer an extremely lively topic for study. One notes, for example, that although at times themselves denounced as sophists in the most dismissive and limited sense of that term, some of the most provocative intellectual figures of the previous century explicitly engaged with the sophists proper, those scandalous figures of the fifth century BCE.[35] Meanwhile in the contemporary university a department of communications will tend to emphasize media courses and sociological methods of analysis. Degree requirements regularly omit even a single course covering either ancient theory or practice. The authors and issues discussed in this volume appear, then, to have received both a very warm and a very chill reception of late.

The present introduction has attempted to argue relatively little when it comes to ancient rhetoric in general. Instead the core thesis has been somewhat different. I have attempted to explain why an introduction to ancient rhetoric is simultaneously an impossible and a necessary task. It is impossible not only because of the intractable mass of strictly rhetorical material to cover, but also because such a volume is inevitably going to take on the characteristics of an introduction to ancient society in general. Conversely, the very features which make it impossible also make it necessary. Just because one cannot say nearly enough does not mean one can get away with saying nothing at all. As with a good speech, so with a good introduction: what I have most attempted to convey is that the present *Companion to Ancient Rhetoric* is itself a good introduction to ancient rhetoric, that this particular approach to the topic provides a useful choice of material, that it has been laid out sensibly, articulated clearly and convincingly, that it has remembered all of the chief points and left nothing too essential to the side, and that, lastly, the reading of it will have been a pleasing as well as an illuminating experience.[36]

Though our own culture has made a significant shift over to the sovereignty of visual signs and a rhetoric of images as against that of words and speeches, we are nevertheless extremely sensitive to questions of rhetoric and persuasion broadly conceived. Perhaps exploring the ancient problematic in some detail – that is, what did they talk about? when? why? and what went unsaid? – will allow for a revisitation of our own discursive regime

[35] See, for example, Deleuze and Guattari 1994: 146–48 on the sophists; Foucault 1997: 346 in praise of the sophists; Derrida 1981: 115–17 on Gorgias; and Lacan 2006: 150 as Gorgianic.
[36] Compare the "peroration" of Crassus' initial survey of rhetorical theory at *On the Orator* 1.203. It is impossible to say it all. Crassus has merely pointed in the direction of the font towards which the thirsty may travel if they wish to drink.

and insight into its family tree. Our own cynicism about rhetoric as "mere rhetoric" and obsession with hypocrisy and manipulation bespeaks an investment, albeit a largely negative one, in the potency of rhetoric. We still cling to the idea that words have power even if the skilled at speaking are no longer assumed to be good men. We worry that essences and appearances have been sundered, and that, ironically, rhetoric really is all too efficacious: while we personally remain unfooled, someone else out there either actually has or is likely to fall for all of this.

In such a context it seems very useful to go back and to explore ancient rhetoric anew. Whether we imagine ourselves as a Third Sophistic, a Renaissance reborn, or the coming of a new community of speech set against that of the old, we will find what others before us have discovered when they decided to take on ancient rhetoric itself as their chosen companion: a set of tools that both enable and constrain and a collection of categories that will work on us even as we work through them. But communication itself is inevitable, community is forever being re-imagined, and politics is the ineluctable destiny of the *politikon zōon*, the civic animal that is man. Accordingly it is very valuable indeed to think through a genealogy of rhetoric, to see clearly its components, their history, their scope, and their interrelationships. The rhetoric of anti-rhetoric was long ago flushed out by the ancient orators: it's just another trope. Don't fall for it. Allow yourself to be persuaded to think carefully about the art of persuasion.

A note on works cited in this volume

This *Companion* is somewhat inconsistent in giving the titles of ancient works. An effort has been made to give an English title for the majority of works. A Latin title often indicates an obscure and untranslated text that in practice will be available only to specialist readers. Papyri and fragments are notoriously inaccessible to the uninitiated. Pretending that one could seek out *Fragments of Greek Tragedy* is misleading when only *Tragicorum Graecorum Fragmenta* will do. However, this rule has numerous exceptions: Statius's *Siluae*, for example, has been translated into English, but translations retain the (untranslatable) title of *Silvae*. The lone concession to modernity is printing *v* for consonantal *u*. Actual speeches almost always have translations, even if something with a title like *Antidosis* seems like it might be a dead end unless you know Greek. The English translations of titles found here will not always match translations found elsewhere, but all of the translations have precedents and they usually align with a general consensus. The English titles provided are often followed in the text by quotations in Greek or Latin. Where an explicit translation is not supplied, the substance of these quotations should be clear from the context. Readers who know Greek or Latin are expected to be familiar with the Greek and Latin titles of the works under discussion. If they wish to follow up on a passage, such readers will labor far less when seeing *Dialogue on Orators* than will Latinless ones who confront the word *Dialogus*.

The Loeb Classical Library is an obvious place to look for a comprehensive collection of English versions of texts. Better translations and notes can usually be found elsewhere in the case of major authors such as Plato, Aristotle, and Cicero. The "Suggested readings" at the foot of individual chapters often advocate specific translations.

PART I

An archaeology of rhetoric

I

NANCY WORMAN

Fighting words: status, stature, and verbal contest in archaic poetry

In book 23 of the *Iliad*, Ajax the son of Oïleus loses a foot race to Odysseus and ends up on the ground with a mouth full of cow dung.[1] On receiving second prize (an ox, fittingly enough), he spits the dung from his mouth (*onthon apoptuōn*) and says, "Damn, the goddess tripped me up; she always stands like a mother by Odysseus and cares for him."[2] His audience of fellow warriors laughs happily (*hēdu gelassan*) at his remark, and the potential for shaming and conflict ends there (780–84). If some speech (such as that of the dilatory Nestor) flows like honey[3] – being by implication persuasive, well composed, and fair-minded – other utterances fill the mouth with bile and splatter their targets. The one mode is lofty, judicious, and even perhaps divine; the other is agonistic, scrappy, and tied to the body and the earth.[4]

While this "praise and blame" model for understanding early speech performance is clearly too schematic, it serves as a necessary starting point for assessing archaic awareness of verbal tactics.[5] The scene from the *Iliad*, although clearly not an extended speech, offers an example of jocular tactics that constitute a mild but telling form of abuse in an agonistic setting. The incident as a whole, trivial and brief as it is, points to a conundrum crucial in reconstructing awareness of speech techniques before the advent of prose writing and rhetorical treatises on speech composition – namely,

---

[1] ἐν δ' ὄνθου βοέου πλῆτο στόμα τε ῥῖνάς τε, *Iliad* 23.777.

[2] ὢ πόποι ἦ μ' ἔβλαψε θεὰ πόδας, ἣ τὸ πάρος περ | μήτηρ ὣς Ὀδυσῆϊ παρίσταται ἠδ' ἐπαρήγει, *Iliad* 23.782–83.

[3] *Iliad* 1.249 (καὶ ἀπὸ γλώσσης μέλιτος γλυκίων ῥέεν αὐδή); cf. Hesiod, *Theogony* 83–84 and further below.

[4] Eustathius associates this incident with the iambic poet Hipponax's abuse of a female target as a "crap hole" (*borboropēn*) (iv.835.13 V. D. Valk).

[5] See especially Nagy 1979 for this approach to the archaic lexicon.

why the happy laughter? Why is Ajax's performance successful in defusing the incident and bonding with the audience?

Richard Enos has suggested that before the advent of rhetorical theory, all assessments of speech performance were in essence stylistic.[6] What one said would have, on this reading, registered as one aspect among many of how one spoke. Thus Ajax Oïleades, nonchalantly leaning on his prize and spitting dung from his mouth, makes the mild joke that he has lost to a mama's boy, and wins a laugh not so much for the joke alone as for the gesture as a whole.[7] Anyone who has read Homer can attest to the broad embrace of such phrases as *kata moiran, ou para moiran,* and *ou kata kosmon,* which all point to an assessment of how appropriate or (more literally) "in order" a given locution is.[8] But what, exactly, is being assessed as fitting: the speaker's vocabulary, deportment, gracious nods to interlocutors; his use of familiar arguments, their arrangement, their moral status? Sometimes such phrases seem to mean, in essence, "I agree with you and share your perspective"; at others, especially in negative usage, they appear to critique manners.

This conflation of verbal style, visible performance, and moral content is a crucial characteristic of stylistic assessment in archaic poetry, one that shaped later oratory and rhetorical theory in essential ways.[9] This means that speech was assessed in its performance by a speaker and that non-verbal elements contributed to its impact. Although the formulaic and conventional nature of Homeric epic limits distinctions among speakers' styles to some extent, Adam Parry and others have demonstrated the degree to which characters in Homer are shaped and assessed by their verbal tactics.[10] And the earliest rhetorical treatises, generated by sophistic

---

[6] Enos 1993: 60. This is notably opposed to traditional classicists' approaches. Cf. Solmsen 1954, who emphasizes content; Kennedy 1957, who argues that the focus on styles was a later invention; and Cole 1991: 42–43, who essentially follows Solmsen in maintaining that there was no perceived gap between thought and its expression in speech. See also Toohey 1994: 153–62, who argues that Homeric speeches exhibit rhetorical structure.

[7] The effect of the whole would include that it is aimed at Odysseus, since he is such an agile manipulator of insults and so all the more valuable as a target. See further below.

[8] See *Iliad* 1.286, 2.214, 8.146, 9.59; *Odyssey* 4.266, 8.179, 14.363, 14.509, 20.182. Karp 1977 argues in detail for rhetorical awareness in Homer, although he does not address any style/content distinctions. Cf. Martin 1989; Kennedy 1994: 13–14; Toohey 1994; Cole 1991: 40–44, who regards Homer and the archaic poets more generally as "pre-rhetorical" or "arhetorical."

[9] Havelock 1963 famously emphasized the orality of the classical period as well, at least up until the end of the fifth century (i.e. before Plato). See also the edited volumes by Bakker and Kahane 1997; Worthington 1996; Worthington and Foley 2002; Mackie 2004.

[10] Thus Kennedy, whose surveys of ancient rhetoric have introduced the material to generations of scholars, is clearly wrong to claim that the Homeric poet does not

training in the fifth and fourth centuries, appear to have received Homeric speakers in this way, treating them as a means of differentiating among styles (e.g. "Nestor" [verbose] versus "Odysseus" [dissembling]).[11]

Subsequent theory and practice preserves this emphasis. Aristotle may have relegated style to the third book of his treatise on rhetoric and denigrated its importance, but neither his predecessors nor his successors shared his perspective. For Isocrates even arguments may constitute elements of style, as when he treats rhetorical syllogisms (*enthumēmata*) as ornamental.[12] Similarly, the Hellenistic theorists Demetrius, Dionysius of Halicarnassus, and Cicero all focus largely or entirely on stylistic categories in their discussions of oratory and orators. And yet scholars have been slow to acknowledge the distorting impact that Aristotle's disdain for style had on the reception of ancient oratory and rhetorical theory.[13]

Further, in Homeric epic most speeches are made in agonistic contexts, where the possibility of conflict and indeed physical violence is often palpable.[14] Sometimes characters in threatening circumstances employ laudatory epithets, elevated compliments, or other seductive verbal tactics.[15] More frequently, however, speakers' persuasive tools range from derogatory inference to direct invective. Whether warriors vaunt on the field of battle or dispute in assembly, their threats, taunts, and slanderous labels broadcast superiority and coerce actions.[16] Odysseus is the hero most capable of resolving conflict by means of manipulative compliments and insults that achieve the allegiance of the interlocutor or the audience. He also often engages in didactic gestures, chastening his verbal opponents or using them as examples for others.[17] Although he becomes a negative figure in fifth-century tragedy,

---

differentiate speakers by diction and composition (e.g. Kennedy 1994: 13); although he cites Martin's 1989 work he seems to ignore its implications. Cf. Parry 1964. Cf., e.g. Nagy 1979; Martin 1989; Pucci 1998; Worman 2002.

[11] See Kennedy 1957; Karp 1977; Worman 2002.

[12] See "to embellish/embroider one's whole speech" (*holon ton logon katapoikilai*), *Against the Sophists* 16.

[13] See Worman 2002. Scholars tend to focus their efforts on the first two books of the *Rhetoric*.

[14] See Ong 1982: 43–45, who regards this agonistic mode as a typical characteristic of oral cultures.

[15] Odysseus is very adept at this rhetorical game: e.g. *Iliad* 9.225–306 and 19.155–82, 216–37 (Achilles); *Odyssey* 6.148–85 (Nausicaa), 14.149–64, 462–506 (Eumaeus), and 19.165–202, 221–48 (Penelope).

[16] E.g. *Iliad* 2.243–64 (Odysseus), 3.38–57 (Hector), 4.334–49, 368–400 (Agamemnon); *Odyssey* 2.35–145 (Telemachus and Antinoos), 8.165–85 (Odysseus), 17.215–32 (Melanthius). See also high-status female characters (e.g. *Iliad* 3.424–36 [Helen], *Odyssey* 13.291–310 [Athena]).

[17] See Svenbro 1976: 50–59; Pucci 1987: 157–208; Worman 1999.

the verbal dexterity, strategic mentality, and talent for coercion and control that the Homeric poet attributes to him make him an obvious prototype for the classical orator.

The challenge, then, is to expose the ways in which archaic poets treat speech performance as an embodied social practice. This approach highlights as well how conflict shapes tactical choices, and what the figure of Odysseus reveals about early awareness of such choices. It is importantly informed by performance theory, which emphasizes the perceptible strategies by which one marks out one's status within the community. The sociologist Pierre Bourdieu has famously argued that language is effectively a "body technique" associated with an "overall way of using the mouth." How one talks is thus one element in a set of oral habits, which, in combination with other physical features such as dress and deportment, constitute what Bourdieu calls bodily *hexis*. And nicely enough for this discussion, he uses the example of the Homeric *skēptron* to indicate the important role that the accoutrements of power play in authoritative speech performance.[18]

Few traditional scholars have argued for a focus on this embodied practice; nor have many understood how rooted it is in archaic settings.[19] In fact, no one has articulated the extent to which the history of scholarship on classical oratory reflects (quite uncritically) ancient theorists' persistent misrecognition of oratory's agonism and performative physicality.[20] Thus while Cicero's famous triad of oratory's goals (*mouere, docere, delectare*; *Orator* 69) has been received as accurate (if clearly idealized), this discussion treats rhetoric *in practice* as a coercive response to conflict and reveals that contentious strategies in archaic speech performance influence classical oratorical strategies quite broadly.[21] Dispute (*neikos*) and mockery in Homer and to a lesser extent the coercive schemes depicted by Hesiod and Pindar contribute to shaping a strain of rhetoric that is in essence cautionary, controlling, and – indeed – forcefully didactic.[22] Thus, contrary to received wisdom on the topic, the language of abuse has a more fundamental role to

[18] Bourdieu 1991: 86 and 109–13. See also Schechner 1985; Herzfeld 1985; J. Butler 1990. Versions of this approach include Martin 1989 (although he relies more on speech act theory); Gleason 1995; Goldhill and Osborne 1999.

[19] But see Gleason 1995; Bassi 1998; Gunderson 2000; Worman 2002.

[20] See Bourdieu 1977: 4–6 on the notion of "misrecognition" (*méconnaissance*), which obscures the true nature of social relations and practices.

[21] Even "honeyed" styles and laudatory strategies seek to offset potential violence: cf. Pindar, *Pythian* 2.51–56, *Nemean* 8.20–39; Isocrates, *Evagoras* 1–11.

[22] Although other archaic poets do not appear to be as overtly concerned with critiquing speech performance, see Solmsen 1954; Havelock 1963: 97–114; Walsh 1984: 22–36; and especially Martin 1984.

play in the forging of oratorical techniques than do elevated or laudatory modes.[23] Closely associated with wisdom poetry and chastening at its core, archaic abuse points the way to the regulating, admonishing role that orators assumed in democratic Athens.

Rhetorical correctives in Homer

There are numerous carefully organized, persuasive speeches in the Homeric epics, many of which the consummate verbal strategist Odysseus achieves. Some of these are not as warmly received as their fine formulations would anticipate; Achilles, for instance, is rarely susceptible to Odysseus' well-oiled pragmatism.[24] Other speakers display their characters and social statuses through penchants for verbal dilation (e.g. Nestor [*Iliad* 11.655–803, *Odyssey* 3.254–328], Phoenix [*Iliad* 9.432–605]) or self-indulgent humbug (e.g. Agamemnon [esp. *Iliad* 19.76–144]). These epics also, however, indicate awareness of rhetorical strategies that arise directly out of conflict and that come to constitute the core of democratic practice, for better or worse. I address two intersecting strategies, both of which the Homeric poet associates with the figure of Odysseus.

Slander and audience allegiance

If Ajax Oïleades achieves allegiance with his audience in a moment that might otherwise have erupted in conflict and abuse, a famous scene early in the *Iliad* stages the opposite effect. When in book 2 Thersites stands up from among the mass of soldiers and criticizes Agamemnon's leadership, a number of signals in the framing of the scene leave little doubt that this criticism will not be well received.[25] Not only is the speaker ill formed in body, the individual indignities of which the poet details (2.217–19); he is also hated by Achilles and Odysseus, Homeric epic's signature heroes (2.220). His speaking style matches his body: it is literally "disordered" (*epea ... akosma*; *ou kata kosmon*, 2.213–14). Although he assembles many of the same points that Achilles has already made in indicting Agamemnon's greedy behavior (1.149–71), his speech elicits verbal and physical abuse

---

[23] N.b., Cole 1991: 47–54 devotes a chapter to decorous strategies from archaic poetry (e.g. the *ainos*), and then finally concludes (54) that these had little impact on classical rhetorical practices.

[24] See Worman 2002: 67–74.

[25] On the figure of Thersites see, e.g. Egbert 1969; Nagy 1979: 259–62; Rose 1988; Thalmann 1988; Martin 1989: 110–13; Seibel 1995; Marks 2005.

from Odysseus, and his fellow soldiers greet it with derision (2.243–77). As is clear from this and other incidents in Homer, the notion of *kosmos* is wielded aggressively as a coercive measure that regulates both speech and behavior; and if this ordering is not pursued appropriately, it must be imposed.

Odysseus calls the ugly, disorderly soldier *akritomuthe* ("unmeasured in speech"), while acknowledging that he is a "clear-voiced orator" (*ligus ... agorētēs*) (2.246). The combination of attributes suggests that Thersites is accustomed to speaking out, although neither his status nor his stature would seem to encourage this boldness. He is an abuser of kings and as such cannot be promoted, either by the audience internal to epic or by the genre's own audiences.[26] Although it has become popular to understand this moment as exposing class hierarchies, J. Marks argues that Thersites is not so much lower rank as a peer who introduces abuse into the assembly.[27] He thus resembles iambic figures such as Archilochus and Hipponax and, like them, insults his peers. As an iambic intrusion into the epic setting, his contentious style is itself mocked and highlighted as radically unsuccessful, by both the narrator and Odysseus.

Let us consider in more detail how Odysseus achieves this effect. First, he does not address primarily the content of Thersites' speech, focusing rather on who he is and how he says what he says. He tells him not to wish to do battle with kings (*erizemenai basileusin*), that there is no one worse than him (*ou gar egō seo phēmi khereioteron broton allon | emmenai*) on the campaign, and that he should hold his tongue (*ana stom' ekhōn*) and not abuse the leaders (*sphin oneidea te propherois*) nor promote going home (2.247–51). That is, Odysseus presents the speech performance as outrageous in itself, out of line for any soldier but especially for one so hideous and shrill. He emphasizes the category of speech in which Thersites engages, repeating words for strife, abuse, and reproach (*erizemenai, oneidea, oneidizōn, kertomenōn*). He rounds off this emphatic labeling with some abuse of his own, threatening Thersites with being stripped naked, beaten back from assembly (*peplēgōn agorēthen*, 264), and sent weeping among the ships of the Achaeans.

Finally, Odysseus complements envisioned with actual violence, striking Thersites on his back and shoulders with the speaker's scepter so that he crumples and his eyes fill with tears. A welt rises where the scepter struck and he sits down shaken (265–69). Although pained, the men laugh happily at the spectacle (*hoi de kai akhnumenoi per ep' autōi hēdu gelassen*, 270),

---

[26] Again, see Nagy 1979: 259–62.

[27] Marks 2005. This is Nagy's essential point, of course, but he also appears to assume the lower-class status.

approving Odysseus' barring of "this word-slinging slanderer" from assembly (*ton lōbētēra epesbolon eskh' agoraōn*) and wagering that Thersites will not again engage in verbal battle with kings (*neikeiein basilēas oneideiois epeessin*) (2.275–76). This physical wielding of authority is essential to the masquerade in which the speaker engages in order to cement his power over his opponent. Odysseus must mark himself visibly as separate and different from Thersites, since both are clearly loud and well-spoken orators.[28] The scene is as ugly as the man it targets, and the poet underscores both the hideous, twisted body of the disorderly speaker and its brutal abuse.

In keeping with this focus on the debased body, the prominence of words that mark this as a vituperative exchange, both in Odysseus' response and in the framing of the scene, makes it abundantly clear that this conflict is importantly instructive. The narrator labels Thersites' speech a *neikos* (i.e. "dispute," cf. *neikee*, 224; *neikeiōn*, 243), a distinction that the soldiers confirm (cf. *neikeiein*, 276). Many quarrels erupt in the course of the Homeric epics, but Thersites' *neikos* and its reception is something else altogether.[29] Indeed, the scene bears more resemblance to orators' invective and audience manipulation in the Athenian assembly and is thus especially useful for this discussion. The elements are all there: a sharp and pointed distinction between speakers, who nonetheless share an ultimately sullying penchant for verbal wrangling and insult;[30] the control of audience perspective by the more authoritative speaker, who achieves this by (slanderously) isolating his enemy as a slanderer; the lurking threat of physical debasement that further distinguishes the target as not sharing the group's perspective or promoting its best interests.

This type of exchange possesses, again, an essentially didactic quality.[31] Its coercive, violent tenor aims at leaving no doubt as to whom the mass of soldiers ought to support (i.e. the leaders [*basilēes*]), as well as who is suited to speak in assembly and why (i.e. the leaders because they are leaders).[32] This assembly of soldiers and the warriors who rule them is no democracy, of course, but the didactic use of invective and threat anticipates quite precisely the ways in which orators in the classical period align themselves

[28] See Bourdieu's remark: "The spokesperson is an impostor endowed with the *skeptron*" (Bourdieu 1991: 109).
[29] Contrast verbal wrangling (i.e. "flyting") and see Martin 1989; Parks 1990; Hesk forthcoming.
[30] Note that Thersites and Odysseus were later associated (Sophocles, *Philoctetes* 438–44), and that Thersites is not depicted as ugly or deformed in Apulian vase-painting (Marks 2005: 2–3).
[31] N.b., the verb *neikeō* often encompasses reproaches aimed at prodding warriors into battle (e.g. *Iliad* 4.241, 336, 368 [Agamemnon], 5.471 [Sarpedon]).
[32] See *Iliad* 2.203–206; Hesiod, *Theogony* 81–93.

with their audiences by means of insulting example – that is, by working to exclude their opponents and enemies from the realm of citizens fit to speak in assembly. Like any fine oratorical wrangler, Odysseus makes good use of this agonistic moment by insulting the insulter, threatening his exclusion from the group, and thereby solidifying his status as advisor to kings while he achieves allegiance with both the audience of soldiers and his fellow leaders. It is an instance of singular oratorical skill and occurs at a moment when conflict and disintegration seem imminent. Further, it reveals the brutality with which verbal and thereby social hierarchies are sustained, a realpolitik component crucial to understanding archaic rhetorical strategies and too often over-looked by scholars. Finally, classical writers clearly receive the incident as uniquely significant, and in particular relation to speaking abilities.

For instance, when Aeschines argues against Ctesiphon's proposal to crown Demosthenes as a public benefactor, he presents a picture of a shrill, repulsive public speaker whose body is also threatened with abuse, remarking wryly that no tragic poet would represent the Greeks crowning Thersites, since Homer depicts him as "unmanly and a panderer" (*anandron ... kai sukophantēn*, 3.231). Money hunger, gluttony, over-imbibing, and rapacious talk tend to fall together in these depictions, as do cringing flattery, effeminacy, and love of luxury. The too obviously greedy or craven speaker cannot hope to win his private cases or support for his public proposals. Thus both orators seek to encourage their audiences effectively to close ranks against such speakers and align themselves with the man clearly on the side of good habits and good leadership.

We might compare as well Thucydides' and Aristophanes' depictions of the reputedly brutal, loud-mouthed, and debased demagogue Cleon. In Thucydides Cleon is the "most violent and persuasive" of demagogues (*biaotatos kai pithanōtatos*, 3.36–38), who renders audiences incapable of making calm and careful decisions. Aristophanes identifies him repeatedly with an aggressive, slanderous style that likewise intimidates the mass of citizens. In *Peace* the greedy "tanner" (see *bursopōlēs*, 648) has rendered the city so desperate that it "snapped up every bit of slander."[33] In *Wasps* and *Knights* Cleon and his kind take advantage of the demos by pandering to citizens' taste for brutal displays of political might by orators who pillory any who oppose them.

Audiences are supposedly in thrall to such aggressive speakers, since they sustain their allegiance through oratorical pyrotechnics that insult and ostracize their opponents. In these depictions the demagogue's slanderous

---

[33] ἄττα διαβάλοι τις αὐτῇ, ταῦτ' ἂν ἥδιστ' ἤσθιεν, *Peace* 643.

and brutal style may sometimes achieve its effect, but his detractors seek to demonstrate that because of such tactics (including both his verbal style and his deportment) he is the one who ought to be excluded from the ranks of leadership.[34] That is to say, "Cleon" in these narratives serves as the peer outsider, the worst of the demagogues, just as "Thersites" in epic tradition represents the worst of the leaders who came on the Trojan campaign. And if in fourth-century invective "Solon" cuts the figure that everyone wants to imitate, "Thersites" is his opposite: the embodiment of the enemy orator, a threat to citizen and state.[35]

Likeness and decorum

Underpinning this strategy of allegiance and exclusion is a consistent recognition that the persuasive speaker must engage in a plausible and appropriate self-presentation. Once again, Odysseus is the figure who arouses awareness of such concerns. His versatile and often debased physicality repeatedly raises questions about how like or unlike he is to a noble type (e.g. *Odyssey* 4.249–51, 6.242–43); and since arguments from probability (*to eikos*) are based on assumptions about likeness, his presence signals questions about not only probability but also the problem that likeness poses within the rhetorical moment.[36] While it would seem that a speaker ought to appear dignified and beneficent to gain trust (as Aristotle would later argue),[37] in part through arguments that give the impression of being likely and reasonable, in both archaic and classical settings the need to "perform as" raises broader anxieties about the putative match between deportment and verbal decorum.

Further, notions of what is probable are closely tied to assumptions about what is appropriate or fitting.[38] Odysseus' famous dismissal of the handsome Euryalus in book 8 of the *Odyssey* reveals the problematic relationship that appearance has to status and verbal authority. When the young man insults him by declaring that he does not look like an athlete

---

[34] If Thersites' physicality in the *Iliad* is unconventional, so reputedly was Cleon's performance style. He is depicted as speaking too loudly, with his cloak thrown back and/or garments hitched up (*Constitution of the Athenians* 28.3; Plutarch, *Nicias* 8.3); cf. Aeschines' depiction of Timarchus' delivery style (1.26). See also chapter 5 of Worman 2008.

[35] See further in chapter 2 of Worman 2008.

[36] See further in Worman 2002: 121–22, 176–77; see also Bassi 1998.

[37] Aristotle names wisdom, virtue, and goodwill (*phronēsis kai aretē kai eunoia*) as components of a persuasive self-presentation (*Rhetoric* 1378a8).

[38] Aristotle denotes suitability by *prepō/prepon* and associates it with style and character (e.g. Aristotle, *Rhetoric* 1408a, 1417a).

(*oude ... daēmoni phōti eïskō athlōn*, 8.159; *oud' athlētēri eoikas*, 8.164), Odysseus responds by pointing out that those who are beautiful in appearance do not always speak fittingly. Invoking the decorous mandates inherent in terms such as *kharis* and *kosmos*, Odysseus declares that a man may look good but speak gracelessly (*ou hoi kharis amphi peristephetai epeessin*), just as he, Euryalus, has roused the stranger by addressing him in an unbecoming fashion (*eipōn ou kata kosmon*) (*Odyssey* 8.174–79).[39]

Plato explicitly makes the connection between likeness and arguments from probability in the *Phaedrus*. He argues that writers of speeches are unscrupulous (*panourgoi*) because they conceal (*apokruptontai*) the nature of the soul (271c1–3; cf. 261e–262b). Such deception hinders the proper kinds of matching that ought to be at work in oratory: that between the speaker's style and the listener's type of soul (272a; cf. 277c).[40] This constitutes the good kind of similarity, one quite distinct from those that sophists such as Tisias and Gorgias employ in *eikos* arguments, which persuade the masses because of their "likeness to the truth" (*homoiotēta tou alēthous*, 273d4). The invocation of Sicilian sophists who argue from probability as a cloak for the truth clearly aligns the discourse of likeness with elaborate, deceptive speakers who educate their elite students to affirm appearances over realities.

In his prosecution of Aeschines' conduct on the second embassy to Philip, Demosthenes sustains a similar focus on visible style versus true character. He also echoes Aeschines' earlier invocation of Solon's contained deportment (*Against Timarchus*, 1.25–26), by lampooning his opponent's use of it (*eisō tēn kheir' ekhont' anabeblēmenon*, 19.251) as a negative example of how a public speaker ought to comport himself. Not only does Aeschines' verbal flamboyance broadcast his excessive type; his imitation (*emimēsato*) of the great statesman's physical disposition (*tou skhēmatos*) also renders visible (by contrast) his own profligacy (19.253). In fact, Demosthenes claims, Aeschines' deportment includes a debased alteration of Solon's that reveals his true motivations: he holds his hand out, but with the palm up – for taking bribes (255).[41]

Kings' rhetoric in Hesiod

The exchange in Homer between Odysseus and Euryalus centers on Odysseus' portrait of the man of unprepossessing appearance whose words are

[39] See Worman 2002: 22, 59–60, 93–99.
[40] Cf. Antisthenes, fr. 51 Caizzi.
[41] See further in Worman 2004 and Worman 2008 (ch. 5).

crowned with eloquence. The passage resembles one in Hesiod's *Theogony*, when the poet describes the speaking style of the good leader. This leader is a man chosen by the Muses, who pour sweet dew on his tongue, so that honeyed words flow from his mouth.[42] The people all admire him as he makes "straight judgments" (*itheīeisi dikēisin*) and wisely resolves serious conflicts (*mega neikos epistamenōs katepause*) (86–87).[43] Both passages are about leadership and the right conferred upon the man of noble birth to speak in assembly; in the language of the discussion above, this would be the man who most resembles a noble type and who can thus lay claim through his visible performance to that right while denying it to others. Only the *Odyssey* passage, however, emphasizes the mismatch that may occur between the visible stature or manifest status of a man and his verbal decorum.

While elsewhere in Hesiod the awareness of abuse of kingship is evident, the passage in the *Theogony* preserves the notion that a sweet, modest, and just speaking style is handed down from the god through the conduit of the Muses, cementing the tie between Zeus and aristocratic leaders.[44] Further, even though the poet emphasizes elsewhere that the path of virtue is prefaced by sweat,[45] since it is long, steep, and rough at the beginning,[46] the man who pursues this rough road is "entirely noble" (*panaristos*) and full of good advice, while he who listens to such a well-spoken man is also good (*esthlos d' au ka'keinos hos eu eiponti pithētai*) (293–95). Thus both speaker and audience may be right-minded and share in fair judgment, but this mutuality is not easily come by and can be coerced if necessary, as the *ainos* of the hawk and the nightingale reveals (202–12). Indeed, as in Homer mutuality may only occur among aristocratic peers; the brutal rhetoric of the "hawk" (i.e. the king) belongs to the assembly and marks the relationship between the leaders and the mass of citizens – including, apparently, the mewling "nightingale" (i.e. the bard).

---

[42] τῷ μὲν ἐπὶ γλώσσῃ γλυκερὴν χείουσιν ἐέρσην, | τοῦ δ' ἔπε' ἐκ στόματος ῥεῖ μείλιχα, *Theogony* 83–84. Cf. again Nestor's honeyed speech (*Iliad* 1.249).

[43] The passages share one line: "… with sweet modesty, and he stands out among those gathered" (αἰδοῖ μειλιχίῃ, μετὰ δὲ πρέπει ἀγρομένοισι, *Odyssey* 8.172; *Theogony* 92); cf. West 1966 on *Theogony* 94–97).

[44] See Martin 1984; Walsh 1984: 24–25 argues that this divine gift does not ensure truth, even though it seems reasonable to expect that fine words from a just speaker would be true. Note that Odysseus makes this bond explicit in reproving the mass of soldiers directly before the assembly in which Thersites speaks (2.203–206).

[45] τῆς δ' ἀρετῆς ἱδρῶτα θεοὶ προπάροιθεν ἔθηκαν | ἀθάνατοι, *Works and Days* 289–90.

[46] μακρὸς δὲ καὶ ὄρθιος οἶμος ἐς αὐτὴν | καὶ τρηχὺς τὸ πρῶτον, *Works and Days* 290–91.

The harsh didacticism of this picture leaves little room for the more subtle problems that attend persuasion: the leaders' own roles in coercing allegiance, for instance; or the speaker's need to appear like a noble man, with its suggestion of the possibility that this may be an impersonation.[47] Hesiod's depiction focuses more on moral correctives than persuasive tactics, with the potential for conflict – for, in fact, the insult and slander that lies just to the side of fair practice – functioning as the threat. The rhetorical dynamics in both Hesiod and Homer less commonly involve a gracious exchange of compliments and arrival at a mutually beneficial solution than they do an aggressive, combative sparring edged with violence. Further, if these dynamics were not proto-democratic in their functioning, they gained purchase in the classical period from the fact that Athenian practices were not themselves very democratic. Elites, some of whom refashioned themselves as popular demagogues, orchestrated decisions in both the courts and the Assembly in a manner that resembled the high-handed and brutal strategies of heroic warriors: fictionalizing, slandering of opponents, and manipulating allegiance thereby.

The slandering Odysseus in Pindar

It is a curious aspect of the development of democratic rhetorical practices that Odysseus becomes a rogue, even as orators are appropriating his techniques.[48] This negative depiction may have initiated with Pindar, for whom Odysseus serves as the prototypical lying, slanderous rhetor. While Pindaric epinikia rarely address the abusive tactics that became associated with Odysseus and so central to democratic practice, as praise poems in service to a rigidly sustained aristocratic hierarchy they continue the didacticism that dominates archaic rhetorical practices.[49] Here once again the notion of *kosmos*, while apparently merely decorative, cements the compulsory and hierarchical ordering of civic relations. Both the poet's composition and the celebrated victor should be an adornment for the city (*Nemean* 6.53, 2.8); and the poet's own poem reiterates this necessary function (*poikilon | kosmon audaenta logōn*, fr. 194.2–3).

This decorative ordering possesses an ambiguous power, since grace (*kharis*) can render the unpersuasive persuasive (*apiston emēsato piston | emmenai to pollakis*, *Olympian* 1.31–32). The ability to fashion graceful

---

[47] Havelock 1963: 107–109 emphasizes the good leader's dependency on the formal characteristics of this gift of the Muses, especially formula and meter.

[48] See Worman 1999.

[49] See Kurke 1991: 163–94.

verbiage effectively masks the brutalities of power; and Pindar himself is deeply complicit in this masquerade. This potentially suspect charm opens out on appearances, fictionality, and the possibility of deceit, as the passage directly preceding this one indicates (*dedaidalmenoi pseudesi pokilois exapatōnti muthoi*, *Olympian* 1.30). We may compare here charges against the sophists, famous for a charisma that many thought concealed devious argumentative tactics. Unlike Pindar, however, the sophists' claims to be able to teach such tactics disturbed the aristocratic elite, since such claims in themselves demystify social authority apparently bred in the bone.

Elsewhere Pindar associates this deceitful mode with Homer and his hero Odysseus. In *Nemean* 7, for instance, he introduces the contest between Ajax and Odysseus over Achilles' arms by invoking Homer's lies (*pseudesi*) and the deceit inherent in cleverness (*sophia | de klepte paragoisa muthois*, 22–24). Odysseus plays the role of the slandering liar chiefly because he verbally overruns the nobler but silent Ajax, the bulwark of the Achaeans.[50] Pindar's dismay at the power of the clever man's language indicates his attachment to aristocratic notions of innate (i.e. noble, heroic) social authority and his suspicion of tactics (whether poetic or political) that might dislodge this hierarchy. Again, many classical writers with aristocratic leanings question in similar terms the strategies of sophists, whom they represent as agile, decadent liars with political ambitions.

The portrait of Odysseus in *Nemean* 8 conjoins the theme of deceit with that of abusive rapacity. Odysseus "grabs" (*haptetai*), "bites" (*dapsen*), and "skewers" (*amphikulisais*) Ajax (*Nemean* 8.23–24) with his arguments as if he were a side of beef, his imagery now prefiguring the representation of the abusive hero as a grasping sophist in classical representation.[51] Odysseus embodies the confluence of these two modes and indicates why they might be thus conjoined: the verbal manipulator plays a mercenary, even shameful role within the heroic idiom. His figure gives the lie to aristocratic assumptions of nobility and natural ascendancy, revealing the instinct to the strategic appropriation of authority, to self-preservation, and to privileging the body's base needs over the hero's honor. The cruder implications of this connection between slander and persuasive fabrications repeatedly come to the fore in the dramatic and oratorical texts of the classical period. Witness, for instance, the sophistic chef who attempts to orchestrate deceptions and threatens to eat his interlocutors in Euripides' *Cyclops* and

[50] See Walsh 1984: 38–42; Pratt 1993: 121, 128. A similar tradition developed around Palamedes (e.g. Plato, *Apology* 41b; Xenophon, *Apology* 26).
[51] On the Pindaric imagery see Steiner 2001.

Attic comedy.[52] In Demosthenes' depiction of Aeschines, the voluble orator is similarly mercenary and aggressive – shouting profanities, fighting for scraps, and gobbling iambs.[53]

Conclusion: rhapsodes versus orators?

The rise of democracy during the classical period in Athens provided numerous settings for the implementation of rhetorical strategies on a daily basis. Sophistic training in argumentative techniques contributed to the growing sense of rhetoric as a *tekhnē* – a body of knowledge with discernible rules and tactics.[54] Although sophistic displays seem to have been modeled on the grand gestures and elaborate dress of the Homeric rhapsodes, some of their techniques became influential in more contentious settings: the use of arguments from probability, for instance, and the deceptive strategies by which the weaker might appear the stronger argument.[55] Except for the funeral oration (*epitaphios*), most public opportunities for delivering speeches called more for negative campaigning, as it were, than for the grand, gracious utterances of laudation among peers.

Athenian orators made frequent use of fictionalizing and abusive tactics that denigrated their opponents' status and stature, both in forensic cases and in the Assembly.[56] They often openly mocked and slandered their opponents, deploying gossip and hearsay as stepping stones to the most serious accusation: that their targets had behaved in ways unbefitting of Athenian citizens. This could often be witnessed in these enemy citizens' very bodies, disposed as they might be in various revealing attitudes in notorious spaces around the city. Mockery of such visible elements forged allegiances with citizen audiences who themselves assumed their right to speak as a basis for verbally ostracizing others. Such derisive tactics debased a speaker's characteristic usage and delivery and thereby threatened not

---

[52] E.g. Aristophanes' *Knights*; Cratinus, *Odysseuses*; Callias, *Cyclopes*.

[53] E.g. in *On the Crown* Aeschines bawls out "cart language" (*hōsper ex hamaxēs*) like a slinger of *aiskhrologia* (βοᾷς ῥητὰ καὶ ἄρρητ' ὀνομάζων) (18.122); he is also a "crumb-snatcher" (*spermologos*, 18.127) and an "iamb-eater" (*iambeiophagos*, 18.139).

[54] Plato's apparent problems with this notion notwithstanding (see esp. Plato, *Gorgias* 462a–463d); compare Aristotle's more positive picture (*Rhetoric* 1355b26–1356a1).

[55] See Eupolis, *Flatterers*; Aristophanes, *Clouds*; Plato, *Ion*.

[56] See V. Hunter 1990; Halliwell 1991b; Carey 1994b and Carey 1994a; Hall 1995. Halliwell points out (288–93) that although there was at least one law against slander in classical Athens, it does not seem to have prevented the kind of character abuse exercised in public and private orations.

only his public career but even his very ability to speak. They thus threw into sharp relief the vulnerability of democratic decision-making and policy.

If these strategies were in fact among the most influential and powerful tools to be appropriated by orators from archaic and aristocratic tradition, democratic practice in Athens must have been in a constant state of threat. And this does seem to have been the case: throughout the late fifth and fourth centuries in Athens, elite factions worked to wrest control from each other, while orators served as their public faces. The rogue demagogue (or proficient orator), modeling his tactics on the fabricating and slandering techniques of Odysseus and his sophistic descendants, pilloried his enemy as a Thersites, urging his audience to align themselves against such debased participants in the public arena. And like the soldiers in the *Iliad*, citizen audiences seem often to have approved such tactics, and to have done so without the anxious laughter.

Indeed, Aeschines depicts a freer response in the Athenian assembly, when he presents Timarchus as such a reprobate that even his policy arguments evoke derision. As Aeschines tells it, when Timarchus made reference to certain spaces in the city, his fellow citizens roared with laughter: "When he mentioned 'the repair of walls' or 'tower' or 'someone taken off some-where,' straight away you shouted and hooted and yourselves uttered the proper name of his acts, which you all well knew."[57] In Aeschines' portrayal, Timarchus' very words reveal that he is unfit for public office. Moreover, Aeschines makes the equation that underscores why these insults carry so much weight in the fourth-century struggle for control of Athenian foreign policy: Timarchus' sullying of his body equally sullies the city (*kataiskhunōn to sōma to heautou kai tēn polin*, 1.40), which (by implication) threatens its safety and dominion.

These tactics of pillory and exclusion from the right to speak in assembly form the core of classical oratory in practice, however much Aristotle might emphasize the importance of projecting beneficence or later theorists that of employing pleasant vocabulary and cadences. Such emphases obscure the hostile and didactic targeting of the speaking body in these confrontations, as well as its roots in archaic settings. They obscure as well the social hierarchies that rhetorical strategies both depend on and seek to mask. A "Thersites" can thus serve both as the Homeric hero's perfect target and as the orator's perfect metonym for citizen debasement. The orator's

---

[57] εἰ γὰρ μνησθείη τειχῶν ἐπισκευῆς ἢ πύργου, ἢ ὡς ἀπήγετό ποί τις, εὐθὺς ἐβοᾶτε καὶ ἐγελᾶτε, καὶ αὐτοὶ ἐλέγετε τὴν ἐπωνυμίαν τῶν ἔργων ὧν σύνιστε αὐτῷ, 1.80, cf. 1.84. As Carey notes in his translation of this speech: "The passage is full of sexual double meanings that are lost on the modern reader" (Carey 2000: 51 n. 86). Compare Fisher 2001: 216.

gesture, like that of Odysseus, aims at the opponent's silence and isolation. Recognizing the rigorously embodied agonism that achieves this isolation is essential to reconstructing a history of rhetorical practice.

Suggestions for further reading

There are not many good discussions of rhetorical strategies in preclassical settings, but see Cole 1991; Enos 1993; Kennedy 1994: chapter 1; and Worthington 1994. Martin 1989 is very perceptive about how speaking styles are shaped in Homer and in many ways more useful, as is Hesk's work on flyting (Hesk 2006). Both make use of a "speech in performance" model, as in somewhat different ways do Bassi 1998 and Worman 2002. The edited collections in the series Orality and Literacy in Ancient Greece have advanced understanding of how oral settings shape ancient discourses well into the classical period (e.g. Bakker and Kahane 1997; Worthington and Foley 2002; Mackie 2004); see also Goldhill and Osborne 1999.

2

ROBERT WARDY

The philosophy of rhetoric and the rhetoric of philosophy

We are the speaking animals. To take a leaf from Aristotle's book, the permanently mute or unremittingly taciturn are inferior beasts or superior gods; to be a person is to be gregarious, and to associate in the human fashion is to speak among ourselves.[1] Indeed, creation and discovery of the individual self are conditional on locating this self among other selves; but since these others are nodes in a linguistic network, a society of speakers, acquisition of a language and entry into a community necessarily proceed in tandem.

This skeletal delineation of linguistic essentialism will strike some as at best tendentious, at worst grotesquely unscientific, bereft of empirical foundations. No matter: for overwhelmingly many others, the absolute centrality of language is a truism so conspicuous as barely to deserve acknowledgment, before one passes on to the burgeoning questions to which it immediately gives rise: is all thought linguistic? Do the expressive resources of all languages come to the same sum, or do different languages manifest characteristic (dis)advantages? With such linguistic relativism, we are moving from what appears to be strictly theoretical to issues with ethical import; consideration of the possibility that language might encode, enshrine, confirm, or even partially comprise various sociopolitical asymmetries takes us further along the spectrum. Participants in such debates may hotly disagree, while fundamentally agreeing that language is always, inevitably at the core of their dispute. Profound insight, or profound delusion: if the latter, this chapter is a modest foray into the pathology of our exaggerated logocentric proclivities. Either way, the ultimate ancestor of this presumption that language is of paramount importance is Greek meditation on – and squabbling over – *logos*.

[1] Adapting *Politics* 1253a2–4.

What is in a word? When it is *logos* – the word of words – much. *Logos* is polysemic: it possesses neither a single, simple signification, nor an ambiguous one which can be taken in different, unrelated ways. *Logos* can mean: a phrase or sentence; a larger discourse consisting of sentences; what is expressed in that discourse; a mathematical ratio; most abstractly, any structural arrangement or pattern. At the semantic heart of *logos* lies the verbal meaning, and one branches out to the other significations from the fact that the words which constitute a meaningful phrase are not a random jumble but rather are arranged in a significant pattern. Thus a simple sentence makes sense, and it makes sense because of the grammatical relations between its words. A speech or piece of writing makes sense because of the various meaningful relations, narrative, logical, whatever, which obtain between its constituent sentences. If one considers those narrative and logical relations in abstraction from their verbal expression, one arrives at *logos* as reason or rationale; and *logos* as ratio or proportion ties together two or more quantities.

But we should do more than register the polysemy of *logos*; we must also realize that to claim that the *raison d'être* of Greek philosophy is the explication of this semantics is scant exaggeration. How so? First, the step from thinking about how one makes proper sense at one or another scale of discourse to deciding how one ought to communicate is short and inevitable. Therefore enquiries into *logos* are fraught with normative suggestions; this is contentious legislation, not dispassionate lexicography. Second, the semantic web of *logos* binds together strands of talk and of what we talk about. Therefore enquiries into it abound with assumptions concerning the organized nature of things, and corresponding prescriptions for how best to convey their truth. Third, to set about the articulation of *logos* is to head towards a *logos* of *logos*. Therefore the logocentricity and self-reflective methodology of Greek philosophy also go hand-in-hand. But fourth, if the philosophers feel themselves to be philosophers just inasmuch as they have created a science of *logos*, they will be predisposed to look askance at unschooled use of it. And suspicion of ordinary incompetence could and would harden into downright enmity towards a bogus rival. Rhetoric will set up as another science of *logos*; a predominant philosophical reflex will be to argue that since a veritable science of *logos* cannot fail to be through-and-through philosophical, this is scientist flummery.

Accordingly we run across no shortage of early Greek thinkers who are equally confident that right *logos* – to which they often claim privileged access – reigns supreme, and adamant that that authentic *logos* is more or less inaccessible to hapless ignorance. Some star examples. Parmenides depicts himself as the recipient of a remarkable divine revelation: an austerely ratiocinative goddess purports to establish that reality is static and unified, so that the phenomena we seem to perceive are altogether delusive. She demands: "judge by *logos* the contentious test I have expressed" (Coxon fr. 7). The goddess does not define *logos*: but since her demonstration takes the form of a rigorous deduction, it is plausibly inferred that one aspect of her *logos* is the argument's logical progression, the other, complementary aspect is the reason we are to apply to her reasoning. But, notoriously, Parmenides does not confine himself to what is, conveyed through and to *logos*: "now I put an end to persuasive *logos* and thought about reality/truth,[2] and from this point do you learn mortal opinions by listening to the deceptive composition of my words" (Coxon fr. 8). The point is not that the *logos* was not linguistic: rather the distinction between it and the "deceptive composition" to come must reside in what the words concern, what they presume, and how they develop. But why the unsettling invitation, if *logos* is indeed "persuasive"? Because the *logos* is "trustworthy" and so "fit to persuade," even if it (sometimes? all too often?) fails to do so?

If Parmenides' content is revolutionary, the form in which he elects to couch it is traditional, quasi-Homeric epic verse. Why would he have chosen to do so, given that his philosophical predecessors and contemporaries are among the first exponents of prose? We might conjecture that the reason for his choice is the fact that epic was the then prestige genre, especially if we shift our focus from Homer to Hesiod. The Hesiodic muses, who are capable of delivering both truths and treacherously plausible falsehoods (*Theogony* 27–28), are the role model for the philosophical goddess who supplies first *logos*, then deceptive verbiage. But note two telling contrasts. First, the precise identity of Parmenides' goddess is unclear; but it is clear that she is a supreme deity. The Hesiodic muses are relatively minor goddesses who function as intermediaries between the higher order of Olympian gods and mortals; the Parmenidean goddess is herself at once a major power, and the authoritative source of truth. Second, Hesiod's transition from the prefatory hymn to his main theme consists of imperatives addressed to the muses. It is possible but not obligatory to conceive of the remainder of the *Theogony* as the muses' own words. But the reader of Parmenides is left in no doubt that, after the poem's introduction, all the rest is the goddess in her own voice instructing Parmenides. The polemical thrust of this narrative device is unequivocal: Parmenidean philosophy has usurped the prestige of Hesiodic epic, or should do so, if we

---

[2] The Greek *alētheia* is sometimes best translated "truth," sometimes "reality": here one hesitates to choose.

have it in us to comprehend the divine *logos*. A shrewd gambit, this – one might even be tempted to describe it as a piece of belligerent rhetoric.

"Listening not to me but to the *logos* it is wise to agree that all things are one," proclaims Heraclitus, the first and foremost philosopher of *logos* (Kahn fr. 36), although he is no more willing (or able?) than Parmenides to furnish us with an explicit articulation of what the *logos* might be. With the best will in the world, how is even the most attentive and biddable of his audience to perform this curious trick? If I pay Heraclitus no heed, will I not remain deaf to the *logos*? Or is it that we initially attend to his message but then transcend his particular utterances to hearken to the universal *logos*? Regardless of the substantive content of this mysterious injunction, it exemplifies what we would doubtless label a complex "rhetorical" strategy: salient reference to the (mal)functioning of the relation between speaker/writer and listener/reader,[3] leavened with a willfully paradoxical behest, backhanded encouragement to grasp the ownerless, cosmic language of the real.

Our third example, Gorgias, indubitably figures on any list of prominent *devotees* of *logos*, but whether he belongs there as a congener of Parmenides and Heraclitus, or in some other capacity, is a nice question. In later antiquity "sophistry" was fathered on him; but "sophistry," no less than "rhetoric" itself, is originally a Platonic-Aristotelian term of art (or invective). Yet notwithstanding the anachronistic hazards, picking up the pejorative connotations of "sophistry" does appear to be the apt response to the author of *On What Is Not*, which pretends: "there is nothing; even if there is something, it is unknowable; even if it both is and is knowable, nevertheless it cannot be revealed to others" (*About Melissus, Xenophanes and Gorgias* 979a12–13). This nihilism trumped makes Heraclitus seem in comparison an accommodating director. Thus it is not difficult to see why sophistical paternity is ascribed to Gorgias; but we must not without further ado designate him a "sophist" (even *avant la lettre*) rather than a "philosopher." Parmenides, after all, is the father of Greek philosophy: but who – try as they might – *can* believe what his goddess says? This is an appropriate comparison, since Gorgias unmistakably couches *On What Is Not* in the logical idiom of Parmenides: venerable philosopher or archetypal sophist, whose *logos* is not outrageously unpersuasive?

---

[3] There is no consensus over how "oral" as opposed to "literary" Heraclitus' work was. A more intriguing question concerns Heraclitus' "linguification" or "textualization" of the world: for if we should listen to the *logos*, then nature itself speaks to us in its own tongue. Lest that appear a strained inference from a metaphor, consider this suggestive declaration: "eyes and ears are poor witnesses for men if their souls do not understand the language [literally, "if they have barbarian souls"]" (Kahn fr. 16).

No less provocative is Gorgias' *Encomium of Helen*. Therein he undertakes to rescue the reputation of traduced Helen; he will effect a "refutation" of her slanderers by "adding a *logismos* to my *logos*" (*Encomium* §2), that is, by enumerating all possible grounds for her absconding with Paris, and systematically arguing that she deserves absolution on all counts. *Elenkhos*, translated "refutation" here, is the same Greek word used by Parmenides for "test" in fr. 7, and to be used by Plato for Socrates' dialectical examinations. The term is not limited to philosophical contexts; it frequently applies to forensic (dis)proof, as in Gorgias' fantasy rallying to Helen's cause. In Plato, the disputatious wrangling of the courts will come to stand for anti-philosophy, specious mock argument targeted on victory rather than truth. So does Gorgias' text offer a specimen of quasi-judicial argumentation designedly at odds with the philosophical standards extravagantly flouted in *On What Is Not*? But to look ahead once more, since the Aristotelian taxonomy will distinguish between forensic rhetoric and epideictic, or laudatory display, should the *Encomium*, which is, after all, an encomium, not rather count as display? Fake forensic is genuine epideictic. "I wished to write the *logos* as an encomium of Helen, but as an amusement for myself" (§21): one might infer that Gorgias is just teasing, that effort spent on the generic identification of the *Encomium* is effort ill-spent on light humor. Consequently the assertion that "*logos* is a great ruler" (§8) is not to be taken at face value; make nothing of the facts that the Greek for "ruler," *dunastēs*, is usually a political term, and that a ready tongue could make a potent political tool or weapon.

The effect of Gorgias' joke is confusion; and different sorts of deliberate confusion emerge as his tactical and strategic goals throughout. Intention: can he be serious? How do we gauge seriousness; what bearing should the producer's intention have on our interpretation of the product? Methodology: even our little broad-brush survey shows that philosophers are keen to discriminate between those types of thought and language which they endorse – and the gullible, pernicious remainder. In *On What Is Not*, Gorgias confronts us with argument reminiscent of the philosophical project, but deployed to deadly parodic effect – or is that not his intention? Genre: is *On What Is Not* serious philosophical nihilism, or light relief from Parmenides? Were it in earnest, what kind of discourse is the *Encomium of Helen* pretending to be?

Logos itself: the *logos* of Heraclitus seeks detachment as it speaks impersonally of the world – or is the world, as it speaks. It alone should be heeded. The *logos* of Parmenides is divine and (or because?) pre-eminently rational and logically forceful, unlike mortal opinions relayed by deceptive words. But the *logos* of the *Encomium* which "accomplishes divine deeds"

(§8) – that is, controls emotion – is not an exceptional species. On the contrary, Gorgias is concerned to emphasize that all controversialists are alike in their manipulation of opinion (§13), which Parmenides had prized apart from *logos*. The *logos* of the goddess is (or should be?) persuasive because its truth is necessarily borne home by logic. "I searched out myself," says Heraclitus (Kahn fr. 101): which might indicate that were we to emulate him, we too might paradoxically withdraw from reliance on other people in our conformity with the universal *logos*. "So many men have persuaded and do persuade so many about so many topics by shaping false *logos*!," warns the *Encomium* (§11) – or is it crowing? The explanation of all this general deception serves to excuse Helen's individual error. The seductive *logos* which persuaded her to elope was irresistible (§12); to persuade simply is to force an impotent soul to comply with the insidious behests issued by the owner of the dominant *logos*. If logical compulsion is rationally inexorable, by the same token erotic beguilement will always, so it seems, take us in.

The philosophers are correct to insist that *logos* works; but they are incorrect to suppose that there is anything to choose between *logoi*, homogeneously threatening to the vulnerable or useful or amusing to the strong. A most emphatic difference between Gorgias and, in their different manners, both Parmenides and Heraclitus, is that his omnipotent *logos* is assuredly linguistic. The (other?) philosophers' *logoi* do incorporate verbal accounts, which, however, are exemplary by virtue of their mapping onto intrinsically rational, objective structures, which validate those accounts. In sharp contrast, the *logos* of Gorgias, illustrated as it is by superficially heterogeneous persuaders, is the common verbal currency of the marketplace of undifferentiated persuasion. From the philosophical perspective, this will appear to be a disconcerting conflation of the trivial and the overweening: it is all just verbiage, but words conquer all.

Philosophers must ask themselves: if (their) *logos* is so strong, why is it in danger of being obscured or even impersonated by unworthy rivals? Why does its beneficent influence not automatically make itself felt? Is it that *logos* in the sense of our rational equipment is routinely corrupt, only rarely up to the job of following reason as it traces the lineaments of what is? The two halves of Parmenides' poem will come to epitomize the unstable subordination of rhetoric to philosophy, or, for those not won over by the rigors of the incredible *logos*, the ironic rebellion of plausible rhetoric against less than specious philosophy. Since, as noted, the two halves of the poem stand in respectively for the true and the false declarations of the Hesiodic muses, the irony might be doubled: if new-fangled philosophy stole the trappings of ancient epic, so in its turn philosophy may have sired Oedipal rhetoric.

The tension – remarkably fruitful in the event – between the conviction that unadorned right reason will necessarily, if only eventually, prevail, and a besetting anxiety lest false yet efficacious persuasion subvert the truth, creates the opportunity for Gorgias' joke. This joke was to become rhetoric's riposte to the arrogant pretension of philosophy – according to the rhetoricians; and rhetoric's not so funny menace to philosophy's vital separation of licit from illicit attempts to persuade – according to the philosophers.

By this juncture one might feel inclined to complain that my focus has been too narrow, my preamble confused. Too narrow: the agenda I have set is exclusively philosophical, with the likely unfortunate consequence that the subsequent discussion will be skewed towards philosophical preoccupations, rather than remaining open to rhetorical aspirations which, so far from intersecting with, are likely to diverge markedly from the paths of the philosophers. This and related complaints come under the rubric of question-begging. Confused: as my awkward way with tenses in what precedes ("was to become ... ") testifies, have I not gone well ahead of myself in talking of "rhetoric" (or "sophistry"), surveying the (mis) appropriation of *logos* with distortive hindsight? This and related complaints come under the rubric of anachronism.

There are some unusual competencies whose connection to ordinary habits of mind, or to abilities innate or routinely acquired, is exiguous: proficiency in building particle colliders might not be even a grand extension of piling up rocks; doing set theory is only a very distant relative of doing humble sums. Others elude easy categorization: is philosophy the most esoteric of disciplines, or a regressive indulgence of the infantile wonder we all once shared, but the non-philosophers outgrew? Finally, some capacities patently elaborate on what was already accomplished untechnically, if to a lesser degree and less consistently: military colleges refine savagery, and cartography redefines, but does not create, our sense of place. Rhetoric might seem to be clearly like that: as bludgeoning the opposition in violent conflict precedes recourse to martial arts, so talking over the other side is prior to cultivation of and reflection on rhetorical techniques. If we truly are the speaking animals, then we have always striven to speak to some effect.

But on closer inspection, the robust conclusion that rhetoric *merely* enhances pre-existent verbal facility will not quite do. First, no one will allege that formal rhetoric is actually necessary for success in a verbal contest; but that it is not necessary for reliable success is not nearly so obvious, most especially in societies where the ruling expectation is that certain persuasive opportunities are the *de rigeur* occasion for displays of what that culture recognizes as verbal art. Second and much more important, the coarse-grained conclusion glosses over both the cardinal distinctions and connections between theoretical insight and practical know-how. Some of the latter can be found in the absence of the former; but the extent of this concession should not be exaggerated. Doing, understanding, and evaluating may split up unproblematically for a great range of performances, from athletics to literature. But not so for all. There are activities descended from entirely natural or straightforward socialized pursuits which cannot be undertaken in the absence of a productive awareness of what, by cultured convention, is to count as participation in those activities; for them, expert understanding stipulates what can be done and regulates what is done well or badly. Rhetoric might be more like that.

On this basis we shall be able to deal briskly with the two objections. To address the specific complaint that I have been anachronistically preoccupied with what is not (yet) "rhetoric." Eschew the snappy but vapid answer "but all discourse is already rhetorical" – so none is. If "rhetoric" is to have a place in our conceptual toolkit, then it must, at a minimum, afford particular purchase on a set of *explananda* whose grouping together is not arbitrary. The set of suasive speech acts fills that bill; but selection of a well-formed genus is not enough. Eloquence as such is not "rhetoric"; whence we derive the bland contention that there is not yet Greek archaic, not ever Chinese rhetoric, if we are speaking accurately (this is, of course, not tantamount to denying the existence of skillful archaic or Chinese oratory). In the Greco-Roman world, the *praxis* of competitive public discourse in law courts and political assemblies, and in other formal or semi-formal venues (e.g. at festivals, in *gumnasia*), gradually evolves; the body of material which grows up symbiotically with such primary discourse, whether theoretically aimed at analysis or practically aimed at improving the chances of winning, or both, is the "rhetoric" we are looking for. Thus it is that where this *praxis* is not to be found, rhetoric too remains absent. To repeat, this hardly means that other cultures lack their own modes of persuasion, or ignore the study of these modes; but just as non-Greek discursive, meditative, self-reflective investigations are not *ipso facto* "philosophy," so it is only the peculiarly Greek inflection of global eloquence which delivers the concept we want, one whose specificity in styles of reasoning and speaking fit it for the task of fine-grained cultural understanding.

So much for "elsewhere." In the nature of the case, "before" is much fuzzier. Since rhetoric supervenes on an evolving *praxis* with which it interacts, it would be stupid to search for clean, abrupt transitions between nascent and full-blown phases of rhetoric. But avoidance of pedantic excess should not make us forget that we neglect the difference a name makes at our peril. To express the issue crudely but neatly: first comes eloquence; then the magisterial philosophers of *logos* arrive, only to be ruffled by the maddeningly tangential, sort of humorous harassment of Gorgias; and then Plato puts Gorgias down in his very own, but restricted and inferior place; Plato does so by putting a name to what the *Gorgias* has Gorgias say he does: "rhetoric."

We have already seen off the absurdity that sophisticated rhetorical analysis provides our sole access to effective means of persuasion. So I am not saying that before the Platonic Socrates formulated the first explicit definition of rhetoric – "the craftsman of persuasion," with the power "to produce persuasion in the soul of hearers" (*Gorgias* 453a) – no one won over an audience competently. The pre-Platonic incompetents would include, bizarrely enough, Gorgias himself, to whom Socrates, in dialectical partnership, attributes this very definition, or, if one prefers, on whom he fobs it off. The huge difference this act of naming and defining makes originates in the duty incumbent upon Platonic characters to try to know whereof they speak; in this instance, to capture the very essence of rhetoric. This is already to broach the other specific complaint, that I have been too narrowly focused on an agenda set by philosophy, so that questions are begged in advance against rhetoric. The rejoinder is that ancient bookstalls may or may not have been littered with technical manuals snatched up by Greeks eager to hone their oratorical skills; but, before the epochal episode of Gorgias' provocation and Plato's reply, questions were not quite there to be begged. Which is to say that rhetoric is the illegitimate offspring of philosophy; before the bastard was christened, it was not altogether identifiable, to be assiduously cultivated and extolled, or vehemently rejected and abhorred.

Earlier I adverted to the inaccessibility of *logos* to mediocre people. That it is out of the reach of the many might seem mildly paradoxical, given the premise that *logos* holds unchallengeable sway in human interaction. For what stupendous obstacle impedes their forming even a fumbling grasp of what is working all about them? Or is it that *logos* works, all right – but always above their heads? If so, does the elite's near monopoly of persuasive power cohere happily with the notion that the common folk are also speaking animals: how so, if *logos* is above and beyond them? Be that as it may, after the transformation wrought by Gorgias and Plato, the outlook for *logos* in the Platonic dialogues becomes both less paradoxical and more bleak. That *logos* is inherently difficult to apprehend is no longer the sole or chief ground for the many's remaining ignorant of it: the predicament is much more sinister than that. Since philosophy is not so much the royal road as the only route which can take us to the truth, antagonism directed against philosophy comes to the same thing as aversion to *logos* and truth; and philosophy is now seen as constantly assailed by manifold threats arising from overt hostility to its redemptive potential, or covert subversion of its credentials by fraudulent claimants to wisdom.

Plato marks a decisive break in the history of *logos*. Socrates in the *Republic* informs us that the maligned professionals whom politicians dub "sophists" are proficient in nothing else, and nothing more, than common opinions; if application of their slight art helps the speaker to convince an assembly to follow his bidding, that is only because the sophistical orator is so thoroughly imbued with run-of-the-mill beliefs and desires, which he must deeply indulge, so as to superficially reorder. This meagre, cunning parasitism is as remote from truth as the host which it placates and hoodwinks (*Republic* 493a–c). If rhetoric is a sort of knowledge, it is but a mean one: its subject is not what really is, but what seems to be, to those whose opinions count least. Correspondingly, its feeble methods yield shallow psychological know-how, but no understanding of what the soul is and might be trained to become.

The characteristic maneuver of the *Phaedrus* is ([in]sincere?) retraction, disavowal, recantation; and there, it is sometimes claimed, Socrates performs a volte-face in his judgment of rhetoric. The assumption is that the outright condemnation of rhetoric in the *Gorgias* is, if not withdrawn, at the very least heavily modified, and paired with a novel vision of rhetoric reformed, a knowledgeable rhetoric which philosophers might countenance. To ascertain whether the *Phaedrus* does open up a space for philosophical tolerance of rhetorical *logos*, I shall interleave excerpts from it with references to pertinent passages in the *Gorgias*.

At the outset of the dialogue Socrates professes to be akin to Phaedrus in their shared passion for *logoi* (*Phaedrus* 228b–c). This is in fact an ironic displacement of the derogation of rhetoric familiar from the *Gorgias* and the *Republic*, since in the sequel the Lysianic oration with which Phaedrus is obsessed will be rubbished. But in a later section, Socrates raises the question of how to produce a good *logos* and himself proposes the answer that its author must have knowledge of the truth (*Phaedrus* 259e). Phaedrus' cautious reaction is to cite, but not openly approve, what he "has heard", namely that persuasion comes from knowledge of what the speaker's audience considers the truth, not from what is actually true (*Phaedrus* 260a). This is a Platonic allusion back to the *Gorgias* (not to exclude the possibility of a secondary reference to the *Republic* passage just discussed), where the broad definition of rhetoric as "the craftsman of persuasion" is qualified by specifying that rhetorical conviction concerns issues of justice and is produced "in mobs" (*Gorgias* 454b). Socrates wrings the concession from Gorgias that this conviction is not knowledge, but rather a state of ignorant belief instilled by an orator himself ignorant of what he speaks about (*Gorgias* 458e ff.), just as in Phaedrus' citation of the theory of unknowing rhetoric.

The reprise of themes from the *Gorgias* extends further. Since orators operate in the political arena, what they are ostensibly ignorant of is moral qualities; but Gorgias cannot stomach this shaming indictment. He insists that were a pupil thus morally and politically ignorant, he would instruct him. But is he implying both that the master Gorgias does have such knowledge *qua* rhetorician, and that its possession is a necessary condition for rhetorical competence as such, or that simple decency obliges him to ensure that inhibitions act as a prophylactic against amoral or immoral exercises of rhetorical power? Neither option is attractive. That rhetoric *qua* rhetoric obeys the tenets of morality is implausible; that it should be lumbered with moralistic encrustations seems like an *ad hoc* defense against the imputation of culpable ignorance; and both options fatally attenuate rhetoric's leading attraction, which is precisely the promise to confer unbridled persuasive dominance. Dangerous rhetoric is sexy, tamed rhetoric is boring. In the *Phaedrus* parallel text, Socrates invokes a personified, moralistic Rhetoric who indignantly expostulates: ignorance is no precondition of rhetorical speech; rather, an orator should get hold of Rhetoric only after he has obtained the truth (*Phaedrus* 260d). This is the counterpart of the second option, which Polus, Gorgias' pupil in the *Gorgias*, castigates as a weak-minded, unnecessary concession to barren conventions.

It is at this point that the *Phaedrus* moves in an unfamiliar direction. Yet another aspersion which the Socrates of the *Gorgias* had cast on rhetoric was that it is not a veritable science, but rather nothing more than a paltry, trifling empirical "knack." He denies the "technical" credentials of rhetoric by arguing that since it is empty flattery designed to please, it cannot sustain theoretical development and regimentation (*Gorgias* 463b: how the atechnical conclusion flows from the hedonistic premise is opaque). The Socrates of the *Phaedrus* transparently refers to this accusation, and contends both that truth is essential to genuine science, and that engagement in philosophy is essential to verbal competence (*Phaedrus* 260e–261a). This contention is compatible with the old rejection of rhetoric, on the grounds that it lamentably fails to satisfy these conditions; but now Socrates lays out an argument to the effect that since authentic (viz. ideal) rhetoric is verbal competence, it taps sources of truth and accords with philosophy.

The new definition of rhetoric: it is "a kind of leading of the soul through *logoi*," in gatherings both public and private (*Phaedrus* 261a). Phaedrus is taken aback, and this broadening of rhetoric's scope should give us pause: does this not sound suspiciously like the self-defeating inflation of rhetoric until it coincides with discourse in general? But the similarity is only apparent, for Socrates' innovation is to detect properly "rhetorical" situations beyond formal courts and assemblies; that is not because rhetoric on his conception is topic-neutral, but rather on account of his perceiving ethical and political repercussions where others do not, above all in the "privacy" of dialectical encounters. But in the first instance the scientific status of rhetoric on this new conception is paradoxically supposed to follow from the psychic "leading" being misleading. Socrates elicits agreement to the commonplace that a skillful forensic pleader will, if he wishes, make the same things appear just or unjust to the same people on different occasions, and that likewise the scientific political orator gives the same things a good appearance to the city at one time, a bad appearance at another. And someone who manages to mislead others while remaining undeceived himself must have an exhaustive understanding of resemblance and dissimilarity. Since deception occurs when we wrongly take one thing for another, but we do not mistake things which differ grossly, a scientifically deceptive speaker competently negotiates the most subtle likenesses and discrepancies (*Phaedrus* 261c–262a).

This volatile combination of propositions is not intended to deceive us even momentarily. First, the sketch of the speaker who knowingly sows misapprehension is nothing like actual politicians, of whom the damning diagnosis of the *Gorgias* and *Republic* continues to hold good: they are self-deceiving manipulators, bound to the victimized masses by the very ideological chains they forge and reforge. They cannot knowingly and voluntarily substitute simulacra for realities, since they themselves fail to comprehend the divisions of reality. But second, nor can the features of the sketch be assembled into a portrait of an ideal orator. Later Socrates draws a parallel between proper rhetoric and proper medicine (in the *Gorgias*, rhetoric had instead been detached from beneficial medicine and associated with harmful cookery, 463–64). Just as a doctor worth the name must not only be able to affect the body but also know what impact his interventions will have on bodily welfare, so too a rhetorical expert must not only lead the soul but also know how his persuasion will contribute to psychological well-being (*Phaedrus* 270b). We began with knowledge of the objects concerning which people were to be deluded; have we not surreptitiously shifted to the deceived subjects? No; and for a reason which dissolves the strange combination. Successful persuasion depends on aligning scientific taxonomies of types of soul with types of discourse naturally congruent with these psychic species (*Phaedrus* 271a–d); but satisfactory knowledge of the soul only comes with an understanding of "the nature of the whole" (*Phaedrus* 270c).

"You will not find out the limits of the soul by going, even if you travel over every way, so deep is its *logos*" (Kahn fr. 35): as in Heraclitus the *logos* conceals and reveals itself both in the cosmos and in the soul, so in the *Phaedrus* psychological expertise collapses into universal philosophy; therefore only perfect philosophers would be able to muster scientific rhetoric. They could engage in deception, but why would they? Philosophy entrains an obdurate commitment to the pursuit of truth, which is incompatible with small-minded mischief; only philosophers could scientifically mislead, but they never would. This is the rhetorical instantiation of the general Socratic paradox that consummate villainy requires knowledge: but since knowledge brings virtue, only the good could be really, heroically bad – an unrealizable counterfactual.

Thus this is not even an incomplete rehabilitation of the rhetoric anyone has experienced in the public or private places of Athens, which, just as in the *Gorgias* and the *Republic*, is the sphere of slaves practicing on slaves for their mutual gratification (*Phaedrus* 273e–274a: unless, perhaps, Socrates was present); what philosophy would have for *real* rhetoric remains largely imaginary.[4] But not entirely so? Platonic readers often have the uneasy sense that the real, the best arguments for the extraordinary theses propounded, endlessly recede behind the words that are there to be read; that might be because the dialogues are themselves proffered as examples of philosophical rhetoric, vehicles for propelling the seduced reader towards a better, elusive, *logos* – which the dialogues themselves never instantiate. Why the tantalizing deferral? Since Plato is the author who persists in remaining hidden, the destabilizing effect is ineliminable: we are enjoined to assimilate what the dialogue contains, but only so as to dispense with its catalytic preliminaries. This is to present us with an image of philosophy as not so much a master discourse, as the only fully meaningful one, which legitimate subaltern *logoi* respectfully gesture towards, in the course of discharging their protreptic, propaedeutic, wholesomely "rhetorical" function. Otherwise the *Phaedrus* remains at loggerheads with rhetoric as it is recognizably practiced.

That grubby, aberrant rhetoric is … *not* philosophy – but apes it; or if innocent of this presumptuous counterfeit, nevertheless feigns an authority legitimately wielded by philosophy alone. The same cannot be said of the parent philosophy by its despised progeny rhetoric. Or can it? Cicero slyly

---

[4] Compare Socrates' inflammatory boast at the end of the *Gorgias* that he is Athens' only true politician (521d–e); or the view that Kallipolis, the utopia of the *Republic*, is the true polity – which is not to be found on earth (592b).

suggests that the Plato who authored the *Gorgias* "was most an orator when heaping scorn on them" (*On the Orator* 1.47). Why so? If the rhetorical tradition ventures neither to incorporate philosophy, nor to repudiate it lock, stock, and barrel, it also never baldly ignores it; indeed, grappling even in a perfunctory manner with how rhetoric is (not) related to philosophy is obligatory for works which aspire above the lowly status of handbooks. For Cicero, eloquence is impossible without knowledge; but on the other hand, expertise, including philosophy, borrows from rhetoric what is needed for persuasive exposition, without which it falls miserably flat (48–50). This is a careful revision of Gorgias' avowal that rhetoric unfailingly vanquishes the experts on their own ground – when it comes to persuading the inexpert (*Gorgias* 456a–c); discreet, well-informed Ciceronian speech is tailored to the rhetorical requirements of that branch of knowledge for which it wins acceptance from those who would otherwise stand recalcitrant. This says what, exactly, about Plato's superbly rhetorical vituperation of rhetoric? Just that he knew whereof he spoke, and said it fittingly? If so, the teasing hint of self-refutation evaporates, since the refutation of Gorgias in the *Gorgias* is predicated on the admission that orators are ignorant of how things truly are, as opposed to how their auditors wrongly take them to be. Any rhetorical strategy of accommodation with the strenuously cerebral posture of philosophy becomes implicated in compromise with daunting philosophical criteria for earning a full rational warrant. If such compromise is not to prove ineffectual, then the clever apologist must prevaricate on whether rhetoric can or should meet the extreme epistemological demands of philosophy: if a positive answer is enunciated, then we are off on the trajectory of the *Phaedrus*; but if there is a clear negative answer, rhetoric is condemned out of its own mouth of ignorance before philosophy's bar, where ignorance is the capital crime.

Since there is no neutral territory on which philosophy and rhetoric can meet, would it not be much more prudent for rhetoric to occupy a position of indigenous strength, favorable for disengaging from or disparaging philosophy on its own, rhetorical, terms? Not a viable option. The felt prestige of philosophy in antiquity precluded the stratagem of withdrawal to secure home ground; whether this is merely a contingent, brute fact about ancient culture or a deep fact about still prevailing conceptions of rationality and persuasion is not easy to discern. The Ciceronian strategy rests content with an ancillary, if crucial, role for rhetoric in its relation to philosophy. A considerably more aggressive stance would fix on the allegation that all the philosophical truths worth knowing are susceptible to a rhetorical presentation which shows them to better advantage than ineloquent philosophy could ever achieve unaided. That strategy would approximate more closely to an assimilation of philosophy by rhetoric, since it might seem that its rhetoricization would carry no countervailing disadvantages. But many philosophers would not be disposed to accept the allegation. A bad argument for resistance: much philosophy includes technical material which cannot be dispensed with; and if this material is to be preserved unadulterated, its sheer technicality will prove rebarbative to rhetoric. Of course philosophy bristles with technical notions, as does the law; but technicality is no barrier to rhetorical presentation of a legal case. Indeed the master orators of antiquity were said to shine all the more brightly when dealing with such unpromising topics.

A better, if inconclusive, argument for resistance: philosophical material is generated in a dialectical matrix, so that anything which might interfere with its tenor – elegant ornamentation, say, superadded to the lucidity which *naturally* belongs to logical argument – is a bad thing. "When Zeno of Citium was asked how dialectic differs from rhetoric, he clenched his fist and spread it out again, and said, 'like this' – characterizing compactness and brevity as the hallmark of dialectic by the clenching, and hinting at the breadth of rhetorical ability through the outspread and extension of his fingers" (Sextus Empiricus, *Against the Professors* 2.7 = Long and Sedley 1987 31E). One should not, however, form the impression that the uncompromising Stoics were any more hospitable to garden-variety rhetoric than the Socrates of the *Phaedrus* – quite the contrary. Since rhetoric no less than dialectic is a "science of speaking well" (Diogenes Laertius 7.41–44 = Long and Sedley 1987 31A4), it is reserved as the exclusive domain of the Sage. Wearing his cap of expert dialectician, he correctly discusses "*logoi* conducted by question and answer." Wearing his cap of expert rhetorician, he utters appropriate truths in "continuous *logoi*." If these truths are, on occasion, perforce punctuated by calculated incitements to draw a false conclusion or fall into emotional perturbation, that is *faute de mieux*: the Sage calculates that the upshot of the deception is the best available outcome; and in any case, the audience is self-deceived, since theirs is the responsibility for succumbing to vicious temptation (albeit to virtuous effect). The Sage is a lonely exemplar whose unconventional ascendancy, like Socrates', utterly controverts current mores.

That, of course, is not the end of the story: philosophies which shun what they regard as redundantly elaborate argumentation will be more amenable to rhetorical expression; and yet others will look for a *via media*. This chapter has afforded only a few glimpses of the protracted interchange between philosophy and rhetoric, but it does so in the hope that its examples of interplay are symptomatic. Aggregating more texts would bring to light a great number of ingenious modifications and refinements in the wary self-positioning of the Greco-Roman philosophical and rhetorical traditions, with and against each other. But we would also see that the key question is resuscitated again and again: does rhetoric, at best (at worst), supplement philosophy, or, at worst (at best), threaten to supplant it? Anyone will guess that this question holds the attention of philosophers; what we should reflect on is the surprise that it has proven equally captivating to rhetoricians, whom we might have anticipated would have preferred to disown their remonstrating senior relatives.[5]

Suggestions for further reading

Both Coxon 1986 and Kirk, Raven, and Schofield 1983 furnish helpful discussions of the meaning and implications of Parmenides' divine revelation. Bollack 1965 contains stimulating observations on early philosophical adaptive exploitation of the epic tradition. Kahn 1979 remains the classic study of Heraclitean hermeneutics. Buchheim 1989 is the best source for Gorgias; and the interplay between Gorgias and Plato is pursued at length in Wardy 1996. Ferrari 1987 develops a subtle reading of the *Phaedrus*. Nightingale 1995 is very good on Platonic contrastive self-definition.

---

[5] Warm thanks to John Henderson, Steven Makin, and David Sedley for their helpful input, and especially to Erik Gunderson, from whose creative acumen and editorial patience I have benefited enormously.

3

MALCOLM HEATH

Codifications of rhetoric

The classical tradition opens with an epic of war and speech. The fighting in the *Iliad* is interleaved with talk that decisively influences both its course and its significance to those involved. These two facets of heroic life underlie the syllabus which Peleus prescribed to Achilles' tutor, Phoenix: "You were a child, with no knowledge yet of leveling war or of debate, where men win distinction. So he sent me out to teach you all these things, to make you a speaker of words and a doer of deeds" (9.440–43). Achilles later acknowledges that he has not learned these two lessons equally well: "I, a man without equal ... in war, though there are others better skilled at debate" (18.105f.). He is right: the catastrophic consequences of his mishandling of the assembly in book 1 show why skilled speech was important. It is no surprise that Peleus thought this skill worth *learning*; that he thought it could be *taught* foreshadows a distinctive feature of later Greco-Roman culture.

The nearest we come to observing Phoenix's teaching style is in the Embassy, where he gives Achilles specific injunctions (9.486f.); highlights significant features of the situation, contrasting them with hypothetical alternative scenarios (9.515–22); predicts the consequences of particular courses of action (9.602–605); and, above all, draws to his pupil's notice examples on which to model, positively or negatively, his behavior. He does not rely on explicitly formulated general principles. Likewise in teaching skilled speech, he would not have needed to articulate principles in an abstract general form, let alone to systematize them. Practical skills can be taught by showing the pupil models from which, his attention guided by particularized injunctions and evaluative feedback, he can implicitly assimilate appropriate habits of performance and judgment. But the systematization of explicitly articulated principles for skilled speech was to become another characteristic feature of Greco-Roman culture. This chapter outlines the history of that process, its goals, and its achievements.

In Plato's *Phaedrus* Socrates jokingly attributes technical handbooks on speech to Nestor and Odysseus, "composed at Troy when they had nothing to do." Phaedrus discerns an allusion to more recent experts (262b6–c3). How far these early rhetorical texts had progressed along the road to codification is unclear. Phaedrus has borrowed a composition of Lysias which he wishes to memorize and emulate (228d6–e5), revealing a teaching practice that still relies on learning from examples. It has been argued plausibly that texts such as Gorgias' *Helen* and *Defense of Palamedes* were condensed models of useful techniques.[1] Antiphon's *Tetralogies*, sets of speeches demonstrating techniques for arguing each side of three cases of homicide, are a striking instance. Because the three cases invoke different kinds of defense (respectively denying the fact, maintaining that it was accidental, and claiming justification), the complete package not only illustrates a range of technical means of persuasion but also implicitly anticipates what would later be explicitly theorized as *stasis* (issue).

We cannot be sure whether or how the lessons implicit in such models were made explicit in oral teaching. Aristotle suggests that Gorgias used simply "to hand out rhetorical speeches to be learned by heart," which he scornfully compares to trying to teach someone how to avoid sore feet by showing them lots of different shoes (*Sophistical Refutations* 183b36–184a8). Aristotle claims that contemporary teachers of "eristic" argument do the same as Gorgias, whereas he has created a genuine art of reasoning. He knows that people were already able to reason, and to speak persuasively; the function of an art (*tekhnē*) is to grasp reflectively the explanation of the success that can be achieved spontaneously or through acquired habit (*Rhetoric* 1354a1–11). Logic and rhetoric elicit from pre-existing practices an explicitly articulated framework of principles that will enhance the natural human capacities which those practices express.

Aristotle boasts that he developed his art of reasoning single-handedly from scratch; by contrast, the articulated rhetoric of his day was the product of a long process of incremental improvement to which many individuals had contributed (183b29–33). *Phaedrus*, too, suggests that an emergent analytical tendency had already led to the articulation of general principles in "the books written on the art of speeches" (266d5f.). Socrates summarizes a prescription for the structure of a judicial speech, including elaborations of the basic scheme (266d7–267a2). Similarly, there is evidence of an attempt to formulate refined distinctions between various persuasive resources (for example, between direct and indirect praise: 267a2–5).

---

[1] Cole 1991: 71–94.

Model-based teaching has already begun to be placed in a framework of explicit norms and classifications.

Plato's review of the handbooks satirizes the superficiality of existing rhetoric, absorbed by nit-picking trivialities while neglecting dialectic and psychology, the foundations of true persuasion. In the *Gorgias* he mounts a more aggressive critique: rhetoric is not an art but a mere "knack," like pastry cookery (462b6–463b6). This denies the possibility of codification in principle; if rhetoric lacks any rational standard (464e2–465a6), it cannot be theorized. This presented later rhetoricians with a radical challenge. The vision in the *Phaedrus* of an ideal rhetoric that might in principle be codified was more encouraging. But that, too, was a radical position: Plato's ideal could never be realized. The many Platonists who taught rhetoric in later centuries would pay tribute to Plato's aspirations, but the detailed content of their teaching was taken over with only superficial modifications from a long and increasingly sophisticated tradition of technical rhetoric rooted in the work of Plato's opponents.[2] But we are hampered in tracing that tradition in detail by huge gaps in the evidence. Greek theory underwent a final, far-reaching transformation in the second century CE. Since the products of a developing discipline tend to obsolescence, and a practical discipline typically discards the obsolescent, our knowledge of intermediate stages of the tradition is limited and patchy.

The best starting point is the *Rhetoric to Alexander*,[3] written in the decades 340–300 BCE, and preserved in the Aristotelian corpus though certainly not by him. We do not know enough to say that this treatise was typical of late-fourth-century rhetoric, but its limited intellectual penetration (and lack of ethical scruple)[4] suggests that it was probably less untypical than Aristotle's *Rhetoric*. At first glance, its overall structure seems familiar: like Aristotle, the author discusses what later rhetoricians would call invention (1–22), expression (23–28), and arrangement (29–37). But the treatise's programmatic announcements (notably in chapter 6) betray no awareness of that structure, combining items we would assign to invention and expression in undifferentiated lists. The execution appears intolerably clumsy unless we suspend our preconceptions. Then a clear two-part structure

---

[2] M. Heath 2004a: 73–78; M. Heath forthcoming.

[3] Chiron 2002.

[4] Cope is appalled by its "utter unscrupulousness and disregard of truth and justice" (Cope 1867: 459). Admittedly, the author explains how to secure false testimony without the witness risking prosecution (1432a3–10). But he is not the only rhetorician to prefer subterfuge to defeat: M. Heath 2004a: 212. Its realism may help to explain how the treatise survived long enough to gain (somewhat ironically) the protection of Aristotle's name.

emerges: first an analytic (*kata merē*, 1436a28) survey of techniques for speaking; then their ordered integration in the body (*sōmatoeidōs*, 1436a29) of a complete speech.

The author proposes a scheme of seven species of speech (1421b8–10), ascribed by Quintilian in the *Institutes* (3.4.9) to Anaximenes of Lampsacus and by Syrianus (2.11.17–2.12.2 Rabe) to Aristotle. Neither can make sense of the scheme; in particular, they struggle to reconcile the "investigative" (*exetastikon*) species with the canonical three kinds of oratory (deliberative, judicial, epideictic). In fact, the species do not categorize speeches, but things that speakers do in speeches. Hence they may be used in combination with each other (1421b10f., 1427b22–24), and they cross between various contexts of speech. If praise and blame are *usually* found in displays rather than contests (1440b12f.) they must *sometimes* be found in contests; so they are not equivalent to "epideictic." Likewise, exhortation and dissuasion occur in public addresses to the people (*dēmēgoria*), but also in private discussions (*homiliai*, 1421b17–19). Including private discussions alongside "demegoric" and "dicanic" contexts seems to have been standard in fourth-century theory (Alcidamas, *On the Sophists* 9; Plato, *Phaedrus* 261a8f., *Sophist* 222c9–11). But they are absent from the treatise's opening sentence, which focuses on the canonical trichotomy of kinds of "political" speech (1421b7f.). Quintilian and Syrianus clearly did not read that sentence in its present form, since they associate the seven species with a *dichotomy* (omitting epideictic). The dichotomy still neglects private discussions but otherwise does less violence to the content of the treatise, in which "demegoric" and "dicanic" are most naturally taken to refer to deliberative debate and judicial dispute as contexts for speaking rather than as kinds of speech. The opening sentence is therefore not authentic.[5] Later readers' familiarity with the three kinds rendered the thought opaque; so they misread and, where necessary, rewrote the text. That should serve as a warning: we, too, run the risk that expectations created by the most familiar codifications will distort our reading of other, less familiar technical treatises.

Aristotle's *Rhetoric* comes closer to meeting our expectations. The structural division absent from the *Rhetoric to Alexander* is present: thought, diction, and order are explicitly identified as distinct aspects of speech to be dealt with (1403a34–b8). And Aristotle adopts the trichotomy of deliberative, judicial, and epideictic kinds as a fundamental principle (1358a36–b8). He divides each kind into two, so six of the species of the *Rhetoric to*

---

[5] Mirhady 1994.

Alexander have been distributed across the three kinds; the investigative kind, indigestible to Quintilian and Syrianus, has disappeared. Admittedly, many unclarities and structural oddities remain. Aristotle was prepared to acknowledge the incremental advances made by earlier rhetoricians when advertising his own achievements in logic; when writing about rhetoric he evaluates his predecessors less positively. They have given most attention to techniques for exciting emotion, which are external to the art; only *pisteis* (proofs?) are intrinsic, and the "body" of proof is the argumentative structure which Aristotle calls "enthymeme," about which his predecessors have said nothing at all (1354a11–18). Yet a key element in Aristotle's theory is the claim that *pisteis* (forms of persuasion?) may be based on the character of the speaker, emotion elicited in the hearer, or argument (1356a1–33), and book 2 analyses emotions at length: a disreputable alternative to *pistis* has become a respectable *pistis* in its own right. This is unexpected, but only mildly disconcerting: readers of Aristotle know that his surviving works were not written for publication and have the loose structure of work-in-progress. The resulting difficulties are usually more than compensated by Aristotle's astonishing intellectual depth. In rhetoric, however, that depth carries a cost. The trichotomy is presented (1358a36–1359a5) as a "necessary" consequence of there being three kinds of hearer (decision-maker, juryman, observer), and is further correlated with three times (past, future, present) and three goals (advantage, justice, honor). Quintilian rightly describes this correlation as concise, elegant and mistaken (3.4.16). A deliberative speaker would find more practically useful advice in the *Rhetoric to Alexander* than in Aristotle's excessively schematized *a priori* construction.

This may explain why the *Rhetoric* never enjoyed especial prominence in the later rhetorical tradition. Aristotle's influence was generally indirect and did not necessarily stem from the *Rhetoric*.[6] Ancient rhetoricians, teaching a practical skill, were constrained by considerations of practical usefulness; modern scholars, whose interest in rhetoric is historical rather than practical, distribute their admiration according to different criteria.[7] This has allowed Aristotle's *Rhetoric* to acquire a misleading salience in modern eyes. Nevertheless, it is clear that Aristotle's ideas had some influence on the development of rhetorical theory in the early Hellenistic period. His differentiation of thought, diction, and order is a first step towards later formulations of rhetoric's five parts (also known as the orator's five

[6] Solmsen 1941.
[7] I have found the experience of teaching practical courses on ancient rhetoric illuminating: M. Heath 2007.

tasks): invention, arrangement, and expression need the addition of delivery and memory. Aristotle touched on delivery only in passing (1403b21–1404a8); his colleague Theophrastus wrote a book on it (not necessarily focused on rhetoric), and Stoic rhetoric adopted this quartet (Diogenes Laertius 7.43). We do not know when memory was added to complete the quintet. The trichotomy of speeches into judicial, deliberative, and epideictic was said to have owed its currency to Aristotle (Cicero, *On Invention* 1.7; *On the Orator* 2.43; Quintilian 3.4.1). Aristotelian influence was presumably exercised through Peripatetic and Stoic philosophers, who according to Quintilian (3.1.15f.) made a greater contribution to rhetoric than the rhetoricians themselves in the period between Theophrastus and Hermagoras of Temnos.

The evidential deficit is especially frustrating in the case of Hermagoras (c. 140–130 BCE).[8] Obsolescence ensured that by the first century CE there was uncertainty about which books he wrote (Quintilian 3.5.12–15), and our sources give incompatible accounts of his doctrine. Confusion has been compounded by the existence of later homonyms.[9] We therefore know much less about Hermagoras than we would like, or is often supposed. A celebrity of whom little is known provides scholars (prone to finding putative lost sources more interesting than extant texts) an irresistible opportunity for speculation. One certainty is the importance of Hermagoras' contribution to the theory of *stasis* (issue). This theory classified the different kinds of dispute with which orators deal: one might distinguish, for example, questions of fact (did he do it?), definition (was this murder?), and quality (was it justifiable?). We have seen an implicit anticipation in Antiphon, and its rudiments appear in both the *Rhetoric to Alexander* (1427a22–30) and Aristotle (1416a6–20). So Hermagoras did not invent the theory but elaborated it. His most distinctive contribution may have been to link the theory to a diagnostic apparatus for identifying the precise point of decision and the key line of argument in each case. This apparatus was to have a complex history, undergoing repeated reconstructions before its ultimate abandonment.[10] Nevertheless, the prominence which Hermagoras' innovations gave to issue-theory decisively changed the shape of subsequent rhetorical theory.

Direct access to Hellenistic theory comes through two Latin treatises of the first century BCE, the youthful Cicero's *On Invention*,[11] and the *Rhetoric*

---

[8] Date: Brittain 2001: 298–307.
[9] M. Heath 2002.
[10] M. Heath 1994 provides details.
[11] Achard 1994.

to Herennius, a work of unknown authorship.[12] These vividly illustrate the extent to which the project of codification had advanced in the centuries since Aristotle. Both begin from what are now well-established fundamental doctrines: the three kinds of speech and the five parts of rhetoric (*On Invention* 1.7, 9; *Rhetoric to Herennius* 1.2f.). The *Rhetoric to Herennius* uses the five parts as the organizing framework for a comprehensive treatment of the subject. Cicero's concluding statement that further books were to follow (2.178) suggests that his project was equally comprehensive in scope though never completed.

Cicero regards invention as the most important of the five parts (1.9). The author of the *Rhetoric to Herennius* concurs, devoting more than two whole books to it; the remainder of book 3 covers arrangement (3.16–18), delivery (3.19–27) and memory (3.28–40); expression occupies book 4. The brevity of the section on arrangement follows inevitably from the decision to organize the treatment of invention around a speech's standard parts: if the structure of a speech has been covered under invention, little is left over for arrangement. Both authors adopt this approach, but it was not the only possibility. A summary of commonplace rhetorical teaching in *On the Orator* (1.138–45) implies that treating the parts of a speech under arrangement remained a familiar option at that dialogue's dramatic date (91 BCE).[13] But their transfer to invention has one practical advantage: each part performs a different job, and invention is accordingly different in each. It was reasonable to subordinate the abstract logic of the five parts of rhetoric to expository and pedagogic advantage.

One important difference between the two treatises indicates that the search for a satisfactory expository structure had not reached a stable end-point. In the *Rhetoric to Herennius* issue-theory is embedded *within* the framework of the parts of a speech: the classification of issues and a significantly modified form of the diagnostic apparatus are first introduced in connection with proof and refutation (1.18–27). Cicero introduces the issues (1.10), along with the Hermagorean diagnostic apparatus (1.18f.), *before* the parts of a speech. This is a more satisfactory procedure: analyzing the dispute and identifying the crucial line of argument are basic to the whole speech. As Quintilian notes (3.9.6–9), arguments have to be worked out before any of a speech's parts can be developed.

Decades later, Cicero presented a larger, more philosophically informed conception of rhetoric in his most original work, the dialogue *On the*

---

[12] Achard 1989. The work is usually assigned to the late 80s BCE; I think a later date is possible.

[13] Wisse 1989: 88–93.

Orator (55 BCE).[14] As the title indicates, the focus is on the orator rather than the art of rhetoric. The programmatic question (1.5) is whether eloquence depends on arts, as Cicero believes, or on natural talent and practice, as his brother maintains. Note "arts," not "art": it is common ground that the theoretical systems of school rhetoric are of limited importance (1.23); derogatory references pervade the whole work, and *On Invention*, based on Cicero's early technical training, is mentioned dismissively (1.5). But Cicero's positive claim is much bolder: the (ideal) orator needs "a knowledge of all the important subjects and arts" (1.20). A provisional list (1.16–18) includes psychology (a branch of philosophy: 1.53f.), history, and law. So this work is not, fundamentally, a codification. Nevertheless, Cicero in a letter describes books 2–3 as containing a technical discourse (*tekhnologia, Letters to Atticus* 4.16.3). The two main speakers between them sketch out a complete system. The five parts of rhetoric provide a conventional framework, and much routine technical doctrine is covered in outline. The objection to the school theories is not that they are wrong, but that they are trivially self-evident, limited in application and incomplete (e.g. 1.145f., 2.77–84, 133, 162). Cicero's main concern in this sketch is therefore not the system as such, but how the standard systems are transformed by the distinctive features that arise from his enlarged conception of rhetoric. Three points merit particular notice.

First, Cicero emphasizes general as against particular questions. Whether homicide is justifiable is a general question (*thesis* in Greek technical language); whether *this* person was justified in killing *that* person in *these* circumstances is a particular question (*hupothesis*). The youthful Cicero rejected Hermagoras' claim that general questions fall within the ambit of rhetoric (*On Invention* 1.12–14). Now he sees general questions as fundamental, since every circumstantially specific particular case is an instance of a general question (*On the Orator* 2.133–42). The point is stated clearly in another mature work: "the orator – not an ordinary one, but this outstanding orator – always removes the discussion, if he can, from particular times and persons, because the discussion can be made broader about a class than about an individual, so that whatever is proved about the class must necessarily be true of the individual" (*Orator* 45).

Secondly, he develops a system of "topics," abstract-argument schemata (such as the inference from class to particular case) which can be used heuristically for finding arguments in any given case. Aristotle's *Topics* and *Rhetoric* were the ultimate source for their use in both dialectic and

---

[14] May and Wisse 2001.

rhetoric, as Cicero knew; but he does not attempt to reproduce Aristotle's teaching here or in the more extensive treatment in his own *Topics*. Close parallels show that he drew on a source also used by one of the rhetoricians excerpted in a later Greek compilation known as the Anonymus Seguerianus.[15]

Thirdly, Cicero rejects the view, standard in recent technical theory (e.g. *On Invention* 1.20–22, 100–109; *Rhetoric to Herennius* 1.7f., 2.47), that securing the audience's good will and arousing their emotion can be localized in the introduction and epilogue respectively (2.311f.; cf. 2.78–84). Instead, he sees these as general forms of persuasion alongside argument, and as permeating the whole speech. This doctrine is visibly related to Aristotle's three sources of persuasion, though not identical: the shift from the speaker's character to the audience's good will reflects the influence of more recent theory, despite the rejection of its localization of non-argumentative forms of persuasion.[16]

Where did Cicero get these ideas? The discussion of general questions was part of Peripetatic and Academic dialectical training; a philosopher teaching rhetoric would naturally view the practice as a useful training for rhetorical argument, too. The topics also suggest a philosopher introducing dialectical elements into his teaching of rhetoric. The only direct evidence for recent philosophical rhetoric is provided by Cicero's *On the Divisions of Oratory*, probably written a few years after *On the Orator*, and explicitly presented as an outline summary of Academic rhetoric (139); it takes the form of a dialogue between Cicero and his son, in which Cicero purports to be casting an existing Greek scheme into Latin. The system may be adapted from that of Philo of Larissa, head of the Academy, who taught technical rhetoric in the 90s (*On the Orator* 3.110; *Tusculan Disputations* 2.9). *On the Divisions of Oratory* includes both topics (5–8, 109) and thesis (61–68, 106). But the topics are not treated at length; and thesis, though elaborately categorized, is not given the central role it has in *On the Orator*. Further, *On the Divisions of Oratory* discusses the arousal of emotion only in connection with the introduction and epilogue (8, 27), which is wholly inconsistent with Cicero's new position. The distinctive features of the theory presented in *On the Orator* therefore do not reproduce the Academic rhetoric summarized in *On the Divisions of Oratory*. We should not be surprised. Cicero claimed to have drawn on the whole of "ancient" rhetoric (*Letters to his Friends* 1.9.23), which does not suggest dependence on recent philosophical

---

[15] On the background to thesis and topics in Cicero: van Ophuijsen 1994; Brittain 2001: 296–343; Reinhardt 2000; Reinhardt 2003.

[16] Fortenbaugh 1988.

or technical rhetoric. Equally, it is not surprising that he does not simply reproduce material from much older theorists. Cicero was not an antiquarian, and he could not ignore the fruits of three centuries of sophisticated theorizing. The image that should guide our thinking is of a mature practitioner, well versed in contemporary rhetorical theory and willing to exploit its resources, finding in Aristotle and Plato (*Phaedrus* is evoked at 1.28) an additional set of resources to help to develop ideas arising out of his own experience and study into a new, independent synthesis.[17]

The change in Cicero's fundamental concept of rhetoric is striking. However, this unique opportunity to watch one individual's development over a whole career also allows us to observe his theoretical position develop at a more detailed level. In *On Invention* he follows the diagnostic apparatus developed by Hermagoras; in *On the Orator*, briefly (2.132), and more clearly in *On the Divisions of Oratory* (101–106), he presents a modified version, closer to that of the *Rhetoric to Herennius*; *Topics* sees a further modification (93–95). Cicero was not mindlessly reproducing different sources, for the direction of change is not random: close inspection reveals progressive attempts to eradicate inconsistencies that were inherent in the original version.[18] That Cicero found it worth keeping up with such highly technical developments puts his critique of theory in proportion; he must have thought that getting the theory right had some value. Quintilian, too, records his change of mind on a complex technical debate about the number of issues (3.6.63–68). He, like Cicero, was a successful practicing advocate, yet found these apparently arcane matters worth getting right. We should not glibly dismiss technical rhetoric as insignificant or (in the pejorative sense) merely academic.

Cicero's mature position failed to gain support from his successors. Quintilian gives perfunctory assent to the importance of general questions (3.5.14f.; cf. 10.5.11), but the idea did not penetrate deeply into his thinking. Pedagogic constraints may have played a part: Cicero acknowledged that young people enjoy particularized declamations more than general theses (*Letters to Quintus* 3.3.4). But there is also a substantive point. What is proved about the class is necessarily true of the individual, *if* the individual is a member of that class. In real cases, the circumstances will be too complex for their proper categorization to go uncontested; a competent opponent will lead the debate back to the ambiguities of the particular

---

[17] The extent of Cicero's direct use of Aristotle is controversial: Wisse 1989; May and Wisse 2001; Fortenbaugh and Steinmetz 1989; Fortenbaugh 2005. Platonic influence: Schütrumpf 1988; Schütrumpf 1994.

[18] M. Heath 1994.

circumstances. Quintilian also reverted to a parts-based treatment of invention. If, as Cicero came to believe, the means of persuasion cannot be localized, then invention cannot be based on the parts of a speech; so he abandoned the structural pattern common to *On Invention* and the *Rhetoric to Herennius* and restored the parts to arrangement. Quintilian, though recognizing the importance of non-argumentative means of persuasion,[19] is content to discuss non-argumentative resources in connection with the epilogue, with the rider that they can also be used in other parts (6.1f). The structural divergence, though apparently superficial, reflects a fundamental difference in the way invention is conceived.[20]

Although Quintilian does not follow Cicero slavishly, his ambitious project is unmistakably inspired by *On the Orator*: a comprehensive technical discourse is framed by a comprehensive account of an orator's education. Book 1 covers pre-rhetorical education, book 2 the staple exercises of rhetorical training, both elementary (the *progumnasmata*) and advanced (declamation), along with a range of meta-rhetorical topics. Book 12 surveys the orator's subsequent career, including further study – where, for example, the usefulness of legal knowledge is addressed (12.3). Within this frame, book 3 introduces the five parts of rhetoric (3.3), which again provide the overall framework for the technical exposition, and the trichotomy of kinds (3.4); this is followed by a complex discussion of the issues (3.6) and the diagnostic apparatus (3.11). Books 4–6, on invention, are largely structured around the parts of a speech. Book 7 is assigned to arrangement. Style, in books 8–9, is supplemented by a discussion in book 10 of reading, imitation, and composition as means of acquiring and maintaining facility – another indication of Quintilian's constant focus on the orator's education. Book 11, on memory and delivery, completes the coverage of the five parts.

Quintilian's project is even more complex than this summary suggests, however, since he does not simply expound a systematic theory; he includes extensive reviews of the diverse and contradictory opinions of earlier theorists (1.pr.2). His aim in surveying and sifting the tradition is to achieve the best theoretical synthesis. Quintilian is not a precursor of Volkmann, Lausberg, or Martin. Modern scholars codify *ancient* rhetoric for the purposes of historical understanding; Quintilian and his colleagues sought to codify *rhetoric* in order to make systematic sense of an essential practical

---

[19] Quintilian (5.14.32) thought that contemporary Greek orators (by contrast with their Roman counterparts) were excessively fond of tight argumentation. Some will find this hard to reconcile with conventional images of the "Second Sophistic": M. Heath 2004a may help to solve the puzzle.

[20] Wisse 1989: 80–88, 129f.

skill and render it more accessible to students and practitioners. This difference means that Quintilian's codification can be as misleading to modern scholars as Aristotle's if used incautiously. Quintilian's systematization has no canonical status within the diverse and constantly changing dialogue through which ancient specialists pursued better ways of understanding rhetoric, and of articulating their understanding. We should take care not to read his predecessors or his successors through the potentially distorting grid of Quintilian's account.

Quintilian's decision to maintain the customary assignment of the parts of a speech to invention meant that he, like the author of the *Rhetoric to Herennius*, faced the problem of what to do with arrangement, now largely devoid of content. Book 7, which purports to treat arrangement, is largely concerned with lines of argument appropriate to each issue and each kind of speech. This material has little to do with arrangement, and its position here is even more vulnerable than the order adopted in the *Rhetoric to Herennius* to the objection that the overall line of argument needs to be worked out before one starts to work up the parts of a speech. Once again, the division of rhetoric into five parts fails to model a viable process of speech production. Greek theorists of the second century CE and later developed a more satisfactory solution. But extant works on rhetoric from this period are predominantly monographs on special topics, and careful study of the relationship between different kinds of treatise is needed to reveal the implicit overall conception of the discipline as a whole. Since the specialist works of this period generally had a close relation to teaching, this can also help us understand the course of rhetorical instruction.[21]

The *progumnasmata* were in a sense preparatory to, not part of, rhetoric (Quintilian, too, treats them outside the technical discourse in books 3–11).[22] The first and foundational part of rhetoric proper was issue-theory, which after undergoing a profound transformation in the second century,[23] now provided a systematic guide to mapping out the argumentative structure of a case. There were numerous treatises *On Issues* or *On Division* (the technical term for the analysis of a case into its constituent heads of

---

[21] See M. Heath 2004a: 215–54 for more detailed discussion of the structure of the rhetorical curriculum in this period, and 255–76 on the technical literature. M. Heath 1997b gives a worked example of the processes involved in invention. There were specialized monographs in earlier periods (Quintilian 4.pr.7), and comprehensive works in this period, such as Longinus' incompletely preserved *Art of Rhetoric*; significantly, this is not pedagogical, but a reference work, serving as a mnemonic (*hupomnēma*, fr. 48.313–23 Brisson–Patillon = 192.14–193.1 Spengel–Hammer).

[22] M. Heath 2004a: 219f.

[23] M. Heath 2004a: 4–19.

argument); the tendency to refer to them by the simple title *Art* reflects the fundamental status that issue-theory had acquired within rhetoric. The extant example is Hermogenes *On Issues*, which became a standard textbook.[24]

Students who progressed beyond this stage learned next how to embody the argumentative strategy in a complete speech. Treatises on this subject are usually cited under the titles *On Invention* or *On the Parts of a Political Speech*. But they were not a mere continuation of the early handbooks on the parts of a speech decried by Plato (*Phaedrus* 268d7–269d9) and Aristotle (*Rhetoric* 1354b16–19): their place in a developed curriculum structure gives them a different significance. Nor do they correspond to invention in the theory of five parts of rhetoric. Greek sources from this period generally work with some variant of a three-part scheme: a preliminary analysis (*noēsis*) establishes the nature of the case, up to and including the identification of its issue; invention works out the detailed articulation of material in each part of the speech; arrangement considers whether the default order (*taxis*) should be varied in the light of the special requirements of the individual case (*oikonomia*). Expression is variously assigned to invention or arrangement. Delivery may be paired with expression, added as a fourth part, or omitted as being a matter of natural talent rather than art; memory is usually omitted, for the same reason.[25] This explains the inclusion of expression and delivery in the treatment of the parts of a speech in the Anonymus Seguerianus, and of style in book 4 of [Hermogenes'] *On Invention* – puzzling anomalies if we cannot see beyond the five-part canon.

The dominant position of issue-theory did not go unchallenged. A third-century rhetorician named Phrynichus described the theory as "drivel," and taught his students to speak through unstructured improvisation. This view, which our sources mention only to dismiss, exemplifies a persistent counter-tendency in ancient rhetoric. Quintilian engages with opponents who regard his project as pointless (2.11f.).[26] It is unclear how far these anti-theorists were a construct of pro-theoretical polemic. At any rate, we must not confuse the extreme dismissal of theory attributed to them with the nuanced position of Cicero's *On the Orator*, which gives qualified assent to the mnemonic usefulness of theoretical precepts (1.145f.). Cicero's insistence that theory is only the distillation of practice would have evoked little dissent, since rhetorical theorists themselves affirmed its premises. Everyone

---

[24] M. Heath 1995.

[25] Sources include the second-century Zeno (*ap.* Sulpicius Victor 315.5–14 Halm), the fourth-century Athanasius (*Prolegomenon Sylloge* 175f. Rabe), and anonymous prolegomena (*Prolegomenon Sylloge* 199–202, 234–36 Rabe).

[26] M. Heath 2004a: 23; Winterbottom 1995.

recognized that there were limits to theory's capacity to specify what works best in practice: what works best is situation-dependent, and situations are infinitely variable. So codification can never be *exhaustive*: an effective speaker must be adaptable (Quintilian 2.13). Nor can codification ever be *conclusive*: there is always the prospect of gaining a better understanding of what works. Good teachers encouraged their students to take a critical attitude to textbook doctrine.[27] Thirdly, codification was never thought to be *sufficient*: no one becomes an orator without frequent exposure to models, written and live, and constant practice (Quintilian 7.10.5–9).[28] Model-based teaching, and the teacher's feedback on performance, provided our starting point and remained central to ancient rhetorical training at all times. Practice is the one indispensable component in the acquisition of a practical skill. Rules can provide a useful framework for acquiring the skill through exercise. A teacher able to articulate general principles can supply that framework and can use it to explain the successes (and failures) of the models and the rationale of his feedback on the student's practice. But without practice, the rules are nothing.

Ancient attempts to codify rhetoric therefore aimed to give a systematic account at the level of general principle of what had been found through experience to work best in practice. That was largely seen as constant: whatever accommodations might be needed to contemporary conditions, the great classical orators were the enduring yardstick of best practice. But even if rhetoric, in the sense of best practice, was a constant, rhetoricians knew that rhetoric, in the sense of theory, changed over time. That was a natural consequence of the attempt to articulate better the principles implicit in the practice of the classical masters. Innovation was prized: rhetoricians were proud to claim credit for new discoveries. [Apsines] expresses this with pleasing modesty: he is bringing his own offering to a contributory banquet (*eranos*, 1.2). Others were more arrogantly self-assertive, for the process was competitive. That carried risks: competition provided a stimulus to progress, but also to excess. If innovation brings kudos, an incentive attaches to innovation for its own sake. But fashionable novelties and dogmatic *a priori* pronouncements could expect only transient success, since innovation had to stand a twofold practical test. Theory had to be able to generate recognizably successful practice, and had to be pedagogically effective. Cicero's *On the Orator* was an exception to the generally close connection of rhetorical codification to teaching; Quintilian's experience as

---

[27] M. Heath 2004a: 195–203, 234.
[28] M. Heath 2004a: 234–53.

a teacher ensured that his model of the "perfect" orator was more securely anchored to reality than Cicero's ideal. It is characteristic that, after a lengthy and difficult justification of his new position on the intricate problem of the number of issues mentioned earlier (3.6.66–82), he sets out a less technically accurate but more accessible account, suitable for use by teachers of beginning students (3.6.83–85). In this practical and pedagogical focus, at least, Quintilian does not mislead us about the nature of ancient attempts to codify rhetoric.[29]

Suggestions for further reading

There is no substitute for reading the primary sources! Since we are fortunate enough to have a comprehensive treatment by a successful orator and teacher, who includes surveys of other theorists' opinions and his own reflections on rhetoric and its pedagogy, the obvious place to start is Quintilian; there is an outstanding five-volume version by D. Russell in the Loeb Classical Library: *Quintilian. The Orator's Education* (Cambridge, MA, 2001). But, as I have emphasized, there was no such thing as a definitive or canonical codification. Quintilian's predecessors can be sampled in Cicero *On Invention* or the *Rhetoric to Herennius* (both available in the Loeb series) the *Rhetoric to Alexander* – there are English translations by H. Rackham (Loeb) and E. S. Forster, in J. Barnes (ed.), *The Complete Works of Aristotle* (Princeton, 1984). But English versions of these three works are not up to date, and not entirely reliable; the Budé editions are far superior. Aristotle's *Rhetoric* is best approached through the revised edition of G. A. Kennedy, *Aristotle. On Rhetoric: A Theory of Civic Discourse* (New York, 2006). Looking in the other direction, late antiquity has handed down the largest corpus of rhetorical theory, but also the least thoroughly studied (the secondary literature contains some astonishingly misleading claims about rhetoric in this period). Its most conspicuous innovations were in the theory of argument and in stylistics, illustrated by the two extant works of Hermogenes: *On Issues*, translated by M. Heath (Oxford, 1995), and *On Types of Styles*, translated by C. W. Wooten (Chapel Hill, 1987). M. Heath, *Menander: A Rhetor in Context* (Oxford, 2004) tries to map the territory (but most readers will wish to pass over the densely technical central chapters). Do not forget that rhetorical texts are primarily practical: so do not simply read them – trying out their recommendations to see how well they work in practice is the key to understanding.

---

[29] On the continuing practical relevance of later Greek rhetorical theory see M. Heath 2004a: 277–331.

PART II

The field of language

4

CATHERINE STEEL

Divisions of speech

Rhetoric is, above all, a system which offers the prospect of organizing and classifying the apparently limitless variety of human speech. In turn, there are different ways in which one can understand the system of rhetoric, and other chapters in this *Companion* approach the issue through the different categories of speech that are established or the processes by which rhetoric takes shape in the writings of different theorists.[1] The concern in this chapter is with the divisions within rhetoric itself, which are used to structure both its theoretical treatments and its educational practices: it offers an overview of rhetoric as a system, a dazzling, and at times baffling, elaboration of the process of public speaking developed over centuries.[2]

The level of detail involved in treating structures comprehensively offers great scope for individual writers on rhetoric to create their own distinctive approach and, in consequence, their appeal as teachers, by choosing which areas to emphasize and elaborate upon. Moreover, the level of elaboration varies from one area of rhetoric to another; by concentrating on areas of particular contestation, we can see how the increasing subdivision of rhetorical theory marks out areas of authority and anxiety in the practice of oratory.

Divisions of areas of inquiry are not natural or incontestable. In Plato's dialogue *Phaedrus*, the character of Socrates identifies two processes as being fundamental to his capacity to speak and think: divisions (*diaireseis*) and collections (*sunagōgai*). Correct use of division is contrasted with the practice of a poor butcher, who hacks bits off rather than following the existing structure of joints.[3] Plato is, of course, referring here to dialectic rather than rhetoric; indeed, later in the same dialogue he ridicules the

---

[1] See especially Chapters 4 (Heath) and 8 (Hesk).
[2] Standard accounts of rhetoric include Vickers 1988: 1–82; Kennedy 1994; S. E. Porter 1997: 3–167; Lausberg 1998.
[3] Plato, *Phaedrus* 265d2–266b5.

concern of rhetoricians with the division of speeches. But the Platonic image is nonetheless a good way of beginning to think about the ways in which rhetoric organizes its material. Rather as there is no universal agreement about the best way to divide up animal carcasses for human consumption, so there existed in antiquity a variety of competing methods of structuring rhetoric; but individual rhetoricians support the rightness of their chosen structure with a conviction which underscores the importance of organizing knowledge as a means to claim authority.

Establishing a structure for rhetoric by dividing it up into distinct areas can be seen to serve two important ends. On the one hand, it makes the subject more comprehensible, and thus more teachable; and didactic capacity is at the heart of the enterprise of rhetoric, whose origins are the desire of individuals to learn how to speak effectively. It is, arguably, in the well-organized textbook that rhetoric has its distinctive being. But, on the other hand, systematization also contributes to intellectual credibility. Unlike most other *tekhnai* or *artes* such as medicine, architecture, or even cookery, rhetoric did not have a distinct field of knowledge of its own. Rather, it offered techniques which could in theory be applied to any discipline. Rhetoric's lack of specific content led to debates about its very status as an *ars*, an argument articulated with ruthless clarity in Plato's *Gorgias* and much disputed subsequently, as Quintilian's summary of the problem indicates.[4] Intellectual prestige as well as pedagogical imperatives demanded that rhetoricians establish methods and structures which encapsulated exactly what it was they claimed to do, and teach.

Nonetheless, the process of organizing rhetoric was regarded by some writers who handled oratory with skepticism or even hostility. When Cicero "replaced" his early work *On Invention* with *On the Orator* its systematic exposition of the parts of rhetoric is cramped and dismissive. His *On the Divisions of Oratory*, which does handle the different parts of rhetoric systematically, is in the form of a catechism for his teenage son.[5] Quintilian's *Institutes* use the standard division of rhetoric as their basic organizing principle but the work contains frequent references to the dangers of excessive complication and the importance for students of relating their work to practical outcomes.[6] Discussing the divisions of rhetoric left ancient theorists of speech vulnerable to charges of a narrow-minded and pedantic concern with detail at the expense of the orator's accomplishment of his task. It is not a coincidence that the same area of inquiry should be both

[4] Quintilian, *Institutes* 2.17–18.
[5] On the *Oratorical Divisions*, see Arweiler 2003.
[6] See, e.g. 3.8.67–70.

a place where rhetoric defined itself and a source of vulnerability: both aspects relate to the difficulty of establishing rhetoric as an intellectual discipline with its own subject matter.

The earliest systems of rhetoric seem to have used the different parts of a speech as their basic structuring device.[7] Aristotle in the *Rhetoric* extends this approach by incorporating the parts of a speech into a wider scheme which involved a set of tasks which an orator had to undertake; and this subsequently undergoes substantial elaboration into a highly complex method for managing the whole process of verbal expression. The usual list of tasks contains five: invention, arrangement, style, delivery, and memory. In other words, an orator is to gather together the arguments which support his case, to put them in the most effective order, to find the right words to express them, to work out the gestures and tone of voice that will support the communication of these arguments best, and, finally, to remember them.

This seems to be a simple structure, but there were many possibilities for complication. There was no complete agreement on terminology in either Greek or Latin, though a slightly more consistent vocabulary developed in the latter. The order of the five was not fixed beyond debate: memory was movable, with some theorists putting it after invention and others after arrangement, and so was style, which in some versions comes immediately after invention, and in others fifth.[8] Some added other parts: judgment, following invention (judgment being the process of deciding whether arguments are worth including), and order.[9] Within the standard five-part division, each element was subjected to enormous elaboration.

Some writers supplemented this system with further material. Cicero in *On the Divisions of Oratory* divides his material into three parts: in addition to the *uis oratoris*, or "resources of the orator," which corresponds to the five-part system outlined above, he considered "the speech" and "the question."[10] Under "the speech" he handles what in other treatments could be included under *dispositio*, that is the parts of a speech; under "the question," material relating to *inuentio*, particularly the theory of topics which he elaborated later in *Topics*. Another triad consisted of the art, the artist, and the work, though in most works the section on art is by far the most extended;[11] for Quintilian, however, the

---

[7] Plato, *Phaedrus* 266d–268a gives a flavor of the degree of elaboration, and technical language, offered by the sophists; see Cole 1991.

[8] Quintilian, *Institutes* 3.3.10.

[9] Quintilian, *Institutes* 3.3.1–15.

[10] Cicero, *On the Divisions of Oratory* 3.

[11] Lausberg 1998 §42.

artist and the work receive detailed separate attention, albeit much more briefly than his coverage of the art, in the final book of the *Institutes*: and his focus on the artist enables him to put forward a strong argument for the moral demands upon the orator.[12] And treatments of rhetoric also incorporate the threefold categorization of speech according to its audience and purpose, that is, into judicial, deliberative, and epideictic speeches.[13]

Each of these divisions can be further divided to a great degree of complexity and can stand as an independent object of study. But before thinking about the parts of oratory it is worth reflecting on the artificial barriers which this process establishes between linked elements of the process of preparing a speech. It is impossible to separate entirely the finding of arguments from their arrangement; choice of style depends on judgments about the kinds of arguments which a speech will employ; and delivery must accord with style. Rhetoric divides and classifies in order to develop a set of teachable recipes but in so doing undermines its capacity to deliver an organic whole.

"Invention" is the usual rendering in English for the first of the orator's duties, from the Latin *inuentio* or "finding," itself a direct borrowing from the Greek *heuresis*; "research" would perhaps be a more helpful term, though "invention" is sanctioned by nearly five centuries of English usage. The focus of most rhetorical treatises in antiquity was not on the process of investigation and thought which could generate material; invention offered instead a minute process of classification of the ways in which a situation could be analyzed in order to identify all possible lines of argument. It was an area subject to enormous expansion in many of the surviving treatises: only style approaches it in terms of the relative amounts of space devoted to each part of rhetoric.[14] And, particularly in Roman writers on rhetoric, the intersection between rhetoric and law generated an enormous volume of discussion of invention in relation to forensic oratory.

There was, however, no single method of handling invention shared by all theorists of rhetoric and handbook writers. Aristotle structured his account around "means of persuasion," *pisteis*, with a definition of rhetoric itself as "let rhetoric be defined as the capacity to see, in relation to a particular

---

[12] On book 12, see Austin 1954.

[13] For this division, see Chapter 6 of this *Companion*.

[14] For example: two out of the three books of Aristotle's *On Rhetoric* deals with invention; rather more than half of the *Rhetoric to Herennius*; and three and a half books of Quintilian's twelve-book *Institutes*.

subject, the available means of persuasion."[15] He establishes an immediate distinction between "artistic" and "inartistic" means of persuasion, in which he is probably drawing upon earlier handbooks; this is the distinction between proofs which the orator himself devises and proofs which are already present as material relating to a case, such as witness evidence or the text of laws. Inartistic proofs receive only a brief treatment. Artistic proofs are subject to a threefold division in accordance with whether they arise from the character of the speaker, or from engendering a particular emotional response in the listener, or from arguments: a triad often summarized as ethos, pathos, and logos. Character in relation to the speaker is dealt with relatively briefly: a speaker will be persuasive if he displays practical wisdom (*phronēsis*) and virtue (*aretē*) (1378a8), and here, naturally, the reader needs to refer to Aristotle's ethical theories. This aspect of character was perhaps relatively straightforward in Athenian oratory because in the law courts defendants spoke on their own behalf; advocacy, as in the Roman criminal system, greatly complicated the use of character.[16] The character of the audience is also considered, with a set of remarks about the characteristics of different groups of people such as the young, or the wealthy. Aristotle's treatment of the emotions consists of a systematic analysis of fourteen feelings and states of mind, arranged in seven pairs; armed with Aristotle's analysis, the orator will be able to create these emotions in his audience in ways which will assist his case, though the actual treatment does not seem specifically designed for a rhetorical treatise. In dealing with logical arguments which the orator can devise, Aristotle uses the distinction between inductive and deductive reasoning. In rhetoric, inductive reasoning relies on the accumulation of arguments to support a general claim: so, for example, one could argue that steps should be taken to stop the king of Persia from conquering Egypt, because Darius invaded Greece after he had conquered Egypt, as did Xerxes (1393a32–1393b4). But examples should be used in a supporting role; the more important kind of argument is the rhetorical syllogism, or enthymeme, which differs from the syllogism proper in using premises which the audience will accept, and in not spelling out all the steps in the argument where they can be easily understood.

The development of post-Aristotelian rhetorical theory is obscured by the absence of surviving works, but in the earliest surviving Roman works from the early first century BCE indicates that a rather different approach to

---

[15] Aristotle, *Rhetoric* 1355b25–26: ἔστω δὴ ἡ ῥητορικὴ δύναμις περὶ ἕκαστον τοῦ θεωρῆσαι τὸ ἐνδεχόμενον πιθανόν.

[16] On ethos and its later developments, Wisse 1989; Ciceronian advocacy, May 1988; Paterson 2004; Riggsby 2004.

invention had become accepted. Cicero's *On Invention* and the anonymous *Rhetoric to Herennius* follow the *status*-theory of the rhetorician Hermagoras, active in the middle part of the second century BCE. The *status* was the "point at issue," that is, the question which the two sides disagreed about. The *status* could be a question of fact, such as "did the defendant strike X?" But it could also be a question of law: "was the defendant's attack on X assault?"; or of procedure: "does this court have jurisdiction over this offense?" Quintilian's discussion of *status* in the third book of the *Institutes* gives a very clear idea of the level of complexity which theorists had brought to this field in relation to forensic oratory; the analytical structures for deliberative and epideictic oratory remained much simpler and, in consequence, the amount of space devoted to them in rhetoric handbooks much smaller.

Cicero used *status*-theory in his early work on rhetoric, *On Invention*, but later replaced it by other approaches. In *On the Orator* he emphasizes the importance of ethos and pathos, using the Aristotelian tradition, and the need for the orator to be philosophically trained. In the *Topics* he addresses the distinction between general and particular questions (*thesis* and *hupo-thesis*), for example between "is it right to kill a tyrant?" and "is it right to kill Caesar?" Although Hermagoras had claimed that rhetoric dealt with both categories, rhetorical training had in practice concentrated on the latter and left the former to philosophy.[17] By offering a systematic account of how to find arguments about *theseis*, and by claiming Aristotle as his direct model in so doing, Cicero was making a claim for the intellectual status of rhetoric; and he was also offering a systematic method for dealing with material which his own oratorical career had demonstrated to be so useful.[18] The evolution of Cicero's thinking on invention over the course of his long public career must have its origins in his practical experience, particularly of forensic advocacy; but it also demonstrates the flexibility of rhetoric which allows Cicero to approach it in a variety of ways. This flexibility, indeed, supports his desire, in the later 50s and the 40s BCE, to establish himself as an authoritative exponent of what emerges, through his writings, as a complex and extensive field of rhetorical theory.

[17] Reinhardt 2003: 3–52.
[18] At *Topics* 85, Cicero offers as an example of a definitional *thesis* the question whether eloquence or civil law is more valuable, which he answered – in favor of eloquence – so effectively in the *For Lucius Murena*. Nonetheless, *theseis* had little impact on most subsequent rhetorical training: Quintilian, respectful of Cicero, does discuss them (3.5.5–16) but briefly, and indicating that there was a view that general questions were not useful to public speakers (3.5.12); see Heath's chapter in this volume.

The second of the orator's duties was arrangement, which follows invention since one must gather one's material before putting it in order. As indicated above, this appears to have been the area which rhetorical theorists first attempted to systematize. Aristotle has little time for arrangement, treating it last and insisting upon simplicity: "the essential parts are the proposition and the proof; these are the parts which really belong, and at most the introduction, proposition, proof, and conclusion."[19] Later the treatment of arrangement became tangled up with that of invention: since different material is required for different parts of a speech, treatments of invention assume the normal order of a speech as they discuss what is appropriate for each part. The author of the *Rhetoric to Herennius*, for example, begins his treatment of invention by identifying six parts of a speech and then says, "in order to make the subject easier to understand I have been led to discuss the parts of a speech and fit them into the theory of invention."[20] In turn, when he reaches arrangement, there is little to say: he recapitulates the parts of speech already used under invention, offers a few miscellaneous observations on circumstances which can justify the omission of one of the usual divisions, and concludes with the familiar point that the strongest arguments should come at the beginning and end of the proof, and weaker points should be placed in the middle.[21] Quintilian's section on *dispositio* (book 7 of the *Institutes*) is more substantial, but it is not really about the arrangement of material at all: instead, this book offers a supplement to the theory of issues outlined under invention which illustrates how the identification of the disputed point or points is translated into argument. Arrangement itself, in the sense of the structure of a speech, is handled under invention.

Cicero in *On the Orator* opens the section on arrangement by having his speaker Antonius draw a distinction between what emerges from the facts of the case itself and the considerations which the orator's judgment can bring to the case:

> That we should make some prefatory remarks, then lay out the case, then prove it by establishing our arguments and refuting those of our opponents, and finally come to a conclusion and make our final statement – this the very nature of speaking demands; but how one puts together what needs to be said

[19] Aristotle, *Rhetoric* 1414b7–9.
[20] *Rhetoric to Herennius* 1.4: *quo res cognitu facilior esset, producti sumus ut de orationis partibus loqueremur et eas ad inuentionis rationem adcommodaremus, de exordio primum dicendum uidetur.*
[21] *Rhetoric to Herennius* 3.16–18.

in order to establish and convey our case – that above all requires the orator's judgment.[22]

Rhetoric's contribution – seen as the identification of different parts of a speech – is dismissed as simple common sense; the important matter is what the orator's experience contributes. Antonius goes on to make a series of remarks which are both theoretically novel for this period (the revival of the Aristotelian concern with character and emotion at all stages of the speech) and grounded in Roman, rather than Greek, practice (such as the reflection on how best to divide material among multiple *patroni*).[23] This section neatly encapsulates some of the dominant concerns of *On the Orator*: to put the orator's experience above rhetorical theory, to ground Greek material in a Roman context, and to demonstrate the superiority of a wide-ranging understanding of rhetoric over a narrow and rule-bound approach. And it also shows the limitations of rhetorical theory in handling the reality of actual cases – limitations which could not be eliminated by ever-increasing complexity.

Arrangement provides a good place to explore the encounter between theory and practice because this duty – unlike the other four – seems to offer an exact fit between its prescriptions and their practical manifestation in a speech. That is, invention, and as we will see, style and delivery also, offer an exhaustive list of possibilities to equip the orator to deal with any situation. But no single case will require all the possible arguments which invention covers, or indeed all the figures of speech or kinds of gesture covered by style and delivery. Arrangement, at least in its simpler models, does seem to offer a template for an entire speech: it will have an introduction, a statement of facts, a section of proof, and a conclusion. And yet, in two respects particularly, actual practice strayed from theory: in the omission of entire parts of a speech, and in the failure to establish clear divisions between different sections.

Quintilian's firmly practical discussion of the parts of speech in books 4 to 6 of the *Institutes* is well aware of these issues. Introduction, narrative, proposition, and partition can all, potentially, be omitted if the specific situation demands it; only the proof section and the epilogue are essential.[24]

[22] Cicero, *On the Orator* 2.307–308: *nam ut aliquid ante rem dicamus, deinde ut rem exponamus, post ut eam probemus nostris praesidiis confirmandis, contrariis refutandis, deinde ut concludamus atque ita peroremus, hoc dicendi natura ipsa praescribit; ut uero statuamus ea, quae probandi et docendi causa dicenda sunt, quem ad modum componamus, id est uel maxime proprium oratoris prudentiae.*
[23] Wisse 1989; Fantham 2004.
[24] Aristotle even denied that an epilogue was always needed (1414b5–6).

His treatment of *narratio* is indicative. Most teachers of rhetoric regard it as essential: but they are wrong.[25] There are a variety of situations where narration is not necessary: when both sides agree on the facts of a case; or when the judge already knows the facts; or when the defendant cannot deny the facts and is using a defense not of fact but of law, Quintilian's example being a man who has incontrovertibly stolen money from a temple, is being prosecuted for sacrilege, and is offering the defense that the money was private property and therefore no sacrilege has been committed.[26] But he goes on to explain that – unlike other writers – he does not regard absence of narration as following necessarily from a denial of charges, as it may still be useful for the orator to narrate what did happen. Moreover, he points out that narration is not useful simply to inform the jury: a well-constructed narration will also make the jury disposed to believe its truth. Cicero's *On behalf of Sulla* offers an excellent example of the omission of a *narratio* in actual practice: the speech starts with a lengthy digression about Cicero's own involvement in the case, and with activities of Sulla irrelevant to the charge, and then moves directly to demolishing the prosecution's case.[27]

Most treatments of arrangement assume that the distinctions between different sections are completely clear; though Quintilian characteristically identifies the potential difficulty, at least in relation to moving from introduction to whatever follows: it is a mistake either to conceal the transition or to make it too abrupt, and cleverness which draws attention to the actual point of transition is "a frigid and childish device of the schools."[28] And as soon as one considers the text of an actual speech, identifying different sections can be more difficult. In the case of Cicero, one indication of this is the existence of different systems of section numbering.[29] And, to take an example almost at random: where does the *exordium* of the *On behalf of Archias* finish? Is it after *asciscendum fuisse*, as most editions print, leaving the *narratio* to start neatly with Archias' childhood? Or is it a sentence earlier, at *genere dicendi*, which lets the exordium conclude with a rousing and extended appeal to the jurors' learning and generosity and starts the *narratio* with a reassertion of Archias' citizen status and a promise, immediately fulfilled, to prove this? An interpreter might conclude that it was less important to impose the

[25] Quintilian, *Institutes* 4.2.4.
[26] Quintilian, *Institutes* 4.2.5–8.
[27] On the omission of a *narratio* in the *On behalf of Sulla*, and its other structural peculiarities, see Berry 1996: 42–49.
[28] Quintilian, *Institutes* 4.1.76–79.
[29] On these, see Glucker 1984; Fotheringham 2007.

rules of rhetoric on a passage such as this, and concentrate rather on understanding how Cicero complicates his transitions in order to give a speech a compelling and persuasive overall unity.[30]

The place of memory in the order of the five duties is variable, but there is great consistency about its importance, given the convention in ancient law courts and assemblies for speech without notes. The earliest systematic treatment is in the *Rhetoric to Herennius*, which offers a detailed prescription for developing an artificial memory. It involves the orator in creating images for himself of "backgrounds" – examples suggested are of a house, or the space between columns, or an archway – which are memorized in a fixed order; against these backgrounds can then be placed images representing events or words which the orator needs for a speech. These are kept in order by the order of the backgrounds; and the backgrounds can be reused once a particular case is over. How far orators used such systems, and how far their memory skills enabled them to achieve exact verbal recall, is unclear, despite the importance of the issue for the relationship between oral performance and written records of oratory. And although particularly good or bad memories among orators were noted, in general this was the part of rhetoric least debated: memory was essential, and in general, it seems, orators acquired it.[31]

Delivery is perhaps the most difficult of the orator's duties to assess. It is a common trope among rhetorical writers that it is the most important of them: "delivery alone is supreme in speaking: without it, the greatest orator cannot be of any account, and a moderate speaker who is trained in this field can often defeat his superiors."[32] In this, ancient theorists are at one with modern research demonstrating the importance of non-verbal as opposed to verbal communication. And the importance of oratorical delivery as an area where issues of gender and status could be articulated and debated has been acknowledged in recent scholarship.[33] But the approach of ancient rhetorical theorists to delivery can appear alien, offering a complex and highly formal system which seems as though it must have been incomprehensible to any listener not already familiar with it. Delivery was divided into two parts: voice and gesture. For the author of the

[30] On Cicero's transitions, see Fotheringham 2004 and Fotheringham 2006.

[31] Curio (cos.76 BCE) had a very bad memory (*Brutus* 217); Hortensius' was superb (*Brutus* 301). See further Small 1997.

[32] Cicero, *On the Orator* 3.213: *actio ... in dicendo una dominatur; sine hac summus orator esse in numero nullo potest, mediocris hac instructus summos saepe superare.* Cf. *Rhetoric to Herennius* 3.19; Quintilian 11.3.2.

[33] Dugan 2005: 147–69; Corbeill 1996; Aldrete 1999.

Rhetoric to Herennius, a number of subdivisions follow. So, "voice quality" has three aspects: volume, stability (*firmitudo*), and malleability (*mollitudo*); malleability covers three possible tones of voice, namely conversational, argumentative, and expansive. Conversational tone has four variants: dignified, explanatory, narrative, and joking. Argumentative tone can be either sustained or broken, and expansive tone either hortatory or pathetic.[34] The author then proceeds to explain what is involved in each of these types of tone.[35] For example, in the joking conversation tone "one should shift one's words from the dignified conversation tone to decent merriment by means of a gently wavering tone and a discreet indication of a smile, but without the slightest hint of excessive laughter."[36] The author then turns to the movements which accompany these different tones: so, "for the broken argumentative tone, one must extend one's arm rapidly, walk up and down, occasionally stamp one's right foot, and maintain a fixed and keen glance."[37] Quintilian's discussion of delivery is even more detailed and, whilst it too is based around a structure of voice and movement, employs a different set of subdivisions, and in the case of movement surveys each part of the body. Hands have the most prominent position: "As for the hands – without which delivery would be mutilated and enfeebled – one can scarcely say how many movements there are, since they almost match the supply of words."[38] And, after some general considerations, possible hand gestures and their meanings are elaborated in great detail. For example, the gesture of raising the hand, with the fingertips bunched together, towards the mouth is used to convey mild surprise, or sudden indignation, or fear and pleading;[39] and one can express surprise by turning the hand upwards, closing the fingers one by one, starting with the little figure, and then reversing each of these movements until the hand is open and face down once more.[40] The range of hand gestures which Quintilian describes, and the emotions which they convey, are even more striking when the physical constraints of these gestures are observed: in

---

[34] *Rhetoric to Herennius* 3.20–24.

[35] *Rhetoric to Herennius* 3.24–25.

[36] *Rhetoric to Herennius* 3.25: *leuiter tremibunda uoce, cum parua significatione risus, sine ulla suspicione nimiae cachinnationis leniter oportebit ab sermone serio torquere uerba ad liberalem iocum.*

[37] *Rhetoric to Herennius* 3.27: *sin contentio fiet per distributionem, porrectione perceleri brachii, inambulatione, pedis dexteri rara supplausione, acri et defixo aspectu uti oportet.*

[38] Quintilian, *Institutes* 11.3.85: *manus uero, sine quibus trunca esset actio ac debilis, uix dici potest quot motus habeant, cum paene ipsam uerborum copiam persequantur.*

[39] Quintilian, *Institutes* 11.3.103.

[40] Quintilian, *Institutes* 11.3.100.

most circumstances only the right hand can be used, and it should not be raised above eye level, or lowered below the chest, or go further right than the right shoulder.[41]

However difficult these accounts of delivery are, it is clear that formalized gestures and modes of voice delivery were an accepted and important element in the entire package of oratorical performance. There is a striking passage in Quintilian's section on delivery where he takes the opening of Cicero's *On behalf of Milo* and offers a vocal commentary upon it; Quintilian had no advantage over modern readers in terms of direct access to how Cicero might have delivered a speech – quite apart from the peculiar situation of the performance of the *On behalf of Milo* – but, faced with a written text, his ease with the shared norms of rhetorical delivery enable him to assert with confidence what Cicero must have done.[42]

Style is the remaining duty of the orator, and it is with the treatment of style that rhetoric reaches perhaps its greatest complexity and variety, as well as its closest links with genres of writing other than oratory. It is also the area of rhetoric which provoked the bitterest disputes between rival practitioners: if speech is an index to character, and style offers the greatest scope for manifesting choice in oratory, then attacks on style lead directly into attacks on rivals.[43] Before considering some specific examples of styles in dispute, however, an outline of theories of style will he helpful. Aristotle opens his treatment of style by identifying two key principles of style: "let the virtue of style be clarity (for speech is a kind of sign, and if it is not clear it will not be performing its function) and appropriateness, neither flat nor in excess of the subject's worth."[44] He also demands grammatical correctness ($1407a19–1407b25$) and includes some observations on figures of speech such as metaphor and simile. Theophrastus codified these points in his lost treatise *On Style* into the four headings of clarity, appropriateness, correctness, and ornamentation; brevity was added by Diogenes of Babylon; and these categories, with various modifications, structure discussions of style in many later writers on rhetoric. Ornamentation in particular becomes an extremely large area, since the category of figures of thought and speech is capable of great elaboration. Indeed, it is tempting to read Cicero's treatment of these at the end of *On the Orator* (3.202–208) as the

[41] Quintilian, *Institutes* 11.3.112–13.
[42] Quintilian, *Institutes* 11.3.47–51.
[43] Seneca, *Letters* 114.1: *talis hominibus fuit oratio qualis uita.*
[44] Aristotle, *Rhetoric* 1404b1–4: ... ὡρίσθω λέξεως ἀρετὴ σαφῆ εἶναι (σημεῖον γάρ τι ὁ λόγος ὤν, ἐὰν μὴ δηλοῖ οὐ ποιήσει τὸ ἑαυτοῦ ἔργον), καὶ μήτε ταπεινὴν μήτε ὑπὲρ τὸ ἀξίωμα, ἀλλὰ πρέπουσαν.

work's final critique of the handbook writers, as Crassus merely offers a long list, without examples, and when reproached by Cotta dismisses the topic as a matter of common knowledge; but their use, however, "is a very demanding matter, the most difficult in the whole business of oratory."[45]

Alongside a division around the virtues of style is found a division into types of style. Though there were competing structures, this approach was based on the idea that there were different levels of style, with the more elevated being used for rousing emotions and for grand climaxes and a lower, simpler style being appropriate for narrative.[46] Types of style were used in the analysis of literary genres other than oratory, and they are arguably the dominant strand in ancient literary criticism; within the study of oratory, types of style became associated with a further method of structuring rhetoric, that is, in terms of tasks of the orator.

There are three of these: the orator must be able to teach his audience, to please them, and to move them.[47] Cicero lines up these three tasks with the three styles in *Orator*: "there are as many styles of speaking as there are tasks of the orator."[48] The simple style is to be used for teaching, the middle for pleasure, and the grand in order to move. For Cicero, this structure enables him to argue that the perfect orator must have a mastery of all registers, and therefore that Atticism, at least as understood by his critics, is not sufficient since it does not encompass the grand style. Other writers on rhetoric, not facing the same attack, do not need to make this move; and though this tripartite division continues to be used, it is usually absorbed under the issue of the appropriateness of style.

The dispute between Atticism and Asianism is one example of an intense focus on rhetorical style as a means for participants to explore a much wider set of cultural concerns. In the Atticist–Asianist debate, we can trace a debate concerning the best way of incorporating Greek disciplines into Roman intellectual life, however much the surviving – Ciceronian – evidence suggests that the focus was on Cicero's own reputation.[49] Another familiar example relates to the language of the Second Sophistic in both Greece and Rome, where word choice becomes extraordinarily loaded,

---

[45] Cicero, On the Orator 3.209: ... *grauissimus est et in hoc toto dicendi studio difficillimus.*

[46] Demetrius offers four styles, two kinds of higher style (the grand and the forceful) and two of the lower (the elegant and the plain); the threefold style (grand, middle, and simple) is used by the author of the *Rhetoric to Herennius*, who also considers the faulty manifestation of each (the swollen, the slack, and the meagre).

[47] E.g. Cicero, Orator 69; Brutus 185.

[48] Cicero, Orator 69: *quot officia oratoris, tot sunt genera dicendi.*

[49] Steel 2006.

since it acts as an index of the speaker's ability to participate fully in the recreation of classical Athens through language. But, though the second century CE may be marked by an obsessive concern with word choice, the phenomenon itself is not without ancient precedent: Caesar was deeply concerned with the theory and practice of correct Latinity (as his ruthless self-discipline in word choice in the *Gallic War* demonstrates), Cicero records solecisms, and there is a revealing anecdote about Theophrastus (who came originally from Lesbos): he was addressed as "stranger" by an old Athenian woman once she had heard him speak.[50] Identity is at stake in language on every occasion of utterance.

Such, in outline, is the structure which rhetoric imposed on the act of public speaking. It is, first and foremost, a system which approaches speaking from the perspective of the educator – and those about to be educated: rhetoric displays its pedagogical concerns in its fundamental organization as a method for writing a speech. What the rhetorical handbooks promise is a recipe, a set of instructions which, if followed in the right order, will enable someone to do the job of an orator. This pragmatic concern with outcomes is the main reason for its limited usefulness as a critical tool for understanding surviving examples of oratory. It is not so much that rhetoric cannot deal with the complexities of real life: the handbooks and the surviving examples of rhetorical exercises engage with highly detailed and elaborate scenarios.[51] In part, indeed, complexity may reduce usefulness; judicial rhetoric always receives the lion's share of space, precisely because legal material lends itself to ever more detailed analysis, whereas deliberative and epideictic rhetoric are usually passed over much more cursorily. But the chief drawback of rhetoric as an analytical tool arises from the obvious point that great orators achieve greatness – and survival for their works – precisely because they can transcend the commonplace and the rule-bound. Nonetheless, rhetorical theory was the underpinning of ancient oratorical practice from its origins, and any attempt to understand speech in antiquity must begin by taking its building blocks seriously.

Suggestions for further reading

General treatments of rhetoric as a system can be found in G. A. Kennedy, *A New History of Classical Rhetoric* (Princeton, 1994) and B. Vickers,

---

[50] Cicero, *Brutus* 172. Quintilian, *Institutes* 8.1.2 has the same anecdote, but with an intriguing twist: the old woman identified him as a non-native because he spoke *nimium Attice* – "in too Attic a way." You just can't win, it seems.

[51] M. Heath 2004b.

In Defence of Rhetoric (Oxford, 1988); H. Lausberg's *Handbook of Literary Rhetoric: A Foundation for Literary Study* (Leiden, 1998) is a comprehensive reference work. Translations of ancient rhetorical works are generally available in the Loeb series; also noteworthy are Kennedy's translation of Aristotle's *Rhetoric* (Oxford, 1991), May and Wisse's of Cicero's *De oratore* (*Cicero: On the Ideal Orator*, Oxford, 2001), and Russell and Winterbottom's of a variety of texts, including Tacitus' *Dialogue on Orators* (in their *Ancient Literary Criticism*, Oxford, 1972). A number of key texts have been the subject recently of substantial commentaries; particularly helpful are Reinhardt's edition of the *Topica* (Oxford, 2003) and Winterbottom and Reinhardt's of book 2 of Quintilian (Oxford, 2006), and these also provide extensive further bibliography.

5

JAMES PORTER

Rhetoric, aesthetics, and the voice

> The voice is speaking, but the speaker is reading.
> (Susan Stewart)[1]

The history of rhetoric in three easy lessons

In the eighth book of his *Lives of the Philosophers*, Diogenes Laertius relates an anecdote about Pythagoras in the light of which Pythagoras seems to have perfected if not the art of rhetoric, then at least its essence. The account is of a most unusual rite of passage. According to Diogenes, and the story is repeated by Iamblichus in his own *Life of Pythagoras*, Pythagoras used to lecture for long periods to his pupils, whether hidden behind a curtain or lecturing only at night in utter darkness (Diogenes Laertius 8.15; Iamblicus, *Life of Pythagoras* 72). "For five years [his disciples] would keep silent, merely listening to his speeches without seeing him, until they passed a test. From that point on they were allowed into his house and were able to see him" (Diogenes Laertius 8.10). How many speakers in antiquity (or at any time) could hold an audience captive like this for an evening, let alone for five years? To be sure, Pythagoras was not an orator and his lectures were not oratory. But he grasped a fact about rhetoric that would define it for centuries to come: rhetoric was the art of managing the voice.

Nevertheless, it was not Pythagoras but rather two figures from epic, Nestor and Odysseus, who would come to embody the spirit of rhetoric in the ancient imaginary, albeit in two distinct ways. Nestor, the elder states-man of the Homeric Greeks, was endowed with a mellifluous tongue and the gift of gab: he was the embodiment of persuasion. His sagacity was announced by his solemnity, his gait, and his age. Once he opened his lips, this physical impression was confirmed. Odysseus, by contrast, was the master of deception, though you would never guess this from the way he looked. Outwardly unheroic, small in stature, even ungainly, he also seemed idiotic and incapable of speech. Yet once "he let the great voice go from his chest" (*Iliad* 3.221; trans. Lattimore), his eloquence not only proved disproportionate to his appearance (much like Socrates after him) but it

---

[1] Stewart 2005: 233.

actually changed the way he looked: as he spoke, he grew taller, thicker, and more handsome. Pythagoras, on the other hand, took speech to a new dimension. Dispensing with appearances altogether and occulting himself from his pupil audiences, he appeared to them in a disembodied form, as a pure voice. His pupils, reduced to silence, were given over to an utter absorption of their master's voice (*meteikhon tōn logōn dia psilēs akoēs*; Iamblicus, *Life of Pythagoras* 72). Whence the name of his lectures, *akousmata*: they were oral deliverances, saturated with the voice.

While the later rhetorical tradition would remember Nestor and Odysseus but not Pythagoras as its mythical prototypes (Plato, *Phaedrus* 261c; Cicero, *Brutus* 40; Dionysius of Halicarnassus, *Art of Rhetoric* 9.6; Tacitus, *Dialogue on Orators* 16.5; Quintilian, *Institutes* 12.10.64–65; Menander Rhetor 416.1; schol. AbT *Iliad* 3.212 *ex.*; etc.),[2] it was Pythagoras, not his Homeric predecessors, who revealed the logic of the voice by which rhetoric works (and had always worked) its magic. Furthermore, the passage from Nestor to Odysseus to Pythagoras can be read as a progression in the development of oratorical self-awareness. In the first stage, body and voice are symmetrical: the voice appears the way the body appears. In the second stage, the voice predominates over the body, capable of changing the latter's appearances. In the third and culminating stage, the voice *replaces* the body, or better yet, *it becomes a body in its own right* – though what results is a paradoxical kind of body, one you can no longer see and touch but can only hear and feel. Here, the voice is eminently seductive. It may be that "the hidden voice structurally produces 'divine effects,'" which would help to account for the cult of divinity that surrounded Pythagoras.[3] But there are further aspects to this story.

The emergence of the voice in the guise of disembodied *logos* represents the triumph of the voice as an aesthetic phenomenon in its own right, its liberation from the constraints of sight, though not from the body per se. The voice when it is heard has a body of its own: it has pitches, melodiousness, timbre, rhythms, and other euphonic qualities. Pythagoras availed himself of all these aesthetic features of the voice, and indeed of the phenomenon of the voice itself, in order to produce an attachment in his pupils to his teachings, which famously leaned in the direction of disembodied realities – mathematics, the soul beyond death, cosmic but not mundane harmonies – but not in the direction of the earthly body. Perhaps that is why his house was called the "Temple of Demeter" and the porch leading to

---

[2] Further, Radermacher 1951: 6–8. (Menelaus is added once the three *genera dicendi* are established and require three epic ancestors.)
[3] Dolar 2006: 62; Riedweg 2005.

it the "Museum" (Diogenes Laertius 8.15). After Pythagoras, rhetoric would aspire to the condition of the veiled philosopher embodied in his voice: it would strive to become all voice. But it would never achieve this same degree of purity, mystery, or magic again.

Named *rhētorikē* in Greek and *oratio* in Latin, rhetoric is the art of speaking well, whether for the sake of persuasion or display, while its instrument is the voice. Rhetoric by definition and by necessity extended its purview to sounds *simpliciter*, and above all to their point of articulation on the body or within the material of language that gives rise to sound, be this "according to the shape of the mouth," "the place of contact <of the lips and teeth>," or in the gaps, spacings, clashings, or blendings of letters (Aristotle, *Poetics* 1456b31–34; cf. Dionysius of Halicarnassus, *On Composition* 14; *Rhetoric to Herennius* 3.20–22; Quintilian, *Institutes* 1.1.37). Rhetoricians never lost sight of the homonymy of their discipline and their instrument: "*Pronuntiatio* is called *actio* by many people. It seems to have acquired the first name from its voice-element (*a uoce*), the second from its element of gesture. Cicero in one passage calls *actio* a 'sort of language' [*On the Orator* 3.222] and in another 'a kind of eloquence of the body' [*Orator* 55] … So we are free to use both names indifferently" (Quintilian, *Institutes* 11.3.1; trans. Russell). Yet Quintilian's easy conflation begs the question of how the voice, in its gesticulations, *looks*. The invisibility of the voice is one of its greatest lures, but also the source of endless anxieties: the barely material voice has powers of penetration that render it insidious and dangerous (Plutarch, "On the Study of Poetry" 14F; Aulus Gellius 11.13.10; Plato, *passim*). Gorgias was capitalizing on these same anxieties when he boasted that "*logos* carries out its effects" either "by means of" or "in" "the smallest and most invisible [or "least apparent": *aphanestatōi*] body" (*Helen* §8). A question begged by Gorgias, no doubt consciously, is whether *logos* names what the voice is or only what it does.[4] But in abstracting *logos* from its appearances he was making a move worthy of Pythagoras. What is more, or the same thing, the voice (as Pythagoras reminds us) is a kind of eloquence of the body even when the body is not visibly present. This condition of absence can pertain most notably to the written voice, which is an area of ancient rhetoric as well.

Rhetoric, whenever it is conscious of its appearances, is inescapably an aesthetic practice. The two kinds of inquiry – theories about rhetoric and theories about music, poetry, painting, sculpture, and architecture, and their associated practices – were in fact closely intertwined in antiquity.

---

[4] J. I. Porter 1993.

Their relationship is a study in interdisciplinarity, but also a study in materialism and the pursuit of the immaterial, at whose critical juncture the voice lay. The aim of this chapter is to sketch out these relationships and their changes over time, from the first beginnings of rhetoric to the Second Sophistic. The story begins with the ascendancy of the voice as an object of theoretical inquiry and as an applied practice. It ends in classicism.

The aesthetic function of rhetoric

The centrality of speech to ancient life guaranteed the prominence of rhetoric as a pursuit and a profession. Inevitably rhetoric became the meeting ground for a variety of practices in antiquity. In particular, it was a place where inquiries into the aesthetics of speech and writing could be explored in theoretical and practical detail, above all through case studies in both speech-production and in literary and stylistic criticism. The analysis of speech and writing was the province of no discipline in particular, least of all in a pre-disciplinary world like antiquity, and most excitingly from the end of the fifth century into the fourth, when fields of inquiry were least formed and most in flux. Rhetoric was a key contributor to these inquiries.

Consequently, the traffic between rhetoric and adjacent fields was intense. Discoveries and insights made in one area were quickly transferred to the next. Rhetoric was often the site of these discoveries, especially early on – whether in language, grammar, criticism, music, performance (encompassing acting, gesture, and vocal range), psychology (encompassing theories of imagination, physical and mental effects both conscious and unconscious, willed and unwilled: empathy, identification, pleasure and pain), or physiology (never clearly sundered from psychology). Though refinements never ceased to be made, in later centuries rhetoric was perhaps less of a productive force than it was a reproductive one. Above all, its spheres of activity shifted as they were harnessed to changing circumstances – to the increasingly obsessive problems of acculturation, especially given the Greek heritage of rhetoric (all of its tools, its language, and many of its *exempla* and ideals, derived from the Greek past), expressions of Roman-ness (*Latinitas*) or Greekness (*hellēnismos*), and attitudes towards the past, and in particular, as the heritage of the past grew heavier and even at times a burden, classicism.[5]

---

[5] Out of a vast literature, see Adams 2003 (Latinity); Goldhill 2001 and Whitmarsh 2001b (Greekness); Woolf 1994 (hybridity); Alcock 2002 (the memory of the past).

Throughout all, rhetoric continued to dwell upon its aesthetic function, however many distant ends rhetoric may have served – be these expressing or achieving virility, self-promotion, the attainment of distinction and social rank, the air of culture, or an ethnic passport. Always primarily a way of articulating practices in the ancient world, rhetoric became a way of articulating their aesthetic dimensions as well, not least given its special place in the field of human expression.[6] By definition a mode of turning attention back upon the very resources of expression (its classic modality was to be directed to the audience or else towards the medium of language itself), rhetoric was to this extent a self-designating and self-conscious medium. And in performing this function, rhetoric, ever one of the primary mediums for exploring the relationship between language, thought, the unthought, and behavior, became increasingly instrumental in articulating new forms of ideological attachment for ancient cultural subjects. Aesthetics, here, was highly functional as well.

The ascendancy of the voice

Pythagoras discovered (anecdotally, at least) the power of the voice as an isolated phenomenon. Much the same discovery was made, albeit slowly, in the performative traditions, starting with rhapsodes and passing into rhetoric. Bards were always conscious of the versatility of the voice and its seductive, imitative powers (*Homeric Hymn to Apollo* 171–75). One of the indices of this passage into rhetoric proper is to be found in the semantics of *hupokrisis*, which gradually came to mean *oral delivery*, while originally it meant *acting* and *gesturing*. The history of this evolution is at best dimly lit, but from Aristotle we can grasp the outlines of a general picture. The information comes from the opening of the third book of the *Rhetoric*, an astonishing document, as it reads like a short speculative history of rhetoric in one of its more prominent aspects. In a word, rhetoric emerges here as a theory and practice of the voice, of speech directed to the listener (*pros ton akroatēn*), whereby language comes to be viewed as a resource of sound worthy of independent speculation and treatment.

Aristotle traces this development along two lines, that of style (*lexis*) and that of delivery (*hupokrisis*), in both cases starting with the poets, who first instigated both tendencies (*Rhetoric* 1404a20). The lessons of the poets, he says, were then generalized by being transposed into the sphere of prose.

---

[6] See Habinek 2005a, for an intriguing sociological account of rhetoric's province over "special speech" in antiquity.

Theoretical inquiry followed. To piece back together this history is not only to retrace some of the lost filiations between rhetoric and its neighboring practices. It is also to observe how the theory of language both narrowed and deepened as it turned inward and confronted its own resources.

First, there came a poeticization of speech and writing in the figure of Gorgias. Subsequently, attention was drawn to the question of what Gorgias had added to his language in order to make it poetic (*poiētikē*), and the answer seemed to lie in language itself: *lexis* (style, diction, expression). For just as "the poets, while speaking sweet nothings, seemed to acquire their reputation through their *lexis*, it was through this [viz. through the emphasis on *lexis*] that a poetic style (*poiētikē lexis*) first came into existence [in prose as well], for example, that of Gorgias" (1404a24–26; trans. Kennedy). Theoretical attention gradually came to focus on this sundering of expressiveness and sense as an abstract idea in its own right, indeed on the very fact of its possibility, which produced yet another abstract idea, the category of style or *lexis* itself (the term is unattested prior to Plato Comicus [fr. 99.2 K.–A.], *c.* 420–390). It fell to Gorgias' pupil Licymnius of Chios to recognize, somewhere around 400, that "verbal beauty lies either in the sounds or in the sense, and ugliness the same" (*Rhetoric* 1405b6–8). This feat, obvious to us, paved the way in later centuries for a theoretical justification of euphony as a self-sufficient criterion of verbal beauty, unless this step was already being taken by Licymnius himself. Licymnius, a mere shadow, seems to have excelled at crossing rhetoric with poetry, disastrously according to both Plato and Aristotle (*Phaedrus* 267c; *Rhetoric* 1414b17). His dithyrambs, Aristotle says, are more suited to reading aloud than to enacting. But as such, they border on aesthetic decoration at the expense of meaning. The sheer senseless materiality of sound cannot for Aristotle or Plato be allowed to take primacy over meaning, to say nothing of the analysis of bodily gestures.

A parallel development appears to have taken place in the realm of *hupokrisis*, or delivery, which gradually detached itself from its origins in drama and came to be transferred over to the art of rhetoric. Dramatists at first acted in their own plays (1403b23–24), but owing to the increased complexity of the stage and, no less importantly, to the powerful appeal of delivery (to which Aristotle's *Poetics* bears witness), they then turned these roles, and their voices, over to professional actors. The need for practical manuals arose,[7] and eventually parallels to rhetorical delivery

---

[7] Cf. Diogenes Laertius 2.103 on a certain Theodorus (§4) who apparently wrote a "very fine" work on vocal training. Could he be the actor mentioned in Aristotle, *Rhetoric* 1403b23–24 and noteworthy for his voice? See Cope 1867, *ad loc.* and Burkert 1975, who, however, fails to mention this notice in Diogenes Laertius.

were noticed, for instance by Thrasymachus in his *Appeals to Pity* (1404a14). But apparently no substantive technical treatise on rhetorical *hupokrisis* existed down to Aristotle's day, even if handbooks on acting and uses of the voice and vocalization in poetic contexts (for instance, tragic and rhapsodic recitations) had been developed, such as that by Glaucon of Teos (1403b21–26). Theophrastus would fill the gap in the next generation.[8]

Aristotle is a reluctant witness to the phenomenon he retails: duty-bound, he offers valuable clues to the way in which the study of style and sound came to be conceived, even though he remains dismissive of the final value of vocalization in rhetoric despite, or more likely because of, its immense and undeniable powers. Aristotle's phrase, a virtual sigh, "But nevertheless, [delivery] has great power" (*all' homōs mega dunatai* [1404a7]), seems to echo Gorgias' famous statement in his *Helen* (§8), "speech is a great dynast" (*logos dunastēs megas estin*). And yet the passage from acting (gesturing) to vocalization (delivery) in the meaning of *hupokrisis* is in one sense not a transition at all, since the two activities are mutually co-involved, at least in the arts of language.

Even so, the true focus of Aristotle's history is neither delivery nor acting, but the domain of the voice (*ta en tēi phōnēi*). The breathy substance of voice lay at the source of the language arts that would eventually culminate in an exclusive attention to the voice: "Voice, the most mimetic of all our parts, was there to start with. Thus, the [verbal] arts were established: rhapsody and acting and the others" (1404a22–24). Later on, writers of prose would realize the fruitfulness of the conjunction of delivery and *lexis*, treating them nearly as functions of each other, as in Dionysius of Halicarnassus: "Here the style itself (*lexis*) shows what kind of delivery (*hupokriseōs*) is needed for it" (*Demosthenes* 54). At the same time a space would be preserved for the virtues of reading aloud without declamation. Aristotle, going the other way, would define the true virtue of *lexis* not in terms of its subservience to sound, but in its transparency to meaning: clarity (*to saphes*) and naturalness – the seeming artlessness – of expression, the final aim of rhetoric being persuasion and demonstration (1404b1–2, 18–19; cf. *Poetics* 22). And he would cling to the genre boundaries between poetry and prose, resisting their virtual conflation and the tide of popular opinion (1404a28–29), which was bewitched by the new poetic qualities of rhetoric (as in the case of Gorgias), even as he recognized the essential rhythmic quality of all well-turned *lexis*, rhythm being one of the deepest features of language (1408b30–31; 1409a22–24). In his very resistance to the power of the voice and in his attempt to contain its effects, Aristotle

---

[8] See Diels 1886: 32–34; Fortenbaugh 1985; frr. 666, 681–92, 699–704, 712–13 FHS&G; Csapo and Slater 1995: 221–74.

supplies us with evidence of its separation in theory and in practice, as had Plato before him. Both are generally hostile to the material, sensuous, and phenomenal aspects of language: for them, the job of the voice is to express, transparently, rational thoughts (Plato, *Republic* 397b; Aristotle, *Poetics* 19).

Once sundered and so justified, the idea of language *qua* sound or voice took on a life of its own. It seems to have attracted independent attention among theoreticians, as in Democritus' studies *On Sounds, On the Beauty of Words,* and *On Euphonious and Harsh-Sounding Letters* (Diogenes Laertius 9.48) or in Plato's *Cratylus.* Orators, such as Demosthenes, employed the services of actors to improve their vocal skills or were themselves trained as actors (like Aeschines), but they also seem to have been versed in the technical analysis of the voice. Aeschines singles out Demosthenes' delivery, which is abetted by his exploitation of pitches (*ho tonos tēs phōnēs*) (Aeschines 3.210). Demosthenes could repay the compliment, labeling Aeschines "euphonious," as though this were a dubious distinction (Demosthenes 18.285; 19.126; 19.337–39). Aristotle's account of voice in the *Rhetoric* betrays some of the same technical language, which no doubt stems from the musical tradition, but also from the researches of Hippias, Prodicus, and Thrasymachus and possibly from early analyses of poetry which have been lost. The Hibeh musical papyrus, speculated to date from the early fourth century and to be by Alcidamas of Elaea, is further proof of these crossovers.

Alcidamas himself did much to bring attention to the voice. Under the guise of attacking prepared speeches in written form and in the name of improvisational speechifying, Alcidamas was in fact promoting a conception of the vivacity of the voice, which was inherited and long-standing: speech ideally ought to be animated (*empsukhos*) and alive (*kai zēi*), supple and mobile (*[ouk] akinētos*), opportune, accomplished, and harmonious (*eukairōs kai mousikōs*), and showing signs of energy (*energeia*). What is more, all the attributes of speech pertain to writing, which is an (audible) image of speech: for underlying every written text is a voice that animates it (Alcidamas, *On the Sophists* 28, 32). The thought was central to ancient conceptions of language (cf. *Carmina Epigraphica Graeca* 286; Aeschylus, *Tragicorum Graecorum Fragmenta* 78a, col. 1.5–8 (Radt); Plato, *Phaedrus* 276a8–9). According to later grammarians, writing is "voice capable of being articulated into (written) language" (*engrammatos phōnē*) (schol. Dionysius Thrax 120.37 Hilgard).[9]

---

[9] Cf. *Papyri Osloenses* 2.13 (text of Janko 2000: 185 n. 2); Crates of Mallos *ap.* schol. Dionysius Thrax 316.24–26; Diogenes Laertius 3.107 and 7.56; *Divisiones Aristoteleae* 38, cols. 1.4 and 2.6 Mutschmann; [Plato], *Definitions* 414d1; Sextus Empiricus, *Against the Professors* 1.100; etc. The idea has its origins in the sophistic movement and in tragedy (Euripides, *Erechtheus* fr. 369 [*Tragicorum Graecorum Fragmenta* (Nauck)]).

Such a view is either derisible as an expression of logocentrism or else it admirably celebrates the vitality of all language. *Voice* is a name for this vivacity – for that which brings speech to life and puts it in touch with the senses, rather than with rational meaning per se. The aesthetics of language pays tribute to this insight into vitality. Rhetoric is one of its enshrining practices.

Eventually, an entire branch of literary criticism would come to be devoted to the way language sounds, above and beyond the subdivision of grammatical research into a special topic devoted to the voice (*peri phōnēs, de uoce*).[10] Rhetoric was once again involved in this evolution, which brought with it an increasing isolation of the voice. We might compare Cicero: "For on the question of voice (*de uoce*) I am not yet speaking of points that concern delivery, but about a matter that seems to me to be connected with utterance as such," by which he means the mechanics of utterance, the regulation of the "tongue and breath and actual tone of voice (*uocis sonus ... ipse*)" (*On the Orator* 3.40–41; trans. Rackham). To isolate the voice was to concentrate on its aesthetic qualities: brightness, strength, clarity, loudness, liveliness, its capacity for being well acted or well delivered, and the like, all of which have a long afterlife in criticism, though all this terminology can be traced in fourth-century Attic orators (e.g. Demosthenes 18.259, 313; 19.199, 206, 216). Similarly, Isocrates shows himself to be fluent in the vocabulary of literary criticism, for instance in his mention of the accessories of "voice and the variations of delivery" (5.26) and in his general awareness of the proximities of literary prose and poetry: he describes his output as being "closer to works composed with rhythm and music than to court-room speeches," and as affording his audience [lit. "hearers": *hoi akouontes*] pleasures akin to those of poetry (15.46–47). Being the proud products of writing designed not for declamation but for delectation, and frequently taken to task for this, Isocrates' texts nevertheless exhibit a *simulated* orality ("But since the impulse to speak out freely has struck me and I have loosened my tongue ... there's no keeping silent"; 12.95–96).[11] In short, already by the early fourth century there existed a kind of theoretical reflection on the subject to which Dionysius of Halicarnassus, possibly in imitation, would later devote a treatise (*On Composition*), while reflection on delivery, especially as this pertained to the voice, became an accepted element in the rhetorical handbook once delivery was canonized by Theophrastus.

[10] See Ax 1986.
[11] For a longer view, see Whitmarsh 2006.

As Aristotle recognized, poetic language was changing; it was approaching the language of speech. The language of prose, for its part, was seemingly going in two directions at once: it was taking its cues from the earlier poets, and it was following the natural progression of poetic *lexis* as this began descending to the level of the everyday (1404a29–39). Aristotle was critical of the first tendency, which seemed anachronistic and absurd (1404a35–36). But what about the second tendency? It would be up to later generations to decide, and to attempt a genuine poetics of prose. Sound (*phōnē*, the voice) might appear too reductive and narrow a category to fulfill as many promises as all of this, but the limitations of the category are precisely where its generative power lay. The focus on sound provoked reflection about poetics proper, that is, about language as an aesthetic phenomenon rivaling poetry and music. It helped to bring attention to poetry as an artifact of a craft or art (*tekhnē*), and consequently to poetic technique. This focus on sound posits – if not reductively and absolutely, then at least provisionally – the possibility of an analysis of language as a material substance with claims to relative autonomy, and it brings to bear the reasons why one might want to take up such a view. At its most extreme, focusing so intently on speech and writing as aesthetic phenomena worked to suspend considerations of logical structure, meaning, content, and morals altogether, clearing the way for a different kind of apprehension, one that depended upon an irrational grasp of the perceived phenomena of language, through the ear (*hē alogos aisthēsis*). The voice here was a continuum of breath, palpable and enjoyable per se. This is the aesthetic flip-side to Gorgias' isolation of the abstract essence of language as *logos*. Euphonism, always an integral element of style, in some quarters came to define all one needed to know about language in order to appreciate its arts and excellences. The extremism of this approach merely brought to the fore what was an operating assumption of all of ancient literature: literature contains a voice that reading, aloud or with subvocalization, releases. The euphonist critics preserved by Philodemus, who included Crates of Mallos and a host of otherwise mainly unknown Hellenistic predecessors, promoted such a view, as did Dionysius of Halicarnassus in their wake. Intent on discovering the music of the voice, these critics dissolved all genre boundaries, including those between poetry and prose, into a stream of sounds. Sound, thus reinvented, was at once a durable material object yet endowed with an ephemeral life, and at the limit passing over into the domain of the ineffable. Sound, here, became sublime.[12]

---

[12] J. I. Porter 2001.

Arts of the sensuous and the imaginary: rhetoric and criticism

Owing to their common pursuit of the sensuous aspects of language, rhetoric and art criticism enjoyed a close proximity in antiquity. Ever the omnivorous consumer of knowledge, rhetoric traditionally felt entitled to cohabit the same space as any number of arts. Quintilian, typical of his profession, pleads for maximal elbowroom: "The musical theorist Aristoxenus divides what concerns sound into rhythm and melody, the former comprising the 'modulation,' and the latter the tone and the quality of the sound. Now are not *all* these essential to the orator?" (Quintilian, *Institutes* 1.10.22; trans. Russell). Similarly, rhetoric requires expertise in grammar, but for the same reasons it also requires expertise in music, astronomy, philosophy, and eloquence (1.4.4–5). The visual arts, not mentioned here, are well attested elsewhere as another annex of rhetoric, and understandably so. The arts of the imaginary require intense visualization (*enargeia, ekphrasis, euidentia, demonstratio*).[13] Taste and connoisseurship are likewise skills shared in common, and these imply a honing of perception and judgment, as well as a shared vocabulary of description.[14] Thus, *euruthmia* (orderly flow, proportionality) and *summetria* (balance, commensurability) are used in musical, poetic, sculptural, and architectural contexts throughout antiquity to capture – not always identically conceived but nonetheless suggestively parallel – aesthetic properties of objects or their perception, while *phantasia* enjoys an equal latitude in labeling a range of subjective processes, from mere appearances to their coalescence in a unified sensory or else imaginary impression.

To take the least obvious of these applications: poets, Isocrates says (9.10), "bewitch their audiences with their shapeliness (*tais euruthmiais*) and symmetries (*tais summetriais*) alone," that is, even absent compelling ideas, an insight that recalls Gorgias (and later Plato), but which is nonetheless dressed in terminology that may have been borrowed from the visual arts. Quintilian picks up the same thread centuries later: "Moreover, an apt and becoming movement of the body – what the Greeks call *eurhuthmia* – is essential, and cannot be obtained from any other source. A large part of the subject Delivery depends on this." He goes on to add music to the orator's quiver of tools: "Again, will not the orator, as a priority, take trouble about his voice? What is so specially the concern of music as this?" (1.10.26–27; trans. Russell). But this is nothing new (Dionysius of Halicarnassus,

[13] See Zanker 1981; Theophrastus F687 FHS&G.
[14] See Pollitt 1974 (indispensable, though by no means complete), and its predecessors (Overbeck 1868; Jex-Blake, Sellers, and Urlichs 1896); also useful: Benediktson 2000.

Demosthenes 48). Visual analogies are frequent throughout the critical tradition. "Whenever painters perfectly fashion (*apergasōntai*) a single body and shape from many colors and bodies, they delight the sight." Gorgias here (*Helen* §18) presents the image of an attractive body (like Helen's), one that is manifestly made-up, whether of body parts, as in the famous parable about Zeuxis combining the features of the five most beautiful women of Croton (Cicero, *On Invention* 2.1–3), or of paint pigments, said by Empedocles to produce a deceptive appearance (*apatē* [Diels–Kranz B23.9]). Both images (Helen and the painter's icon) furnish visual delight; both can be seductive and pleasurable (but also painful [*Helen* §18] or painfully pleasurable [§9]); both embody a kind of unrivaled and irresistible perfection; both resemble the illusions of rhetoric (Plato, *Sophist* 234c, *Republic* 586b–c), but also those of poetry (*Helen* §§8–9).

Building metaphors likewise abound (indeed, just now, painting was itself a kind of construction). Architecture was a conventional analogue to verbal composition from the age of Pindar onwards. While couched in the competitive language of durability (poetry as monument), the conceit in fact helped to bring out the material and palpable qualities of words. In Roman rhetoric, avoidance of hiatus is sometimes termed *coagmentare*, or "cementing," though smooth surfaces of sound are not always a desirable quality (Cicero, *On the Orator* 3.171; *Orator* 77–78; *Brutus* 68). But often they are. Suetonius records how Caligula once criticized Seneca's style as lacking this binding quality: it is "like sand without lime" (*Caligula* 53.2). Words can be thought of as a *structura* when they are joined together (*iuncta, coniuncta, apta*). They need to be squared (*quadrata*) and polished (*polita*). They sit on foundations (*fundamenta*). And in general, to compose in language is to be like a "builder of words" (*architectus uerborum*), the way the Stoics are in philosophical argument, though not in oratory (*Brutus* 118). It is to build a monument, *exaedificare*, though not always a splendid one (Cicero, *On the Orator* 1.164, 2.63, 3.175; *Brutus* 33; *Orator* 149, 220, 224; Quintilian, *Institutes* 2.5.9 [*leuis et quadrata*]; Tacitus, *Dialogue on Orators* 22.5, ironically, with reference to Cicero).

The epigraphic and ecphrastic tradition of "speaking objects," likewise of early date, helped to solidify further the connection between words, presented as sensuous objects of experience, and three-dimensional objects.[15] Thus, for [Longinus], "[selection] makes grandeur, beauty, old-world charm, weight, force, strength, and a kind of luster bloom upon our words

---

[15] See Steiner 2001 on the early traditions; J. I. Porter forthcoming on this and on later traditions.

as upon beautiful statues; it gives things life and makes them speak" (*On the Sublime* 30.1–2; trans. Russell). Often, verbal architecture rivals physical architecture:

> The special character of the austere style of composition is this: it requires that the words shall stand firmly on their own feet and occupy strong positions [*staseis iskhuras*; "like columns": Roberts] and be seen on all sides; and that the parts of the sentence shall be at considerable distances from one another, separated by perceptible intervals (*aisthētois khronois*).
>
> (Dionysius of Halicarnassus, *On Composition* 22; trans. Usher, adapted)

The last passage is remarkable for the way it visualizes a critical conceit about language, not only for the degree of vividness it imparts to the scenario, but also for the kinds of transformations it brings about. Words are turned into building materials, and then the gaps between them are magnified in such a way that they become three-dimensional objects jutting off the page and so too microscopically surveyable in their minutest textures. Needless to say, the gaps in question consist not of space, but of *time*. The transformation thus wrought is twofold: a visualization of a text requires (i) its spatialization, which is to say its translation into a spatial image. But that, in turn, requires, or rather is equivalent to, (ii) a temporalization, or translation of space into time. Finally, as this entire textual landscape is imagined under the sign of its being read aloud, in question at any moment are fewer whole words, gaps between them, and *khronoi* in the technical sense of the term in conventional (Aristoxenian) rhythmical theory (time durations), than they are vocalic and intervocalic sounds, silences (pauses), and lengths of *breath* (Dionysius of Halicarnassus, *On Composition* 22). After all, "harsh and dissonant collocations" is a reference to effects of sound, and especially those which are productive of grandeur, or *megethos*. It is as if the very effort to describe sound in all its sensuousness required a collapsing of space and time, as with the language of eurythmy and symmetry above.

In appealing to images from other arts, rhetoric also borrowed from their languages. Conceivably, the flow of ideas went in both directions, but this is harder to ascertain. Musicology may have been immune to influence owing to its intense specialization starting with Aristoxenus. In the visual and plastic arts, little survives beyond a handful of titles. The rhetorical tradition is far better preserved.[16] Indeed, rhetorical treatises are one of the major sources of evidence for the visual arts and especially for visual art theory in antiquity. Stylistic categories are likely to have been shared (grand, middling,

---

[16] See Pollitt 1974.

refined, and various shades in between; see Dionysius of Halicarnassus, *On Composition* 23, *Isocrates* 3), as were grand narratives of the arts, best exemplified by Pliny's judgment that art more or less had ceased to be produced (*cessauit ars*) after the first decade of the third century BCE, and only revived (*reuixit*) after 156/153 BCE (*Natural History* 34.52). Similar stories could be told about Atticism. All belong under the general heading of classicism.

Classicism

As the centuries wore on, the aesthetic function of rhetoric never diminished, though its ulterior purposes evolved. The voice that rhetoric guarded in custodial fashion aged like an old photograph: encrusted with time, sepia toned, curling at the edges, increasingly hallowed and even holy, the voice became a museum object, enshrined for display, emulation, and worship. And yet the preserved voice of the past could appear simultaneously old and new: its sound was at once aged and fresh, archaic and present. To read a text was to breathe life back into it and to hear the past come alive before one's senses. Quotation was a way of parading and especially performing the past, but it was also a form of reanimation. Likewise, imitation was frequently a way of ventriloquizing classic orators. This logic was shamelessly exploited by Second Sophistic rhetors, who frequently boasted their ancestral ties to long-dead historical figures (as did the Second Sophistic itself). Herodian desired to be known as "one of the Ten" (the canonized Attic orators) and was identified with Critias. Proclus of Naucratis, an Athenian from the post-Hadrianic era, gave declamations in the style of Hippias and Gorgias. Philostratus tells of the Thessalian rage for Gorgianizing (Philostratus, *Lives of the Sophists* 501–503, 564, 604). Aelius Aristides dreamt he was Demosthenes declaiming to the Athenians (*Orationes* 47.16 Keil).

The archaizing aesthetic was programmatic under the empire. Readers and aspiring writers are frequently enjoined to appreciate "the patina of antiquity" (*ho arkhaios pinos*) or the *color uetustatis* of classical texts. *khnous* ("powder," "film," "bloom," or "down") and *umbra* are frequent synonyms, at least in some authors (especially Fronto and Gellius). Elsewhere, architectural metaphors take the place of sculptural ones, to the same effect. The appeal to the visual domain is once again an allusion to sound: texts were not only ancient, but they also "looked," felt, and sounded so. Antiquity of sound is central to the concept of linguistic purism (*hellēnismos* and *Latinitas*), and it lies behind the *sonantia uerba et antiqua* that Pliny and others so admired (*Letters* 1.16.2). But not all were in agreement. Cicero disparages the *rustica uox* that affects the sound of greater antiquity, though he knows the virtues of *pinos* too (*On the Orator* 3.41–45; *Letters to Atticus* 12.6a [*eupines*], 14.7 [*pepinōmenai*], 15.16 [*pepinōmenōs*]). The feeling is doubtless tied up with the complexities of the Roman tongue's appearing ancient in the mirror of Greece, as well as with the dilemmas of wanting to be modern and free of the burdens of the past. Quintilian nervously follows suit (2.5.23–24).[17] *Pinos*, after all, means both venerable old-world charm and filth or dirt.

The antiquity of a language and its heritage, which is rooted in the very aesthetic perception of language, is bound up with ideology and with communal identities. It is the sheer materiality of the voice, its euphonic properties (and, we might add, its direct availability to feeling), rather than anything it says, that does the work of capturing the past on this conceit. Benedict Anderson notes how ritual hymns and national anthems "provide occasions for unisonality, for the echoed physical realization of the imagined community."[18] In Greece and Rome, these echoes took on near-religious dimensions. "Antiquity is commended to us by a certain majesty and, I might almost say, religious awe (*religio*)," Quintilian preaches (1.6.1; trans. Russell; cf. 10.1.88: *Ennium sicut sacros uetustate lucos adoremus*; Horace, *Epistles* 2.1.54: *sanctum est uetus omne poema*; [Plutarch], *Moralia* 10e). Pliny, Martial, and Statius speak in similar hushed terms about Vergil (Pliny, *Letters* 3.7.8; Martial 8.55.3; 12.67; Statius, *Silvae* 4.4.54–5, *Thebaid* 12.816–17), while the conceit of libraries as a kind of temple was widespread (see Pliny the Elder, *Natural History* 35.2.9–11), not least thanks to the Roman imperial habit of locating major public libraries next to temples, perhaps on the model of the Alexandrian Museum and its two adjoining libraries.[19] What one hears in a classical or classicizing text is thus a *relation* rather than a sound or set of sounds by itself. What is heard, above all, is the sound of a cultural and historical *difference*.

As the canon of Ten Orators gradually became fixed, probably in the second century CE,[20] rhetorical manuals increasingly played the part of guardian of the tradition. Contests over hierarchies within established canons were frequent and inevitable: reasons for inclusion had to be articulated, nor did canonization mean agreed-upon rankings. The purview of rhetoric included stylistic criticism, anthologization, collections of ancient sound-bites, and rules of all kinds – rules about correct pronunciation,

[17] Further, Farrell 2001: 65–70.
[18] B. Anderson 1991: 45.
[19] Citroni 1998; Zeitlin 2001: 212; Casson 2001.
[20] Douglas 1956.

about how to avoid *faux pas* in writing, rules about decorum (aptness of language to meaning or character), about judging quality and effectiveness, and most insidiously of all, rules about what pleasures and other emotional habits to feel, to adopt, or to assume – thus inscribing postures and tastes in the subjectivities of its audiences.

To study ancient rhetoric in any of its periods is to study the recesses of classical culture, its most fundamental ideologies and beliefs about meaning and experience. Aesthetics, and notably the aesthetic dimensions of rhetoric, are the materials through which such behaviors are "sutured":[21] through these, culture appears to cohere, and its subjects can form passionate attachments to their culture (Thucydides 7.63.3; Plato, *Menexenus, passim*; Demosthenes 15.35; Cicero, *On the Laws* 2.3–4).[22] Thus, while the ideals of classicism had a fixed, burnished, and timeless appearance, they were in fact the product of endless disputes and squabbles. The harder one looks at them, the less credible they seem. Was Demosthenes a better prose stylist than Lysias? Was Cicero better than both of these? Was Athens the center of the world or was it a quaint museum of faded splendors in another, now Roman world? Rhetoric was frequently the public medium in which such questions could be raised. And in its finest moments it could be seen either to solve these questions or else to render them, for a moment of aesthetic bliss or more durably, whenever its lessons were absorbed into one's *habitus*, irrelevant.[23]

Suggested further reading

Rhetoric and identity: M. W. Gleason, *Making Men: Sophists and Self-Presentation in Ancient Rome* (Princeton, 1995); E. Gunderson, *Staging Masculinity: The Rhetoric of Performance in the Roman World* (Ann Arbor, 2000), *Declamation, Paternity, and Roman Identity: Authority and the Rhetorical Self* (Cambridge, 2003). Y. L. Too, ed., *Education in Greek and Roman Antiquity* (Leiden, 2001). Orality and the voice: A. Krumbacher, *Die Stimmbildung der Redner im Altertum bis auf die Zeit Quintilians* (Paderborn, 1920); H. Ll. Hudson-Williams, "Isocrates and Recitations," *Classical Quarterly* 43 (1949) 64–69 and "Impromptu Speaking," *Greece and Rome* 18, no. 52 (1949) 28–31; S. Usener, *Isokrates, Platon und ihr Publikum: Hörer und Leser von Literatur im 4. Jahrhundert v. Chr.*

---

[21] Miller 1977; S. Heath 1981; Silverman 1983: 194–236.

[22] See Loraux 1986a; Connolly 2001; Wohl 2002; J. I. Porter 2006.

[23] This chapter is drawn from J. I. Porter, forthcoming. Thanks above all to Erik Gunderson for his shrewd editorial counsel.

(Tübingen, 1994). F. Dupont, "*Recitatio* and the Reorganization of the Space of Public Discourse," in T. Habinek and A. Schiesaro, eds., *The Roman Cultural Revolution* (Cambridge, 1997), 44–59. W. Johnson, "Toward a Sociology of Reading in Classical Antiquity," *American Journal of Philology* 121 (2000) 593–627. J. Rée, *I See a Voice: Deafness, Language, and the Senses – a Philosophical History* (New York, 1999). Rhetoric and other arts: L. van Hook, "The Metaphorical Terminology of Greek Rhetoric and Literary Criticism," diss., University of Chicago (1905); W. Kroll, "Randbemerkungen," *Rheinisches Museum für Philologie* 62(1907) 86–101. Hellênismos, Latinitas: S. Saïd, ed., ΈΛΛΗΝΙΣΜΟΣ. *Quelques jalons pour une histoire de l'identité grecque: Actes du Colloque de Strasbourg, 25–27 octobre 1989* (Leiden, 1991). S. Swain, *Hellenism and Empire: Language, Classicism, and Power in the Greek World, AD 50–250* (Oxford, 1996). J. Wisse, "Greeks, Romans and the Rise of Atticism," in J. G. J. Abbenes, S. R. Slings, and I. Sluiter, eds., *Greek Literary Theory after Aristotle: A Collection of Papers in Honour of D. M. Schenkeveld* (Amsterdam, 1995), 65–82. Second Sophistic rhetoric: E. L. Bowie, "The Greeks and their Past in the Second Sophistic," *Past and Present* 46 (1970) 3–41; Thomas Schmitz, *Bildung und Macht: Zur sozialen und politischen Funktion der zweiten Sophistik in der griechischen Welt der Kaiserzeit. Zetemata* 97 (Munich, 1997); Swain; Gleason (bibliography, above). Classicism: J. I. Porter, ed., *Classical Pasts: The Classical Traditions of Greece and Rome* (Princeton, 2006). S. Settis, *The Future of the Classical* (Cambridge, 2006).

6

ERIK GUNDERSON

The rhetoric of rhetorical theory

Theories regularly enjoy a specific rhetorical advantage: their audience generally comes to them pre-persuaded that theoretical accounts are authoritative and that well-articulated theory has a masterful tale to tell about practice. For a writer of an overview of a subject, this disposition makes for lighter labors. Neutral, factual, true: an objective account of practice persuades us that theory itself is to be trusted.

It is clear, though, that I am here to put you on your guard, even at my own expense as the authoritative authority. For I am here to persuade you that theory persuades. Specifically, there is no such thing as "The theory of rhetoric." Instead there are various performances that have been labeled by their authors as "The theory of rhetoric." And these performances, to the extent that they are effective, yield a conviction on the part of their audience that the theory they encounter is "The Theory," that the author of this theory is an authority, and, most importantly, that the prestigious, potent, and culturally contested domain of rhetorical practice has been fully compassed by it.[1]

If we look at Quintilian's *Institutes* we will find a text that is explicitly rhetorical.[2] The contents of the arguments are exemplified by the form in which they are presented. It is, then, important to read the *Institutio Oratoria* as a rhetorical performance if we are to appreciate the message

---

[1] The multiplicity of theories of rhetoric is documented in a number of essays in this volume, but see especially Heath.

[2] Kennedy remarks in passing: "Quintilian sometimes likes to illustrate a technique at the same time that he describes it (e.g. IX,ii,6)" (Kennedy 1969: 73). Zundel 1981 offers a book-length study of the style advocated as well as employed by the *Institutes*. Readers who wish to follow up on this essay should consider consulting Zundel's work. Zundel himself owes a significant debt to Seel 1977 and his remarks on Quintilian's style. See especially Seel 1977: 90–96.

of the *Institutes* itself.[3] As a rhetorical performance the *Institutes* betrays traits of deliberative, forensic, and display oratory since it not only concerns itself with the expedient, the just, and the noble but even attempts to unite them. When united, both the theory and the rhetoric of the *Institutes* combine to delimit a specific territory for good and legitimate speech that simultaneously exiles from its borders other possible discourses as illegitimate or even as "untrue."[4]

An education does not merely inform a man; it makes him who he is. This is presupposed throughout antiquity. Ancient education came in a variety of forms, though. Quintilian himself was the first person to head a publicly established school at Rome and to receive his salary from the state treasury. Vespasian, keen on "restoring" the principate after the chaotic end of the Neronian era, took an interest in education.[5] Well-born children had long attended prestigious private schools and emerged from them as gentlemen of distinction. Quintilian's school, though, was formally an element of the political sphere.[6] Rhetoric teachers had once been expelled from Rome as a threat to its sociopolitical traditions, now one was on the public payroll. The politics of a rhetorical education extend well beyond political politics, of course. In addition to the specifically political valences of such an education, one has to note as well that schooling tends to be a schooling in "manly excellence." The cultural logic of social status and even of gender itself is herein implicated.

In any number of dimensions Quintilian can be described as a "canonical" author. In fact, one of his chief aims is to ensure the canonization of Ciceronean style against other contenders to the title of authoritative Latin.[7] But he also canonizes a certain version of education itself. And the form of this education is perfectly adjusted to its contents. In the *Institutes* we find an apparatus for producing and reproducing manly excellence at Rome. Moreover the *Institutes* archives and comments on the tradition of rhetorical training that precedes it. Hence a close examination of Quintilian reveals as well much about rhetorical theory more generally: all of the

---

[3] Note as well that Quintilian himself writes rhythmical prose (Kennedy 1969: 93). Like the great preponderance of ancient texts, this one is also designed to please to the ear. See Norden 1915: 1.

[4] See Hesk in this volume.

[5] Suetonius lists the financing of education among Vespasian's grand public projects (*Vespasian* 17–19).

[6] See Colson 1924: xxvi–xxvii for a summary of the educational principles of Quintilian himself.

[7] But both Ciceronean rhetoric and the political world for which that rhetoric was adapted have long since passed. See Dugan in this volume.

various possible stances have been laid out within its pages. The *Institutes* archives these other theories of rhetoric as part of its own performance of rhetorical-*cum*-theoretical mastery. I take the *Institutes* to be, then, not just "a" case study, but rather something that aspires to be "the" case study when it comes to the theory of making a case. Lastly, the rich afterlife of the *Institutes* reveals that the efficacy of this apparatus was not limited just to Rome in the Flavian era.

Before I end my own prologue and transition to my narration, then, let me note the following: Quintilian offers a theory of prologues.[8] In book 4 of the *Institutes* Quintilian specifically notes that the opening should win over the listener and pave the way for the remainder of the speech. Most authorities, says Quintilian, insist upon the following: the audience should be made well-disposed, attentive, and receptive to instruction (*beneuolus, attentus, docilis*).[9]

Naturally Quintilian's advice on prologues is detailed and varied, and it includes items such as the question of whether one is to display or to hide one's eloquence given that it may affect the question of the good will of the audience.[10] A careful student of the advice will, though, come to an arresting conclusion: this theory corresponds to a practice we have already seen in our earlier reading of Quintilian's own text, and a practice we will see again. That is, while the opening section of the fourth book of the *Institutes* is dedicated to instructing the reader about the theory of prologues, the *Institutes* itself has a prologue.

The preface to the first book addresses Marcellus Vitorius, the man to whom the text is formally dedicated.[11] Quintilian is helping Marcellus educate his son. And this first book is about elementary education. Quintilian himself appears in this prologue as a character, as a good man, experienced at teaching: he has retired after twenty years of instruction. The fourth book, the book on prologues, itself opens with a prologue. Here we see a good man doing his duty and are asked to feel sympathy for him. Quintilian claims that he had already been anxious about what people will make of this work of his. But now Quintilian has more to worry about: the emperor Domitian has entrusted Quintilian with the education of his sister's grandchildren.[12] Quintilian recognizes as well the overwhelming mass of the

---

[8] Quintilian, *Institutes* 4.1. For more on the different segments of a speech, see Steel in this volume.

[9] 4.1.5.

[10] 4.1.9.

[11] 1.pr.6: *quod opus, Marcelle Vitori, tibi dicamus.*

[12] 4.pr.1–2.

Institutes as a whole. Though it may tire him, he has to soldier on.[13] The preface to the fifth book addresses the issue of "teaching" (*docere*) as opposed to "moving" (*mouere*) an audience. Since the fifth book itself will be about teaching, Quintilian makes sure to render his audience "well-disposed, attentive, and receptive to instruction" by assuring them that the potentially controversial topic of moving the passions has not yet arrived. One is accordingly free to sit back and to absorb Quintilian's instructions as to how to instruct an auditor. The sixth book, the book on stirring the passions, begins with a stirring prologue. Quintilian laments the death of his son. The book is no longer a legacy that can be left from a father to his child, but rather it is a gift from Quintilian to any who would become his adoptive children. The *Institutes* is his reason for living,[14] but the ends he serves are no longer really his own: the book readied for a son is now left as a legacy for others.[15] The twelfth and final book begins with a preface: Quintilian needs to make one last push. In the discussion of the character of the orator we will behold the innermost mysteries of oratory.[16] Quintilian here declares himself to be an innovator.[17] In his earlier books he followed others; here he sails out onto a vast sea alone.

These various prologues each fulfill the various dictates of the technical discussion of the art of prologues as found in the fourth book of the *Institutes*. In fact we discover an ironic and self-aware quality to them. Even where the prologues are most "moving," the practiced ear detects in them consummate artistry and not raw emotion. The prologue to the book on "teaching" the auditor is cool and collected. The prologue to the book on "moving" the auditor offers the most lachrymose and effusive version of the narrative voice that we can find in the whole of the *Institutes*. As a character who inserts himself into his own text, Quintilian in the prologues resembles the advocate who inserts himself into the prologues of his own cases. And the *Institutes* has specific advice for such a speaker.[18] Quintilian tells him to "Show yourself a good man."[19] Use the material itself to win the sympathy of the judges.[20]

[13] 4.pr.7.
[14] 6.pr.14.
[15] 6.pr.16.
[16] 12.pr.3.
[17] Kennedy 1969: 123 shows that Quintilian is not so novel as he pretends. This is all the more reason to see the passage as "rhetorical." See Zundel 1981: 91–101.
[18] For Cicero's Antonius both the character of the client and the character of the speaker matter. The speaker's own character is an object of persuasion. And an element of this persuasion is the very style he chooses to employ. See Cicero, *On the Orator* 2.182–83.
[19] 4.1.7.
[20] 4.1.23.

Avoid looking overconfident.[21] Cultivate the art of looking artless."[22] There are different kinds of speeches, and one needs to know how to make sure that in a doubtful case the audience is well disposed, that in an obscure one it is ready to learn, and that in an unglamorous one it is attentive.[23] Quintilian practices what he preaches: the prologues to the various books of the *Institutes* are each adapted to their corresponding circumstances.

The *Institutes* is not just about rhetoric, then. It is itself rhetorical. Moreover it exemplifies its own theory of rhetoric. To read the *Institutes* is to learn something about good oratory even if one were somehow to segregate the form of the text from its contents. But such a separation is pointedly impossible. Rather than offering a naked set of rules, Quintilian adorns his text. Rather than offering a melancholy anatomy of oratory, he fleshes out his precepts about rhetoric with rhetoric itself. There is something perverse in stripping oratory down to its sinews and bones, says Quintilian: that kind of analysis is infinite and almost sadistic in its will to know.[24] Authors who write in this manner think themselves clever and seek to project a certain image of themselves.[25] But undue subtlety and excessive analysis are vices. Conversely stopping short and building back up are hallmarks of Quintilian's good taste and discretion. His text is both analytic and synthetic, both a body decomposed and one recomposed, both a dead book of rules and a living, breathing piece of rhetoric in its own right. Quintilian's text both "embodies" and "bodies forth" this paradox of the body-of-rhetoric and rhetoric-as-body. Such, then, is my argument as to the spirit of Quintilian's argument.[26]

After my prologue about prologues it is time for me to proceed directly to a narrative of the rhetoric of rhetorical theory. We will take a brief look at Quintilian's past and then at Quintilian's present. My exposition of this history aims to persuade you that rhetorical theory had long been making a case for itself.[27] I hope to make my account clear, brief, and plausible. These are the virtues, after all, of a good *narratio*.[28]

---

[21] 4.1.33.

[22] 4.1.56.

[23] 4.1.41.

[24] 1.pr.24. The bodily metaphors all come from Quintilian: *nudae artes, ossa, nerui.*

[25] 1.pr.24: *nimiae subtilitatis adfectatio.*

[26] Compare Gunderson 2000: 187–222 on Cicero's *On the Orator*. See Heath in this volume for the notion that Quintilian's *Institutio* is inspired by the *On the Orator*.

[27] Note that a "persuasive exposition" is itself one of the definitions of a rhetorical narration offered by Quintilian in his discussion of the theory of *narrationes*, 4.2.31: *expositio rei factae aut ut factae utilis ad persuadendum.*

[28] 4.2.31: *lucida, breuis, ueri similis.*

Even if we look at our earliest authorities, we already see that theories of rhetoric emerge in a contested intellectual space that is also a contested political space. Plato's *Gorgias* is dedicated to redefining oratory and the theory of oratory. The conversation begins with one way of looking at things, and it ends with another. The rhetorical wonder Gorgias is mastered by the philosophical wonder Socrates. The message in the text is the same as the message of the text: one is to be persuaded not by the *logos* of sophistry but by the *logos* of philosophy.[29] The former *logos* is mere words, the latter *logos* is reason itself.[30] And, despite their displeasure with being forced to accept this conclusion, unless Socrates' interlocutors can come up with better *logoi*-as-arguments, then they will just have to accept his definition as to the real force and scope of the art of words. *Logoi* ought not just to evince the aesthetic virtues of arrangement and order, *taxis* and *kosmos*, they should engender these real virtues in the soul of the listener.[31] In this way Socrates, with typical irony, can declare himself to be almost the only "real politician," that is, a man of the city who speaks to improve the soul of his citizen-auditor.[32]

Aristotle's *Rhetoric* opens by declaring the irrelevance of previous works on the subject. Proofs, he says, are the only element of oratory that admits of real formalization. Other authors tend to omit them. Other authors spend the bulk of their efforts on elements that lie outside the essence of rhetoric itself. These authors explore stirring the emotions of the audience.[33] Of course Aristotle himself has to persuade his reader that a discussion of rhetoric should be thus limited. He needs his audience to accept certain propositions about what constitutes a proper "art." A proof is a kind of demonstration. A rhetorical demonstration is an enthymeme. And enthymeme is a sort of syllogism.[34] Therefore, according to this syllogism about proofs, rhetoric is a subset of dialectic. Naturally, a philosopher is most qualified to discuss it. And we should not be surprised to see Aristotle enjoining us to define rhetoric as "the capacity to discover the possible means of persuasion concerning any subject."[35] If Aristotle himself has found the means to persuade us about rhetoric, then we will accept this

---

[29] A key move comes early: "What kind of *logoi* are you talking about?" (Plato, *Gorgias* 449e). See also Wardy in this volume.

[30] Another crucial moment: rhetoric is a practical skill, but not a systematic knowledge, an *empeiria* but not a *tekhnē* (Plato, *Gorgias* 462c).

[31] See Plato, *Gorgias* 504a and compare Plato, *Gorgias* 507b.

[32] Plato, *Gorgias* 521d.

[33] See Aristotle, *Rhetoric* 1354a10–17. The same point is made again shortly at 1354b17.

[34] Aristotle, *Rhetoric* 1355a4–9.

[35] Aristotle, *Rhetoric* 1355b25–26: Ἔστω δὴ ἡ ῥητορικὴ δύναμις περὶ ἕκαστον τοῦ θεωρῆσαι τὸ ἐνδεχόμενον πιθανόν.

definition, a definition that includes what most authors exclude and excludes what the others include.

The debate over the definition of oratory is perhaps the single most important element of the rhetoric of rhetorical theory. The quality of whole texts hangs in the balance. Philosophers are, not surprisingly, most sensitive to this matter of first principles. And philosophers appreciate that if one is going to make a case for oratory – or, as regularly happens in philosophical discussions, against it – then the definition of oratory itself will be a decisive moment in this debate. Of course Quintilian is writing his *Institutes* roughly half a millennium after the debate about oratory began. The interventions of Plato and Aristotle were by no means decisive, and their arguments by no means conclusive. Quintilian's own approach to the problem of the definition of oratory instead embraces this history and makes of it a sort of prestigious legacy that itself encourages us to take rhetoric seriously if only because of its very antiquity.[36]

A substantial portion of the second book of the *Institutes* is given over to such issues. Section 15 of that book offers a survey of the various definitions of oratory that others have given. Isocrates, Gorgias, Plato, and Aristotle all make appearances. But so do a host of other authors. Quintilian moves through the variety of definitions and reveals the various modifications that many of them underwent in the face of criticism. Thus Isocrates' "power of persuasion"[37] was refined by some to "the power of persuading via speech."[38] Here one can object that prostitutes and flatterers do the same. "Leading the judge where one wishes" is an inadequate definition because failing to win one's case might mean failing to be an orator.[39] Then we find Aristotle's definition and various modifications made to it.[40] Next comes a number of variations on a theme: very specific definitions about persuasion in a civic context.[41] We also find belittling or snide definitions such as "the art of deception."[42] Quintilian next slows down and offers a reading of various moments from Plato's *Gorgias*. Quintilian likes the way that Plato is insisting on the addition of ethical goodness to the definition of oratory.[43] This resonates with Quintilian's own insistence throughout the *Institutes*

---

[36] Compare Porter's remarks concerning classicism in this volume.
[37] 2.15.3.
[38] 2.15.10.
[39] 2.15.12.
[40] 2.15.13–17.
[41] 2.15.18–23.
[42] 2.15.24.
[43] 2.15.26–29.

that the orator be a "good man." And Quintilian's survey of definitions draws to a close with more ethically minded ones. Finally Quintilian chooses his own preferred definition: "Rhetoric is the art of speaking well."[44] The word I have translated as "well" is *bene*, and Quintilian makes explicit that only an (ethically) good man can speak (morally) well. Any Latin-speaker is likely to assent immediately to the proposition that *bene* implies *bonus*.

One ought to note that *bonus* has class valences as well: the word can mean "gentleman." But the socially embedded quality of the "goodness" of good rhetoric is a notion that extends beyond the peculiarities of Latin idiom: something like it has haunted oratory for centuries and across cultures. This issue crops up throughout the present volume. As Worman makes clear, the speech of a warrior elite is a moment in rhetoric's genealogy this is never fully forgotten. Conversely Rosenbloom depicts a deracinated "tongue" of socially unconnected demagogues that horrified the Athenian dramatists. One can also contrast to the "good man" the multiply "impossible" figure of the disabled man presented by Wohl. And, more generally, Connolly shows us rhetoric as a species of symbolic violence that "ennobles" discourse even as the aristocratic genealogy of this same discourse is disavowed. Nevertheless, as Batstone points out, the *uir bonus* is himself just a *persona*, a mask, a role, and a self enacted rather than some fundamental essence. As such, then, the space for critique, re-staging, or even failure always remains open. Not, of course, that Quintilian encourages us to pursue any of these avenues. He was speaking only of the definition of oratory.

Quintilian himself has no interest in inventing a definition for oratory. He notes that some others have a warped zeal for making "new" definitions of terms that are merely the same old definitions reworded.[45] Instead Quintilian acts as a sort of judge over the Case of the Definition of Oratory. Having given ear to all the sides, he chooses: "Rhetoric is the art of speaking well." Naturally Quintilian is not just a judge but an advocate as well. His artful summary has steered us towards a conclusion that will be the same as his own.

Quintilian's practice as a rhetorical theorist fulfills the dictates he lays down for an orator. An orator ought to teach, to move, and to delight his audience.[46] If we examine these activities individually, we will find that Quintilian labors to achieve each of these ends.[47] On the one hand

[44] 2.15.34: *rhetoricen esse bene dicendi scientiam.*
[45] 2.15.37.
[46] 3.5.2: *tria sunt item, quae praestare debeat orator, ut doceat, moueat, delectet.*
[47] See Zundel 1981: 52–147 for a more detailed discussion. See Zundel 1981: 164–72 for his more general remarks.

it is clear enough that Quintilian's predecessor Cicero achieves all three in his *On the Orator*. That text is a grand dialogue about oratory filled with wit, elegance, and erudition. It is written by a master orator at the height of his powers and, though it teaches, it never smacks of the textbook.[48] On the other hand there is no shortage of books that Quintilian himself would describe as "bare textbooks" (*nudae artes*).[49] An endless array of taxonomies and definitions is the cornerstone of the pointedly unadorned style of these works. "There are three classes of political oratory ..." "The task of an orator is ..." "Delivery is ..."[50] Such authors stick to the matter, and the words follow.[51] The words are copious and authoritative. For the most part, there is little debate archived within these textbooks: the author offers a true story of oratory that effaces its own status as a story. This non-narrative is presented as a collection of definitions. There are facts to be conveyed. The reader's job is to soak it all in.

Quintilian, though, regularly reports on the debate surrounding his technical topics. He teaches us the state of the question and then invites us to cast a verdict upon it. Quintilian even asks us not to ask of him that he be the sort who lays down laws of oratory bound tight by the chains of immutable necessity.[52] Thus even as there is no shortage of raw definitions within the *Institutes*, one would seldom mistake it for the far drier *Rhetoric to Herennius*.[53] Moreover so many definitions are flagged as belonging to a

---

[48] Courbaud 1967: xv–xvi lauds the *On the Orator* as a literary masterpiece, especially when set beside the pedantry of works such as Quintilian's. See also Dugan 2005: 81 on the "this is not a textbook" quality of the *On the Orator*. See Fuhrmann 1960 on textbooks in antiquity and their modes of exegesis. The *On the Orator* is also self-aware about the matter of the rhetoric of rhetorical theory. And so too does it insist that we readers appreciate this rhetoricity. For example, at *On the Orator* 2.39 Catulus interrupts to remark how eloquently eloquence has just been praised.

[49] 1.pr.24.

[50] An endless supply of footnotes could arise here. But for the first, see the opening of the so-called *Rhetoric to Alexander* (*tria genē tōn politikōn eisi logōn* ... 1.1). Next see the opening of the pseudo-Ciceronean *Rhetoric to Herennius* (*oratoris officium est* ... 1.2) as well as the opening line of Julius Victor's *Ars Rhetorica* (*oratoris officium est* ... 373H). Finally see again the *Rhetoric to Herennius* (*pronuntiatio est* ... 1.3) and also Julius Victor's *Ars Rhetorica* (*pronuntiatio est* ... 440H).

[51] I am alluding to Cato's famous rhetorical advice: "Hold fast to the matter at hand, and the words will follow" (*rem tene, uerba sequentur*; *De Rhetorica* fr. 15).

[52] 2.13.1.

[53] See, though, the opening of book 4 of the *Rhetoric to Herennius* (4.1–10): here the author explores the use of examples in rhetorical texts. He offers a highly rhetorical analysis and refutation of the rhetoric of other rhetorical theorists.

specific author or school that one can never completely lose sight of the notion that there is not an "ontology of oratory" but instead a collection of perspectives and disputes that surround the description of rhetoric itself. In this the *Institutes* resembles a forensic speech where one needs to sift through the various stories about what really happened on the day that Milo killed Clodius. And the audience is expected to come to a verdict of its own, a verdict advocated by Quintilian himself.

Rather than presenting a "rhetoric of fact," Quintilian instead prefers to evoke the idea of "utility." Usefulness is the touchstone with which Quintilian regularly tests the variety of teachings he explores. Quintilian's theory is hence always in dialogue with practice. There can be no book of simple rules, because spotting the expedient is something akin to being a good general.[54] Once again we feel the latent presence of the rhetoric of the "good man." Given that the phrase *uir bonus* is evocative of military prowess and an old aristocracy of martial virtue, metaphors drawn from war play into the overarching sense that what matters most is elite *savoir-faire* rather than a dutiful pedantry.[55]

Handbook writers forbid the use of the figure of apostrophe in the exordium. Quintilian shreds their argument: they forbid it not because it is illicit, but because they think it inexpedient. However, sometimes the trope is genuinely useful. And thus we ought to employ it for the very justification which was once cited against it: utility. Quintilian directs our attention to Demosthenes' *On the Crown* and Cicero's *On behalf of Ligarius*.[56] Theodorus and Apollodorus have two different rigid systems. Theodorus claims that you should always apply your commonplaces to individual points at issue. Apollodorus claims that breaking things up like this is wrong: you need to instruct the judge before you stir his passions. Quintilian finds the whole debate absurd and the hallmark of a kind of cult of the rhetorical handbook: nobody seems willing to be guided by what is useful for the specific case at hand.[57] Quintilian's guide will not be such academic theories, but rather what he has seen the best orators do.[58] This argument, though, redounds to Quintilian's own credit: he too once was an orator and not just a teacher. Moreover, even within the realm of teaching itself,

---

[54] 2.13.2–4. Quintilian is hardly innovating when he makes a connection between oratory and war. Compare Cicero, *On the Orator* 1.157.

[55] Compare Cicero, *On the Orator* 2.16–20.

[56] See 4.1.64–66.

[57] Compare the remarks of Antonius in Cicero's *On the Orator* 2.77–83: Greek precepts tend to be too fixed and too myopic.

[58] 5.13.59–60.

he has vast stores of practical experience that he can bring to bear.[59] In fact, the very first point Quintilian makes in the whole of the *Institutes* is that he has now retired after twenty years of teaching.[60]

We can see that Quintilian is teaching us a certain kind of lesson, namely how to be properly taught. One is properly taught when one attends to the useful. However, the useful is always also noble. This is a second lesson Quintilian needs to impart. We are not looking for raw advantage, but rather pursuing the sorts of ends that a good man always pursues: *bonus* and *bene* converge yet again. This logic is applied to rhetorical ornamentation. Dressing up one's oratory is always liable to charges that it has been overdone: superfluity and effeminacy are the main vectors of criticism. Quintilian argues that proper rhetorical adornment is always both functional and virile. Thus the well-made argument of the good man is akin to the virile beauty evinced by the muscular body of an athlete: "True good looks are never divorced from usefulness," says Quintilian.[61] All of the language that surrounds "good" and "well," though, is consistently attached to a broader set of associations: manliness, military prowess, and mastery.

If we look at the second duty of the orator, "delighting his audience," we will observe that indeed Quintilian does seek to give us a certain sort of pleasure. In fact the constant evocation of military metaphors within the *Institutes* forms a kind of subtext to the text as a whole: it is agreeable to behold the sublimity, the magnificence, the luster, and the authority of oratory. We applaud the man who displays it to us. Thus what Quintilian says of Cicero's adorned rhetoric and the applause it won is itself applicable to his own text.[62] Among Cicero's virtues was the "luster" (*nitor*) of his oratory. This same word appears regularly in the catalog of recommended authors and texts that Quintilian offers in his tenth book. It is a stylistic effect an orator ought to seek to achieve. It is also an effect that Quintilian has sought to produce. He says as much of his own *Institutes*. "Bare textbooks" are unadorned.[63] His own work has a certain luster to it (*nitor*).[64] A book that is agreeable to read will be read. And Quintilian

---

[59] See 7.1.3.

[60] 1.pr.1.

[61] See 8.3.6–11. This segment ends with the maxim just quoted: *numquam uera species ab utilitate diuiditur.*

[62] 8.3.3: *sublimitas profecto et magnificentia et nitor et auctoritas expressit illum fragorem.*

[63] The *nudae artes* of 1.pr.24 are recalled by the use of *nuda* in 3.1.2: Quintilian wonders if his book is not about to turn into that kind of book when he takes up the dry, technical material at hand.

[64] 3.1.3. See also Zundel 1981: 5–6, 52–53, and 162–64.

evokes Lucretius' famous simile of the honeyed rim around the cup of bitter medicine. As, then, poetry sweetened philosophy so does rhetoric sweeten rhetorical theory. To the extent that one finds the *Institutes* to be an arid and jejune text, this sensation represents a stylistic failure on the part of Quintilian. He sought to compose a beautiful text. Of course this beauty is a virile beauty, the beauty that flashes from a sword held firmly in a general's hand.

Issues of "teaching" and "delighting" the audience of the *Institutes* are fully implicated with the question of "moving" it. Whatever one concludes about the real thrust of the rhetorical quality of the *Institutes*, there is no denying that the text is filled with the very rhetorical effects that it teaches. Pointed questions, imagined objections and their refutation, anaphora, metaphors and similes appear everywhere in the text. One might even consider the whole of it to be an exhortation. Accordingly the discussion of tropes (8.6) as well as those chapters concerning various figures (9.1–3) can be used to interpret the construction of the very work that teaches us about them.

Fear is a powerful motivator. Quintilian makes the wrong way of doing things seem utterly absurd. The most striking examples come in the discussion of delivery. There transgressions come off as ridiculous.[65] Quintilian re-stages others' self-staging as absurd rather than grand.[66] The virility–effeminacy antithesis is a rhetorical ploy used throughout the *Institutes*. The right way of doing things is invariably martial and manly. The wrong way is regularly decried as womanly and weak.[67] See, for example, the long and overheated discussion of the evils of declamation in Quintilian's own era.[68] The antithesis he draws is between the manly man and the eunuch. Some might have a taste for the latter, but such is the product of a depraved judgment. Quintilian's own rhetoric becomes the most heated just where the cultural debates are keenest. After all, declamation did have its fans, and Quintilian's beloved Cicero was often left to gather dust in libraries. This whole excursus winds up being an example of a rhetorical elaboration on the theme of rhetoric itself. It is strategically located at the close of the

---

[65] Zundel 1981: 66 notes that Quintilian tends to shift from his regular, expository style to a more rhetorically elaborate mode precisely where he critiques others.

[66] See 4.2.39 and any number of passages from 11.3. Gunderson 2000 explores this topic in detail. See especially the second chapter.

[67] Quintilian is hardly alone in making this kind of argument. Any number of parallels could be drawn from the corpus of rhetorical theory. Consider, for example, the way we are meant to cringe at the idea of a soft and womanly voice at Cicero, *On the Orator* 3.41.

[68] 5.12.17–23.

section on argumentation. Today one no longer assents quite so readily to gender-baiting arguments. However, such thundering examples ought to make us sensitive to a more pervasive effect: Quintilian's ubiquitous deployment of "good taste" and "sound sense" and the figures that embody them is meant to guide us ineluctably towards specific conclusions.

The most pervasive trope Quintilian employs in order to move us, though, is the appeal to authority. With few exceptions, anything Cicero did is adduced as an example of an excellent means of achieving any number of ends. As a choice example of this phenomenon I could myself cite the way Quintilian cites Cicero when giving examples of how to use examples in oratory.[69] In many ways the *Institutes* is but an inverted commentary on Cicero's orations. Rather than moving through a speech like the *On behalf of Ligarius* sentence by sentence we are instead given a taxonomy of rhetoric that has the *On behalf of Ligarius* and other speeches mapped onto it.

Cicero, though, is not just an author of orations; he is also an author of rhetorical theory. In fact, Cicero is both Rome's best orator and its best theorist.[70] Quintilian regularly cites Cicero's opinion about technical issues when he wishes to settle disputes.[71] Quintilian accordingly feels it necessary to linger and to disentangle things when Cicero takes one position in one theoretical text and another in another.[72] And, in general, critiques of elements of one text of Cicero's are made by means of appeals to some other text of Cicero's. Such moments are rare, though. Instead Quintilian regularly gives Cicero the last word when it comes to technical discussions. And in book 9 at the end of his introduction to the topic of figures Quintilian even inserts long verbatim quotations from Cicero's *On the Orator* and *Orator.*[73] Quintilian therewith wholly cedes his own authority to Cicero's: Quintilian cites these discussions "lest I cheat my readers of the judgment of that superlative author."[74]

Authority commands our assent. In a related fashion "character" is a species of argument. "Ethos" matters. And a complex interrelationship between morals and passions lies at the heart of the issue of moving one's

[69] 5.11.11. Note also Quintilian's parenthetical (rhetorical) question: "And where else would I take them from?" (*nam unde potius?*).
[70] 3.1.20.
[71] See, for example, 2.4.8: "My opinion is not odd. Compare Cicero ..."
[72] See, for example, 3.3.7 and 3.11.18.
[73] See 9.1.26–36 and 9.1.37–45. These two citations run for roughly five pages of the Oxford text.
[74] 9.1.25: *ne fraudarem legentes iudicio maximi auctoris.*

audience.[75] Once again, this point can be made both within oratory proper as well as in the case of Quintilian's rhetoric of rhetorical theory. We expect that the character of a speaker will emanate from his speech, and we demand that this character be morally upright.[76] It is particularly at the opening and closing of cases that we expect the kinds of ethical and emotional fireworks that Quintilian is discussing. And, Quintilian argues, being ourselves stirred is the surest way to achieve them.[77] In fact, he attributes a significant measure of his own fame as an advocate to the way he himself felt the emotions he was representing.[78] Not coincidentally, we learn this last detail at the end of the section on moving the passions.

Once again we see theory and practice converge: the contents of the advice for orators harmonizes with the form that contains that same advice. Quintilian's sixth book opens with the most emotional material in all of the *Institutes*, namely the description of the loss of his own son. According to the rules of a good exordium, this material is extraneous to the case at hand even as it leads us into the case proper, namely, the dispute as to how to stir the emotions. Furthermore the character that appears at that juncture is that of a good man and a good father. Amidst his tears we behold, nevertheless, a Quintilian ready to rededicate himself to taking all of his readers under his wing and to showing them the paternal affection and solicitude that he can no longer offer to his own son. The sense of the presence of Quintilian, good man and good teacher, regularly appears at the beginnings and at the ends of the various divisions of his work. The twelfth book, the end of the *Institutes* as a whole, is a sort of peroration. And this peroration is "ethical": the topic of the book is the character of the orator. This is not, though, a discussion of the representation of goodness in and by oratory. We are examining the actual goodness of the orator. Thus the advice on yourself feeling as you would have others feel returns with a vengeance. This message affects both the orator and the teacher. The one is taught to be good if he would seem it. The other subtly persuades us that, yes, in fact, he himself has long followed his own advice. The "good man" designates the place where both good theory and good practice have come into alignment, where an enlightened virtue gives life to a compelling torrent of words whether these last are an oration proper or an account of oratory itself.

My own peroration, then, ought to be both stirring and ethical. You can see the chief theme of it coming a mile away. The *Institutes of Oratory* is

[75] See the opening of 6.2.
[76] 6.2.13.
[77] 6.2.26.
[78] See 6.2.36.

meant to leave you persuaded. It seeks to persuade you that it knows the secrets of persuasion. On the one hand, these secrets are not secret at all. The text rehearses a variety of technical details available in other works by other authors. However, we do need a steady guide. There is so much out there available to us. There are so many *Companions to Ancient Rhetoric* already in print. Accordingly we also need to become convinced that our guide is a good guide, and that his adjudication of disputed technical issues renders the right verdict. We need to be sure that we are being taught the right things.

On the other hand, there is something more subtle going on, and Quintilian's own evocation of the language of mystery cult is a rhetorical trope that is no mere trope.[79] Except at a council of the wise, persuasion is needed. And persuasion occurs when instruction, pleasure, and passion have all been artfully made to converge. Quintilian makes the case for the veracity of his own instruction by conveying it in a manner that provides pleasure and passion as well. The *Institutes* is well written. It has polish. It is no mere textbook. But it is not enough to declare that these adornments are just some sort of showy raiment set upon a sinewy mass of facts. Instead there is something else animating the whole, a sense of mystery, of interiority, of "presence." One is stirred: something is happening here; something ethical; something good; something manly. One is left with the sense that the text has not just a body but that it has a soul as well, an *animus* that animates and gives life to what would otherwise be an inert corpse-*cum-corpus* of facts.

All of the talk of fathers and sons, generals and soldiers, teachers and students is meant to stir "us." And by "us" it is by now clear that Quintilian presupposes an audience that no longer exists quite as he imagined it. He is addressing a community of men who live within a specific social fraction of a specific social formation: elite males who have both real and cultural capital available to them. They seek to add to their resources by becoming masters of a skill that promises mastery. Rhetoric promises to make its students "more themselves," to articulate, to consolidate, and to legitimate their sense of themselves as powerful and important. In this sense, then, there are no innocent readers of rhetorical theory.

But it is also the case that there is no way one could write an innocent account of rhetorical theory. The catalog of prior authors on the topic is

---

[79] Others sometimes treat oratory as a mystery and this is bad: see 5.13.60. However, Quintilian uses the same images of his own teaching. See 5.14.27, 6.2.26, and especially 12.pr.3, which inserts this sort of language into the final movement of the whole of the *Institutes*.

extensive.[80] Quintilian notes that often all that is really left for him to do is to gather what has come before and to take a position within the old debates.[81] Quintilian's comprehensiveness becomes his distinctive virtue, and a "testimonial as to his industry" (*curae testimonium*). Of course this *testimonium* is not just an attestation of personal merit but also a bearing-witness more generally: "Here it is, rhetorical theory." Theory is itself something precious, a heritage left to us from antiquity, and a legacy to be handed on to one's real and surrogate children. Quintilian's theory is itself rhetorical, but then again, rhetoric itself has long since smacked of rhetorical theory: speakers have all gone through the same system of education and accreditation.[82] And the way Quintilian reads Cicero only consolidates this sense that the practice is destined for theory and the theory for practice.[83]

For me there are in the end three important ideas one can take away from an encounter with the *Institutes*. First, that rhetorical theory is itself rhetorical. Second, that Quintilian has embraced this complexity and involution. And, third, that he expects as much of us as well. Though it is clear that there is much to give a person pause in this situation, it is less clear that one has any choice but to accept this burden. Innocent accounts of oratory are unavailable. Innocent students of oratory are nowhere to be found.[84] A debate about the nature of debate is inevitable, and we might as well enter into it with our wits about us, because a variety of clever speakers are always about to come forward and attempt to win us over to their side.

Suggestions for further reading

If a reader has elected to read this essay in isolation from the rest of the pieces in this volume, then the next place I would send him or her is through the whole of this *Companion*. Those pieces offer the specific context within which this piece is meant to be read. The contributions of Heath, Hesk, and Steel, though, are likely to prove the most immediately interesting for those who are primarily interested in rhetorical theory itself. But for those who

---

[80] See especially 3.1.

[81] 3.1.22.

[82] Compare Goldhill in this volume.

[83] Compare Cicero, *On the Orator* 2.5: eloquence necessarily requires both technical instruction (*doctrina*) and even a well-rounded education more generally (*omnis sapientia*).

[84] The elaborate framing of works such as Cicero's *On the Orator* and *Brutus* as well as Tacitus' *Dialogue on Orators* themselves serve to highlight this issue: the author of the text has a personal relationship to the contents of his own text.

wish only to think about the rhetoric of rhetorical theory Zundel 1981 and Leeman 1963 should be consulted. Booth 2004 might be of interest for its engaged narrative of the rhetoric of rhetoric.

To the reader who is prepared to do somewhat more extensive and far-flung further reading, then I would suggest a collection of paired readings that set ancient and modern texts next to one another. The task here is not to take the modern text as an authoritative commentary on the ancient one, but instead to appreciate how questions of form and content are yoked. And by yoked I mean to indicate a coupling that is both internal to any individual text as well as that more complex and dynamic yoking of the two that emerges in the dialogue between the ancient and the modern text when set side by side. I omit Quintilian from my list below in as much as I hope that the above essay will be read in conjunction with his *Institutes*. Here then, are my pairs. First is the *Rhetoric to Herennius* and Lausberg 1998. One should read the first book of the former and the convergent segments of the latter. Lausberg's index will reveal such readily. Next one should read the first book of Aristotle's *Rhetoric*, or, at a minimum, *Rhetoric* 1.1–4. One would compare Kennedy 1963. The role of the term "persuasion" should be noted closely in both cases.[85] A third pairing would be the first book of Cicero's *On the Orator* set beside the sixth chapter of Gunderson 2000. And finally one should read Plato's *Phaedrus* with an eye to its extremely elaborate overall argument and the manner in which rhetoric is situated within a much wider set of issues. As a companion piece I would recommend Derrida 1981.

---

[85] The disjunction between Kennedy 1963 and Kennedy 1972 is largely a function of that single term.

7

JOY CONNOLLY

The politics of rhetorical education

Classical rhetorical discourse staked its claim for pedagogical authority on the basis of a string of ideas first and most memorably articulated by Isocrates – that speech is the capacity which, distinguishing human from beast, enables men to live harmoniously in communities, according to nature; that speaking well is thus the summit of human endeavor, helping to establish the rule of law and uphold just government; and consequently, that training in eloquence is the best education, transforming that which makes us human into the stuff of near-divine excellence (*aretē*).[1] This, the essence of Isocrates' rhetorical theory, became the model *apologia* for later writers, notably Cicero, who sought an ethical basis for their configuration of education around rhetorical training. Centuries later, Isocrates' thought inspired the early modern European revival of classical pedagogy, engendered at a time when political and economic upheavals rendered it necessary to redefine the goal of education as creating active citizens rather than, as before, nobles, professionals, or priests.

The gist of his claim seems *prima facie* easy to dismiss. If the political community is the natural setting for the morally good life, as classical thinkers tend to agree, then moral judgment must be a key element in political action. But what exactly does learning to speak well have to do with learning to be good, let alone learning to apply moral goodness to deliberation regarding good action? It is precisely on this point that Plato inaugurates the long battle between what he calls "philosophy" and "rhetoric," both terms whose

---

[1] The ascription of the invention of city life and law to eloquence is attested in Isocrates, *Nicocles* 5, *Antidosis* 253–57; Aristotle, *Politics* 1253a7–9; Cicero, *On Invention* 1.1–5, *On the Orator* 1.32; and (with less emphasis on politics) Quintilian 1.pr.9–20, 12.2.21 (but see Quintilian's denial of the first premise, *cur tamen hanc primam originem putet* [*Cicero*], *non uideo*, 3.2.4).

early contours owe much to Platonic usage.[2] As Robert Wardy discusses in greater detail elsewhere in this volume, Plato criticizes the sophists for advertising as a kind of moral education their technical instruction in arguments that, as he sees it, shape opinion rather than true knowledge. Plato's Protagoras asserts that he "makes men into good citizens," but he cannot sustain his definition of virtue (Protagoras 319a); his Gorgias, when pressed to explain the rhetorician's responsibility to teach right from wrong, is quickly led into a tangle of contradictions (Gorgias 458e–461a).[3] Far from teaching virtue, Plato contends, sophistic rhetoricians push a tainted mix of deceit, inanity, and flattery – much the same charges Aristophanes had leveled at Socrates in his Clouds. But before taking a closer look at the rhetoricians' elaborate defensive strategies, beginning with Isocrates, it is worth asking how the discursive knot binding virtue, politics, and eloquence together was tied in the first place.

Rhetorical training, invented as a cure for political antagonism, reflects the internal antagonisms that are constitutive of politics. Its bid for pedagogical authority should be seen in the context of ancient perceptions of what politics is – and what political ideals conceal.[4] Consider the normative formulations of Aristotle's Politics. Aristotle constructs his definition of the political on the capacity that distinguishes humans from the rest of the beasts: reason and speech. With moos, grunts, and howls, animals can express pleasure or pain, but only humans, with their unique capacity to speak rationally, can examine the causes of pleasure and pain and communicate their thoughts to one another, minimizing the likelihood of violent conflict, maximizing the good of all, and thus transforming their community into one whose rule may rightly be called "political" (1252a1–1253b1).

In the Confessions, Augustine tells this story by way of autobiography. As a baby he was like a beast, able to express pleasure and pain only by uttering inarticulate noises and violently flinging about his arms and legs (1.6.8). Growing up, he learned to express his will in words, thus entering "the society of human life" (uitae humanae societatem, 1.9.13). Far from harmonious, however, the society of speech turns out to be stormy

---

[2] The word rhētorikē is first attested at Gorgias 448d9. Halliwell 1994: 224 suggests that its earliest surviving appearance is to be found in Alcidamas' On the Sophists and raises the possibility that Alcidamas anticipated Isocrates in promoting a "philosophy" of rhetoric as a generalizing mode of education (paideia) that would include literature and history.

[3] I am persuaded by Ford 2001 against collapsing the categories of "sophist" and "teacher of rhetoric" (see especially 87–89).

[4] On antagonism and its concealment, see further Laclau 1988: 254–56; Butler, Laclau, and Žižek 2000.

(*procellosam*), and the site of the arts of speech, the schoolroom, is worst of all. "O God my God, what miseries and mockeries I experienced there, when it was put to me that to live the right life for a boy was to obey my teachers, so that I might excel in the tongue-arts" (*linguosis artibus*, 1.9.14). The vividly recalled beatings and other acts of intimidation that accompany Augustine's education powerfully suggest that the violence that characterized his earlier existence persists, if in another form. Speech has not replaced or eradicated beastly infantile violence; it has simply shifted violence to the modality of rule: in Augustine's case, the rule of the teacher of grammar and rhetoric over the bullied student; in Aristotle's, the rule of the free adult man, exerted in different ways over other free men, women, children, and slaves.[5] The sign of the human, eloquence is also the sign of the acceptance, willing or not, conscious or not, of some types of violence in favor of others.

The traditional Greek account of the origins of rhetoric clarifies the point and carries us into the public sphere. One Corax, the story goes, possibly with the help of a friend or student named Tisias, invented the first handbook of rhetoric as an aid to legal disputation in the chaotic wake of the establishment of democracy in Sicily during the second quarter of the fifth century BCE.[6] By transferring the violent struggle between the classes into the civil venue of the law court, Corax's tongue-arts ameliorate the material devastation of civil strife and offer the promise that justice will be done. While they can and do claim the legitimacy of popularly established law, the forensic and deliberative institutions boosted by Corax's work also become the venue for elite competition and class exclusion, by strengthening the economic and social dominance of the rich and by aiding in the official silencing of the disadvantaged, foreigners, women, and slaves.

The stories of Corax and Augustine remind us that even as the art of eloquence genuinely enables and comes to epitomize peaceful, civilized life, it distracts us from the violence of the civilizing process. Pierre Bourdieu explains this strategy of distraction as the product of symbolic violence, a phrase he applies to the process by which societies and individuals systematically reproduce social and cultural inequalities, especially those relating to gender and class.[7] Education is a principal way in which members of a society internalize, accept, and come to consider natural the ideas and practices that sustain the *status quo*. This is a violent process, as Bourdieu

---

[5] The virtue of the citizen is to know how to rule and be ruled well (*Politics* 1277a25–b24).

[6] The earliest extant reference to Tisias appears in Plato, *Phaedrus* 273a; Aristotle mentions Corax (*Rhetoric* 1402a) and Tisias (*Sophistical Refutations* 183b) and discussed both in his lost *Synagoge Technon*. Further discussion in Cole 1991 and Schiappa 1999.

[7] Bourdieu 1990.

sees it, because it enables coercion and subordination; it is symbolic insofar as the violence is latent and operative on the level of personal self-conception or subjectivity. It is important to emphasize that Bourdieu's concept of symbolic violence does not imply mass self-deception or passive acceptance of propaganda "from above." On the contrary, its ideas and practices make the perception of individuality and an attitude of freedom understandable and sensible *only* within the context of collective inequality.[8] The system's justification is built into the system. This works in rhetorical practice as well as theory. As Peter Wilson has persuasively argued in his critical examination of rhetoric's rhetoric of civil harmony, the egalitarian ideology perpetuated in and by Athenian oratory conceals the real material inequalities that divided the inhabitants of the city-state.[9]

To admit the latent presence of violence in the normative discourse of politics is one of those things that is just not done (though the orator's favorite trick of denying expertise can function as a form of acknowledgment, distancing the orator from the dangerous territory of class difference). Instead, canonical classical ancient thinkers recover and refigure politics as the highest form of human endeavor. They define it as the pursuit of the collective good and treat moral judgment as an essential element in political action.[10] Aristotle strengthens his hand in the *Politics* by enrolling the forces of conventional belief about gender into the argument, with his claim that politics is the natural domain of men. Men, and men only, possess the natural capacity to rule that may and should be translated outside the household into the public arena of the city-state.[11]

Politics need not be defined as a moral pursuit. Aristotle and his colleagues could have expressed themselves in, say, purely utilitarian terms.[12] But they chose virtue – more narrowly, virtue defined as a masculine property – and their political theorizing thus lends normative moral legitimacy to a system imbricated in, even as it presents itself as the alternative to, violence.

The history of rhetoric's aggressive identification of eloquence with civic virtue is usually related as the child of the paideutic competition between the rhetoricians and the philosophers of fourth-century Athens, or as a

---

[8] Bourdieu 1988: 21.
[9] Wilson 1991: 173–74.
[10] Aristotle, *Politics* 1252a1; similar sentiments in Plato, *Republic* 519e, and Cicero, *On the Republic* 1.39.
[11] Aristotle, *Politics* 1252a24–34, 1260a2–23.
[12] Geuss 2005 thoughtfully explores the disadvantages in Kant's and Rawls' identification of politics with morality.

reaction to criticisms that linked the rhetorician's craft with that of the actor or the pedant.[13] I am suggesting that rhetoric's claims on virtue are responding to deeper issues than the purely discipline-focused critique suggests, namely to the homology between the symbolic violence of political thought and rhetorical education. Just as canonical theory's notion of politics as the highest human endeavor glosses the violence of political action, so rhetoric helps to conceal the instabilities and inequalities involved in political rule by identifying the arts of persuasion with virtue and beauty. This function explains why rhetoricians accounting for their discipline tend to depoliticize it. Removing rhetoric from the context of its local political conditions, they place it under the rubric of ethics and aesthetics.

We may now return to Isocrates' response to the skeptical Plato – an important early step in the history of rhetoric's self-identification with the good and the beautiful. Isocrates developed a carefully calibrated language of advocacy for his profession. He never claims to teach virtue to a pupil born depraved; the best he can do is nourish good tendencies in good men (*Against the Sophists* 21; cf. *Antidosis* 194–95, 274–75). In agreeably rounded if repetitive phrases whose form performs content, he elaborates the omnipresent Greek association between beauty and goodness (concisely captured in the multivalent word *kalos*) into an argument for rhetoric's unique qualities as an educator of good men. His program of instruction is a *psuchēs epimeleia*, or "care of the soul" that cultivates wide historical knowledge, cultural refinement, skill with discerning and defending that which is probable, and the capacity to speak gracefully and moderately, in ways proper to the occasion (*Against the Sophists* 8). In a significant move, Isocrates declares that learning to speak mellifluously and melodiously (*eurhuthmos, mousikos*) is the best training (*epimeleia*) in moral goodness (*epieikeia*). His appropriation of the values and practices of traditional Greek pedagogy, especially *mousikē* and *gumnastikē*, marries the "middling" values of Athenian democratic culture with a refusal to apply the rigorous standards of Socratic dialectic to the dynamic uncertainties of the political realm.[14]

Where Plato has struck readers such as Nietzsche as manifesting a destructive desire for unitary knowledge, Isocrates enters the great Greek debate over epistemological standards with what appears at first to be a call for flexibility and multiplicity. The sophists of a generation earlier had already mapped this territory. Gorgias claimed that humans use language

---

[13] On acting: Graf 1992; Fantham 2002.
[14] On "middling" culture, see Morris 1996.

to approximate the world, a practice that would never enable perfect correspondence between speech and reality. So long as particular words and the conventional beliefs they convey make sense to the community of speakers using them, they meet the conditions of communication in the public sphere (*Helen* 13). Similarly, Plato's Protagoras argues that "whatever appears to be right and honorable" to the civic community "is really right and honorable, so long as it believes it to be so" (*Theaetetus* 167c). Isocrates acknowledges the risk that *doxa* will not always be correct (*Panathenaicus* 248) but he argues that "in dealing with matters about which they take counsel, men ought not to think that they have exact knowledge of what the result will be; rather, they ought to look towards contingencies as men who exercise their best judgment (*doxa*) but are not sure what the future has in store" (*On the Peace* 8).

Isocrates' views on epistemology are circumspect. Political decisions, he knows, must be based on knowledge. Human affairs being what they are, this knowledge is not a fixed set of data, but a fluid array of facts, opinions, convictions, preconceptions, and expectations. Where Plato attacked rhetoric's built-in tendency to flatter the people's desires or baseless opinion (*doxa*) instead of probing the truth (*alētheia*) of the matter, Isocrates is content with the good-faith efforts of experienced men – wise men (*sophoi*) – who judge the best course of action on the basis of opinions about the probable that they develop with *phronēsis* (*Antidosis* 271; cf. *Panathenaicus* 30). On this basis he is able to claim that public speeches are the proper context for determining proper action. "How could people judge well concerning the past or take counsel about the future if they do not scrutinize the arguments of opposing speakers and make themselves the impartial audience of both sides?" (*On the Peace* 11).

In keeping with his emphasis on the unpredictability and variety of human circumstance, Isocrates' system of rhetorical training self-consciously resists systematization. Against those rhetoricians who offered lists of fixed rules for argument (*Against the Sophists* 10–12), he encourages students to look to the political decisions of the past (*Panegyricus* 141) and keep the common good firmly in mind (*Antidosis* 231–36). Far from disregarding them, Isocrates idealizes the *dēmos* as a collective of potential students. The fictional works he presents as models for deliberative orations before the Athenian assembly recall the speeches in Thucydides' history in their complexity, ambition, and breadth of scope. "Greedy for *logoi*" (*Antidosis* 311), Isocrates' Athenian audience is capable of rational analysis (*philosophēsete kai skepsesthe*) about political causation, say, regarding the decline and fall of states (*On the Peace* 116). The people, and no less the orator who addresses them, must cultivate intellectual flexibility, stay alert to contingency and indeterminacy, and recognize the right moment to act (*kairos*).[15]

These factors mean that Isocrates' account of rhetoric continues to play an important if largely unacknowledged role in democratic thought. "At the heart of strong democracy," Benjamin Barber argues, "is talk, the mediator of affection and affiliation as well as of interest and identity, of patriotism as well as individuality ... it is talk that makes and remakes the world."[16] Theorists of "deliberative democracy" have rediscovered classical rhetoric as a politically imaginative resource, an instrument by which public discourse may be enriched and broadened to include voices traditionally banished to the margins.[17] Takis Poulakos remarks that Isocrates' pedagogy seems to create "the possibility for guiding the community rhetorically by reconstituting its conventional *doxai* and by redefining its traditional truths" in the public eye.[18]

But Isocrates' words also make a velvet glove that hides the iron fist. In the context of the Greek project of self-definition over and against non-Greeks, he appears as an early culture warrior defending the Greek-speaking world against the barbarians. His *Panegyricus*, an exhortation to the Athenians to take up their historical mantle as the leaders of Greece, praises Athens as the center of philosophy and the arts who "revealed" to the rest of the world, notably the barbarian nations bordering Greece, the force of *logos* (*Panegyricus* 47). As Niall Livingstone has shown, the *Panegyricus* treats education as the justification for the military expansion of the Greek world. Livingstone sees a direct analogy in the speech between Isocrates' smooth, "unifying authorial voice" and "the individual city or ruler endowed with the hegemony of the Greeks."[19] His willingness to extend Greekness to those who share its mindset (*dianoia*) rather than its race (*genos*) welcomes "barbarians" into the civilized world on condition that they submit willingly to Greek cultural imperialism (*Panegyricus* 50).

Moreover, for all his praise of Athens, Isocrates is no champion of democracy per se. The anti-democratic flavor of his views, slightly tempered by his declaration that democracy is by some measures the most successful regime (*Areopagiticus* 70), is clear from Isocrates' insistence that Athens' fifth-century prosperity grew from Solon's decision to grant governing

---

[15] K. Morgan 2004 helpfully explores the ethical and political tensions resulting from Isocrates' embrace of *amphibolia* and *eutrapelia* ("flexibility of mind").
[16] Barber 2003: 173, 177.
[17] Young 2000: 62–68.
[18] Poulakos 2004: 61.
[19] Livingstone 1998: 275–76.

authority to propertied men whose leisure makes them best suited to rule (23–26). Rhetoric, it seems, abhors the lottery, and it loves the well-off. Goldilocks-like, Isocrates carves out a space for rhetoric in the moral and political experience of the citizenry without locking rhetoric into extreme claims either to final epistemological authority or to allegiance to any single political regime.

Good or bad governance lies not in the particular nature of regimes, institutions, or laws, but in the nature of the men who govern. It is this belief that allows him, without fear of inconsistency, to praise the excellence of monarchy (*Nicocles* 15), offer the leadership of the Greeks to Philip of Macedon (in the *Philippics*), and replay almost *verbatim* the encomium of *logos* in a speech originally addressed to the Cypriot prince Nicocles (*Nicocles* 6–9) in a professional *apologia* directed to Athenian critics and responsive to the Athenian democratic context (*Antidosis* 253–57). The *Panathenaicus*, a model panegyric designed for students' imitation, is neat proof of Isocrates' ability to transform localized politics into global (if originally Greek) ethics. The virtues it praises – a quick intellect, respectability, honesty, self-control, and modesty – might apply to citizens of virtually any regime (32). It treats charm, familiarity with accessible language, and above all, consistency as correlative with the putatively Greek political norms of civility, consensus, and good judgment. This *paideia*, in the act of bridging the gap between aesthetics and ethics, erases the particularities of politics.

On a more complex and contradictory level, Isocratean rhetoric discloses certain tensions that normative political thought tries to suppress. In the context of democratic Athens, Isocrates intends eloquence to improve rational decision-making among and by all citizens, but the aesthetics of his rhetoric acts as its own ideology, an ideology in perceptible tension with its democratic origins and impulses. The Isocratean sentence, for example, with its balanced, rotund fullness, implies closure, the sense that everything has been said, *and said beautifully at that*, perpetuating a conventionalism that says: he who speaks this way (and only he who speaks this way) is speaking the right way. Isocratean rhetoric rewrites the aristocratic aesthetic of balance and self-control as the model of a moderate, rational, civil politics. This pose reinforces traditional class limits on participation and shuts out the irrational, the unharmonious, the unsettling, and the unfamiliar. It amplifies, broadcasts, and makes utterly familiar the very propositions that may need the intensity of intellectual reflection that only a more critical politics might provide. Isocrates has already closed that door by making philosophical dialectic into a kind of incivility, along (presumably) with shouting, violence, or other mass action (one of the core values of Isocratean rhetoric is the value placed on the speaking individual over and above the listening mass).

Precisely because Isocrates promises to build his arguments upon *doxa*, his refusal to interrogate the underpinnings of popular opinion make his *paideia* the perfect instrument for essentializing social structures. To Bourdieu, whose theory of symbolic violence proposes that the reproduction of social inequalities rests on the assimilation of certain material factors as "facts of life," "what any normal person would think," Isocrates' commitment to the perpetuation of *doxa* is a fine example of rhetoric's powers of social discipline. This is true "euphemization," making nice words do the work of naturalization that leads to the legal definition of acceptable behavior.[20]

Largely due to the influence of Werner Jaeger's magisterial history of Greek education, *Paideia*, Isocrates' advocacy of the civilizing power of *logos* in the service of Panhellenism has long been understood as a confrontational response to Plato's *Gorgias* and *Phaedrus*. His unwavering belief in the peculiar power of rhetorical persuasion to train men to judge right from wrong and his refusal to ground his theory of argument in an objective definition of truth do distinguish him from the theoretical philosophizing advocated by Plato.[21] We may now see, however, that Isocrates' blurring of aesthetics and ethics, and his substitution of pan-Hellenism for local political allegiance, brings him closer, in spite of himself, to the Platonic perspective. Just as Plato explores the relationship between soul and state in *Republic*, so Isocrates draws an analogy between the constitution (*politeia*), the soul of the city, and prudent judgment (*phronēsis*), the soul of the body (*Areopagiticus* 14) – a virtue theory Isocrates disembeds from any particular politics and implies is the property of those comfortable men who share his moderate, rational, civil tastes.

Isocrates' intervention is crucial for the subsequent history of rhetorical education in late Republican and early imperial Rome, where Cicero would claim that "*eloquentia* is the highest virtue" (*On the Orator* 3.55). Though Republican Rome was not a democracy, public speaking played a crucial role in elite efforts to channel public opinion and garner electoral support.[22] Forensic speeches showcased political issues of the day, and magistrates regularly defended policy, proposed laws, praised allies and attacked rivals in public meetings known as *contiones*, which could easily develop into violent confrontations.

---

[20] Bourdieu 1990: 110.
[21] Halliwell 1997; also see Cooper 2004.
[22] Morstein-Marx 2004.

In a series of works written during a time of profound political crisis, Cicero transformed Isocratean rhetoric into a program of moral and political education specifically designed for the leading men of the Republic.[23] Though the loss of most Hellenistic rhetorical theory makes certainty impossible, it seems clear that his work represents a major departure from recent developments in Greek rhetoric, such as Hermagorean status theory or Theophrastus' survey of *ethos*. Where Isocrates' defense of rhetoric as a discourse of virtue disembedded rhetoric from its city-state context, Cicero carefully plugs rhetoric back into the local system. His three-book dialogue *On the Orator* uses the voices of the great men of a generation past to make the polemical case that oratory is the most noble pursuit for Roman men; his history of oratory, *Brutus*, rewrites Roman politics as a history of public speaking. His effort reveals the immense strain of marrying the inculcation of elite masculine Roman values – a task he eagerly claims for rhetoric – with the transformation of the student into a speaker whose posture, gestures, beliefs, and arguments make him the living embodiment of the *concordia ordinum*, the harmony of classes praised in Cicero's letters and political works.

Cicero's reclamation of politics means that he directs a new kind of attention towards the living, breathing, speaking body. "The orator should control himself by the poise of his whole torso and by the manly inclination of his side" (11.3.122): this is Quintilian's paraphrase of a line from Cicero's *Orator* (59). Underpinning the two Romans' emphasis on moderate and graceful deportment was the cultural association of a particular set of behaviors, attitudes, and gestures – Bourdieu, drawing on the Latin term, calls the whole assemblage *habitus* – with a particular class. If, to paraphrase Fitzgerald, the very rich like to seem different from you and me, the rhetoricians helped to brand the differences of elite *habitus* as signs of inner virtue. In their work, the ideal orator *moves* differently from everyone else. His graceful gestures, erect posture, and measured stride collectively signify his *dignitas*, making him the visible opposite of the workman or slave who hastens or sidles from task to task. As many scholars of gender and sexuality have noted, Cicero and Quintilian are policemen of behavior and style, encouraging students to cultivate a "naturally" masculine attitude, and punishing those who had the look and sound of the slave, the foreigner, the ill-educated man, or the woman.[24]

---

[23] The argument of the next section is explored in greater detail in Connolly 2007a.

[24] On gender and rhetorical performance: Corbeill 1996; Gleason 1995; Richlin 1997; Connolly 1998; Gunderson 2000; Connolly 2007b.

To behave like a member of the lower classes is, in an important sense, to become them. Louis Althusser illustrates his point with the example of Pascal's doubting Christian, who genuflects and moves his lips as he prays in an effort to inculcate orthodox belief.[25] Cicero's long list of pedagogical injunctions – speaking good Greek or Latin, reading the right books, quickly grasping the conditions (*status*) under which the case must be argued, identifying the proper approach (*color*) to an argument, moving and gesturing the "right" way while speaking, in short, showing that you *are* the kind of man you wish to *seem to be* (Cicero, *On the Orator* 1.87) – are rituals conspiring to make subjectivity spring up from materiality. This subject, summoned by particular ideological imperatives, proceeds to make ideology work: his behavior in the assembly or the forum reinforces and justifies the entrenched authority of his gender, class, age, or nation. "What is called the *sense of honor*," Bourdieu argues, "is nothing other than the cultivated disposition inscribed in the bodily schema and in the schemes of thought," through which each agent automatically engages in daily practice consistent with the social logic that formed him.[26]

Hence Cicero and Quintilian warn against moving like a woman, and they gaze anxiously upon flexible, jointed body parts (especially the neck, wrists, and hips) and leaky bodily orifices (eyes, mouth, and nostrils). "To 'crinkle the nostrils,' as Horace has it, or to flare them, twitch them, probe them with a finger, to snort through them with a sudden exhalation, stretch them wide, or rub across them with the flat of the hand: these actions are improper," Quintilian observes (11.3.80). His desire to train young men to keep their openings closed and their secretions hidden makes sense in light of ancient medical treatises' comments on the fluxes and flows that permeate the cold, wet, female body.[27]

In passages such as these we glimpse a risk of rhetorical education that our sources only indirectly acknowledge, namely that the attention the student learned to lavish on himself might boomerang, transforming him into a self-absorbed fake, no different from the mime-artist or the perfumed, cosmetic-caked woman or eunuch he was repeatedly told to detest and avoid.[28] Especially in the Roman context, where political conditions meant that

---

[25] The example is discussed in Dolar 1993; Butler 1995; and Wingrove 1999: all are concerned precisely with the difficult problem of materiality and ideality in Althusser's theory of interpellation.

[26] Bourdieu 1977: 15.

[27] On women's bodies: Hanson 1990.

[28] Prize examples in Cicero: *Orator* 59, 78, *Brutus* 36, *On the Orator* 1.231, 3.100; Quintilian 1.8.2, 1.11.102, 2.5.7–9, 2.11.2, 5.12.17–21, 8.3.6–11, 9.4.142.

a small elite regularly faced a large public, the distribution of power between speaker and audience was of paramount concern. The "act" of performance placed the orator into a (notionally) unfamiliar position of submission, like a slave, a woman, or an actor, judged on the satisfaction he gives to the probing eyes and ears of his audience (*On the Orator* 1.118–21). It is partly to bolster the orator's sense of mastery in these challenging conditions that he is constantly exhorted to be, or at least look like, a man.[29]

But the rituals of social practice should also be seen, following Giorgio Agamben, Judith Butler, and others, as structures of possibility that leave open paths towards future change and resistance.[30] From this perspective, the constitutive flexibility and slipperiness of language and performance, enacted in the creative experimentation of rhetorical exercises such as declamation (see below), supplies the means by which rhetorical education sustains conditions of freedom.

This is precisely the path taken by Cicero, pushing against the bias of class and gender, in his commitment to a Republican politics that rests on the voluntary partnership of the people with the traditional governing class.[31] If his ideal orator seeks to guide the people, his training also sets limits on his own will to power. His speech cannot command but must sway his audience, using arguments and strategies that are meaningful in the context of communal belief and practice. When Cicero warns his orator to speak in language the crowd can easily understand, he is exhorting him to stay true to the demands of communal belief and usage.[32] To do this, the orator follows his body: he must watch and listen to the audience and modify his speech accordingly. Unlike the Stoic or the philosopher, whose arid arguments repulse listeners, the orator "tastes" the experiences of his audience and gives blood and color to their verbal representation (*On the Orator* 1.56, 218, 223). The orator embodies the strength and integrity of the Republic: he is not an actor, "who simply mimics reality," but "an agent of reality" (*actor ueritatis* vs. *histrio ueritatis, On the Orator* 3.214). This body reflects Cicero's image of the Republic: authoritative, controlled, rational, learned, and stable, but also accessible, responsive, emotional, and dynamic. The orator who wishes to give counsel to the Republic must know his Republic, Cicero says (*mores ciuitatis*), "but since this frequently changes, one's style of speech must change too" (*On the Orator* 2.337).

---

[29] On the performance of masculinity in Roman rhetorical discourse, see further Corbeill 1996; Gleason 1995; Connolly 1998; Gunderson 2000; Dugan 2005.

[30] Agamben 1993: section 11, cited and discussed by Butler, Laclau, and Žižek 2000: 26.

[31] On Cicero's treatment of the *concordia ordinum*, see Asmis 2004.

[32] Cicero, *On the Orator* 1.54, 1.108; on the universal appeal of gesture, 3.221–23.

Cicero's presentation of argument in book 2 of *On the Orator* is punctuated with elaborate Isocratean protestations of asystematicity: good men need no petty rules – though Cicero goes on to survey them (77–84, 123–24, 133). By contrast to Isocrates, however, whose phrasing is almost compulsively balanced and who rarely reveals a sense of humor, Cicero defends passion and (especially in the character of Caesar Strabo, in *On the Orator* 2) clearly loves a joke.

No less important than the body are the intellectual habits instilled through rhetorical training. Here Cicero takes a page from Hellenistic Greek rhetoric, where the practice of developing arguments *in utramque partem*, "for both sides," furnished students a sense of easy familiarity with bending language to their desires, a familiarity that also promised a certain mastery over contingency. The student well versed in the techniques of arguing both sides of a problem, especially through his familiarity with commonplaces, was best prepared to make his case (*On the Orator* 2.130–41). Arguing *in utramque partem* compelled the student to take stock of legal and political situations from more than one perspective. He trains himself to draw on a range of sources to make his judgments: rumor, testimony, opinion, values, emotions and understands the changeability of belief and feeling.[33]

In his embrace of the Hellenistic rhetoricians' increasingly finely tuned divisions of argument and stylistic equipment (such as tropes and figures), Cicero's early treatise *On Invention* aligns rhetorical instruction with the habits of mind required to sustain civil law. Status theory, beginning with the Hellenistic rhetorician Hermagoras and finding its first extensive Latin discussion in *On Invention* and the anonymous *Rhetoric to Herennius*, provided the student with logical tools with which to disentangle complex questions of legality, morality, and procedure.[34] Dry reading, perhaps, but these treatises' implicit confidence in the power of language to bring order to a chaotic world strengthens the idea that the law court and the forum are the source of worldly justice, and that the student's own language is identical with the language of logic and Roman law. Both status theory and the multiform rules of *elocutio* and *actio* may be seen as a response to the latent violence of civic conflict that plagued Rome through most of the first century BCE.

No practice better combined the training of body and mind than declamation, the advanced exercise that drew together all five parts of oratory,

---

[33] On evidence: *On Invention* 2.46, 47, 54, 56, 72; on mutability, *On the Orator* 1.108.
[34] Connolly 2007b.

including performance, and that became a favored venue for competition and entertainment among elites during Cicero's lifetime (at the latest). The most striking aspect of declamatory exercises, especially the *controuersia*, or fictional law-court case, is its sensationalism.[35] Rapists, adulterers, parricides, torturers of sons, poisoners, pirates, misers, and kidnappers populate the pages of the elder Seneca, Quintilian, and other declamation-collectors. Why? Robert Kaster argues that the fantastic nature of the declamatory theme helped to assure the student that convention and tradition were sufficient to meet the most unexpected situations. Seeking to explain the particular prominence of rape, he concludes that rape represents an unusually intense and violent strike against the social order, and the declaimer uses all the resources of reason and emotion he can muster to clean up the mess – after all, this is precisely the task for which the declaimer is being trained.[36]

Our richest sources for declamation emerge when the political order, after decades of civil war, was being altered to suit the demands of dynastic autocrats, the Julio-Claudians and the Flavians. In the elder Seneca's description of his favorite declaimers, the task of rhetoric seems also to have altered. Instead of seeking balanced and rotund charm, the declaimers aim for the pointed, the unusual, the experimental – what Ruth Webb calls "imaginative engagement within set bounds."[37] As the violence of Republican politics is unveiled and exchanged for autocratic violence, the performances of declamation mirror the process of fracture.

Under these unpredictable political conditions, language was one area of expertise that offered a relatively safe means of exercising *libertas*. The case of the teacher M. Pomponius Porcellus is telling. When a certain Ateius Capito insisted that the emperor Tiberius' choice of word was good Latin, or that if it were not, it certainly would be from that day forward, Porcellus retorted: "You can give citizenship to people, Caesar, but not to words" (Suetonius, *Lives of the Rhetoricians* 22). The declaimers may be seen as exploring avenues of change and resistance. The declaimers joked about logic (Albucius Silus: "Why is a cup broken when it falls, but a sponge, if it falls, is not broken?," Seneca the Elder, 7.pr.8) and tested the limits of convention. In a *controuersia* involving a man who raped two women, where one of the victims demands the rapist be punished with death, while the other demands marriage, most of the declaimers poke fun at the topic, to Seneca's dismay: "I congratulate you, virgins, that dawn came so quickly!"

---

[35] Lamented, and to a certain extent explained, by Gunderson 2003.

[36] Kaster 2001: 325–28.

[37] Webb 2001: 304.

"You ask what brought an end to his rapes? Day"; "He was just preparing himself for a third – if only night had not ended!"

Cicero's effort to make Republican citizens under the sign of rhetoric represents a politicized anomaly in the history of ancient rhetorical education. After the violent consolidation of autocratic power by the Julio-Claudian Caesars, Quintilian translates the Isocratean treatment of rhetoric as pan-Hellenic virtue into terms suitable for the Roman imperial context. The political conditions of late first-century Rome are rendered opaque, in favor of ever more scrupulous attention to the division and codification of speech.[38] As the *Institutes* concludes: "If [my teachings] fail to be very useful to young students, at least – and this is my real aim – they should encourage good will" (*at certe, quod magis petimus, bonam uoluntatem,* 12.11.31). One Ciceronian priority remains crucially important to Quintilian: the law. In the last, most wide-ranging book, which is devoted to the nature of the orator's character (12.pr.4), his default genre of speech is forensic, and *aequitas* is a persistent theme.[39] Shifting the orator's political responsibilities to the law court, Quintilian harnesses all the resources of history, literature, philosophy, and experience to the maintenance of law and order.

One of the limits of working with rhetorical treatises, themselves so preoccupied with the distinction between writing and speaking, is the silence of the student. We have seen that Greek and Roman rhetoricians defended a range of highly idealized claims about the universal virtue of eloquence. One wonders whether they fostered discussion on the problematical role of speech in democratic and Republican politics. What is the dividing line between popular consensus and coercion? On what legitimate basis may a system that privileges language as the mark of the human exclude some voices and not others? Where does rational argument end and demagoguery begin? And so on. Allied as it is with the ruling order, classical rhetoric offers few opportunities for critical reflection on the inequalities it helped to sustain. But its own emphatic celebration of the virtues of law, equality, and freedom should not be seen as hypocritical or naively idealistic. On the contrary, rhetoric reminds us soberly of the interpenetration, and perhaps the co-dependence, of education and oppression, and the powerful role of virtue in making sense of a violent world.[40]

---

[38] On the increasingly elaborate structures of rhetoric, see Heath and Steel in this volume; on Quintilian's politics: T. Morgan 1998b.

[39] Forensic speaking: 12.1.11 (*omnem orationem*), 12.1.24, 12.1.34–45, 12.8.1–15, 12.9.8.

[40] I would like to thank Erik Gunderson for his keen and helpful comments on the draft of this chapter.

Suggestions for further reading

In this large and growing field, it is worth singling out articles by Catherine Atherton on the grammarians, Teresa Morgan on Quintilian, and Niall Livingstone on Isocrates, each of which explores rhetoric's role in enforcing social rules and forming notions of political action (collected in Too and Livingstone 1998). Poulakos 1997 and Haskins 2004 are important contributions to the revival of interest in Isocrates, while Ober 2001 helpfully guides the reader through the larger debate over education in fifth- and fourth-century Athens. Corbeill 2001 traces the connections that rhetoric makes with traditional Roman cultural practices, and Fantham 2004 usefully discusses Ciceronian rhetoric in its elite social and political context. Kaster 1988 remains the best guide to the role and responsibilities of the grammarian in late antiquity.

PART III

The practice of rhetoric

8

JON HESK

Types of oratory

Aristotle's *Rhetoric* is our first surviving work to divide oratory into three types (*eidē*) or species (*genē*): "deliberative" (*sumbouleutikon*); "forensic" or "dicanic" (*dikanikon*); "epideictic" or "display" or "demonstrative" (*epideiktikon*).[1] This threefold classification is an important structuring principle in the philosopher's attempt to establish that rhetoric is a proper "art" (*tekhnē*). Aristotle's vision of rhetoric is that it be a practical discourse; an important counterpart to philosophical dialectic in a real-world setting where a speaker is seeking the best available means of persuasion in the face of mass audiences (Aristotle, *Rhetoric* 1358a36–b8).[2]

Aristotle explains that there are three types of *rhetorikē* because there are three kinds of "hearers" of speeches (1358a37–b6): epideictic oratory is directed at the spectator (*theōros*), who judges the ability of the speaker. The hearer of forensic oratory judges things that have already happened while the "deliberative" hearer is a judge of things to come. Aristotle goes on to give each of the three types a distinctive mode: deliberative oratory is either hortatory or dissuasive. Forensic oratory is either accusatory or defensive. Epideictic oratory offers either praise or blame (1358b8–13). In line with the remarks on "judgment" the three types also treat different aspects of time (1358b14–19). But when it comes to epideictic oratory, Aristotle's penchant for tidiness comes under strain: while he deals primarily with matters of the present, the display orator might also recall past events or anticipate the future. Finally, Aristotle gives each of the three types of

---

[1] Aristotle's threefold scheme is likely to be a systematizing elaboration of previous "sophistic" handbooks. See Plato, *Phaedrus* 261a1–262c3 with the chapters of Heath and Wardy in this volume.

[2] See Heath and Steel in this volume for important comments on the distinctiveness, influence, and shortcomings of Aristotle's analytical approach to rhetoric. For debates over the "agenda" of Aristotle's *Rhetoric* and the question of its coherence, see the discussions and suggested further reading in Rapp 2002 and Kennedy 2007: 13–17.

oratory an "end" (*telos*) about which the audience must make their judgment (1358b22–28). The *telos* of deliberative oratory is "the expedient or the harmful" although it may also invoke justice/injustice and honor/disgrace as additional considerations. Forensic oratory naturally has "justice or injustice" as its *telos*. Again, there may be other auxiliary considerations which the forensic orator can refer to. Epideictic oratory is primarily concerned with "the noble" (*to kalon*) or "the shameful" (*to aiskhron*) but other concepts can be deployed with that *telos* in mind.

Aristotle probably sketched this typology in the mid fourth century BCE – right in the middle of an active tradition of rhetorical theory, pedagogy, and practice in classical Greece. We should therefore not be surprised that it offers a good "fit" with the most important contexts in which persuasive oral discourse was used on mass audiences in Greek *poleis*. And the fact that Aristotle's typology was anchored to real audience types and *telē* means that it is a very effective tool for classifying most practical examples of Greek and Roman oratory. The first aim of this chapter will be to show how some of the details of Aristotle's analysis can often enhance our understanding of the practical speeches.

Although Aristotle's typology shaped and influenced subsequent Hellenistic and Roman theory and practice, some later rhetorical writers criticized it for being too narrowly circumscribed by the performance contexts of the classical *polis*.[3] These writers also contested the names and numbers of oratory's species, arguing that the Aristotelian typology failed to encompass or adequately theorize the innumerable forms of speech which real rhetorical situations demanded. Epideictic oratory, for example, was surely not just about praising and blaming: there must also be an account of how to complain, console, pacify, excite, encourage, frighten ...[4] Thus Aristotle's threefold scheme was not always seen as the only, or even the most natural, way to divide oratory into subspecies.[5] And, as the astute Roman interlocutors of Cicero's *On the Orator* point out, the process of mapping rhetorical practice by means of abstract classifications is always one where vital details, nuances, and syntheses become lost or simplified.[6] The second aim of this chapter, then, is to elaborate upon that inevitable gap between an analytic theory based on neat, generalized typologies and the synthetic

---

[3] See Quintilian, *Institutes* 3.4.4–6.

[4] See Quintilian, *Institutes* 3.4.1–16 for a sense of this debate and disagreement. Heath (this volume) offers further detail on other Greek and Roman typologies.

[5] Steel (this volume) also discusses ancient analytical rhetoric's divisions as non-natural and highly contestable.

[6] Cicero, *On the Orator* 2.43–71.

practice of composing and performing real speeches for particular debates, cases, and occasions. We will see that real Greek and Roman speeches are always persuading their audiences in ways which go beyond or complicate the Aristotelian picture.

The two central features of this mismatch between theory and practice are historical specificity and sociological sensibility. The former feature details the way in which particular political, legal, and cultural climates affect our reading of oratory's persuasive operations and the salience of Aristotle's typology. The latter feature details the way in which Aristotle's *Rhetoric* assumes a sociological perspective which is very different from our own. Aristotle can see that successful oratory must take account of the beliefs and values of the audience to whom it is directed: this is why he thinks that it is so important for a speaker to pay attention to the character he projects (1377b21–1378a28). What Aristotle cannot see, and in this he is neither unique nor culpable, is that different types of oratory (and different historical instantiations of those types) have ideological and sociopolitical roles which go beyond the surface requirements of persuading a particular audience in relation to a particular *telos*.

Deliberative oratory

Aristotle stresses that deliberative oratory will often be directed at assemblies.[7] His account fits well with the speeches which we know were delivered in the assemblies of Greek *poleis* in general and Athens in particular.[8] One thinks of the Thucydidean Pericles' arguments in favor of continuing war with Sparta or Demosthenes' assembly speeches designed to rouse Athenians to action against Philip of Macedon. It is important to realize, however, that one usually has to infer that Aristotle would have approved of

---

[7] However, see *Rhetoric* 1358b9–10, where Aristotle explicitly recognizes that deliberative rhetoric can take place in private contexts.

[8] The extant corpus of the fourth-century politician Demosthenes offers us seventeen speeches which were delivered to the Athenian Assembly with the aim of persuading the citizen body to vote for, or against, a particular policy or course of action. This is a minute fraction of the number of speeches which must have been made during the lifetime of the Athenian democracy, although it is likely that the inherently fluid nature of policy debate made the writing-out of pre-prepared speeches of limited use and effectiveness. In the fourth-century treatise *On the Sophists*, Alcidamas argued that the need for flexibility and the on-the-spot creativity in public debates or disputes made written speeches inadvisable. Herodotus, Thucydides, and Xenophon also furnish us with examples of speeches which *purport* to be what was said in the deliberative contexts of assemblies or councils in Athens and in other Greek *poleis*.

a Periclean or Demosthenic political harangue: these two great Athenian *rhētores* get only the briefest of mentions in the *Rhetoric*.[9]

For Rome, we have a bigger sample of real and reported material to go on. Cicero's *Philippics* are perhaps the best, and certainly the last, examples of deliberative oratory used to influence policy before the emperors came along to curtail public deliberation. Although popular assemblies did meet at certain periods in Roman Republican history, the senate was the chief venue where deliberative rhetoric was used to contest power and policy. It was very different from the Athenian assembly in that elite senators addressed each other rather than the Roman "masses" and there were all manner of speaking and voting protocols which reflected the particular importance of rank, patronage, financial networks, and family ties in Roman politics.[10] Of course, such cultural specifics are not anticipated or explored in Aristotle's description of deliberative oratory. One might contrast those moments where Cicero ensures that his ideal orator will take account of quintessentially Roman social practices.[11] But there is still real *value* in comparing Aristotle's description with examples of ancient deliberative practice and the competing descriptions of other ancients. For the comparison reveals a wider and deeper picture of such practice and its differences from the theoretical debates which attempted to describe and prescribe it.

As an example, let us look at Aristotle's emphasis on the specific sorts of knowledge which he thinks a deliberative orator must have. These sorts of knowledge are five in number: *poroi* ("ways and means"), war and peace, the defense of the country, imports and exports, and legislation (1359b20–23). What does it mean for an orator to know about these things? In the case of *poroi*, he must know about the nature and extent of the city's resources with a view to additional fund-raising or appropriate reallocation. And he must know the city's expenditure with a view to making necessary cuts (1359b23–32). The other four areas of knowledge are similarly obvious and rather unglamorous in their specificity: the size of enemy forces, the exact positions of guardhouses, and so on. We might contrast this call for mundane expertise with the more influential emphases elsewhere in the treatise on the need for all kinds of oratory to manipulate "character" (*ēthos*), "virtue" (*aretē*), and emotions (*pathē*).[12] Nevertheless, the prominence of

---

[9] Aristotle's failure to refer to Demosthenes as a model orator may be to do with his close links to the Macedonian court. See Kennedy 2007: 279.

[10] See Steel 2006: 3–24.

[11] E.g. *On the Orator* 2.182 where the patron–client relationship shapes Cicero's treatment of *ēthos*.

[12] See 1377b21–1378a28, 1378a31–1379a2, 1388b30–1391b2.

knowing specific subject matter in Aristotle's account is paralleled in actual deliberative speeches. Here is Demosthenes on the question of how to fund his proposed military expedition to aid Olynthus against the aggression of Philip of Macedon (Demosthenes, *Olynthiac* 1.19–20, trans. J. H. Vince):

> With regard to the supply of money (*poros*), you have money, men of Athens; you have more than any other nation has for military purposes. But you appropriate it yourselves, to suit your own pleasure. Now if you will spend it on the campaign, you have no need of a further supply; if not, you have no supply at all. "What!" someone will cry, "do you actually move to use this money for military purposes?" Of course I do not. Only it is my opinion that we must provide soldiers and that there must be one uniform system of pay in return for service. Your opinion, however, is that you should, without any trouble, just appropriate the money for your festivals. Then the only alternative is a war-tax, heavy or light, as circumstances demand. Only money we must have, and without money nothing can be done that ought to be done.

At first glance, this reads like a straightforward putting-into-practice of Aristotle's advice.[13] But the fit between the theory and the practice is significantly imperfect. For Demosthenes' knowledge does not lead him to make specific proposals. He simply tells the assembly that it can afford a campaign which is imperative. The real rhetorical impact of this section of the speech lies in its synthesis of conviction in the rightness of military action with the impression of in-depth knowledge about public finances. Aristotle's deliberative orator builds a persuasive argument based on proper understanding of the facts which underlie the issues being debated. But Demosthenes' specific argument about finances is not as important as the general impression of expertise, authority, and acumen which his money-talk projects.

This is not to suggest that Aristotle denied the importance of such "general impressions." In a sense, Demosthenes is constructing his *ēthos* just as the philosopher enjoins. But Aristotle never tells us that the type-specific knowledge which deliberative orators need has "character-creation" as its end. Although the analytic theory and synthetic practice of "deliberative" oratory do overlap considerably in the fourth century, the practical material

---

[13] On the other hand, it might have *contributed* to Aristotle's account in the *Rhetoric*. The date of *Olynthiac* 1 is 349 BCE and, according to the standard scholarly view, Aristotle's *Rhetoric* was finished in 336 BCE. However, the *Rhetoric* is often regarded as the culmination of earlier public lectures delivered by Aristotle. For these lectures, see Cicero, *On the Orator* 3.141; Diogenes Laertius 5.3; Philodemus, *De Rhetorica*, *Volumina Rhetorica*, vol. II, pp. 50ff., ed. S. Sudhaus, col. 48. These earlier lectures have been variously dated by different scholars. Allen 2006 offers fascinating new arguments for pinpointing them to 355 BCE.

is not slavishly following the theory and the practical oratory, like the theory, has its own agendas.

Indeed, Aristotle's account of "deliberative oratory" as a discourse that is best grounded in proper knowledge has a decidedly up-beat agenda. This contrasts with the pessimism of other intellectuals who were actively pondering the nature and impact of this type of rhetoric in democratic Athens. Thucydides' earlier account of the Peloponnesian war often depicts deliberative oratory as impotent, ineffective, or morally compromised.[14] In the diplomatic exchange known as the "Melian dialogue" neither side changes policy on the basis of the other's arguments, and state-sponsored slaughter ensues. In the Mytilenean debate, the Athenian *dēmos* is persuaded to alter its policy for the good but only by the slightest of margins. The implication is that wise decisions are made by chance rather than through good argument. In the Athenian debate on whether to invade Sicily, mass delusion and dubious motives conspire to make the most disastrous policy win the day. We must also contrast Aristotle's optimistic but pragmatic analysis with the Platonic Socrates' claim that the speeches of real democratic *rhētores* are a damaging form of specious flattery (Plato, *Gorgias* 462e5–466a3, 517a1–519d7).[15]

The moral foundations of deliberative rhetorical advice were frequently contested in Roman rhetorical theory too. Although he does not mention Aristotle by name, Quintilian follows Cicero in being surprised that some thinkers regard "expediency" (*utilitas*) as the goal of deliberative oratory rather than "the honorable" (*dignitas, honestum*) as well or instead (Quintilian, *Institutes* 3.8.1–4). Thus the ancient theoretical formulation of deliberative oratory's characteristic features and goals was always subject to change and contestation in the light of the historically specific values and ideologies which fed individual writers' agendas.

Forensic oratory

According to Aristotle, the law-court orator must consider the motives, dispositions, and characters of both the wrongdoer and the victim (1368b1–5). This leads him quickly into a definition of injustice as "voluntarily causing injury contrary to the law" where "the law" can either be

---

[14] The question of how far the direct speech of Thucydides' *History* is an accurate representation of what was actually said is vexed. Thucydides' own opaque remarks on the matter at 1.22 have attracted much scholarly debate. See now Greenwood 2006: 57–82 for an excellent engagement with this debate.

[15] For more on the Platonic "quarrel" with rhetoric see Wardy (this volume).

a specific rule from a particular city or a more general law which appears to be agreed universally (1373b1–1374b23).

Aristotle then makes a further division between what a particular written law says and a more general notion of "equity" (*to epieikes*). A law which forbids wounding with an iron instrument has to make a general statement about the instrument – it cannot go into stipulating the exact sizes and kinds of weapon owing to the infinite number of possibilities. But the law's necessary recourse to a general definition ("iron instrument") means that "if a man wearing a ring lifts up his hand to strike or actually strikes, according to the written law he is guilty of wrongdoing." In such cases, Aristotle continues, we must invoke *to epieikes* and look, not to the letter of the law but to the intention (*dianoia*) of the legislator. We must also consider the *proairesis* ("moral purpose," "choice") of the perpetrator. He concludes with the observation that matters of equity should go to arbitration rather than a law court on the grounds that jurors look to the law where an arbitrator looks at equity. Most private court cases in Athens were looked at first by an arbitrator with a view to settling the matter "out of court" (Aristotle, *Constitution of the Athenians* 53–54).

Having discussed ways in which the orator might amplify or diminish the seriousness of a crime with reference to its consequences, its relation to law or even its location, Aristotle goes on to treat the manner in which the orator must make use of five so-called "atechnic" proofs which are largely exclusive to forensic rhetoric (1375a22–1377b12). These external forms of evidence are laws, witnesses, contracts, slave evidence gathered by torture, and oaths. They are to be contrasted with "entechnic" means of persuasion which are germane to all three types of oratory and which are so-called because they require the *tekhnē* (skill) of the orator himself. The "entechnic" means are three in number (1355b35–1358a32): (1) arguments (*logoi*) which can themselves be divided into inductive reasonings by means of examples or deductive "enthymemes" which rely on probability (*eikos*) and "signs" (*sēmeia*); (2) the use of character (*ēthos*) to enhance the image of the speaker; (3) the use of emotion (*pathos*) to put the orator's audience in the right frame of mind.

Despite the fact that Aristotle classifies certain forms of evidence such as laws or witness statements as "atechnic" ("without *tekhnē*"), it is clear that one still must use creative arguments to make them work for one's case. Thus one can use the concept of equity to get round the fact that the written law is counter to one's case, pointing out that the juror's oath is to abide by his "best judgment" (*gnōmēi tēi aristēi*) rather than what is necessarily written down. And if the law is equivocal, "we must turn it about, and see which way it is to be interpreted so as to suit the application of justice."

If the law favors one's case, one must argue that the juror's oath does not allow him to contradict the laws.

Aristotle follows this discussion of "atechnic" forensic proofs with the second book of the treatise, the first half of which discusses the use of emotion and character. Alongside an intelligible and convincing account in relation to his subject matter, the orator must "show himself to be possessed of certain qualities and ... his hearers should think that he is disposed in a certain way towards them" (1377b21–1378a28). Furthermore, the hearers themselves need to be disposed in a certain way towards the speaker. These rationales for "character" and "emotion" lead to extensive analysis of a series of emotions: anger and disdain, mildness, love and friendship, fear, shame and shamelessness, gratitude and benevolence, pity, righteous indignation, envy and emulation (1378a31–1388b30). He then analyses a range of character types related to age, class, wealth, and power (1388b30–1391b7). The second half returns to the issue of *logoi* (logical arguments) which he had begun in book 1. Now, it must be stressed that Aristotle's conceptions of *ēthos*, *pathos*, and *logos* are as much a resource for the deliberative and epideictic kinds of oratory as they are for forensic. Nevertheless, the treatise's first chapter complains that other rhetorical handbooks have promoted the sorts of emotional appeal to jury-members which are not relevant to the case at hand (1354a11–31). And Aristotle himself points to the particular value for a forensic orator of putting a hearer into a certain emotional state of mind (1378b29–31). When discussing the nature of arguments from probability, his hypothetical orators are clearly litigants and his audience is clearly a jury (1402b21–1403a2). So, although Aristotle is determined to differentiate himself from predecessors who make "law-court oratory" stand for "all oratory," Aristotle's "entechnic" means of persuasion have a strong forensic flavor.

Some aspects of the foregoing analysis dovetail remarkably well with the real classical Athenian situation. For example, we know that Athenian jurors were made to swear not only to give verdicts in accordance with the laws and decrees passed by the Athenian assembly and Boule but also, in cases where no laws exist, to judge according the "most just judgment" (*gnomēi tēi dikaiotatēi*).[16] This is very close to Aristotle's reference to "best judgment." When laws seemed contradictory or open to interpretation or obsolete or inapplicable, Athenian speech writers exploited this "interpretability" on behalf of their clients. Indeed, we can see that both Aristotle and the Attic orators project a surprising view of laws as "evidence" and

---

[16] See Demosthenes 24.149–51; 39.40; 20.118; 57.63.

hence as akin to facts or persuasive arguments. By contrast, we moderns would distinguish law as framing the rules under which the facts or arguments are to be considered.[17]

However, Aristotle's analytical remarks are only a partial guide to the ruses of real Athenian forensic oratory. Lysias 10 (*Against Theomnestus* 1) illustrates this point very well. The speech was delivered to an Athenian people's court in 384 BCE: the year of Aristotle's birth. Lysias' client is prosecuting Theomnestus for slander. The latter has publicly accused the speaker of killing his own father during the regime of the Thirty Tyrants. Let me start with aspects of the speech which fit with Aristotle's analysis.

The bulk of the oration is taken up with debunking an argument which Theomnestus had put forward during the pre-trial arbitration (10.6–7): "that it is not a use of a forbidden word to say that someone has killed his father, since the law does not prohibit that, but does disallow the use of the word 'murderer' (*androphonos*)." Theomnestus is thus represented as trying to wriggle out of the charge on the grounds that he did not use the same wording as specified by the law on slander. Lysias' client is quick to pour scorn on this argument (7–9). His key point, however, is that the jury's concern "is not with mere words but with their intention (*dianoia*)" and that "it was too much of a task for the lawgiver to write all the words that have the same effect; but by mentioning one he showed his meaning in regard to them all." Lysias' client continues in this vein – with meticulous illustration from old but unrepealed laws – for another ten sections of a thirty-section speech. Here, we have an example of the way in which a forensic orator is appealing to *to epieikes* as Aristotle defines it.[18] The reference to "intention" (*dianoia*) shows how close is the orator to the philosopher in this regard.

Lysias' client passes swiftly – *suspiciously* swiftly – over the fact that he was too young to have killed his father himself or to have been an oligarchic conspirator who caused his death. He then briefly uses probability argument and emotional appeal: it was actually disadvantageous of him to kill his father because his elder brother was heir to all the family property and indeed had by now "deprived us of all our inheritance" (10.5). In fact, he continues, he has good reasons for wishing that his father was still alive. Thus, within the first few minutes of his speech the speaker finds a way of getting the audience to feel pity for him and to make himself seem like an unlikely parricide. There is a subtle and organic quality to this Lysianic

[17] Harrison 1971: 134–35 and the modifications of Todd 1993: 58–59.
[18] The closeness to Aristotle is also noticed by Usher 1999: 103.

example of *pathos* and *eikos* which Aristotle would have been proud of: they appear to arise *naturally* from the speaker's character and case rather than seeming artificial.[19]

But the content of these strategies is very much geared towards the specifics of Athenian history and collective democratic ideology. Lysias plays to the Athenian *dēmos*'s suspicion of high status and birth by making nobility skin-deep and representing Theomnestus' cowardice as congenital.[20] By contrast, the Aristotelian formulations concerning *ēthos* and *pathos* are much vaguer; they lack the cutting ideological specificity and awareness of recent events of many Athenian forensic character attacks. So Aristotle's conception of the "forensic" type of oratory is not actually as historically determined as it might have been. In fact, Aristotle rarely adduces examples from the Attic orators and seems much more interested in the language and style of dramatists and poets from Homer right down to his own time.

There are other instructive differences between Aristotle's *Rhetoric* and Lysias' speech. Where Aristotle sees *to epieikes* as a concept which is most useful in arbitrations or arguments for leniency, Lysias deploys the concept to attack Theomnestus' attempts at pre-trial arbitration and he certainly is not interested in the exercise of leniency. Furthermore, Lysias' client attacks his opponents' sophistic, technical arguments with very clever-sounding legal arguments of his own. The evidence of other forensic speeches suggests that over-cleverness and sophistry went down badly with juries and provided opponents with an opportunity for democratically charged character assassination.[21] Aristotle himself makes it clear that he is no lover of sophistic-style strategies (*Rhetoric* 1355b17–21, 1401a1–1402a27). And yet Lysias' client does not go in for an Aristotelian-style character attack on Theomnestus' cleverness and seems unconcerned about projecting his own specialist expertise.

This might suggest that recent critics (including myself) have been unduly influenced by Aristotle's anti-sophistry and his stress on character arguments in their readings of Attic speeches. We have overplayed the extent to which arguments which smelled of sophistry were anathema in the Athenian courts. Certainly, there are examples where speakers admit to being *deinos* ("clever") or subtle in order to excuse their sophistication or to show that they were unlikely to behave in the stupidly self-incriminating

[19] See Edwards and Usher 1985: 229–35 for perceptive comments on this aspect of the speech.
[20] See Ober 1989a: 255.
[21] See Ober 1989a: 156–91; Hesk 2000: 209–27.

manner that is alleged by their opponents.[22] *Against Theomnestus* 1 would probably not look so unusual in its "cleverness" if more Athenian law-court speeches had survived. So it is not just Aristotle's approach to forensic rhetoric which imperfectly matches the "practical" Greek and Roman law-court speeches which we have before us. Modern scholars too, when they attempt to encapsulate the typical features of Greek or Roman forensic oratory, for whatever literary or historical purposes, will tend to focus on some speeches more than others or to emphasize recurring strategies at the expense of unique ones.[23]

On the other hand, modern scholarship has developed a plausible historical sociology of Athenian forensic oratory which has little in common with Aristotle's account. Athenian law courts were arenas in which political rivals used rhetoric to discredit and handicap each other's power and influence in the city. They were venues in which physical and/or linguistic slights to personal honor and manhood could be redressed through appeals to democratic values or "unAthenian" identities and activities. They were theaters for inter- or intra-familial feuding via the often violent language of oratory rather than the use of actual violence.[24] And, taken as a whole, it has been plausibly claimed that Athenian forensic oratory was *the* most important mechanism by which Athenian democracy maintained and renewed a structure in which wealthy elites served the masses with their advice and their money whilst remaining very much subject to the deliberative and judgmental power of the people.[25] For the language of Athenian law-court oratory was not merely shaped by the circumstances and legalities of the specific case in question. In addition, those (mainly elite) individuals who found themselves in court had to represent themselves and their past deeds as conforming to an ideal image of the demos-friendly citizen.[26] Thus a requirement to rhetorically project oneself as ideologically "on-side" with mass conceptions of democratic citizenship and the rich man's role in a democracy meant that law-court speeches were a medium through which elites were made to perform, and conform to, the language and ideas of that democracy.

[22] See Antiphon 3.2.2; Lysias 7.12–19; Demosthenes 18.276–77; Aeschines 3.228–29.

[23] However, see the studies of Johnstone 1999 and Rubinstein 2005 for "differentiated" strategies which were determined by whether a speaker was prosecuting or defending and the specific type of case and/or procedure in question.

[24] Athenian court cases as contests of manly honor and contestations of the meaning of manhood: Winkler 1990; Roisman 2005. Law courts as arenas for feuding as opposed to dispute settlement: Cohen 1995 and the more balanced approach of Christ 1998.

[25] Ober 1989a.

[26] For more on this, see the excellent discussion of Wohl (this volume).

These sociological aspects to Athenian law-court oratory cannot be found in Aristotle's *Rhetoric*. This is partly because Aristotle writes for all Greeks. He is not interested in a merely Atheno-centric view of oratory's operations and does not give an account of forensic oratory which speaks to specific forms of law or procedure. And it is partly because no culture (including and especially "our" own) is terribly good at performing sociology on *itself*. Aristotle's representation of forensic oratory assumes that the litigants are there to convince a jury that they are the innocent party and that their opponent is guilty of a crime or else is making a false accusation. We have seen that the details of his analysis are helpful for understanding the assumptions and strategies which underlay real law-court speeches. And yet, they are rarely adequate guides to the synthetic, historical and socio-logical specificities which shape such orations. In weighing up the extent to which Aristotle hits the mark or falls short, though, we are helped towards an identification of the shortcomings of *our own* critical procedures with these texts. Aristotle helps us to see that every single Greek and Roman forensic speech which we have is as significantly unique as it is significantly typical.

Epideictic oratory

In arguing that epideictic oratory is concerned with praise and blame in relation to virtue and vice or what is noble or shameful, Aristotle was clearly imagining the ceremonial contexts of classical Greek civic religious festivals and funerals in which gods, cities, or individuals were praised. Our best-attested subgenre of such civic epideictic is the Athenian *epitaphios logos*. The *epitaphios logos* was a funeral speech delivered by a prominent public figure to commemorate those citizen-warriors who had fallen in the past year's military actions.

However, Aristotle's predecessors and contemporaries show us that official and public prose eulogies were just one of several ways in which rhetorical *epideixis* could be put to work in the classical city. For this genre allowed intellectuals to display and model their rhetorical skills and out-look: the longest element of Gorgias' defense of Helen is also an exposition on the power of persuasive *logos* (*Helen* 8–14). Other "display" speeches from the fifth century turn out to be exploratory rather than demonstrative. Thus the language, style, and strategies of Antiphon's *Tetralogies* are very different to those of real Attic legal speeches. They are "think-pieces" in which "entechnic" forms of argument are tested in different kinds of legal situation and against different forms of "atechnic" evidence. Pupils were meant to criticize and think about these speeches rather than apply or copy them.[27] Indeed, one of Aristotle's intellectual rivals, Isocrates, ends a written "epideictic" speech in praise of Athens with a fascinating coda in which his pupils debate the preceding oration's quality and meaning.[28] In direct contrast to Aristotle, Isocrates collapses the distinction between the theory and practice of epideictic.

Despite being its inspiration, classical Greek civic eulogy is itself poorly served by Aristotle's analysis. Comparison between surviving *epitaphioi logoi* reveals that these speeches were far more than an opportunity, to use Aristotle's terminology, for praising the war dead and blaming the enemies who shed their blood.[29] These speeches were used to project and reinforce a specific ideology of patriotism, collectivity, and citizenship. In order to do so, they not only praised the courage and valor of the war dead *en masse* but also compared their exploits to previous generations of Athenian warriors who had died in past conflicts, thereby locating them within an honorable lineage of collective self-sacrifice. One of the key *topoi* of Athenian funeral speeches is that the war dead are to be envied and emulated. But these speeches also described the values of Athenian public and private life beyond the battlefield. Here, according to Thucydides, is a section of Pericles' oration for the war dead in 431 BCE (Thucydides 2.40.1–3, trans. adapted from those of R. Crawley and C. F. Smith):

> We are lovers of beauty without extravagance and we love wisdom without effeminacy; wealth we employ more for practical use than for boasting, and place the shame of poverty not in owning to the fact but in declining the struggle against it. Our public men have, besides politics, their private affairs to attend to, and our ordinary citizens, though occupied with the pursuits of industry, are still fair judges of public matters; for we alone regard him who takes no part in these duties not as one who minds his own business but as useless. We decide public questions for ourselves and instead of looking on debate as a hindrance to action, we think it indispensable to be instructed by discussion first.

Obviously this is the language of praise. But it is also a projection of an ideal Athens: a model of egalitarianism and deliberative virtue. Indeed, even for Pericles' time, it is clear that many of the "ideals" laid out in this speech were not quite reflected by reality. That is because this speech was designed to *forge* a sense of identity and values around a set of ideal images rather

---

[27] See Gagarin 2002: 103–34.
[28] See Isocrates, *Panathenaicus* 204–68 with the illuminating remarks of Von Reden and Goldhill 1999.
[29] The classic study of the *epitaphioi logoi* is Loraux 1986a.

than merely to reflect the *Realien* of Athenian society and political life. These speeches conjure up an "imagined community" which the real community can inhabit at the level of ideology.[30]

We should not view these funeral speeches as artless or formulaic propaganda. Here is a section of Hyperides' funeral oration delivered in 322 BCE following one of Athens' military encounters in the Lamian War (Hyperides 6.4–5, trans. J. O. Burtt):

> Compare her [sc. Athens] with the sun which visits the whole world and duly separates the seasons, disposing all things for the best, with provision, where men are virtuous and prudent, for their birth and nurture, the crops and all the other needs of life; for so our city never fails to punish the wicked, help the just, mete out to all men fairness in place of wrong, and at her individual peril and expense assure the Greeks a common safety.

Here, the extended simile comparing the city of Athens to the sun is appropriate to a speech praising its war dead. It is consonant with Aristotle's advice on the value of metaphors and similes to all kinds of orator, not to mention his strictures on the need for appropriateness and the avoidance of forced artificiality (1405a2–1407a15). This is Hyperides' own spin on the Periclean speech's claim that Athens is the "School of Hellas" (Thucydides 2.41.1). The simile asks Athenians to conceive of their city as an almost cosmic regulatory force in the wider world. But it is also designed to soften the impact of another very unusual aspect to Hyperides' speech. Unlike other *epitaphioi logoi* which contain impersonal and austere praises of the Athenians *en masse* and where the speaker will mention himself only in passing and individual generals of the past only briefly, Hyperides devotes much of his oration to praising the military and political achievements of the general Leosthenes, who had just perished in the Lamian campaign. Thus the speech deftly balances the projection of *collective* ideology with a clear agenda to memorialize an *individual*. Once again, we see that analysis and typology fail to encompass the specific strategies and circumstances of a single speech.

In Rome the genre of the funeral speech (*laudatio funebris*) also had an ideological significance which takes us well beyond Aristotle's account.[31] And his emphasis on the "showiness" of epideictic genres does little to explain the centrality of declamatory exercises to education, self-fashioning, and enculturation among the Roman elite.[32] Furthermore, these "fake"

---

[30] B. Anderson 1991.

[31] See Polybius 6.52.10–6.54.4 for these funeral eulogies of prominent individuals as paradigmatic mechanisms of Roman acculturation.

[32] See Beard 1993 and Gunderson 2003.

exercises afforded teachers and pupils a simple and focused task with which to practice all manner of entechnic arguments. Thus "epideictic" oratory was a useful teaching tool for engagement in *all three* types of oratory at Rome.

Epideictic oratory also became increasingly important because of the rise of autocratic power. Under an emperor, the chief rhetorical requirement in public life is to find ways of praising him on ceremonial occasions.[33] The younger Pliny's *Panegyricus* was delivered in praise of Trajan on the occasion of Pliny's consulship in 100 CE. It is a very long speech detailing the emperor's virtues and achievements in highly flattering tones: at one point Trajan is styled as fulfilling the role of Jupiter on earth. But Pliny frames his speech as a piece of sincerity free from any need to pander to power (*Panegyricus* 2, trans. B. Radice):[34]

> Away, then, with expressions formerly prompted by fear: I will have none of them. The sufferings of the past are over: let us have done with the words which belong to them. An open tribute to our Emperor demands a new form, now that the wording of our private talk has changed ... Nowhere should we flatter him as a divinity and a god; we are talking of a fellow citizen, not a tyrant, one who is our father not our over-lord.

Here, it is Trajan's very *ordinariness* that is stressed and implicitly praised. In his section on epideictic Aristotle argues that one device of encomium is to compare the recipient of praise with other illustrious and virtuous figures. But making a person seem *superior* to others is also important: "that is why, if you cannot compare him with illustrious personages, you must compare him with ordinary persons, since superiority is thought to indicate virtue" (*Rhetoric* 1368a24–26). In treating Trajan as a "fellow citizen," Pliny actually does the opposite of what Aristotle advises. Once again, we see how Aristotle's approach to the three types of oratory does not always help with specific instances of rhetorical strategy.

Many of the epideictic speeches which survive from Greco-Roman antiquity are as much displays of their author's ingenuity or learnedness as they are a praise or attack on a particular person or subject. A good example of this is the *Encomium on Hair* by the Cynic-Stoic philosopher and rhetorician Dio Chrysostom (*c.* 40–110 CE). Dio tells us that he has decided

---

[33] The roots of Latin panegyric lie in the Republican customs of funeral eulogy and consuls thanking the people for their election. The variety of forms of panegyric is attested in the treatises of Menander Rhetor (third century CE). See Rees 2007 for an authoritative overview and further bibliography.

[34] See Bartsch 1994 and Rees 2001.

to praise the "hair-lovers" (*philokomoi*) because he has woken up with his hair in such a grievous tangle. Those who look after their hair even to the detriment of a good night's sleep are compared to the Spartans who combed their hair before the battle of Thermopylae. Then, Dio argues that Homer most frequently identifies the physical beauty of heroes with reference to their hair. Both Dio's speech and the fourth-century bishop Synesius' much later response to it are full of what one scholar has recently called "high bravura Second-Sophistic *Witz*."[35] They show us how epideictic rhetoric in antiquity is often about so much more than its specified subject matter: in these examples the epideictic genre is a vehicle for a series of declarations of cultural affiliation and self-authorizing displays of skill and knowledge in the fields of Greek literature and history.

The most important figure for showing these subsequent generations of writers that epideictic oratory could be such a rich multipurpose medium was Isocrates (436–338 BCE). Isocratean epideictic offers a distinctive manifesto for Panhellenic unity. His "speeches" – many of which were probably never performed orally – balance vicious attacks on the educational vacuity of other "sophists" with a distinctive (if rather imprecise) vision of practical education, political *logos* and *philosophia*.[36] Sometimes, they deliberately draw attention to the fact that rhetorical writing can be an object of interpretation and debate – that a speech's meaning might not be as obvious as it first seems, that it might be opaque or knowing, and that audience prejudice and subjectivity can vary from person to person. In the *Panegyricus* Isocrates shows how *epideixis* can stake out one's cultural authority. In the *Panathenaicus* he shows how it can be ironic and playful, how it can overtly praise while covertly offering blame, and how it can offer or contest advice without coming near a traditional civic forum of oral delivery and debate.

Later rhetorical thinkers tend to see Isocrates' emphasis on the writing and reading of *epideixeis* to convey political and educational ideas as very much opposed to an Aristotelian tradition of spoken deliberative and judicial oratory. Isocrates' attacks on other unnamed sophists and rhetoricians certainly attests to a fourth-century battle over how rhetoric was to be taught and used. And his decision to make the *writing* of epideictic *the* primary vehicle for his rather aberrant *logos* was always going to conflict with a view that rhetoric is defined by *real* oral performance contexts and *real* institutional structures. On the other hand, Isocrates' distinctive style

---

[35] Goldhill 2006: 154. For more on these texts see Goldhill (this volume).
[36] See Too 1995 and Livingstone 2007.

was in fact very influential upon no lesser a "real" public orator than Cicero himself. The post-classical story of epideictic is as much an Isocratean one as it is Aristotelian and it is a story in which a type of speech is appropriated for many types of *writing*.

Aristotle's identification of three main types of oratory has endured as a useful tool of classification: it is hard to dispense with it even when we try to or want to. Aristotle's remarks on the three types can be enormously helpful for understanding rhetoric's many instantiations from antiquity to the present. But his analysis was limited and has always been keenly contested: neither his contemporaries nor his successors necessarily agreed with his threefold division and its operations. And when we go to the written versions of real examples of Greek and Roman deliberative, forensic, and epideictic oratory, we often find that there is much in them that cannot be explained or predicted on the basis of Aristotle's classifications nor, for that matter, on the basis of the classifications offered by *any other* rhetorical thinker.[37]

Suggestions for further reading

There is no obvious or easy place to go for those who wish to pursue the concerns of this chapter further. More detail on ancient typologies of oratory and some interest in how far partial examples of Greek and Roman rhetoric square with, or depart from, such typologies can be found in G. A. Kennedy, *A New History of Classical Rhetoric* (Princeton, 1994) or in the earlier works by Kennedy to which that book occasionally directs the reader. A sense of the differences between Aristotle's mode of analysis and that of sociologically minded modern scholarship on Athenian forensic oratory can be gained from reading D. Cohen, *Law, Violence and Community in Classical Athens* (Cambridge, 1995). An accessible English translation of the *Rhetoric*, with notes, is to be found in G. A. Kennedy, *Aristotle on Rhetoric: A Theory of Civic Discourse*, second edition (Oxford, 2007). Useful surveys or analyses of the individual genres of oratory and the particular authors discussed in this essay are referred to in the footnotes.

---

[37] I would like to thank Erik Gunderson, Robert Wardy, David Rosenbloom, Victoria Wohl, and Nancy Worman for comments or conversations which helped me enormously with this chapter.

9

VICTORIA WOHL

Rhetoric of the Athenian citizen

> Synonymy, metonymy, metaphor are not forms of thought that add a second
> sense to a primary, constitutive literality of social relations; instead, they are
> part of the primary terrain itself in which the social is constituted.
>
> (Laclau and Mouffe 1985: 110)

Rhetoric fueled Athenian democracy. Public policy was forged through
persuasive speeches, and political power was the prize of oratorical skill.
Citizenship, too, was defined by speech, the citizen's right to speak his mind
freely in the Assembly. But rhetoric also structured the democracy and the
democratic citizen in more profound ways. If, as Jacques Lacan says, the
unconscious is structured like a language, so too is the political unconscious,
ideology. The ways in which citizens talk about themselves and their relationship to the city – the language they use but also the very grammar of
their thought – is a vital part of that ideology. The rhetoric of the *politēs*
(citizen) bespeaks the fundamental structure, the constitutive tensions and
aspirations, of the *politeia* (state).

In Athens the citizen was defined by rhetoric in a very literal sense. One of
the key identifying attributes of a citizen was *parrhēsia*, the right to speak
freely in the public sphere.[1] This included the right of any citizen to stand up
in the Assembly and argue for or against specific proposals, a freedom dramatized in Aristophanes' *Acharnians*, where the everyman hero Dikaiopolis
("Just City") attempts to convince his angry countrymen to make peace
with Sparta. Frank speech, Aristophanes suggests, is not only the citizen's
right but his duty, his contribution to civic justice.[2] The definitional force
of *parrhēsia* for the democratic citizen is suggested both by its imagined
absence in tyrannical regimes and also by its occasional revocation for
Athenians: certain crimes were punishable by *atimia* (disenfranchisement),
which barred a citizen from speaking in the law courts, Council or Assembly.
Atimia branded an individual with the mark of the non-citizen, silence;

---

[1] For discussions of *parrhēsia*, see Sinclair 1988: 32–34; Monoson 1994; Foucault 2001; the
essays in Sluiter and Rosen 2004 (esp. Raaflaub, Carter, Wallace, Balot, Roisman), and now
Saxonhouse 2006.
[2] On citizen identity in this play, see McGlew 2002: 57–85.

it put him in the same category as those other non-citizens – women, slaves, foreigners – who were barred from full public speech.[3]

In Athens' official fora only citizens could speak, and that speech expressed the distinctive qualities of Athenian citizenship. *Parrhēsia* bespoke the citizen's autonomy and freedom (*eleutheria*). It implied that he was his own man, free from compulsion and beholden to no one: this is why women and slaves, who were under another's authority, could not speak in public. Only citizens could speak, consequently all citizens could speak. *Isonomia* (political equality), the essence of Athenian democracy, had its rhetorical counterpart in *isēgoria*, the equal right of all citizens to address the Assembly.[4] This right was enacted in the herald's question that opened every Assembly meeting: "Who wishes to speak?" When the lowly Thersites spoke out against the general Agamemnon in the *Iliad*, he was beaten mercilessly and told to keep his mouth shut (*Iliad* 2.211–77: see Worman in this volume). But in Athens – at least in theory – poverty was no impediment to public speech, an ideal dramatized in *Acharnians* in the scene where Dikaiopolis, dressed in beggar's rags, publicly lambastes the general Lamachus, justifying his right to speak solely on the grounds that he is a "good citizen" (595).

If the citizen was defined by his right to speak, the most powerful citizens were those who spoke well. Athens had no entrenched political elite. Political power depended largely upon the ability to win over the demos to one's point of view by speaking persuasively in the Assembly. Indeed, by the fourth century a "career politician" was referred to simply as a *rhētōr*.[5] Gaining authority through Assembly speeches and defending it in courtroom speeches, *rhētores* were citizens who exercised their *parrhēsia* frequently, skillfully, and successfully. But that rhetorical power was kept in check by the mass audience, which always had the final vote. As Josiah Ober has shown, although Athens' prominent orators comprised a *de facto* elite of status and skill, they were prevented from forming a permanent ruling class by the "ideological hegemony of the masses," whose norms and values set the parameters of successful speech and rhetorical dominance.[6]

---

[3] For the absence of *parrhēsia* under tyranny, see Plato, *Republic* 567b; Aeschylus, *Persians* 591–94. Allen 2000: 230–32 discusses *atimia* as public silencing.

[4] On *isēgoria*, see Euripides, *Suppliants* 438–41; Herodotus 5.78; Ober 1989a: 78–79, 296–98; Raaflaub 2004: 221–25.

[5] Ober 1989a: 105–12; cf. Connor 1992: 116–17; Yunis 1996: 9–12. For recent scholarship on public speech and political leadership in Athens, see Sinclair 1988: 136–61; Ober 1989a: 104–55, 314–27; Yunis 1996; Hesk 2000: 202–41; McGlew 2002: 86–111; Balot 2004.

[6] Ober 1989a, esp. 293–339.

Speaking and listening thus formed a rhetorical counterpart to the alternation of governing and being governed (*arkhein/arkhesthai*) that for Aristotle is the essence of democracy.[7] The perpetual, heated debate over rhetoric in fifth- and fourth-century Athens can therefore be seen as part of a larger debate over the nature of citizenship and leadership in the democracy. Although it sometimes appears to be merely a quarrel over aesthetics (styles of speaking) or ethics (the character of speakers), the rhetoric of rhetoric is always also a political rhetoric with vital political stakes.[8]

The high-profile feud between the orators Aeschines and Demosthenes, for instance, stages a debate over democratic citizenship in terms of rhetorical style and ethics. Both define the good *rhētōr* as a good man and a good citizen, and they agree in general on his necessary qualities: he must be virtuous in his private life, obey the laws, and defer to the sovereign authority of the demos. Above all, he must be transparent and patriotic; his words must reflect his true thoughts, and both must be devoted to the civic good.[9] Each orator claims to embody these ideals in his person and to enact them in his speech. A famous example is Demosthenes' *On the Crown*, a defense of his career as a statesman, a *rhētōr*, and a citizen. Demosthenes vividly re-enacts the critical meeting of the Assembly held while Philip's forces advanced on Athens. The herald opened the meeting with the traditional call, "Who wishes to speak?" No one came forward, "although all the generals and *rhētores* were there, and the fatherland was calling for someone to speak on behalf of its salvation" (§170). Only Demosthenes dared to speak. "I alone did not abandon my patriotic post in that crisis" (§173). Speaking out for the benefit of all, thinking nothing of the risk to himself, he did (he proclaims) "everything befitting a good citizen" (*agathos politēs*, §180; cf. 197).[10]

Demosthenes presents his speech – its brave delivery, sage content, and vigorous style – as the supreme act of democratic citizenship. But Aeschines warns the jury that his opponent's oratory does not reveal a good citizen but instead conceals a bad one (3.174). Demosthenes is a "scoundrel sophist," a "technician of words," a "magician" whose rhetorical trickery is designed

---

[7] Aristotle, *Politics* 1317a40–b17. Cf. 1277a25–b25: the virtue (*aretē*) of a citizen is to know how to rule and be ruled.

[8] See especially Yunis 1996; Hesk 2000. See also Hesk, Worman in this volume.

[9] E.g. Demosthenes 18.219, 277–81, 306–13; 19.337–40; Aeschines 1.22–36; 3.1–4, 168, 215–29, 248–49.

[10] On this scene, see Yunis 1996: 267–77. Compare again Aristophanes' *Acharnians*, where Dikaiopolis delivers his speech with his head on the chopping block.

to deceive the demos and benefit himself at the city's expense.[11] *Mutatis mutandis*, Demosthenes derides Aeschines' past career as an actor and implies that in his speeches, too, he is playing a part (19.337; cf. 19.246–50). It is not diction or tone of voice that makes a good orator, he remarks, but loyalty to the *polis* (18.280). This threat of rhetorical style unanchored by ethical substance echoes throughout Athenian discussions of political rhetoric. We hear it, for example, in tragedy's depiction of the wily Odysseus, who says one thing but means another, and in the public mistrust of the sophists, who were reputed to teach their students how to make the weaker argument seem the stronger.[12] Plato spells out the political dangers of rhetoric divorced from truth: the demos is ruined by speakers who pander only to its desires and whose oratory is pleasurable but not beneficial.[13] Aristophanes literalizes this critique in *Knights* in his depiction of Demos as a foolish old man, "tongue-kissed into silence" (352) by the flatteries of the *rhētores*.

These critiques of democratic rhetoric suggest that there was a civic art of listening as well as speaking. In the debate over Mytilene Thucydides has Cleon – himself a personification of the negative qualities of oratory – accuse the demos of abdicating their duty as democratic citizens by submitting to the charms of oratory (3.37–40). Political deliberation has become mere spectacle that distorts reality and results in disastrous decisions. The fault, he says, lies less with the *rhētores* than the demos: "You are to blame for being such bad judges, you who are habitual spectators of speeches and listeners to deeds" (3.38.4). No longer active participants in democratic debate, Cleon charges, they have become passive spectators and slaves to rhetorical novelty (3.38.5). "Simply put, you are conquered by the pleasure of listening and are more like the audience that sits around watching the sophists than like citizens deliberating the affairs of the city" (3.38.7). The freedom, autonomy, and energetic engagement that characterize the citizen as speaker should characterize him no less as a listener. To listen passively is to be "soft" (3.37.2), emasculated, a slave.

Of course there are myriad ironies to a *rhētōr*'s making a persuasive speech urging his audience to resist persuasive speech. But Cleon's ideal of a manly and resistant audience had its practical counterpart in the *thorubos*,

---

[11] E.g. Aeschines 1.166–76; 3.16, 137, 202–207, 215, 229, 253. Cf. Worman, this volume.

[12] E.g. Protagoras, fr. 80 B 6b (Diels–Kranz); Euripides, *Trojan Women* 283–87; Sophocles, *Philoctetes* 101–11; Aristophanes, *Clouds* 98–99, 112–18, *et passim*; Hesk 2000: 202–91; Worman 2002: 169–92. See also Rosenbloom in this volume.

[13] Plato, *Gorgias* 462d–465e, 500b–503d, 513a–523a. On the antagonistic intimacy between philosophy and rhetoric, see Wardy, this volume.

the loud uproar with which audiences often responded to speeches in the Assembly or law courts. This raucous heckling, as Robert Wallace notes, was itself a form of *parrhēsia*.[14] It was a vocal demonstration that even when he was only listening, the Athenian was still exercising the rhetorical freedom of a good citizen. This is precisely what Aristotle has in mind when he praises the alternation of governing and being governed.

The citizen was thus defined by speech, even when he was not speaking. Rhetoric – including the rhetoric about rhetoric – mediated his relation to his leaders, his fellow citizens, and the city. But these rhetorical practices of citizenship were themselves sustained by a deeper rhetorical logic. The Athenians often boasted that the *polis* is not its land or its buildings, but its men.[15] But what does it mean to say that a city is its citizens? This deceptively simple equation conceals more complex rhetorical operations. Is the *polis* a whole of which the individual *politēs* is the constitutive part, as might be suggested by Aristotle's definition of a *polis* as a multitude (*plēthos*) of citizens (*Politics* 1274b41, 1275b20–21)? Or is the *politēs* a symbol for the *polis*, representing in himself some essential quality of the state? Alternatively, is the city a soul writ large, as in Plato's *Republic* and, if so, is the relationship analogical or somehow organic, statically structural or dynamic and reciprocal? These questions are simultaneously political and rhetorical: they illuminate the rhetorical undergirding of political relations. The rhetoric of citizenship not only has a politics but *is* a politics, for the ways in which citizens speak about their relation to the city and to one another not only reflect but create those relations. Rhetoric opens channels of thought along which real political relations can flow.

The rhetorical substructure of Athenian citizenship can be charted on the double axes of metaphor and metonymy. Metaphors define through substitution; metonyms, through association. The former are vertical and idealizing, as one term is replaced by another within a relatively fixed structure of cultural meaning. An eagle, for instance, represents the United States, symbolizing the abstract ideals of power and freedom that are imagined as the nation's essence. Metonymies, by contrast, work horizontally, linking meanings laterally along chains of related terms. Metaphor looks for something essential within the thing and expresses it in the universalizing form of a symbol: the United States is an eagle. Metonymy takes some attribute of the thing and links it to other things that share that attribute. Instead of a one-for-one substitution, metonymy creates bonds of complexly related

[14] Wallace 2004, esp. 225–26.
[15] Sophocles, *Oedipus Tyrannos* 56–57; Herodotus 8.61.2; Euripides fr. 828 (Nauck); Thucydides 7.77.7.

meanings among symbolically contiguous terms. Functioning as a metonym, the "American" eagle does not isolate a universal truth about the United States but instead situates the nation's qualities in a network of potential associations. Thus, depending on what attributes are foregrounded, the eagle might connote the freedom of flight, but it might also evoke predation on other species, the chilly remove of a mountain eyrie, or even the pitiful prospect of an empty nest.[16]

As the example of the eagle illustrates, the line between metaphor and metonymy is not absolute, and a given symbol can often be read either way. Is a populist leader a metaphor embodying the ideals of his country or a metonym standing for his fellow citizens? These rhetorical figures do not name fixed ontological categories but instead designate different relations of substitution or association, with different political implications. Ernesto Laclau, for instance, has suggested that metonymy is the basic trope of politics, which forges contingent networks of alliances and articulates different sets of interests.[17] Michael Ryan aligns metaphor, with its vertical orientation of meaning, with conservative politics and metonymy, with its web of lateral associations, with progressive politics.[18] We might even go further and say that while monarchy is metaphoric, democracy – especially a direct democracy such as Athens' – is at base metonymic. These political alignments were vividly illustrated in the French Revolution, for example, when the monarchical metaphor – "l'état c'est moi" – was countered by a metonymic distribution of power that made the name "Citizen" interchangeable with every individual's name.

In the case of Athens we might begin to elaborate this political tropology by looking at one paradigmatic (and highly self-conscious) use of metonymy to articulate the relationship between the individual citizen and the democratic city. In his famous court speech against Meidias (Demosthenes 21), Demosthenes forges a web of symbolic associations between himself, the jurors, the laws, and the *polis*. The notion that the city is its citizens appears here both as an unassailable tenet of democratic ideology and as a self-interested legal strategy. Demosthenes charges that Meidias punched him

---

[16] On these two tropes see Burke 1945: 503–17; Jakobson and Halle 1956: ch. 5; White 1973: 31–38; and Ryan 1989: 111–33, from whom I borrow the example of the eagle. Ober (1989b) points the way for the present study in his suggestion that the various institutional parts of the citizen body (the Assembly, Council, and juries) stood in a synecdochic relation to the whole citizen body. I leave aside synecdoche, which can be understood either as a metaphor (a microcosm that contains the essence of the macrocosm) or as a metonym (a part of a whole made up of its parts).

[17] Laclau in Butler, Laclau, and Žižek 2000: 78–79. Cf. Laclau and Mouffe 1985: 141.

[18] Ryan 1989: 111–33.

while he was serving as *khorēgos* (choral producer) at the City Dionysia. This is not merely a private quarrel, Demosthenes argues, but a matter of national security, for in striking him Meidias has assaulted a civic official and thus the city itself: "It was not just me, Demosthenes, whom he insulted that day, but your chorus ... If on any other day Meidias had committed any of these crimes against me as an individual citizen it would be right for him to be punished in a private suit. But if it is shown that he committed this *hubris* against me while I was your *khorēgos* ... he deserves public anger and retribution. For a *khorēgos* was insulted at the same time as Demosthenes" (31, 33–34). Demosthenes is more than just Demosthenes; he stands metonymically for the chorus, which in turn metonymizes both the jury and the demos as a whole.

Demosthenes develops these equations through an analogy. No one who serves in the office of thesmothete has the name Thesmothete, he notes, but "whatever name each man has" (32). If someone insults a thesmothete as an individual, he will be tried and fined, but if he insults him as a thesmothete he risks disenfranchisement "because the man who does this is also insulting the laws and your common crown and the name of the city. For Thesmothete is not the name of any man but the city's name" (32). His point is obvious, but the analogy is devious, because it implies that, just as the title Thesmothete signifies an individual as well as an office, so the name Demosthenes signifies the *khorēgia* as well as the man. "Demosthenes" becomes an official title, "the city's name." In a literal met-onymy, Demosthenes' name becomes interchangeable with that of Athens.

Demosthenes threads the warp of personal identification into the weft of Athens' democratic ideology to create a fabric so tightly woven that a rip in any part threatens to unravel the whole. Like every litigant, Demosthenes works to forge a bond of empathy with the jurors. "As you listen to everything you are about to hear, jurors, ask yourselves what one of you would have done if he had suffered this violence" (108). This identification is the first node in a larger network of associations. Demosthenes asks each juror to imagine himself hurrying home after the trial, glancing over his shoulder in fear of the kind of assault from his enemies that Demosthenes suffered from Meidias. In this vivid picture Demosthenes invokes one of the basic tenets of Athenian citizenship, the physical sanctity of the citizen. David Halperin has shown how the political sovereignty of the Athenian demos was manifested in the corporeal inviolability of each individual citizen.[19] This analogy between citizen microcosm and civic macrocosm is

[19] Halperin 1990.

played out in this speech as a metonymic association among all the parts of the whole: Meidias' attack on Demosthenes' body is a potential assault on every citizen's body and, by extension, on the sovereignty of the Athenian citizen body.

If identification with the jurors links Demosthenes metonymically to the demos it also connects him, through a different set of associations, to the law. The jurors' oath to "vote in accordance with the laws" made each individual *dikastēs* (juror) an agent of *dikē* (justice). Thus by insulting him, Meidias has also insulted the laws (7), and Demosthenes prosecutes not just for his own sake but, as he repeatedly tells the jurors, "on behalf of myself and you and the laws" (20, 40, 213, 222). How could he do otherwise, since he has shown these three – Demosthenes, jurors, laws – to be just three different names, metonymies, for the same democratic ideals?

Finally, he ties these metonymies together in one of the speech's most famous passages. Why do the jurors not fear the sort of attack he himself has suffered? Because as jurors they are "strong and sovereign over everything in the polis." Why are they sovereign? "Because the laws are strong." "And what is the strength of the laws? ... You – if you secure them and make them valid for anyone who asks. The strength of the laws lies in you and your strength lies in the laws" (223–24). The jurors are the laws, the laws are the jurors. Through this rhetorical catachresis, individual citizens are endowed with the legitimacy of the lawful city, and written laws infused with the will of the sovereign demos. At the center of this symbolic union stands Demosthenes. He situates himself at the precise intersection between Athens' political and jurisprudential ideals and the living bodies of its citizens: the two seem to meet in – and thanks to – him. The entire symbolic structure of the democracy is at stake in the jurors' verdict. By defending him (he implies) they will be defending not only the laws but the sovereignty they themselves derive from the laws, not only themselves but the vitality the laws borrow from them. The strength of Demosthenes' argument is that it draws on metonymic connections already deeply embedded in Athenian communal thought and at the same time seems to be the indispensable ligature binding those vital strands.

Of course, Demosthenes can weave himself so seamlessly into the pattern of democracy only by erasing the significant economic and social differences dividing the powerful *rhētōr* from a jury of average Athenians. Peter Wilson has shown the way the speech's overtly egalitarian ideology – in which all citizen bodies are equally inviolable – glosses over the real inequalities that made some bodies more inviolable than others.[20] Rhetorical figures conceal

[20] Wilson 1991: 173–74.

as much as they reveal, and one thing they can conceal is their own politics. Indeed, the very suggestion that the members of the jury might themselves have enemies like the powerful Meidias elides significant social differences.

But Demosthenes works hard to smooth away any rough edges to the equation between himself and the mass jury. He does this, first, by projecting all difference onto Meidias, who is a monster of elite *hubris* and anti-democratic individuality. Second, he empties his own person of any particularity, turning himself into a symbol. Consider, for example, how he depicts – or rather, fails to depict – the central event of the case, the punch. "A man who throws a punch can do many things, jurors, some of which the victim could not report to anyone else – with his posture, his look, his tone of voice ... No one reporting these things could make listeners experience their terror as clearly as the *hubris* appears to the victim and spectators during the actual moment of the event" (72). The punch is described as indescribable, and Demosthenes' wounded body is rendered invisible. It is obliterated as the object of violent assault and even as subjective witness to that assault: the scene is staged as a disembodied hypothetical and its real pain is placed beyond the descriptive language of the speech. Instead, Demosthenes leaves the jurors to imagine the scene for themselves: they are invited to substitute themselves into a picture from which Demosthenes has disappeared.

By emptying himself of any particularity Demosthenes transforms his body into a repository of social meaning, the invisible center of the web of associations he himself has woven. At this moment, metonymy reaches towards metaphor. The logic becomes vertical rather than horizontal, as Demosthenes makes himself a transcendent symbol of inviolable citizenship. Douglas MacDowell expresses the reaction Demosthenes no doubt hoped for: "As he approaches the conclusion of his speech Demosthenes rises above the details of his dispute with Meidias, and is telling a universal truth with both pathos and power."[21] His particular, private, elite body becomes an abstraction, a metaphor that consolidates politics precisely by affecting to transcend them. Social and economic differences are made to disappear. All we see is the universal truth of the egalitarian *polis* and sovereign demos, embodied in the idealized body of the elite citizen.

In Demosthenes 21, the symbolic structure of democracy – the metonymic bonds between citizen, demos, law, and *polis* – is anchored by the

---

[21] MacDowell 1990: 37. This universalizing strategy would be facilitated if, as some believe, the speech was never in fact delivered in court. Freed from the specific context of the trial, the speech's "I" would have been disembodied from the start and thus more easily elevated into a civic symbol.

metaphor of the exemplary individual. This rhetorical strategy has important political implications. To see these, we can turn to a similar metaphoric fixation in Thucydides. In the Funeral Oration delivered by Pericles, Thucydides presents an idealized vision of Athenian democracy. This vision, like Demosthenes', is structured by a metonymic logic, in which the heroism of the war dead, the virtues of the living Athenians, and the greatness of the city are all mutually defining. The city's power is a signifier (*sēmainei*) of the individual citizen's excellence (2.41.2). Conversely, the brave heroes' grave (*sēma*) is a sign (*sēmeion*) of the city's superiority (2.41.4–5, 2.43.2–3). In a city that is supremely autonomous (*autarkestatē*, 2.36.1–3), each and every citizen – as both cause and effect – is personally autonomous (*to sōma autarkes*, 2.41.1). The syntax of this political fantasy is the first-person plural: we Athenians are free and courageous, Pericles says; we are masters over our own bodies which we willingly give for our city. This first-person plural bond culminates in a love affair between citizen and city, as Pericles urges his audience to "gaze upon the power of the city every day and become her lovers," and, as they do so, to remember the dead heroes who made her so powerful and worthy of their love (2.43.1). Eros unites lover and beloved, as each sees itself in the other's eyes. It also unites lovers: all Athenians are equal in their love of Athens and their willingness to die for her.[22]

With its egalitarian first-person plurals and romance of political reciprocity, the text's rhetorical surface reflects the deep metonymic substructure of democratic citizenship that Demosthenes invoked in his speech against Meidias. Of course, Pericles' vision, like Demosthenes', requires certain strategic elisions. Nicole Loraux has emphasized the elitism of the speech and the denial of inequality required to produce its fantasy of a free and autonomous demos.[23] But whereas Demosthenes invites the jurors to see their democratic sovereignty in his own sovereign body, Pericles distributes the city's power to all its citizens: Athens' greatness is not condensed metaphorically into a single *sēma* or *sōma* but is instead metonymically embodied in the *sōma autarkes*, the autonomous person, of each and every Athenian. In this way, the speech's rhetoric of praise imitates what it praises, the democratic city that shares its power and freedom equally among all its citizens.

But the encomium of Athens that Thucydides attributes to Pericles is subtly undermined by Thucydides' encomium of Pericles himself. For while

[22] Wohl 2002: 30–72.
[23] Loraux 1986a: 180–92.

Pericles urges the Athenians to fall in love with the *polis*, Thucydides invites his readers to fall in love with Pericles, and the qualities that the Funeral Oration locates in every Athenian, living and dead, Thucydides suggests are uniquely embodied in Pericles himself.[24] Pericles asked the citizens to gaze upon the power of Athens and remember those who made it great, but for Thucydides Athens was greatest under Pericles (2.65.5). For Thucydides (as for many since), Pericles stands as a unique metaphor for the *polis* at its most perfect – "Periclean" Athens.[25]

Thucydides spells out the politics of this metaphor: Athens under Pericles was "a democracy in name, but in fact rule by the first man" (*logōi men dēmokratia, ergōi de hupo tou prōtou andros arkhē*, 2.65.9). Symbolic substitution – Pericles is Athens – elevates the symbol over what it symbolizes. Indeed, the very qualities that define Athenian democracy in the Funeral Oration become, when condensed in an individual leader, the props for a rule that displaces democracy. Our *politeia* is a democracy, says Pericles, because "we govern freely (*eleutherōs*) with regard to the common good" (2.37.2). But that citizen *eleutheria* is most fully actualized in Pericles, who "restrained the majority freely" (*eleutherōs*, 2.65.8). Pericles' *eleutheria* stands in for the demos's *eleutheria* but also marks its limit: the free demos is "restrained" by its freest member. The means of Pericles' rule, moreover, is his rhetorical prowess: because he spoke for the people's good and not for their pleasure, he "led them more than he was led by them" (2.65.8). The democratic alternation of *arkhein/arkhesthai* comes to a halt. The Athenians' political freedom is displaced by the rhetorical freedom of a superlative *rhētōr* who now speaks for, not just to, his fellow citizens. And the Funeral Oration itself is, ironically, the paradigmatic metaphor of that brilliant rhetorical rule.

Thucydides' portrait of Pericles exposes the antidemocratic implications of imagining one exemplary individual as a metaphor for the *polis*.[26]

---

[24] Pericles was chosen to deliver the speech, Thucydides says, because of his intelligence and prestige (2.34.6; cf. 2.60.5, 2.65.8). These same qualities characterize Athens, which is unique in its combination of speech and action, calculation and daring (2.40.2–3), and enjoys a reputation that spans the known world (2.41.1–5, 2.43.2–3).

[25] Loraux 1986b.

[26] This is not an exclusively elitist dynamic. We might compare Cleon, the populist demagogue who represented himself as guardian of the people, *prostatēs dēmou*. *Prostatēs* implies standing in front of (to protect), but also standing before (to lead), or even, by extension of the meaning of the prefix, standing in place of. The shift from *prostatēs* as a metonym (standing in front of the people who follow) to *prostatēs* as metaphor (standing in for the people he leads) – the shift from representation by association to representation by replacement – marks a slide from demagogue to tyrant.

The citizen who represents the city metaphorically represents – even "rules" and "restrains" – it politically.[27] The rhetoric of the citizen is in a very real sense the politics of the city. Citizenship, as we saw, is determined by who can speak and where, what one says and how one says it. But it is also constructed at a deeper level in the very syntax of Athenian thought, in the tension between the vertical substitutions of metaphor and the horizontal associations of metonymy. This rhetorical substructure is replicated at the institutional level, where, on the one hand, measures of accountability (such as the audit Pericles faced soon after delivering the Funeral Oration, Thucydides 2.65.3) prevented metaphoric condensation of power and, on the other, payment for service and selection by lot ensured that democratic power was distributed metonymically to every citizen. Such institutions helped to maintain an equilibrium between what I am labeling metaphoric and metonymic relations within the *polis*, an equilibrium encoded in the continual alternation of ruling and being ruled, *arkhein/arkhesthai*.

This equilibrium was also negotiated, I have suggested, in the very language citizens used to describe themselves and their relation to the city. If Demosthenes 21 shows a tendency towards metaphoric consolidation around the exemplary citizen, another courtroom speech, Lysias 24, reveals the *polis*'s vital interest in its metonymic bond to the *politēs*. The speech is titled *Huper tou Adunatou*, "For the Disabled Man." The speaker is *adunatos*, disabled, impoverished, powerless. His multiple incapacity blocks idealizing identification of the sort Demosthenes establishes: how could his crippled body symbolize the Athenian citizen body? The speech *Huper tou Adunatou* is both about an *adunatos*, a disabled man, and about an *adunaton*, an impossible metonymy that threatens to expose impossibilities within the metonymic structures of democracy.

The *adunatos* is arguing in the Council for continuation of his disability pension of one obol. This minimal dole – barely enough to live on – was available to Athenian citizens who owned less than three mina worth of property and were physically unable to work. His opponent apparently contends that he is able to work and has enough income to disqualify him from the pension (4). The burden of the speaker's case, then, is to prove his incapacity, and he does so with bitter self-derision. He suggests that the prosecutor is harassing him out of envy (*phthonos*, a word connoting class resentment) because he is the better citizen, despite his disability (2–3). To his opponent's accusation that he is wealthy enough to ride a horse,

---

[27] Spivak 1994: 70–74 offers a sophisticated analysis of the distinction between mimetic representation (*Darstellung*) and political representation (*Vertretung*) and the dangers of blurring that distinction.

he answers sarcastically that he rides a horse because he cannot walk and by that logic it might be held against him that he uses two crutches instead of one (12). Alluding to the practice of *antidosis* (by which one citizen challenged another to assume his tax burden or else accept an exchange of property) he speculates that if he were selected tragic *khorēgos*, his opponent would pay for the *khorēgia* ten times over rather than submit to the exchange of property (9). The cripple is no Demosthenes: for him the idea of being *khorēgos* is just a sad joke.

Of course, the mere existence of this speech, written by one of the most prominent speech-writers of the day, might suggest that the speaker is not quite so resourceless as he claims.[28] But the speaker deflects suspicion of deceit by making his crippled body speak for itself. My opponent will try to persuade you that I am not *adunatos*, he says. But he is insane. "For he has come to dispute over my misfortune as if it were a wealthy heiress (*epiklērou*) and he tries to convince you that I am not such a man as you all see. But you must trust more in your own eyes than in his words; this is the task of sensible men" (14). His disability, he claims, is displayed unambiguously on his body: the councillors have only to look at him to see it. The striking simile to the *epiklēros* figures the speaker as passive and effeminate and ridicules his opponent for squabbling over such a miserable legacy. It also suggests that while the opponent reads his body metaphorically – as something it is not – he and the jury see it for what it obviously is. His crippled body seems beyond rhetorical manipulation, clear and unequivocal proof.

What metonymies can be forged around such an impossible body? The speaker's black humor turns the very possibility of metonymic identification into a veiled threat. Imagine me as an exemplary citizen and target of other citizens' envy, he challenges the jury (3). Imagine me as a *khorēgos*, rubbing shoulders with the wealthiest men in town (9). Imagine me as an archon, a top magistrate. "If my opponent convinces you that I am not *adunatos*, councillors, what's to stop me from being chosen as one of the nine archons? What's to prevent you from taking away my obol on the grounds that I am healthy and awarding it to him on the grounds that he is impaired?" (13). He mockingly invites the jurors to identify with him, to see him as one of them: my opponent says I am not *adunatos*, that I'm no different from him or from you. But if he insists on that identification, what's to say that the basis of similarity is my capacity and not your incapacity: that he – and

---

[28] Consequently, some have argued that the speech was just a rhetorical exercise, never actually delivered in court. Others, however, have suggested that the cripple had a wealthy patron or that Lysias worked *pro bono*.

you – aren't *adunatoi* like me. But the very thought is absurd, he scoffs. Just look at me.

Through these sardonic hypotheticals, the cripple transforms himself into a social *adunaton*, the unthinkable embodiment of a crippled citizenry. He offers his debased body both as a metonym for the bodies of his fellow citizens and as a metaphor for the body politic, and in this way threatens to disable the health and integrity of both. But he offers the jurors a deal. They can be *dunatoi* if they look on him as *adunatos* and give him his obol. If they are to see themselves as they wish to imagine themselves, they must see him as he wishes to be seen, as a cripple. Thus in contrast to Demosthenes' strategy of identification, this speaker employs a strategy of dis-identification, an anxious metonymy in which symbolic contiguity works like physical contamination, spreading the disease of disability. The demos need pay only an obol for the cure.

To trace to the politics of this self-presentation we can follow the money, the single obol that moves between the speaker and the city. For the cripple that obol represents the sum total of his citizenship. This pension was granted him by the vote of the *polis*; it is his civic allotment and to rob him of it, he asserts, would deprive him of "the only share fate has given me in my fatherland" (22). This is the language of political participation. Aristotle defines a citizen as one who has a share in the decisions and offices of the state (*Politics* 1475a22–23). This trial's verdict is the cripple's only share in the city's decisions; it is a test of qualification (*dokimasia*) for the only office he can hold, the office of pensioner (26). The obol, then, stands metonymically for the cripple's desire for a metonymic connection to the city.

This desire is not only the cripple's but also the city's. Demosthenes, as we saw, offered the jurors the fantasy of an inviolable citizen body. In his speech the threat to that body is the *hubris* of a violent elite. The cripple symbolizes a threat to that same fantasy from the opposite direction: poverty. While the Athenians tolerated a good deal of economic inequality, they recognized that extreme poverty could undermine the democratic ideals of *eleutheria* and *isonomia*. Pericles tacitly acknowledges this when he boasts that in Athens poverty is no impediment to political participation (Thucydides 2.37.1) and imagines every citizen as the possessor of a *sōma autarkes*, a body free from necessity or want. It is precisely this autonomy that the dole was supposed to guarantee. Thus the cripple's case tests Athens' commitment to this fantasy of the citizen's *sōma autarkes* and to the political equality it implies. This commitment was in fact one justification of the democratic city. As Solon tells the tyrant Croesus, since life is uncertain and no man truly self-sufficient (*autarkes*), the happiest existence is

provided by the egalitarian city (Herodotus 1.30–32).[29] Lysias' *adunatos*
makes a similar argument. "Since the divinity deprived me of the greatest
things in life the *polis* voted me this money with the idea that everyone
shares equally in good and bad fortune. Would I not be most miserable if my
misfortune robbed me of the greatest goods and then the prosecutor robbed
me of what the *polis* gave me out of consideration for those in my condition?" (22–23). If the obol represents his own wounded attachment to the
city, it also symbolizes the city's self-grounding at the site of the individual's
vulnerability. The city promises to protect the citizen and claims to be just
and equitable by virtue of that promise. The *polis* is no less invested in this
crucial metonymy than the cripple himself: one obol is also the name for
minimal citizenship.

The *adunatos* threatens to interrupt the democracy's grounding metonymies: his crippled body savagely ironizes the fiction that the citizen body
is inviolable and all citizens are equally sovereign through the city. He
threatens to expose as *adunaton* the city's claim to protect all its citizens
and ensure their civic equality in the face of unequal fortune. But he also
gives the *polis* a chance to maintain that impossible fantasy – by giving him
his obol. The cripple does not demand full rights for the disabled or a
redistribution of wealth. He is no revolutionary; all he wants is his obol.
And yet by gesturing to the principles of political equality, the speaker opens
a gap – a failed metonymy – between the *polis* and its egalitarian ideals.
The cripple's rhetoric thus bespeaks an incapacity within the city itself and
hints at the impossibility of its aspirations to democratic justice. Viewed in
this light, the cripple's black comedy is a political tragedy, and he himself,
ironically, is the tragic *khorēgos*.

The cripple offers the Athenians a cheap way out: they can avert this civic
tragedy for a single obol. But if the price is cheap, the symbolic and political
logic of this deal is rich: it is the minimum social contract of the democratic
state, its investment in its most vulnerable citizens. Athens may have liked to
see itself metaphorized in the powerful body of a Demosthenes or a Pericles.
But perhaps the cripple's painful metonymy better expresses what was truly
democratic about Athens, its will to actively maintain a metonymic bond –
if only one as tenuous as an obol – among all its citizens, and to imagine
itself metonymically as always and only the sum of its parts.

Demosthenes and the *adunatos*, from their different ends of the social
spectrum, illustrate the chiasmus of politics and rhetoric that crossed through
the body of the citizen: the Athenian *politēs* is rhetorically structured at every

[29] Kurke 1999: 148–50.

level, and the rhetoric of citizenship (as Thucydides' "rule of the first man" suggests) entails real political consequences. By exposing the intertwined rhetoric of politics and politics of rhetoric, moreover, these speeches remind us that rhetorical criticism is itself a political activity, one that stands to uncover in the tropes and figures of Athenian rhetoric the underlying syntax of the city's democratic ideology.[30]

Suggestions for further reading

The role of public speech in democratic Athens is the subject of a vast bibliography. One might start with Josiah Ober, *Mass and Elite in Democratic Athens* (Princeton, 1989); Josiah Ober and Barry Strauss, "Drama, Political Rhetoric, and the Discourse of Athenian Democracy," in J. J. Winkler and F. I. Zeitlin, eds., *Nothing To Do with Dionysus?* (Princeton, 1990), 237–70; Sara Monoson, "Frank Speech, Democracy, and Philosophy: Plato's Debt to a Democratic Strategy of Civic Discourse," in J. P. Euben, J. R. Wallach, and J. Ober, eds., *Athenian Political Thought and the Reconstruction of American Democracy* (Ithaca, 1994), 172–97; Harvey Yunis, *Taming Democracy: Models of Political Rhetoric in Classical Athens* (Ithaca, 1996).

The scholarship on Athenian oratory tends to fall into three categories: formal rhetorical studies, commentaries on specific speeches, and sociohistorical analyses. The most prominent example in the first category is George Kennedy, *The Art of Persuasion in Greece* (Princeton, 1963). Particularly noteworthy in the second category are D. M. MacDowell, ed., *Demosthenes: Against Meidias* (Oxford, 1990); N. R. E. Fisher, ed., *Aeschines: Against Timarchus* (Oxford, 2001); Harvey Yunis, ed., *Demosthenes: On the Crown* (Cambridge, 2001). Outstanding examples in the third category include David Cohen, *Law, Violence and Community in Classical Athens* (Cambridge, 1995); Matthew Christ, *The Litigious Athenian* (Baltimore, 1998); Danielle Allen, *The World of Prometheus: The Politics of Punishing in Democratic Athens* (Princeton, 2000); Gabriel Herman, *Morality and Behaviour in Democratic Athens* (Cambridge, 2006).

Finally, on the rhetorical structure of the citizen subject see, for Athens, Nicole Loraux, *The Invention of Athens: The Funeral Oration in the Classical City*, trans. A. Sheridan (Cambridge, MA, 1986); and for the modern citizen, Michael Ryan, *Politics and Culture: Working Hypotheses for a Post-Revolutionary Society* (London, 1989).

---

[30] I am grateful to Erik Gunderson and Robert Wardy for their helpful comments on this chapter.

10

JOHN DUGAN

Rhetoric and the Roman Republic

In the Aeneid's first simile Vergil compares Neptune calming raging storm winds to a Roman magistrate who pacifies a seditious crowd threatening arson and stone throwing (*Aeneid* 1.148–53). The mere sight of the man, someone "of consequence because of his deserved reputation for responsibility," causes the crowd, like a pack of animals with their ears pricked up, to stand still. The orator then "rules their souls with his words and soothes their hearts." The epic's first extended trope offers the image of the power of an orator to bridle the passions of an unruly, plebeian mob. Rhetoric here contains dangerous elements in Roman society, putting anarchic forces back into their place like the winds that Aeolus released from their cages. A member of the elite vested with personal authority uses speech to control internal threats to the state. It is a process where the top strata of society rein in those at the bottom, and speech suppresses wild disruptions.

Vergil turns a central trope within Republican Roman rhetoric inside out – exchanging what is figurative (the political storms roiling the state) for literal tempests,[1] while the real presence of the orator becomes, in more than one sense, a figure of speech. The reduction of the Republican orator (or, at least, a *version* of the Republican orator) to an image within the *Aeneid* is symbolic of a cultural shift that took place under the age of Augustus, a regime whose ascendancy Vergil's poem heralds. In the *Aeneid* the orator is an artifact from an earlier age, a person whose previous political and cultural importance has passed into memory. This essay will explore both the special role of oratory within the Roman Republic and, chiastically, how the Republic figures within Roman oratory.

Public speech was crucial to the civic life of Republican Rome. A powerful speech by one individual senator could change the government's whole policy. Eloquent advocates garnered personal fame and power from

---

[1] As the ancient commentator Servius notes on *Aeneid* 1.148.

their triumphs in Rome's politicized courts. The ability to speak with success in the deliberations of the senate, to defend one's clients from legal peril, and to influence popular opinion in the mass meetings where legislation was proposed, could realize an aspiring politician's ambitions. From oratory's practical function in the Republic's government there grew a cultural superstructure, an ideology that presented rhetoric and the Republic as dependent upon one another for their very existence. Long before he appeared in the *Aeneid*, the orator was already a symbol of the Roman Republic, that political system of elective magistracies that Romans believed began with the expulsion of Tarquin, the last king of Rome, conventionally in 509 BCE. This orator becomes canonized as the protector of the Republic against its regression into various sorts of tyranny, ranging from military dynasts to revolutionary tribunes of the plebs. This link between public speech and the Republican form of government is among the most enduring and deep-rooted ideas within Roman culture. So fixed was the notion that the orator was an agent of Republican government that Cicero, in his dialogue *Brutus* (a history of Roman oratory), makes Lucius Junius Brutus, traditionally the founder of the Republic, also Rome's first orator (*Brutus* 53). Similarly, Cicero presents Julius Caesar's dictatorship as the death of oratory in Rome – tyranny and oratory are mutually exclusive within this worldview.[2] In this account, rhetoric attends the birth of the Republic, protects the state at moments of peril, and, finally, perishes along with the Republic with the arrival of Augustus' principate.[3]

Vergil's plebs-pacifying speaker distills two defining qualities of Republican orator: he is a member of the elite and his powers of persuasion derive from his personal authority. The opportunity to engage in public speech – in the senate, law courts, or mass public meetings – was available to few Romans. For this speech to be consequential required *auctoritas*, that combination of esteem, credibility, and status that is characteristic of Roman social thought.[4] Roman legal process depended upon the prestige of the advocate who spoke on behalf of his client. The advocate's status within the community vested his words with an authority that could, and indeed did, take priority over the logical demonstration of a point at issue. Similarly, those who spoke in the senate were a small subset of its members, with a few leading senators called upon in a descending rank of prestige. Run-of-the-mill senators would generally be able to express their opinion only as *pedarii*, walking to join a speaker whose position they

---

[2] On tyranny vs. oratory in Greek and Roman thought see Habinek 2005a: 8–11.
[3] For surveys of Roman rhetoric see Kennedy 1972 and Clarke 1996.
[4] See Hellegouarc'h 1963: 295–320.

supported.[5] This hierarchical arrangement was even part of Roman public meetings. At these *contiones* there was no general discussion of proposed legislation; instead, members of the elite, those vested with *auctoritas* and *dignitas* (social standing), expressed their views to the people, attempting to win their support.[6]

In extreme cases personal *auctoritas* could not only make one's speech persuasive; it could make speech itself superfluous. Scipio Africanus avoided prosecution by noting at trial that it was the anniversary of his triumph over Carthage at the battle of Zama and then leading those in attendance in a procession to the Temple of Jupiter Optimus Maximus.[7] Part of the Roman aristocratic ideology held that the use of persuasive speech was an affront to one's station, and that a supreme position of *dignitas* such as Africanus enjoyed because of his soldiering would free one of the necessity of having to use speech in order to have one's way. This strand of thought within Roman culture maintains that public deliberation, especially the sort of speech which placed the orator's status in doubt because it appeared to resort to verbal trickery that played upon the audience's emotions, implied a deficiency of *auctoritas*. Another anecdote, of another Scipio (Nasica), relates how an aristocrat, in the face of a crowd's grumbling, merely said, "quiet, please, fellow citizens – for I understand better than you what policy is in the Republic's interests" (Valerius Maximus 3.7.3). The recording of such stories of how an authoritative person could change the course of a political debate merely on the strength of prestige shows how this idea appealed to the Roman imagination. These accounts provide some of the historical background that lies behind Vergil's crowd-controlling magistrate.[8]

The identity of the orator is part of a larger imagined community that he constructs in his speech, a *res publica* ("affair of the people") to whose nature and values Roman oratory repeatedly returns.[9] Roman orators rhetorically fashion a version of their state for which their proposed course of action is the natural or inevitable path. Even Scipio Africanus' non- or anti-rhetorical speech imagines a Rome in which a general who saved the state should have to submit himself to standard criminal prosecution. This ability to construct a community again depends upon *auctoritas*: the orator

[5] On procedure in the senate see Lintott 1999: 75–85.
[6] Morstein-Marx 2004 is an important new study of the *contio*. On limited freedom of speech in Rome see the classic study Wirzubski 1960.
[7] Livy 38.50–51; Valerius Maximus 3.7.1e; Aulus Gellius, *Attic Nights* 4.18.
[8] See Nippel 1995: 50.
[9] On the state as an "imagined community" see B. Anderson 1991 and Habinek 1998: 44f.

must have the credibility to engage in large-scale cultural definition and the authority to mark out the essential qualities of the Roman state and its values. This rhetorical manipulation of the *res publica* is present in all genres of Roman oratory. While deliberative speech would inevitably involve questions of the state and its policies, forensic and ceremonial oratory would also routinely engage political issues. Trials, specifically those in the so-called "public courts" (*iudicia publica*), as Andrew Riggsby has persuasively argued, conceptualized crime in terms of harm done to the state as a whole.[10] Even epideictic speech was not divorced from politics. A central goal of the funeral orations of the Roman nobility was to advertise the record of service to the Republic made by the deceased and his ancestors.[11]

However much individual Roman orators might present the nature of the Republic and its institutions and values as self-evident and transparent, in practice we find utterly divergent views of the state and its purpose. While Vergil canonizes the familiar image of a Roman magistrate asserting senatorial authority over the populace, there was a countervailing tradition of popularist rhetoric, a movement associated especially with the brothers Tiberius and Gaius Gracchus (late second century BCE), each a renowned orator who used his powers of speech to advocate for Rome's poor and disenfranchised. While murder by senatorial lynch mobs ended the career of each, the Gracchi represent an alternative view of the state and its function within the Roman rhetorical tradition. The specter of these revolutionary tribunes of the plebs haunts more conservative Roman orators, especially Cicero, where their popularist politics serve as a foil for his support of the senate.

The complexity of "Republican" discourse within Roman oratory – both for the Roman participants and for us seeking to understand it – is augmented by the fluidity of what *res publica* could mean.[12] Compounding this uncertainty is the fact that the Romans never codified their political constitution in writing. This unwritten constitution offered an obvious advantage to Rome's ruling elite, who could make claims about the state without fear of written contradiction.[13] Not just in oratory, where one might expect the opportunistic manipulation of the concept of *res publica* as it suited an individual speaker's persuasive goals, but even within Roman political theory the definition of the state could be remarkably nebulous. Cicero's

---

[10] Riggsby 1999.

[11] See Flower 1996: 128–58.

[12] See Schofield 1995: 66 on the semantic range of *res publica*. Cf. Habinek 1998: 72–73, who emphasizes its economic significance ("common wealth").

[13] See Brennan 2004, esp. 31–2.

dialogue *On the Republic* (*De re publica*), written from 54 to 51 BCE, offers a definition of the *res publica* as the *res populi*: "the affair (or "property") of the public is the affair (or "property") of the people." Even with the further qualifications that Cicero offers – that a *populus* is not just any gathering of people, but one united by law and common advantage – we are still left with a concept of the *res publica* that admits to a range of interpretations.

In speeches delivered in moments of serious political crisis, when the existence of the Republic appears to be at stake, we find particularly rich, often paradoxical, attempts to use rhetoric to fix a version of the state that will withstand assaults on its integrity. When orators present their words as all that stands between the state and obliteration, rhetoric fulfills its most vital political function: the very preservation of the Republic. This sort of oratory rests at the top of the ancient rhetorical theorists' taxonomies of style – the most serious emergencies demand the highest style of speech. The *Rhetoric to Herennius* (an anonymous treatise dating from the early first century BCE)[14] offers a taxonomy of three stylistic registers (*grauis*, *mediocris*, and *adtenuata*) which corresponds to this hierarchy: the high style appears in a case of treason that involves the very existence of the state; the middle makes an inquiry into whether allies revolted from Rome at the instigation of parties within Rome;[15] the simple style tackles a case of illegal assault (4.11–16). The author of this text thus establishes a scale of rhetorical embellishment to match the question involved. Tacitus, writing his *Dialogue on Orators* in the Rome of the emperors, looked back to the Republic as the high point of Roman oratorical achievement. Yet it was, Tacitus argues, precisely the political turmoil of the period that fostered oratorical genius.[16] This "rhetoric of crisis" has both a political and an aesthetic dimension – great matters give rise to great speech, and great speech can safeguard the Republic.[17]

In such high style and high-stakes speeches as the *Catilinarians* and *Philippics*, Cicero negotiates the fundamental issues of the nature of the Roman Republic and the place of rhetoric within it. Here Cicero also does something surprising: he shows himself willing to jettison essential aspects of the Republican constitution in an effort to save the state as a whole. Cicero's willingness to sacrifice aspects of the Republic he deems inessential to its ultimate survival shows the orator's willingness to offer radical reinterpretations of the Republic within his oratory. The series of speeches

[14] On the date of the treatise see Corbeill 2002: 31–34.
[15] See Krostenko 2004 on this middle style.
[16] Tacitus, *Dialogue on Orators* 37.
[17] The "rhetoric of crisis" is Wooten's designation (Wooten 1983).

that Cicero delivered against Catiline mark a decisive and definitive event within the intersection of politics and rhetoric in the Roman Republic. Here Cicero canonizes himself as the staunch defender of the Republic, a figure embodying the best traditions of senatorial authority, guiding the state through dire peril.

The central constitutional question within the Catilinarian crisis and its aftermath is to what extent the senate has the authority to empower the consul to override fundamental civil rights in order to see that the Republic itself survives. In the early stages of the emergency (October 21, 63 BCE) Cicero called together the senate and it issued a so-called "final decree of the senate" (*Senatus Consultum Ultimum*). This decree advised the consul to make sure that the Republic would come to no harm.[18] As Cicero reminds the senate in the first of his speeches against Catiline (*Catiline* 1.4), the SCU, as instrument of senatorial authority, arose from the perceived threat from the popularist tribunes of the plebs, Tiberius and Gaius Gracchus. While the senate first used this decree in 121 BCE to eliminate Gaius Gracchus, the younger of the brothers, the earlier events that led to Tiberius' murder provide context essential for understanding how the "ultimate decree" came into being. In 133 BCE Scipio Nasica, then head of the Roman state religion (Pontifex Maximus), proposed in the senate that the consul protect the *res publica* by taking up arms against Tiberius Gracchus who was rumored to be preparing to seize control of the state as a *regnum*.[19] An expert in law, the presiding consul, P. Mucius Scaevola, refused to do so on the grounds that such action would violate Gracchus' civil rights since he had not been condemned of any crime in a court of law. Undeterred by Scaevola's legal scruples, the Pontifex Nasica, having cinched up his toga as if to perform a sacrifice,[20] led a mob who responded in the affirmative to his call that "all who wish the *res publica* to be safe follow me."[21] This posse stormed the Capitol and proceeded to bludgeon to death Tiberius Gracchus along with many of his followers, ignoring the tribune's sacrosanct status. The scenario is one where a religious authority, acting as a private citizen, used his personal *dignitas* and *auctoritas* to improvise a solution to a crisis in which the political structures of the senate were unable or unwilling to respond.[22]

---

[18] On the SCU see Nippel 1995: 57–69. The term SCU comes from a joke by Caesar (see *Civil War* 1.5.3 and 7.5, and cf. Lintott 1999: 89).

[19] On Ti. Gracchus' aspiring for a *regnum* see Wirszubski 1960: 62 and n. 3.

[20] See Nippel 1995: 58 and cf. Badian 1972: 725–26.

[21] Valerius Maximus 3.2.17. Cf. Nippel 1995: 61.

[22] See Badian 1972.

When the younger Gracchus Gaius seized control of the Aventine with a group of his followers in 121, the senate for the first time issued an ultimate decree advising the consul Opimius to take whatever measures necessary to preserve the *res publica*. This measure, it should be emphasized, like other senatorial decrees, did not have the status of law, but instead was the official advice of the senate.[23] Of dubious constitutionality, the SCU was a measure invented on the fly to respond to an immediate threat to the senate's authority. It did not protect Opimius from subsequent legal action in 120 when he was accused of putting to death a Roman citizen without trial, though he was acquitted.[24] From its inception in 121 until Cicero's use of its authority to execute the captured followers of Catiline in 63, the SCU could not avoid the appearance of being a convenient pretext for the senate to resort to the force of arms when it felt threatened – a device used to suspend the usual functioning of the *res publica* on the grounds that to do otherwise would imperil the state as a whole.[25] As with Rome's unwritten constitution, the SCU allowed orators to debate the nature of the imagined community they sought to protect.

The issue of the SCU and the validity of executions performed in its name was already a matter for legal and political debate before the Catilinarian affair arose. In 63 BCE Julius Caesar had instigated legal proceedings against C. Rabirius on the grounds that he, as consul working under the mandate of the SCU, had murdered the tribune Saturninus in 100 BCE.[26] The tribune of the plebs, Labienus, revived the ancient legal practice (one dating from Rome's regal period) of trying Rabirius before *duumuiri*, in this case, Caesar and his cousin L. Julius Caesar, consul in the previous year. If Rabirius were found guilty, the *duumuiri* would have imposed the extraordinary punishment of scourging and public crucifixion upon the now aged Rabirius for a crime that he was alleged to have committed some thirty-seven years ago. That Caesar chose to prosecute Rabirius for the improper application of the SCU in order to suppress an insurrection nearly forty years ago, and, correspondingly, that Cicero as consul (along with his colleague Hortensius – forming a senatorial legal dream-team) would be called upon to defend Rabirius demonstrates how the SCU and its uses were still a matter of political and legal controversy. At stake was not just the culpability of an elderly and inconsequential senator in a nearly four-decade-old murder, but

[23] See Nippel 1995: 63.
[24] See Nippel 1995: 65. Cf. T. N. Mitchell 1991: 208.
[25] On the legal status of the SCU see Lintott 1999: 90.
[26] Cape 2002: 129–36 offers an illuminating discussion of this case. See T. N. Mitchell 1979: 205–206 for a summary of these events with earlier bibliography.

the limits of the senate's authority to act in crises where it feels it must take extreme action. Moreover, the SCU is negotiated by rhetoric at every stage. Its authorization was debated in the senate; the consul could use oratory to justify his actions while charged with its authority; and an ex-consul might find himself subject to criminal prosecution for misusing the powers the decree granted. The SCU can be seen as a sort of blank check in which the senate grants the consul extraordinary powers, yet for which he could ultimately be held to account.

The office of consul, though emblematic of the Roman Republic, ironically gave its holders extraordinary powers that could allow them to act like kings.[27] The paradox of Cicero's situation in the *Catilinarians* is that the measures he takes in suppressing the conspiracy are ones perilously close to those of a tyrant, that figure against which the Republic and its oratorical traditions defined themselves. While the actual threat that Catiline's conspiracy posed was and is still open to debate, the occasion allowed Cicero to engage the high rhetorical register and present an image of Rome facing as dangerous a crisis as any in history. High-style speech, as Cicero would later describe it in his treatise *Orator*, has the power to overwhelm an audience, uprooting fixed ideas and replacing them with new ones.[28] To eliminate Catiline from the state Cicero uses the leverage of fundamental cultural categories and narratives, not in the parsing of subtle legal distinctions. Cicero takes the intrinsic *auctoritas* of the office, adopts a Demosthenic rhetoric of crisis, and aspires to speak with the authority of a Scipio Africanus. He makes himself the master of a variety of voices: Roman tradition, the Republic, and the Fatherland (*Patria*) as a whole, a technique that allows the state to express its approval for Cicero's use of the senate's ultimate decree (*Against Catiline* 1.18; 1.27–29).[29] Cicero thus confidently presents himself as an unquestionable authority on the powers of the SCU, which, but for Cicero's own inaction (see the rationalization at *Against Catiline* 1.4), would have meant Catiline's execution which had as precedent the deaths of the Gracchi.[30]

The sublime rhetorical register allows Cicero the imaginative license to telescope the history of the Republic, transporting his audience to Romulus'

[27] Cicero presents the power of the consulate in regal terms in *On the Republic* 2.56 and *On the Laws* 3.8 (yet see the comments of Dyck 2004a: 456–57). See also Wirszubski 1960: 21–22. Cf. Cape 1995: 267 on 4.19.

[28] Cicero, *Orator* 97. On the impersonation of the *res publica* as appropriate to the high rhetorical register see *Orator* 85.

[29] See Batstone 1994: 219.

[30] *Against Catiline* 1.3 and 1.4.

foundation of the city to argue that Catiline constitutes the greatest threat in its history. The scene setting for this motif is established by the fact that the senate is meeting, not in the Curia in the Forum, but in the Temple of Jupiter Stator, a cult site of great antiquity reputedly founded by Romulus himself to celebrate a victory over the Sabines.[31] Using this resonant locale Cicero is able to imply, in the first of the *Catilinarians*, that his role in saving Rome is like Romulus' in founding it. Cicero's attempts to rid Rome of Catiline, as Thomas Habinek has argued, becomes like Romulus' elimination of his brother Remus, a scapegoat whose removal will secure the integrity of the state.[32] By the third speech Cicero, with characteristic immodesty, suggests that the people of Rome, both now in the future, ought to hold in similar esteem both Romulus, the founder of Rome, and Cicero, its preserver (*Against Catiline* 3.2). The *supplicatio* the senate offered Cicero emphasized his role as the state's liberator, implicitly linking Cicero with the likes of Brutus, who freed the state from the tyranny of the kings.[33] In the fourth speech Cicero claims that the unanimity of Romans of all classes against Catiline and his followers is like nothing Rome has experienced since its founding.[34] Cicero writes himself into Rome's foundational narrative in the *Catilinarians*, making himself a new Romulus. Here Rome's origin and present meet. Romulus' role within Roman political thought is as the embodiment of Rome's dominant patrician class over and against the proletarian Remus.[35] By striking a Romulean pose, Cicero thus reprises the narratives of the senate's opposition to revolutionary figures such as the Gracchi.

As fratricide and Rome's first king, however, Romulus is a role dangerous for any Roman political leaders to play.[36] With this motif folded into a series of speeches composed in the sublime oratorical register and with claims that the SCU gave Cicero the authority to overlook fundamental civic rights in order to maintain the integrity of the state, the stage is set for Cicero to act tyrannically, or, at the least, to allow his enemies to accuse him of doing so. The imagined Rome that Cicero constructs in the Catilinarians threatens to become a dystopia. When Cicero says that he hopes that Rome's citizenry would have their feelings about the Republic marked upon

[31] See Vasaly 1993: 41–59. Cf. Habinek 1998: 82.
[32] Habinek 1998: 69–87 (esp. 83–87).
[33] *Against Catiline* 3.14.
[34] For Cicero the state should have a harmonious balance between the social classes (*concordia ordinum*). See Wood 1988: 193–200 and Strasburger 1956.
[35] See Wiseman 1995.
[36] See Habinek 1998: 58, with other bibliography.

their foreheads (*Against Catiline* 1.33) he shows an alarming authoritarian impulse. The solution to the secret plotting of Catiline, who appears at the beginning of this speech as marking out for death each member of the senate (*Against Catiline* 1.2), is to imagine a servile citizenry bearing brands that show their political intentions.[37] Such are the perils and paradoxes of powerful rhetoric trained against enemies of the state: Cicero, the would-be defender of the Republic, can become its antithesis, the tyrant. Julius Caesar, in Sallust's version of his speech debating the fate of the captive Catilinarians, subtly hints at the tyrannical precedent that executing the prisoner might set when he expresses the concern that, while Cicero's own conduct is beyond reproach, some other consul in the future might use the senate decree as a pretext for illegitimate violence (Sallust, *Catiline* 51.35–36). Cicero's enemies would less obliquely turn his Romulean stance back against him: an anonymous invective refers to him as the "Romulus of Arpinum" (with scorn for his municipal origin like that which Catiline expressed when he called Cicero a "resident alien"). Cicero himself reports in the *On behalf of Sulla* that Sulla's prosecutor Torquatus called Cicero the "the third foreign king of Rome" (after Tarquin and Numa).[38] Cicero's "regal" rhetoric had immediate negative consequences culminating in his exile for the unlawful execution of the Catilinarians by his enemy Clodius Pulcher, tribune of the plebs in 58 BCE.[39] In Clodius' version of Rome there is no haven for those who kill citizens without trial.

Cicero's attitude towards rhetoric within politics, amid circumstances where the very existence of the Republic is in question, is one of exceptional flexibility in the policies he proposes, so long as those policies, in his judgment, advance the long-term welfare of the state. In this regard Cicero found a foil in Marcus Cato, the staunch defender of traditional Roman Republican values whose speech (according to Sallust) in favor of the execution of the Catilinarians won over the senate. While admiring Cato's patriotism and the consistency of his policies, Cicero found his intransigent adherence to the letter of the law dangerous to the state's best interests. Cicero's Cato (as he famously put it in a letter to Atticus in 60 BCE) "sometimes hurts the Republic out of extraordinary commitment to consistency (*fides*), for he speaks in the senate as if he is living in Plato's Republic and not in Romulus' shithole."[40] Cicero had no illusions about

---

[37] See Batstone 1994: 260.

[38] [Sallust], *Against Cicero* 7: *Romule Arpinas*; Sallust, *Catiline* 31.7: *inquilinus ciuis urbis Romae*; Cicero, *On behalf of Sulla* 22: *tertium peregrinum regem*.

[39] For these events see T. N. Mitchell 1991: 127–43. On Clodius see Tatum 1999.

[40] *Letters to Atticus* 2.1.8. Cf. *Letters to Atticus* 1.18.7.

where he was, seeming to revel in his rhetorical ability to negotiate through this malodorous landscape.[41] Although allies in the issue of the punishment of the captive followers of Catiline in December of 63, a month earlier Cato and Cicero clashed over the matter of accusations of electoral bribery against the incumbent consul Lucius Licinius Murena.[42] Even though Murena was almost certainly guilty of these charges, Cicero took part in his defense in order to assure that a consul sympathetic to his policies regarding Catiline would succeed him.

The defense that Cicero stages pits his own deft rhetorical improvisation versus Cato's dogmatic Stoic inflexibility. In the face of Cato's accusations of inconsistency (Cicero's support of Murena is not in accord with his stalwart opposition to Catiline and the legislation he passed in his consulate against *ambitus*),[43] Cicero parodies Cato's rigid adherence to Stoic ethics as well as the similarly constrictive devotion to the letter of the law of Cato's colleague, Servius Sulpicius. In arguing for a more adaptable, more humane view of legal justice Cicero conjures from Roman historical memory the accusation that the elder Cato (the great-grandfather of this Cato) made against Servius Galba, a case where Galba secured an acquittal by appealing to the sympathy of his judges.[44] Cicero presents this case as evidence of the suspicion that the Roman people have against overly powerful and prestigious prosecutors, thus using Cato's extraordinary *auctoritas*, which Cicero claims he fears more than the accusation itself, against him.

Ultimately the case boiled down to conflicting interpretations of what the Republic requires from its leaders. In the face of Cato's claims that the Republic has called him to this accusation against Murena, Cicero counters that such a view is shortsighted when the still-looming threat of Catiline imperils the very existence of the state. In a gesture like that of Scipio Nasica's request for his audience's attention since he knows better what is in the state's interests, Cicero asks the jurors to listen to him in his capacity as consul, a consul who spends his days and nights thinking about the Republic.[45] In this way Cicero calls upon his consular *auctoritas* in the hope that it will trump Cato's considerable personal *auctoritas*.[46]

[41] See Rose 1995: 375: "the foundation of his whole being is this very commitment to be as involved as possible in the political life of a society that he perceives as hopelessly corrupt."
[42] On this crime (*ambitus*) see Riggsby 1999: 21–49. Cf. M. C. Alexander 2002: 119–27. For an an analysis of Cicero's rhetorical strategies in the *On behalf of Lucius Murena* see Leeman 1982.
[43] *On behalf of Lucius Murena* 3.
[44] *On behalf of Lucius Murena* 59. On this case see Cicero, *Brutus* 89–90.
[45] *On behalf of Lucius Murena* 78.
[46] Cicero explicitly bases his plea upon his consular authority (*On behalf of Lucius Murena* 86).

By defending Murena in this fashion Cicero essentially passes over the question of his client's guilt. He requests that his listeners rely upon his consular wisdom to foresee the longer-term dangers that a successful prosecution of Murena would pose to the Republic, a peril to which Cato, under the sway of Stoic principles and his youthful stubbornness, is blind. Cato's unnatural, harsh intransigence (*On behalf of Lucius Murena* 60), Cicero says, will eventually find itself softened by the experience of the real world that comes with time.[47] In turn, Cato (as Cicero himself reports) cautions against seeking "ultimate power, ultimate authority, the helm of the Republic by soothing people's feelings, softening their hearts, and providing them with pleasures." Cato calls such irresponsible and unprincipled pursuit of power pandering, not statecraft. Murena's trial thus offers two opposing views of Rome: in Cato's, principled adherence to ethical values holds sway; in Cicero's, political pragmatism dominates. Cicero hoped that the emotional impact of such resonant terms as "peace, calm, harmony, freedom, security, life" (*On behalf of Lucius Murena* 78: *pacis, oti, concordiae, libertatis, salutis, uitae*) would trump Cato's stronger legal case, and he proved right: Murena was unanimously acquitted.[48] The jurors assented to Cicero's image of Rome and rejected Cato's.

After his defeat in the civil war against Caesar in April of 46 Cato committed suicide at Utica in North Africa rather than allow Caesar to pardon him with an ostentatious display of clemency. He became a martyr to the cause of republicanism, a paradigm of the Roman statesman's opposition to tyranny even to the point of death. Cicero celebrated Cato's valor in his treatise *Cato*, a work to which Caesar responded in an *Anti-Cato*.[49] The death of Cato, in the words of Catherine Steel, was for Romans an occasion for "discussing the *res publica* and their place within it."[50] Cato's refusal to allow Caesar an opportunity to pardon him signals his refusal to assent to Caesar's hegemony – such granting of forgiveness is the prerogative of tyrants.[51] His principled suicide caused Cicero both admiration and dishonor: in his letters he writes that with Cato dead he is ashamed to be alive.[52]

Instead of suicide, Cicero chose to praise Caesar's decision to show clemency to Marcus Claudius Marcellus (consul of 51), an enemy of Caesar,

---

[47] *On behalf of Lucius Murena* 65.
[48] Quintilian, *Institutes* 6.1.35.
[49] See T. N. Mitchell 1991: 280 and n. 149.
[50] Steel 2005: 34.
[51] See Habicht 1990 on Plutarch, *Cato the Younger* 66.2.
[52] See *Letters to his Friends* 4.13.2, *Letters to Atticus* 13.28.2. Cf. Habicht 1990: 72.

though he had taken no active role in the civil war. Though the name *On behalf of Marcellus* suggests a defense speech, it is instead a panegyric addressed to Caesar, flattering him in extreme terms, going so far as to say he is like a god. In a letter describing the circumstances of the original speech that Cicero improvised in the senate house (and thus breaking a silence of public speech that he had held since his defense of Milo in 52), Cicero calls this so fine a day that he "seemed to see some likeness of the Republic being reborn, so to speak."[53] In the published version, Cicero offers Caesar extraordinary admiration and holds out the promise of even further glory if he should be willing to restore the ruin of the Republic.[54] Cicero hopes that his admiration will sway the dictator to restore some form of Republican government, some constitutional arrangement in which Cicero's voice could still be heard. The *On behalf of Marcellus* gives us Republican oratory at the extreme end of the spectrum: it is not a rhetoric of crisis in which Cicero defends the Republic from peril, but rather rhetoric is used to cajole a tyrant into ceding his power to a Republican form of government. Writing to Marcellus in exile, Cicero goes so far as to hold himself up as a model of responsible action under this new political circumstance, yielding to the current state of affairs.[55] The apparent volte-face that Cicero makes here – lavish praise of a dictator and a willingness to serve a regime, even lending his intellectual labor to the construction a new state,[56] to an extent that his Republican principles ought to have made impossible – has led readers, both in antiquity and now, to suspect that Cicero cannot mean what he writes to be taken at face value. There must be some covert, figured meaning that would salvage Cicero's political consistency.[57] Yet Cicero has repeatedly shown himself as an orator willing to use persuasive speech to salvage some essence of the Republic, while jettisoning the inessential. Cicero's Republic is an imagined community open to constant rhetorical manipulation and negotiation. These bouquets thrown at the feet of the victorious Caesar simply provide an extreme instance of Cicero's confidence in his powers of persuasion to shape political reality.

---

[53] *Letters to his Friends* 4.4.3 (to Servius Sulpicius).

[54] *On behalf of Marcellus* 10.

[55] See *Letters to his Friends* 4.8.2 and the illuminating comments of Steel 2005: 100f.

[56] *Letters to his Friends* 9.2.5.

[57] Dyer 1990, basing his reading on the Gronovian scholiast's claim (Stangl 1964: 295f.) that some read the speech as a covert criticism of Caesar in the form of praise, offers the provocative thesis that the speech goes so far as to encourage its readers to assassinate the dictator. Yet see Levene 1997 and Winterbottom 2002 for convincing arguments for taking the speech on its own terms.

With Julius Caesar's assassination in 44 BCE Cicero re-entered a political arena that granted him an opportunity to renew his consular voice and use his Republican rhetoric, now against Caesar's lieutenant Marcus Antonius. These *Philippics* allowed Cicero to revive his Demosthenic persona and to provide a capstone to his claim to be the near embodiment of the Republic, boasting at the start of the *Second Philippic* that in twenty years there has been no enemy of the Republic who has not also simultaneously declared war on Cicero.[58] Yet even here Cicero was forced to compromise principles in the service of the ultimate salvation of the Republic. He cozied up to Octavian with praise like that he gave Caesar, singing of his divine qualities, presenting him as the hope for the Republic's salvation, and supporting his bid for *imperium*, admittance to the senate, and the ability to run for higher office.[59] Cicero's proscription by the triumvirs and his brutal murder showed that he miscalculated his rhetoric's power to impose his image of the Republic upon this changed political landscape.

Cicero's final stand on behalf of the Republic in his speeches against Antony secured his heroization as the orator who embodied the Republic and its values, his contradictions and compromises largely forgotten. In the lecture halls under the empire declaimers repeatedly returned to the scene of his death, a heroic last stand where Cicero bravely faced the executioner's sword.[60] Seneca, writing under the reign of the emperor Nero, uses Cicero as an example of the capriciousness of fate (*On the Shortness of Life* 5.1):

> M. Cicero inter Catilinas, Clodios iactatus Pompeiosque et Crassos, partim manifestos inimicos, partim dubios amicos, dum fluctuatur cum re publica et illam pessum euntem tenet.

> Marcus Cicero, tossed about amid Catilines, Clodiuses, Pompeys and Crassuses, some out-and-out enemies, others vacillating friends, while he is pitched about along with the Republic, he holds it tight as it sinks to the bottom.

---

[58] *Philippics* 2.1.

[59] See *Philippics* 3.3, 3.5, 5.43. Cf. Habicht 1990: 81: "Cicero violated the constitution and abandoned the principles of republican government which he himself had taught and for which, he insisted, he was fighting right now." Later, Augustus would give nodding acknowledgment to Cicero's rhetoric on his behalf in the *Philippics*. Cf. *Record of his Accomplishments* 1.1: *exercitum priuato consilio et privata impensa comparaui*, and Cicero, *Philippics* 3.3: *firmissimum exercitum ... comparauit* and 3.5, *rem publicam priuato consilio – neque enim fieri potuit aliter – Caesar liberauit*. It is tempting to speculate (with Habicht 1990: 98–99) that Cicero gave Augustus a crucial strategy for his rhetoric of reviving the Republic.

[60] On Cicero's role in these rhetorical exercises see Richlin 1997; Kaster 1998; Dugan 2005: 70–74. On declamation generally see the rich studies of Beard 1993 and Gunderson 2003.

Seneca presents Cicero as a heroic captain going down with the ship of state, a tragic variation of a favorite image for the Republic within Cicero's writings,[61] and so he has Cicero perform a variety of *deuotio*, the practice where a Roman general would sacrifice himself on behalf of his troops.[62] Like Vergil's image of the orator in the *Aeneid*, Seneca's reuse of a nautical trope from Roman Republican oratory signals a cultural shift. In Seneca's essay Cicero's ship of state becomes both a metaphor for death – both Cicero's and the Republic's – and a dead metaphor – Cicero's ship of state had sailed. At the helm Seneca stations an idealized Cicero, whose actual practice, far from sinking into the abyss with his craft, was to toss over-board principles and constitutional provisions deemed extraneous in the hope that such sacrifices would allow the state's ultimate survival. Cicero was confident that, so long as he had a voice in the state, he could use the power of his rhetoric to refashion his Republic even while making such compromises. The paradoxes that this choice brought to Cicero demon-strate the limits of rhetoric to preserve a state lurching toward Augustus' reign.[63]

Suggested further reading

Historical background: P. A. Brunt, *The Fall of the Roman Republic and Related Essays* (Oxford, 1988); M. Beard and M. Crawford, *Rome in the Late Republic: Problems and Interpretations*, second edition (London, 1999); J. Osgood, *Caesar's Legacy: Civil War and the Emergence of the Roman Empire* (Cambridge, 2006).

The Republican Roman constitution: A. W. Lintott, *The Constitution of the Roman Republic* (Oxford, 1999); T. C. Brennan, "Power and Process under the Republican 'Constitution,'" in H. I. Flower, ed., *The Cambridge Companion to the Roman Republic* (Cambridge, 2004) 31–65.

The power of the people and oratory at popular assemblies: F. Millar, *The Crowd in Rome in the Late Republic* (Ann Arbor, 1998); H. Mouritsen, *Plebs and Politics in Late Republican Rome* (Cambridge, 2001); R. Morstein-Marx, *Mass Oratory and Political Power in the Late Roman Republic* (Cambridge, 2004).

---

[61] See Williams 2003: 145.

[62] Cf. Dyck 2004b for Cicero's use of the trope of *deuotio* in the speeches following his exile.

[63] I owe many thanks to Erik Gunderson, whose insightful editorial assistance substantially improved this chapter.

Cicero's political theory: H. Strasburger, *Concordia Ordinum: Eine Untersuchung zur Politik Ciceros* (Amsterdam, 1956); N. Wood, *Cicero's Social and Political Thought* (Berkeley, 1988); E. Asmis, "A New Kind of Model: Cicero's Roman Constitution in *De Republica*," *American Journal of Philology* 126 (2005) 377–416; J. Connolly, *The State of Speech: Rhetoric and Political Thought in Ancient Rome* (Princeton, 2007).

The politics of Cicero's rhetorical works, and Cicero as a cultural figure: D. Konstan, "Rhetoric and the Crisis of Legitimacy in Cicero's Catilinarian Orations," in T. Poulakos, ed., *Rethinking the History of Rhetoric: Multidisciplinary Essays on the Rhetorical Tradition* (Boulder, 1993) 11–30; T. Habinek, "Ideology for an Empire in the Prefaces to Cicero's Dialogues," *Ramus* 23 (1994) 55–67; E. Narducci, *Cicerone e l'eloquenza romana: Retorica e progetto culturale* (Rome, 1997); C. Steel, *Reading Cicero: Genre and Performance in Late Republican Rome* (London, 2005).

The later influence of Roman republicanism: F. Millar, *The Roman Republic in Political Thought* (Hanover and London, 2002); A. M. Gowing, *Empire and Memory. The Representation of the Roman Republic in Imperial Culture* (Cambridge, 2005). M. S. Kempshall, "*De Re Publica* 1.39 in Medieval and Renaissance Political Thought," in J. G. F. Powell and J. A. North, eds., *Cicero's Republic* (London, 2001) 99–135.

11

DAVID ROSENBLOOM

Staging rhetoric in Athens

Why tragic and comic poets, with their divergent approaches to drama, converge in their ambivalence to democratic oratory, is a fascinating question, since on the face of it, dramatists and orators have much in common.[1] Like orators, dramatists were citizens of Athens authorized by the democracy and occupied a prestigious place within the city's speech regime. Dramatists, like orators, competed for victory before mass audiences, though five judges randomly selected from a pool of ten determined victory in dramatic contests, not a majority of spectators.[2] Their audiences, though not identical, overlapped; Demosthenes calls jurors as witnesses to events that transpired in the theater (21.18, 226). As Simon Goldhill writes, "to be in an audience is not just a thread in the city's social fabric, it is a fundamental *political act*."[3] Most scholars believe that performances of tragedies and comedies at festivals in honor of Dionysus, god of wine and life-giving liquids, were in some sense political. How political were they? This essay discusses the anatomy of fifth-century theater's negative engagements with democratic oratory and orators and suggests that its symbolic violence towards democratic speech regimes aroused a potentially anti-democratic nostalgia for a fictionalized time of unitary socioeconomic, political, and

---

[1] Recent treatments of the relationship between oratory and tragedy in English differ on this question. Ober and Strauss 1990, esp. 270, argue that shared symbols in drama and oratory transcended an aesthetics/politics divide and expanded the meaning of citizenship. Bers 1994, esp. 182–90, stresses the normative differentiation of forensic oratory and tragedy against the grain of the genre's increasing openness to it. Hall 1995 stresses affinities between oratory and drama. Halliwell 1997: 141 argues that tragedy testifies to "the ambivalence and instability which underlay Athenian experience of rhetoric." Pelling 2005, esp. 99–100, sees the "misfiring" of rhetoric in tragedy as similar to uses of tragedy in oratory: each serves the other as an exemplar of deviant speech.

[2] See Pickard-Cambridge 1968: 95–99; Csapo and Slater 1995: 157–65. For the audience's role in determining the victor, see Wallace 1997.

[3] Goldhill 1994: 352.

moral orders, the time of the fathers expressed in the slogans "ancestral constitution" and "ancestral laws."

Tragic poets dramatized episodes from Panhellenic myth for a Panhellenic audience; for the most part, they staged a pre-democratic world, which featured institutions and forms of personal authority outmoded and indeed outlawed in contemporary democratic society. Within this frame, tragedies stage the world of the *polis*, political choices (such as to go to war) and their consequences. Political speech and debate, as Aristotle noted (*Poetics* 1450b6–7), were the stuff of tragedy. Hence tragedies can reinforce, question, or even subvert the norms of political life. Indeed, the canonical rhetorical effects of tragedy – the emotions of pity and fear – have political undertones. Tragedy induces civic and civilized emotions. Fear, according to Aristotle, prompts deliberation (*Rhetoric* 1383a6–8). Pity requires self-identification with and differentiation from others' pain and judgments about the moral worth and desert of those who suffer (*Rhetoric* 1385b11–1386a3; *Poetics* 1453a5).[4] Pity was central to the rhetoric of the democratic law courts. Defendants sought acquittal through appeals to pity and sometimes staged supplications at the end of their defenses, displaying their wailing children and family members before the jurors (e.g. Aeschines 2.179–81; cf. Aristophanes, *Wasps* 560–75, 975–81).[5] Pity was a norm of democratic power: the demos was open to compassion for the suffering of the well born, wealthy, and successful who generally litigated cases. Compassion lay at the heart of the city's collective identity. Demosthenes defines "pitying the weak" as an essential element of the *polis*'s character (24.171). Tragedies prompted audiences to pity the strong reduced to weakness by failures of judgment, the brutality of the more powerful, and the malice of the gods and the weak as victims of cruelty contrary to Hellenic law and custom.

By the early 420s political discourse seeks to exclude the core of tragic rhetoric from its arena. When the political orator Cleon, "the most violent of citizens and by far the most persuasive man to the demos," according to Thucydides (3.36.6), adjures the assembly in 427 to annihilate Mytilene for revolting from the empire, he warns the demos not to fall victim to the "three things most disadvantageous to empire – pity, the pleasure of speeches, and noble fairness" (3.40.2). In effect, he defines tragic values as antithetical to those of Athenian imperialism and as obstacles to its interests. Cleon depicts democracy as incapable of ruling an empire and

---

[4] For pity as a judgmental emotion, see Konstan 2001.
[5] See Johnstone 1999: 109–25.

views empire as tyranny based upon force (3.37.1–2). This type of political oratory, which alienates the discourse of power and collective self-interest from the values of tragic performance, partly explains ambivalence towards orators and the rhetoric of politics after Pericles' death in 429.

Tragedians presented plays before citizens and foreigners at the City Dionysia. On the rare occasions when Athens appears on the tragic stage, the city is an object of praise. Even if tragedians were inclined to blame the city, it is unlikely that the demos would allow itself to be criticized before foreigners in a tragedy.[6] Moreover, the case of Phrynichus, who was fined for staging the *Capture of Miletus* after the Persians besieged and sacked the Miletus in 494, set a precedent: tragedy did not remind the Athenians of their "own pains" (Herodotus 6.21).[7] When Athenian-style democracy intrudes into non-Athenian contexts in Euripides, however, the results are lamentable. Such plays as *Hecuba*, *Suppliants*, *Trojan Women*, and *Orestes* pique discontent at the moral failing of democratic speech regimes. Apart from the *Suppliants*, characters and choruses are critics of non-Athenian regimes. Their authority is questionable or they alienate the audience. They are external critics and their voices ambiguous.

By contrast, the comic poet functioned, as Josiah Ober argues, as an internal critic of the democracy.[8] Comedians crafted fictionalized personas for themselves, formally in the parabasis of a play, where the chorus comes forward to address the audience in the voice of the poet, among other voices, and informally, by identification with "heroes" such as Dikaiopolis in the *Acharnians* (377–82).[9] An essential link between comedy and democracy was a feature of debates about comedy's Megarian origins (Aristotle, *Poetics* 1448a29–b3), and comedy was incorporated into the City Dionysia in 486 BCE, within the first two decades of Athenian democracy. Eventually the genre exploited the democratic value of *parrhēsia* ("freedom of speech," literally "saying everything") to a virtually unlimited degree.[10] Comic *parrhēsia* was not necessarily authorized by the demos; rather, comic poets negotiated limits of free speech in their plays.[11] Comic ridicule of named Athenians was fierce and slanderous even at the City Dionysia, when

---

[6] [Xenophon], *Constitution of the Athenians* 2.18 claims that the demos did not allow itself to be mocked in comedy. Isocrates 8.14 states the opposite view.

[7] See Rosenbloom 1993.

[8] Ober 1998, esp. 122–26.

[9] For the parabasis, see Hubbard 1991; for the comic hero, see Whitman 1964: 21–58.

[10] There is evidence that Athens passed laws to limit ridicule of individuals by name in comedy. Halliwell 1991a; Csapo and Slater 1995: 176–80 collect and challenge this evidence.

[11] Goldhill 1991, esp. 188–200.

foreigners were present; it was superlatively obscene, personal, and topical at the Lenaea, a festival for Dionysus which citizens and resident aliens attended (Aristophanes, *Acharnians* 496–508).

At both the City Dionysia and the Lenaea, comedians exploited their freedom of speech to revile with a violence unparalleled for any other citizen a type of democratic orator – the "demagogue" or "defender of the demos" – who pledged love, friendship, and goodwill to the demos and claimed to act solely in its interests.[12] Comedy configured four of its biggest targets of ridicule as orators of this type, also reviling them as men who made and sold commodities or performed services for a living: Cleon "the tanner," Hyperbolos "the lamp-maker," Cleophon "the lyre-maker," and Androcles, mocked as a day-laborer, cut-purse, or prostitute; all but Cleon were killed in politically motivated violence. The three, styled "defenders of the demos," were all murdered in oligarchic violence in 411 and 404.[13] Comedy favors leaders who derived their authority from sources external to their oratory, who do not sell commodities or services, and who do not adopt the rhetoric of a "defender of the demos."[14]

Fifth-century comic ridicule of this type of orator is virtually identical with the discourse of abuse that orators employ against one another in public cases adjudicated in the fourth-century courts: they ridicule one another as slaves, foreigners, uneducated and uncultured, pathics and pros-titutes, sycophants, sophists, bribe-takers, scapegoats, and traitors.[15] Never-theless there are key differences. Comedies suspend the assembly's decrees, rejoice in the closure of the jury courts, where the demos's power was most heavily concentrated, ferociously revile orators of a certain type by name (not merely a single opponent), and violently expel voluntary prosecutors of public crimes as sycophants – malicious prosecutors for profit.[16] The legal trial is a dialogic process between members of a leadership class under the authority of the demos; comedy is one-way abuse of a specific subclass of leaders which undermines the demos's authority.

Hostility towards democratic speech regimes is all the more surprising since Athenian oratory and sophistic teaching on rhetoric influenced the drama of Euripides and Aristophanes, so much so that critics speak of their rhetorical or sophistic drama. Self-conscious rhetorical performances

---

[12] See Connor 1992, esp. 109–10; Finley 1988.

[13] See Rosenbloom 2004a: 88–89.

[14] For comic targets, see Sommerstein 1996. For the "defender of the demos" see Connor 1992: 110–15; Rosenbloom 2002: 292–300; Rosenbloom 2004a: 90–93.

[15] See Dover 1974: 30–33; M. Heath 1997a, esp. 232–33.

[16] For the sycophant in comedy, see Christ 1998: 104–17.

constitute the audience's experience of theater. The clash of speakers, ideas, and rhetorical *topoi* is pleasurable in itself and increasingly becomes so into the fourth century. Euripides incorporated formal debates (*agōnes*) into his tragedies in which characters conduct rhetorical contests; these debates straddle boundaries between sophistic, epideictic, and forensic rhetoric.[17] The rhetorical character of Euripidean drama and its notional connection with forensic oratory did not escape Aristophanes: his Hermes claims that Theoria, the spirit of festival attendance, takes no pleasure in Euripides, "a poet of forensic rhetoric" (*Peace* 534). It is fairer to say that Euripides' tragedy, like Aristophanes' comedy, is both powerfully attracted to and repelled by the power of rhetoric.

The power of oratory: Aristophanes' *Birds*

Consider the case of Aristophanes' *Birds*. This comedy has a fair claim to being the most complete dramatization of the power of oratory and the most thoroughly rhetorical and sophistic drama to survive from fifth-century Athens. Produced in 414 while Athens was engaged in the invasion of Sicily that could expand the city's Aegean-wide naval empire into the western Mediterranean, critics are divided about how to interpret it. Some consider it a sophistic dystopia;[18] others read it as "tragi-comic" ridicule of Athenian democratic naval imperialism;[19] some see it as pure fantasy.[20] The hero of the play, Peisetairos, whose name indicates that he persuades a "comrade" or "partisan" (politically organized "partisans" [*hetairoi*] were a threat to the democracy at this time), is a voluntary exile from Athens who rejects the domination of the Athenian courts (30–45, 108–11) and seeks an "untroubled place" (*apragmona topon*, 44–45) – a keyword for life apart from the intrusions of Athenian democracy and imperialism – among the birds.[21] Instead of immediately enjoying such a life, however, he discovers a "great plan among the race of birds, and power which might come to be, if you obey me" (163–64), and creates a *polis*, politics, and empire among the birds literally *ex nihilo*. He uses all the resources of rhetoric to convince humans' natural enemies, birds, that they were the original divine kings of the cosmos. Starting from his own desire for the life of birds (324, 412–15), and his grief over their loss of kinship (464–66), Peisetairos awakens

[17] For the Euripidean *agōn*, see Lloyd 1992.
[18] Hubbard 1997.
[19] Arrowsmith 1973.
[20] Whitman 1964: 169–99.
[21] For the *apragmōn*, see Carter 1986.

the birds' desire to regain their kingship and divinity at all costs. In the cosmogony of the play, birds are the offspring of Erōs (Desire) and Chaos (Void, 684–707) and were the first creatures in the cosmos. Persuasive speech is a function of a speaker's desire and has the capacity to implant drives for power as a form of justice in mass audiences, even if the language is vacant and self-referential, as it is in the Birds.

Peisetairos advises the birds to form a single polis and to build massive walls around their patch of the sky (179–86, 549–51, 1118–69), threatens to unleash the birds upon humankind to destroy their food supply if they do not worship birds (571–91), and promises wealth and health if they accept this thrifty alternative to worshipping the Olympian gods (592–626, 708–36). Blocking sacrificial smoke from reaching the gods, and reducing them to "Melian hunger" (185–86, 1262–66, 1515–24), Peisetairos finally brokers a deal in which he marries Zeus's heiress Basileia and "has it all," replacing Zeus as ruler of the cosmos, restoring the birds' scepter, and becoming their tyrant (1515–53, 1685–87, 1706–1708). On the wings of desire, through winged words, and by occupying the empty space between earth and the gods, Peisetairos becomes Zeus. The Birds dramatizes the logic of Athenian democratic imperialism as a strategy of mass persuasion. At Athens, fictions of collective identity (e.g. the myth of autochthony) communicate a desire for and entitlement to power; control of the sea, the space between poleis and their food supplies, leverages persuasion. As the birds control the air, the Athenians control the sea, and can "persuade" poleis to do their bidding under threat of combined naval and land block-ades to starve them into submission (cf. Herodotus 8.111.2).

Yet Peisetairos applies this strategy to birds, slaves, and commodities in the current cosmos (13–18, 522–38), both inverting the order of things and restoring a primordial order, placing mortals and immortals under the oldest regime, which is also the newest. In this regard, the Birds resembles the Knights, in which a Sausage-seller proves himself a seemingly more loathsome demagogue than the tanner Paphlagon (Cleon) but transforms Demos into an archaic Ionian aristocrat and sends him back to the fields a happy and self-sufficient man, ending Paphlagon's "radical" democracy (1316–1408). The Birds' Peisetairos is a more nimble sophist, deft political orator, and cunning intellectual than the Athenians, who, according to Thucydides, informed the Melians that they believe the gods are well disposed towards them as invaders rather than the Melians as defenders and victims of injustice, because the Athenian demand for tribute and threat of retributive siege realize a law that applies to gods and mortals "by necessary nature": "to rule wherever one has the power" (Thucydides 5.105.2). Peisetairos enacts this very law in the Birds; but for him, becoming

Zeus also realizes his desire for a place untroubled by Athenian democracy and imperialism, an *apragmōn topos*. The only way of escaping the domination of the Athenian courts and empire is to realize a greater form of power: to become Zeus himself.

That Peisetairos is analogous yet violently opposed to the democratic orators and sophists he resembles becomes increasingly clear as the play reaches its conclusion, the wedding of Peisetairos and Basileia. The chorus of birds sings about places and marvels it has seen in its travels. The last is the "race of tongue-in-belly men," who use their tongues to make a living. Comprising orators and sophists, this barbarian race lives in "Phasisville" – *phasis* is a favorite procedure of sycophants – "along the Water Clock." These villains, Gorgiases and Philips, "reap and sow, nibble and test figs with their tongues ... and from those tongue-in-belly Philips everywhere in Attica the tongue is cut" (1694–1705). This myth of the origins of cutting the tongue from a sacrificial beast is particularly violent: it implies that every time the tongue is cut from an animal, it commemorates and renews its "original" excision from political orators and sophists.

Oratory as tongue

That the *Birds* presents a comic hero who is all tongue – but never associates him with this organ – while also reveling in the excision of orators' and sophists' tongues is emblematic of comedy's ambivalent hostility towards political and sophistic oratory. During the fifth century the trope of rhetoric as "tongue" (*glōssa*) and of eloquence as "good tongue" (*euglōssia*) becomes an important element of a strategy to deprive orators of the intellectual and moral authority required for legitimate leadership. Even as the theater increasingly functioned as a venue for rhetorical performances, drama problematized the tongue as an instrument of domination, an organ of desire, and a means of production – an economic tool that produces speech as a commodity, promising power, pleasure, monetary profit to its auditors and delivering them to its practitioners. The trope of rhetoric as tongue associates orators with a body part that is incapable of standing for a whole body or an integrated body politic; the tongue has cultural associations with symptoms of disease, polluting pleasures, and sacrificial ritual. While a *polis* may speak with a collective voice, it cannot speak with a collective "tongue"; to conceive of oral performance in terms of the tongue stresses the dangerous dependence of the *polis* upon individuals' speech-acts and their power to create realities in momentary performances that nullify the accumulated experience of the past.

The tongue undergoes apotheosis in the fifth century. Aristophanes' Socrates tells Strepsiades, who wants an education in sophistic rhetoric so he can cheat his creditors in court, he will believe in three gods: Chaos, Clouds, and Tongue (*Clouds* 423–24). The comic Euripides likewise prays to "Aether my pasture and pivot of my tongue" along with intelligence and his nostrils to help him prove and refute arguments he takes up in the *Frogs* (892–94). Where Tongue is god, the gods are no longer legal tender (*Clouds* 247–48). Zeus does not exist; Dinos is king (379–411, 816–31, 1468–76). The personification of rhetorical proof and exponent of rhetoric as "exercising the tongue" (1058–59), the Lesser *Logos* of the Aristophanes' *Clouds*, declares that the goddess Justice (*Dikē*) does not exist (904b–906).

The comic poet Cratinus characterizes the tongue as the prime mover in the democratic assembly: "... you bear (*phorein*) a tongue (*glōttan*) of fine ever-flowing speeches (*logōn*) in the demos by which (tongue) you will move (*kinēsei*) everything by speaking" (fr. 327). That the tongue "moves" everything relates oratorical prowess to personal power and makes it a force in the world (cf. Sophocles, *Philoctetes* 98–99); it implies that the tongue controls the demos, recapitulating the paradox that persuasion (*peithō*) is force. The sophist and teacher of rhetoric, Gorgias of Leontini, writes, "the *logos* which persuades the soul, forces the soul it persuades to obey what is said ..." (12). Gorgias describes the *logos* as a "great dynast" (*Helen* 8), comparing its effects to magical spells and to drugs in the body (10–14). Euripides' Hecuba, who discovers the power of oratory in the course of the *Hecuba*, describes *peithō* as "sole tyrant for mortals" (814–19). The power of oratory suppresses the consent of the persuaded, depriving them of freedom and moral responsibility, committing a kind of *hubris* on the audience.[22] Such views of rhetorical power underpin the notion that the demos is not responsible for its votes in the assembly.[23] The orator's tongue is responsible for persuasion and its outcomes. The orator becomes the demos's scapegoat or *pharmakos*, a guilty figure whose ritualized expulsion or death purifies and renews the entire community (e.g. Aristophanes, *Knights* 1121–50, 1397–1408).[24] Rhetoric as tongue stresses an individual speaker's responsibility, but also deprives the demos of moral responsibility and authority.

The defining features of "tongue" are omnipotence and lack of moral authority. Tragic and comic poets label orators *ponēros* and *mochthēros*

---

[22] See Wardy 1996: 62–64.
[23] See, e.g., Aristophanes, *Knights* 1355–57; Lysias 20.20; Thucydides 3.43.4–5; [Xenophon], *Constitution of the Athenians* 2.17.
[24] See Rosenbloom 2002: 329–39; Rosenbloom 2004b: 332–39 with bibliography.

("bad," "base," "vile," "villainous," "immoral") to underscore the latter.[25] Eloquence (*euglōssia*) forms the dividing line between the *ponēros* and his ethical antithesis, the *khrēstos* ("good," "honest," "noble," "authentic").[26] "O Zeus," complains a character in a fragment of Euripides, "why do you give this provision to men, to all villains (*ponērois*) eloquence (*euglōssian*), but to those who are good (*khrēstois*) incapacity in speaking?" (fr. 928b). Characters in Euripidean drama express anxieties that an unjust orator's eloquent slander will defeat a speaker with a just cause because of his verbal clumsiness (*aglōssia*, "lack of tongue," *Alexander* fr. 56; cf. *Antiope* fr. 206). In the *Knights* the Sausage-seller's *euglōttia* – his slanderous tongue – will make him the "greatest of the Hellenes" and enable him to rule the city and empire make "much money" (836–40; cf. *Clouds* 429–30, 445). The equivalence of oratorical prowess and moral failure is a cardinal rule in the game of competitive speech which orators and audiences accept; orators seek to align themselves with honest and straightforward speech and to pin the label "clever at speaking" (*deinos legein*) on opponents.[27]

Theseus extols Athens' democratic institutions of speech in Euripides' *Suppliants*: "This is freedom. Who has some good (*khrēston*) advice for the *polis* and wishes to bring it front and center? The one who is willing to do this is celebrated and the one who does not is silent. What is more equal for a city than this?" (438–41). Theseus praises the democratic speech regime as a realization of the democratic values of freedom and equality. The terms *isēgoria* ("equality of speech") and *parrhēsia* express the sociopolitical importance of these two values in the Athenian democracy: the privilege of all citizens, irrespective of class or status, to address other citizens as equals and to express their thoughts freely.

Dramatic treatment of democratic speech regimes severely test this ideal. That *ponēroi* orators drive *khrēstoi* out of politics is a theme of the period (e.g. Euripides, *Ion* 595–601; Aristophanes, *Frogs* 718–26). The trope of oratory as "tongue" associates it with villainy (*ponēria*). Theseus' praise of Athens' speech regime in the *Suppliants* takes place in counterpoint to his own and the Theban Herald's denigration of the *ponēros* orator.[28] The Herald champions monarchy over democracy; Theseus champions democracy as the demos's monarchy (352–53), but he inaugurates a critique. He excludes the rich (238–39) and poor from the coalition that preserves the social and moral order (*kosmon*, 245) of a *polis*, focusing on "vile

---

[25] For texts and bibliography, see Rosenbloom 2004a: 56 n. 4.
[26] For the *khrēstos*, see Connor 1992: 183–93; Rosenbloom 2004a: 63–66.
[27] See Dover 1974: 25–26; Ober 1989a: 173–74; Hesk 1999; Hesk 2000.
[28] For the politics of the *logos* in the *Suppliants*, see Burian 1985.

protectors" (*ponērōn prostatōn*, 240–43), who "cheat the poor with their tongues," exploiting their envy to harass the rich in the courts, fighting a class war that profits only them.

Possessing the power of speech in the absence of authority derived from some combination of birth, landed wealth, military leadership, education, and culture, the tongue enables those of low socioeconomic origins and moral worth to control the masses and gain entry into the ranks of the elite. "This is a source of disease (*nosōdes*) for the better sort," opines the Theban Herald, "whenever a vile (*ponēros*) man, who was nothing before, possesses rank and status (*axiōma*), because he controls (*kataschōn*) the demos with his tongue" (423–25). Contrast Thucydides' Pericles: "powerful by rank and status (*axiōmati*) and intelligence (*gnōmēi*) ... he controlled (*kateiche*) the masses freely" (*eleutheros*, 2.65.8).[29] Pericles' successors, according to Thucydides, lacked his *axiōma* and had to compete with each other as equals. They sought advantage over one another by speaking to please (*pros hēdonēn*) the demos and yielded power to it (2.65.8–9). For Thucydides "radical" democracy was the creation of orators struggling to fill Pericles' shoes.

Aristophanes depicts orators' pleasing the demos and yielding power to it as a rhetorical stance. Democratic politics is the art of making and selling sausages, "shaking up and mincing together all the affairs of the city together and always winning over the demos by sweetening it up with the rhetoric of cooks" (Aristophanes, *Knights* 214). The orators' flattery, slander, promises of food and increased power and wages, professions of desire, friendship, goodwill, and declarations to defend the demos against conspirators induce false consciousness.[30] The demos fantasizes that its ideological hegemony translates into real kingship, tyranny, world mastery, or divinity, but it is a fiction promulgated to conceal the power, profit, and pleasure of orators. Orators condition the demos to think itself master while they enslave it (Aristophanes, *Wasps* 548–759). Political rhetoric is a knavish diversionary trick, a fog that blinds the demos to the orators' predations (e.g. *Knights* 790–809).

Odysseus' tongue: rhetorical and moral victory

In Euripidean tragedy, Odysseus figures the democratic orator, "always wily and with the mob" (Euripides, *Iphigenia at Aulis* 526). His tongue is a trope

---

[29] See Edmunds and Martin 1977.
[30] See Connor 1992: 99–108; Wohl 2002, esp. 80–92; Rosenbloom 2002; Rosenbloom 2004a: 87–88.

for political and sophistic rhetoric, the cause of irremediable violence and injustice.[31] When Hecuba learns that she has been allotted as a slave to him in the *Trojan Woman*, she vents her outrage: Odysseus is "a polluted trickster, enemy of justice, transgressive beast, who twists all things from there to here and their opposites again with his twofold tongue, making what was an enemy before a friend again" (278–88). Odysseus' tongue "twists" ethical predicates, relativizing them in the manner of sophistic "double arguments." He bases ethics and alliances upon self-interest rather than upon reciprocity or justice. His twofold tongue embodies the inversion of moral order – lies over truth, words over deeds, shamelessness over shame, villainy over nobility, illusion over reality – that enables the group under his control to achieve its interests.[32] Implicit in the Euripidean figure of Odysseus is Diodotus' claim in Thucydides' debate on Mytilene that justice and self-interest are mutually exclusive (3.47.5). Odysseus' tongue figures the democratic speech regime's tragic dislocation of moral order in the determination of collective self-interest.

Odysseus' tongue is an agent of victory in competitive debate before a mass audience. This plays into a *topos* of Euripidean drama: the base man (*kakos*) "wins" verbal contests judged by the masses. Such figures include the "wise but base Odysseus" (*Trojan Women* 721, 1224–25; cf. *Hecuba* 116–39), the Theban Herald's orator in the *Suppliants*, and the anonymous demagogue of the *Orestes* (944). The condemnatory use of the epithet "wise" (*sophos*) to characterize a false or unjust but eloquent speaker is also a Euripidean *topos*.[33] Odysseus' victories in the assembly sanction the sacrifice of Polyxena even though he has a moral obligation to her mother, Hecuba, who accepted his supplication and saved his life (*Hecuba* 218–331); they would permit Polymestor to murder and mutilate his Trojan guest-friend for his gold because he is an ally and killed the last of the Priamidae (850–63, 1132–82); they mandate throwing Astyanax from the walls of Troy so as "not to raise the son of a heroic father" (723). In the *Orestes* the demagogue voices the interests of Tyndareus and argues that Orestes and Electra should be be stoned to death (914–15). In these plays Euripides stages the sorrows of royalty and aristocracy as victims of an orator's formulation and a mass audience's ratification of collective self-interest, emphasizing the violence that its realization inflicts on their persons, families, community, and culture. Characters in these plays subvert this bond to realize private interests, allegiances, and values which have

[31] See also Sophocles, *Philoctetes* 406–408; cf. 98–99; Euripides, *Cyclops* 313–15.
[32] See Rose 1992: 307–308.
[33] See *Medea* 579–87; *Hecuba* 1187–94; *Antiope* fr. 206; *Meleager* fr. 583.

deeper moral content. These plays stage nobility as a response to the cruelty of collective self-interest as formulated and enacted in a democratic assembly.

Hecuba and the Trojan women embody this nobility as something alien to the democratic and Hellenic identity. Radically external critics of democratic oratory, they nonetheless attract the audience's sympathies and elicit its resentments against a regime similar to its own. A barbarian woman, former queen, and slave who has lost everything in the Trojan War and its aftermath, Hecuba criticizes democratic oratory in terms identical to those of Thucydides: orators please and gratify the demos, yielding authority to it; they do not freely express their mind and characters. The *Hecuba*'s chorus characterizes Odysseus as "a wily-minded, sweet-speaking (*hēdulogos*), a demos-gratifying (*dēmokharistēs*) hair-splitter" (131–33; cf. *Suppliants* 412–16). Hecuba constructs rhetoric in opposition to democratic oratory, condemning all orators (*dēmēgoroi*) as ". . . without gratitude . . . you who do not care if you harm your friends, if you say something to gratify the many" (*toisi pollois pros kharin*, 254–57; cf. Euripides, *Orestes* 1155–57). She impugns orators for not being free: ". . . the majority (*plēthos*) of a *polis* or written laws keep them from employing their characters according to their judgment" (866–67). They are afraid to say or do what is right, "and give more to the mob" (868–69). Thucydides attributes Pericles' freedom in controlling the demos to his prestige (*axiōma*, 2.65.8). Euripides' Hecuba tries to convince Odysseus to use his *axiōma* to oppose the sacrifice of her daughter on ethical, legal, and religious grounds (287–92). She maintains that even if *axiōma* delivers a rhetorically ineffective speech, it prevails (293–95). In response, Odysseus warns Hecuba to learn not to alienate "the man who speaks well" (299–300). He conceives of his power as rhetorical performance rather than *axiōma*.

Hecuba's claims do not go unchallenged in the play. The charge that public orators "lack gratitude" contradicts Odysseus' argument before the army in favor of Polyxena's sacrifice. The assembly is split between the view of Agamemnon, who protects Hecuba because of his relationship to Cassandra, not to sacrifice Polyxena, and that of Theseus' two sons, who argue that Cassandra's bed is less valuable than Achilles' spear and that his tomb should be "crowned with fresh blood" (120–28). Odysseus breaks the impasse, arguing that the gratitude the Danaans owe Achilles overrides consideration for a slave's life and that they must avoid reproach among the dead "that Danaans left . . . Troy lacking gratitude (*akharistoi*) towards Danaans who died on behalf of Hellenes" (133–39). Odysseus' *axiōma* is decisive and *kharis* is the basis of his argument. He articulates an uncontroversial ranking of warriors over slaves, men over women, Greeks over barbarians, and public over private obligations.

The sacrifice of Polyxena seems to achieve moral-aesthetic beauty and to emblematize moral order. Polyxena embodies freedom, nobility, courage, and decorum in death; the mass of soldiers toil to honor her as a hero (518–82). Yet when we reflect that Polyxena's sacrifice, Polymestor's murder and mutilation of Polydorus for his gold, and the sack of Troy are sanctioned by this democratic speech regime, it appears that the play attaches greater moral authenticity and depth to the private bond sanctioned by religion and custom than to the public bond between orator and mass audience. Odysseus maintains that distributive justice and the capacity to recruit soldiers in the future hinge upon the sacrifice of Polyxena (306–16); he says he would be satisfied with little wealth, if his burial seemed worthy of himself, because this is a matter of long-term reciprocity (318–20). But these claims do not reconcile the contradiction in his position over his obligation towards Hecuba or address the deeper question of how virgin sacrifice can function in a durable system of distributive justice.

Hecuba trumps these claims: she pins her vengeance on the very existence of *nomos*, the gods derived from it, and moral order in the cosmos (787–805). If Polymestor can murder a guest-friend for his gold and mutilate his body, tossing it into the sea, and others can pillage temples, "nothing is fair (*ison*) among mortals" (799–805). In the *Hecuba*'s version of the sack of Troy, Hellenes burst into Trojan bedrooms while wives put up their hair for bed; they slaughter men in their beds (905–52; *Trojan Women* 562–67). Hecuba's vengeance erases lines demarcating the sack of Troy, the sacrifice of Polyxena, and the murder and mutilation of Polydorus. The drama subverts the army's authority and interests to vindicate a moral order based upon *xenia*, a pre- and anti-democratic value configured in precise antithesis to the values of the democratic speech regime and orator.

Odysseus thus emerges as "sweet-speaking gratifier of the demos" in a pernicious sense: he presents the violent realization of collective interest as the achievement of moral order. The parallel between Thucydides' post-Periclean orator and Hecuba's is again instructive. Thucydides' Cleon argues that the Athenians will realize both justice and rational self-interest if they annihilate Mytilene (3.39–40). By unleashing Hecuba's fury upon a man who murdered a *xenos* for his gold, *Hecuba* plays into a sense of outrage against the democratic speech regime and its orators; indeed Aristophanes uniquely singles out Paphlagon for violating strangers (*Knights* 325–27, 1192–99; cf. *Peace* 632–48). At the end of the *Knights*, he goes to the gates of the city to sell sausages "so that the strangers he harmed may see him" (1407–1408).

Agamemnon justifies collusion with Hecuba against the interests of the army on the grounds that "this is common to all, to a private individual and city, for the bad (*kakon*) to suffer something bad (*kakon*), and the good (*khrēston*) to fare well" (902–904; cf. 592–603, 841–45). This motive meshes with comic depictions of democracy as the domination of *ponēroi* to the exclusion of *khrēstoi* (e.g. Aristophanes, *Frogs* 718–37), Pseudo-Xenophon's refusal to praise democracy because it chooses "to give more to *ponēroi* than to *khrēstoi*" (*Constitution of the Athenians* 1.1), his portrait of the democratic speech regime as *ponēroi* expressing the interests of *ponēroi* (1.6–7), and the depiction of the socioeconomic and political order of Athens in the Aristophanes' *Wealth* as an inversion of moral order, where "temple robbers, orators, sykophants, and *ponēroi* are rich" and *khrēstoi* are poor (26–31). The paradox of the *Hecuba* is that Hecuba's ugly vengeance not only is the culmination of a more authentic and persuasive series of rhetorical performances and a subversion of the interests of the Achaean army but vindicates a moral order which the interests of the Achaean army suppress. Rhetorical victory before a mass audience is by definition the converse of moral victory.

Theater, rhetoric, and revolutionary nostalgia

For us, as for the Greeks, a moral victory is a defeat. Oratory as "tongue" expresses the opportunity cost of democratic, collective self-interest as axiomatically victorious. The trope of rhetoric as "tongue" explores what is lost when speech acts before mass audiences represent, create, and move reality in the absence of valid claims to authority and knowledge external to them. The underlying function of the concept is its potential to provoke disgust. The tongue as an organ of *ponēria* elicits moral revulsion and class-based disdain for democratic rhetoric as the production of commodities which offer pleasure and profit and unleash unholy violence.

Dramatic hostility towards democratic oratory as the inversion of moral order and suppression of nobility activate a potentially revolutionary nostalgia. Euripidean characters lament and subvert the bond between the orator's tongue and the masses in his Trojan plays. In the *Suppliants* Theseus conducts an ideal of Athenian democracy against the degraded reality that slips through fissures in the play's fictionality. The bond between Odysseus' or a demagogue's tongue and the mob is part of the tragic universe, an objective reality that inflicts pain, prompts lament, destroys nobility, and makes victory more ethically problematic than defeat. Yet characters who appear most sympathetic in the face of suffering, "rational optimists" are also deluded.[34] There is no permanent moral order under the auspices of

---

[34] See Mastronarde 1986.

rational and kindly gods. But it does not follow that Euripidean tragedy ceases to yearn for one, whether by presenting the *Suppliants* or lamenting the nothingness of Troy. The *Orestes*, which depicts the democratic assembly as a travesty (884–952) and has its leading characters defy its decree that Orestes and Electra commit suicide, form a private club (*hetairia*), and attempt to kill Helen as responsible for the entire mess (1022–1175), comes as close to scripting revolution as possible in tragedy. Apollo as *deus ex machina* resolves the insoluble conflict between what passes for political and moral order.

Comic nostalgia, by contrast, does not lament the world, but transforms it; its revolutionary potential is greater. The *Birds* recreates a fictionalized primordial order which excludes orators and sophists, symbolically excising their tongues. The *Knights* restores a fictionalized original Athenian democracy, transforming decrepit Demos's body into a youthful and handsome Ionian aristocrat and expelling Paphlagon as a scapegoat (*pharmakos*). This ironic ending – the Sausage-seller returns as *deus ex machina* – renews a time when the bond between demos and leaders was forged in the mess and on the battlefield rather than through "the tongue."[35] In the *Symposium* (189c2–197d7), Plato has Aristophanes praise desire (*erōs*) as a yearning for a lost half; humans were originally whole and round, a unity fused from two. Their power and confidence expressed themselves as *hubris* and they challenged the Olympian gods; Zeus bisected them as punishment. Now they yearn for reunion with their original and completing other half. This myth describes a crucial dimension of plays such as *Knights*, *Birds*, and *Wealth*, where restoration of a self-sufficient and whole body politic is also an expression of *hubris* towards prevailing institutions of domination, from Olympian religion to the democratic speech regime. Underlying this nostalgia is a demand for justice, a yearning to align the *polis*'s socioeconomic, political, and moral orders. These comedies realize a desire for wholeness and fullness by ritually scapegoating *ponēroi* orators and sophists, unifying audience and society around their humiliation and expulsion, and renewing an original moral order. In this context Aristophanes uses the trope of demos as monarch (*Knights* 1329–34).

The oligarchic takeovers of 411 and 404 realize such nostalgia as political revolution. Both takeovers attempted to secure correlation among socioeconomic, political, and moral orders by restoring the authority of the fathers in sociopolitical fictions termed "laws of the fathers" (*patrioi*

---

[35] See Rosenbloom 2002: 318–29; cf. Hesk 2000: 255–58; see Wohl 2002: 110–23 for readings of the irony that undercut the apparent message of the ending.

nomoi) in 411 and "constitution of the fathers" (*patrios politeia*) in 404.[36] Both revolutions followed a comic pattern of renewing an "original" regime to achieve this end. The revolution of 404, enabled by Sparta's demand that Athens adhere to a *patrios politeia*, declared itself as such a movement. According to Lysias, the Thirty came to power "saying it was necessary to make the city pure of unjust men and for the rest of the citizens to turn to virtue and justice" (12.5; cf. [Plato], *Seventh Letter* 324b8–326b4). The initial gambit of both takeovers was to kill democratic orators as scape-goats for the new regime, which was also an old regime. The second takeover brutally purged orators. Sources are unanimous that such violence unified the *polis*: they murdered "both sycophants and those who associated with the demos for their gratification (*pros kharin*) beyond what is best (*to beltiston*), and those who were evildoers and villains (*ponērous*), and when this happened the *polis* rejoiced, thinking that they acted for the best" (Aristotle, *Constitution of the Athenians* 35.3; cf. Lysias 25.19; Xenophon, *History of Greece* 2.3.12). Plato's Socrates incorporates these terms into his definition of rhetoric: the practice of flattery which "aims at pleasure in the absence of what is best" (*Gorgias* 464e2–465a2) and "the gratification of souls assembled together, not at all examining what is best" (501d4–5).[37] The terms that justify the purge of orators are the terms that define rhetoric, or rather, brand it as fundamentally opposed to "what is best" and should be excised for the health and well-being of the *polis*, like the tongues of "Philips and Gorgiases."

The symbolic violence of the fifth-century theater towards democratic orators and oratory was realized as actual violence. This purge was so indiscriminate and so incompatible with the moral pretensions of the oligarchs, that it set an upper limit for *ponēria* as political speech and action; and against this benchmark, the democratic speech regime refashioned and renewed itself in an order that lasted from 403 to 322. Nostalgia prevails in fourth-century public discourse; but the object of that nostalgia is not a unitary socioeconomic, political, and moral order of the fathers that requires the transformation of democracy into a previous form, but for democracy itself, as successfully practiced by the fathers.

Suggestions for further reading

The fullest and most accessible introduction to the Sophists remains W. K. C. Guthrie, *The Sophists* (Cambridge, 1971 = *A History of Greek Philosophy*, vol. III, Cambridge, 1969), though it presents an overly simplified

---

[36] See Ostwald 1986, esp. 367–85, 475–80.
[37] See further Plato, *Gorgias* 501b2–c1, 502d10–503a1; cf. [Andokides] 4.12.

picture of sophistic influence. More sophisticated are G. B. Kerford, *The Sophistic Movement* (Cambridge, 1981) and J. de Romilly, *The Great Sophists in Periclean Athens*, trans. J. Lloyd (Oxford, 1992); the former is highly concentrated, the latter more wide-ranging. John Poulakos, *Sophistical Rhetoric in Classical Greece* (Columbia, 1995) treats the rise of the fifth-century Sophists and their reception in the fourth century. A brief historical treatment of the Sophists can be found in R. W. Wallace, "The Sophists in Athens," in D. Boedeker and K. Raaflaub, eds., *Democracy, Empire, and the Arts in Fifth-Century Athens* (Cambridge, MA, 1998) 203–22.

Euripides' relationship to the sophists is a subject of perennial interest. For a sober treatment of the issues which insists on Euripides' subordination of rhetoric and sophistic thought to his dramatic aims, see D. Conacher, *Euripides and the Sophists: Some Dramatic Treatments of Philosophical Ideas* (London, 1998). W. Allen, "Euripides and the Sophists: Society and the Theatre of War," in M. Cropp *et al.*, eds., *Euripides and Tragic Theatre in the Late Fifth Century* (Champaign, 2000 = *Illinois Classical Studies* vols. 24–25) 145–56 explores Euripides' dramatization of the conflict between morality and power in the *Heraclidae* and *Suppliant Women* as a function of his response to "sophistic ideas." R. Scodel, "Verbal Performance and Euripidean Rhetoric," in M. Cropp *et al.*, eds., *Euripides and Tragic Theatre in the Late Fifth Century* (Champaign, 2000 = *Illinois Classical Studies* vols. 24–25) 129–44 offers a wide-ranging analysis of verbal performance in Euripidean drama, focusing on the potentially contradictory aims of using rhetoric to perform the self and to persuade others. For an overview of the ways in which Aristophanes and other comic poets depict representative sophists and Socrates, see C. Carey, "Old Comedy and Sophists," in D. Harvey *et al.*, eds., *The Rivals of Aristophanes: Studies in Athenian Old Comedy* (London, 2000) 419–36.

Democratic oratory is a much studied topic. The best place to start is J. Ober, *Mass and Elite in Democratic Athens: Rhetoric, Ideology, and the Power of the People* (Princeton, 1989) especially chs. 3–7. He argues that oratory enabled and consolidated the power of the people. H. Yunis, *Taming Democracy: Models of Political Rhetoric in Classical Athens* (Ithaca, 1996) traces the development of models of rhetoric as "effective political discourse" and concentrates on tensions between these models and democratic practices. H. Yunis, "The Constraints of Democracy and the Rise of the Art of Rhetoric," in D. Boedeker and K. Raaflaub, eds., *Democracy, Empire, and the Arts in Fifth-Century Athens* (Cambridge, MA, 1998) 223–40 is a good introduction to the problem of the origins of rhetoric and its relationship to democratic oratory. For attempts to situate comic discourse within the speech regime of democracy, see J. Henderson,

"The *Dēmos* and Comic Competition," in J. Winkler and F. Zeitlin, eds., *Nothing to Do with Dionysos? Athenian Drama in its Social Context* (Princeton, 1990) 271–313; C. Carey, "Comic Ridicule and Democracy," in R. Osborne and S. Hornblower, eds., *Ritual, Finance, Politics: Democratic Accounts Presented to D. M. Lewis* (Oxford, 1994) 69–83. For the subgenre of "demagogue comedy," see A. Sommerstein, "Platon, Eupolis and the 'Demagogue-Comedy,'" in D. Harvey *et al.*, eds., *The Rivals of Aristophanes: Studies in Athenian Old Comedy* (London, 2000) 437–51. For a checklist of targets for comic ridicule, see A. Sommerstein "How to Avoid Being a *Komodoumenos*," *Classical Quarterly* 46 (1996) 327–56. P. J. Rhodes, "Nothing to Do with Democracy," *Journal of Hellenic Studies* 123 (2003) 104–19 doubts an essential relationship between drama and democracy.

12

WILLIAM BATSTONE

The drama of rhetoric at Rome

Drama is generally taken as a representative art: it is not life, but it represents life. It is the art of actors pretending to be something that they are not. Rhetoric is generally taken as the art of using words to persuade and manipulate, irrespective of the truth, essence, and sincerity; it is the art of pretense and the constructed truth. In Rome, in particular, it is primarily the art of lawyers who represent and advocate for their clients, speaking for them, even acting out emotions that their clients are presumed to feel.[1] It is an accident of language that both the actor and the lawyer are called *actores* (after all, herdsmen, bailiffs, and artillery men are also *actores*): the term refers to the one who performs the material task (as opposed to, say, a producer). But the accident underscores similarities: the performances of *actores* as representatives of others (characters or clients) are artistic, manipulative, insincere. They are the ones who hide behind the mask, manipulate the mask, make you see what you do not see.

But orators also represent themselves, their *auctoritas* (personal authority and influence) and their character. The courtroom is the stage where they assume the *persona* of the *uir bonus* (the good or manly man). One version of the *uir bonus* was the sincere speaker, the man of no artifice. But how do you act like *uir bonus*? Cato the Censor, a man who inveighed against Greek rhetoric and influence and had the orators tossed out of Rome, reduced rhetoric to a simple formula: *tene rem, uerba sequentur*! ("Stick to the truth; the words will follow.") But Cato himself studied rhetoric and had his sons learn Greek. The pontiff of sincerity turns out to be wearing a pontiff's mask; that is how you act like a *uir bonus*.

The Latin for "mask" is *persona*, the same term that is used for a lawyer's self-presentation and, indeed, for any entity that has standing in a court of

---

[1] See Kennedy 1968.

law, or any role that one plays or is forced to play in the world.[2] In fact, without a Latin term for "the self," the Roman thinks in terms of his *persona*. Identity itself becomes a game of masks, of *personae*. We will begin with comedy, because here this game is objectified on the stage. The clever slave, always a *seruus malus* ("a bad slave"), plays with the illusion that things are what they are, for he knows that things, including himself, are as they are constructed, that rhetorics born of position, power, desire, and ideology efface the distinction between world and reality, acting and sincerity. The truth of Plautine comedy is that it represents life as already staged, as a rhetorical competition for who gets to say who we are.

This essay is about the ways in which one finds enactment and representation, insincerity and manipulation at play in Roman literature and life, and the purposes that it can serve. This general game of *persona* and with *personae* is played at Rome in author after author and genre after genre. I will be arguing that rhetoric and a drama of self-representation is endemic to Roman identity, and that sincerity itself is just another actor in the drama of rhetoric at Rome. The drama of rhetoric goes, as they say, all the way down.

Act one: the comedy of rhetoric

facit illud ueri simile, quod mendacium est.　　　　(Plautus, *Pseudolus* 405)

Scene one: the trunk-fish

The Rudens, a typical New Comedy of mistaken identity, involves a scene in which two slaves, Gripus and Trachalio, debate the ownership of a trunk found by Gripus in the ocean. To a large extent the play is about ownership and fairness, but this debate is pointless: it does not further the plot; it does not determine ownership; and it does not form the basis of any future decision about the trunk. This can be taken as a sign of Plautine invention, and so a sign that we are dealing with something that goes to the heart of Plautine comedy. It exists for the comic pleasure it brings, and that pleasure is, in large part, a send-up of legal argumentation. But parody is both a form of analysis and a representation; it claims that the thing being parodied can be reduced to this. So, what is Plautus' view of legal argument? An improvisational game with words and *personae*.

[2] Cicero, *On behalf of Lucius Murena* 6: "I have always played gladly the roles of gentility and pity, roles which nature herself taught me; I did not seek that *persona* of gravity and severity, but I sustained it when the republic imposed it."

Trachalio sees Gripus dragging a trunk away in his net. He recognizes the trunk and knows who owns it. So, he pretends he wants advice about a matter that concerns Gripus. If I saw a theft, he says, and knew the owner, should I get half the property in return for not telling the owner. "And more too!" says Gripus. Then, Trachalio explains that he knows who owns the trunk and how it was lost. Gripus improvises:

> But I know how it was found
> and I know the man who found it and who owns it now. (964–65)

By refuting Trachalio's assumption about ownership, Gripus escapes the charge of "theft." He caught it fishing, and the sea is common to all, he says. Trachalio asserts the right of origins: if the sea is common to all, then what comes from the sea is common to all. Gripus, appeals to the common world: how could fishermen make a living if what they caught was common to all. Trachalio complains that it is foolish to compare trunks and fish, and then in a moment of confidence says:

> Either you've got to show me what kind of fish a trunk is,
> or don't take what wasn't born in the sea and hasn't got scales. (990–91)

"What," says Gripus, "you've never heard of a trunk-fish?!" and he brings out his credentials as a fisherman. "They're rare, but you do catch them sometimes." He describes their color and their size.

This extravagant comic fantasy contradicts Gripus' earlier statement to Trachalio when he thought Trachalio wanted something from him: "I don't have any fish, young man; don't think that I do" (941). The contradiction is important because it marks the constructivism of the entire scene as a feature of Gripus' improvisational attitude to the world. That constructivism is also apparent earlier in the scene, when Trachalio asks Gripus to swear that he would play fair:

> TR: Hush, I'll tell you
>   if you'll give your faith to me that you'll not be unfaithful
> GR: I give you faith, I will be faithful, whoever you are. (951–53)

Here, the stilted language of Roman contracts and oaths, a language that reflects Roman legalistic care, may sound like a parody. But it is not, and that serves my point: what we experience as parody is actually realistic illusion, because the "real" world of legal agreement in Rome is flagrantly constructivist.

An oath, a principle of opportunism, an argument about definition and ownership, a trunk-fish, all for no purpose except that it exposes the drama of rhetoric at Rome: things are what you say they are, if you are clever enough to get away with it. Trachalio sums up Gripus' argument as "a cursed mess," a *scelus* (just what comedy prizes) and "giving words" (*uerba dare*, just what comedy loves to do).

The Latin phrase, "to give words," is a common idiom for tricking someone. As such, it points to the special relationship that the Romans felt between words and power: you are within my sphere of influence and even control if you accept my (rhetorical) version of the world. In modern terms we might say that this reflects how all things are determined by position and power, and when you accept my version of things, you have yielded to my world. But even that seems to depend too much on a world which is stable from my perspective. For the Romans, such stability is itself constructed.

Scene two: someone else's self

Tricking your opponent (*uerba dare*), taking possession of what is not your own, and turning things into things they are not is central to Plautus' earliest comedy, *Miles Gloriosus*, but in a far more extreme way.

Palaestrio's art of persuasion convinces Sceledrus that he did not see what he did see. It combines visual and verbal trickery: giving sights, illusions, dreams for Scledrus' autopsy ("I have my own eyes, and I don't need to use someone else's," 347) and giving words, threats, arguments, narratives[3] ("Now they won't give me words, by god, that's for sure," 353). These two types of "argument" correspond to the distinction in rhetoric between signs and proofs. Signs are usually thought of as evidence, but Plautus is already wise to a distinction now made by postmodern historiography: "evidence" is only evidence when it is in an argument; until then, it is a trace, a sign, of something, but what?

Sceledrus thinks he saw, and did see, the soldier's girl, Philocomasium, kissing her lover next door; Palaestrio is protecting Philocomasium and the lover. The first sign is the appearance of Philocomasium from the soldier's house, although Sceledrus just saw her at the neighbor's house. This improbability is supplemented by a narrative that makes the improbable sound verisimilar. The girl says she dreamed that her twin sister was next door with her lover. In an aside, Palaestrio says, "The story is The Dream of Palaestrio" (386). The characterization is perfect. A dream, something seen but not seen, explains the "evidence" by giving words to Sceledrus so that he does not see what he did see. Soon Sceledrus: "There is nothing I can say for sure: I did not see her, although I did" (407).

---

[3] See Quintilian, *Institutes* 5.10.12.

The next stage of the trick is to have Philocomasium go into the soldier's house, slip over to the neighbor's by a hole in the wall, and reappear from the neighbor's house. Since seeing is believing, Sceledrus thinks this must be Philocomasium, but now the vision is supplemented with the "twin's narrative" which confirms Philocomasium's dream. And Palaestrio refers to the two narratives as an *oratio* (466).

The final stage is to have the neighbor take offense at Sceledrus' conclusion. It is the old "what kind of a person do you take me for" attack. It only works because the neighbor has invited Sceledrus to look into the two houses at the same time as he has Philocomasium slip back and forth. So, Sceledrus sees one person, Philocomasium, but thinks he sees twins: he sees what he does not see. And the proof that convinces him that he did not see what he saw depends upon his believing that he sees what he does not see. Sceledrus confesses that he has done wrong; he calls it *iniuriam*. The neighbor ups the ante and tells Sceledrus that from now on he should not even know what he knows (572–73). Case closed.

Palaestrio's manipulation of evidence and cooptation of Sceledrus' insular identity is an effective illustration of how one of the neighbors can change us when we are not looking – or when we are. Our self is, in fact, not our own, but always contested and constructed in its confrontation with others. This contest makes a virtue of not knowing what one knows (Chrysalus, *Bacchides* 791) and not remembering what one remembers (the prostitutes, *Miles Gloriosus* 893). On the comic stage, it is all smoke and mirrors – the only question is whether you are blowing smoke and hiding behind mirrors, or being changed by those who do, the *actores*.

Scene three: law and morals

The *Miles Gloriosus* ends with a punishment, an oath, and a moral. When Pyrgopolynices discovers that he has been tricked by the slave, that the sailor who came to take away Philocomasium was actually her lover, like Trachalio he speaks of "giving words" and "a cursed mess":

MILES: Oh, no! they gave me words;
I see it. Palaestrio, that cursed mess of a man,
tricked me into this delusion. Rightly so, I judge;
if other adulterers were treated so, there'd be fewer adulterers.
They'd be more fearful, less eager. Let's go home. Applaud!
(1433–37)

Pyrgopolynices knows he has been trapped, caught, and punished as an adulterer should be. But he did not commit adultery: the neighbor was not married; his "wife" was a prostitute only pretending to be a "wife"; and Pyrgopolynices did not seduce her; she seduced him. How did this happen? Giving words, the artificial invention of "inartifical proofs," and turning Pyrgopolynices into someone else's self.

Palaestrio plays to the soldier's self-importance and the important secrecy of their plan. When the go-between, Milphidippa, speaks of the soldier, her words need no polish (1000).[4] In fact, Milphidippa's words are so persuasive that Pyrgopolynices begins to desire her mistress, Acroteleutium, sight unseen: "By God, Palaestrio, I'm already beginning to lust after her!" (1004). "But you haven't seen her," Palaestrio protests. The soldier replies: "I believe you and that amounts to my seeing her" (1005). Giving words amounts to giving sight, and this is the function of any speech: "It's possible to give to both sides of a case the following succinct rule: the orator should put the entire strength of his case before the eyes of the judge" (Quintilian 8.3.17). Like the jury, like Sceledrus, so Pyrgopolynices sees what he does not see.

At the conclusion of the *Miles Gloriosus*, Pyrgopolynices is himself the jury: he admits his error (which was not his error), accepts his punishment, and moralizes about adultery. The scene is a complex interweaving of truth and illusion. The soldier sees himself as an adulterer – although in fact he was not and he could not have been one, but, in some other more deeply psychological way, he was. The soldier sees that he has been tricked, "I see that words have been given me" (1434), but he does not see the extent of the trick. He does not see that he has been turned into his desire. This complexity of seeing and not seeing describes the work of the drama itself: the audience both sees what it does not see and sees that it does not see what it sees. The slave improvises a scripted text; there is a soldier, who is punished, as an adulterer. Suppose the actor takes the audience into his confidence. The rhetoric of these masks and inventions is the rhetoric of life.

Act two: the dramatic rhetoric of politics

One may distinguish two kinds of playing in Roman comedy: the strategic and the merely ludic. The rhetoric of politics tends to be of the former variety, and its strategic function is clearly stated by Quintilian:

> I will admit that rhetoric sometimes substitutes falsehood for truth, but I will not allow that it does so because its opinions are false, since there is all the difference between holding a certain opinion oneself and persuading someone

---

[4] *loquitur laute et minime **sordide**, Miles Gloriosus* 100; *nec **sordidis** umquam in oratione erudita locus*, Quintilian 8.3.18.

else to adopt an opinion. For instance a general frequently makes use of
falsehood.   (Quintilian 2.17.19)

What follows is the story of Hannibal's deception of Fabius, Theopompus
dressing like a woman to escape from jail, and Cicero throwing dust in the
eyes of the judges during the Cluentius' trial. Surely, it is not coincidental
that the favorite role for the clever slave in Plautus is that of a general. The
slave is a general; rhetoric is a general: both marshall the forces of appearance and deception for strategic advantage.

Scene one: diebus festis ludisque publicis
(Cicero, On behalf of Caelius *1.1)*

Quintilian notes that it is often useful to assume the role of your client or
someone else involved in the case. Technically this is called "prosopopoeia":
creating a character, donning a mask, putting on a *persona*. In doing this the
legal *actor* becomes a stage *actor*. Quintilian even refers to the stage: "Just
as their case would be more pitiable if they were to speak themselves, so
their case is to some extent more effective when it seems to be spoken from
their own mouths, as is the case with stage actors where the same voice and
delivery under a *persona* is more effective at moving the emotions" (6.1.26).
It is interesting that here Quintilian equates rhetorical effectiveness not with
sincerity, but with the *persona*. Our use of the word "person" derives from
persona and points to the history of one's personal standing.

Of Cicero's many prosopopoeias, perhaps the most familiar and most closely
connected with Roman comedy is the *On behalf of Caelius*. In the exordium
Cicero laments the fact that the jurors cannot enjoy the *ludi Megalenses* that are
going on, which would have included dramas, especially comedies. But soon
it becomes apparent that the speech is itself a compensation for their jury duty.
It is Cicero's own little drama, a *lusus* with the charges and the evidence.

Cicero begins by picking at the prosecution in terms of *personae*, as if the
director had not known what he was doing. Vituperation is not prosecution,
he says (3.6), besides, it should be done with humor. It doesn't suit the
young prosecutor, Atratinus. (Who is the casting director?!) The prosecution should have brought on the *senes seueri* for these accusations. Caelius is
accused of promiscuity: well, aren't all good looking young men? Atratinus,
consider your age. Soon, upon dismissing the actual charges against Caelius,
Cicero turns to their source: the path of gold, poison, and the baths leads to
a promiscuous woman, Clodia, and her jealous heart.

Cicero fashions his own *personae* from the comic stage, in roles familiar
from Terence's play *The Brothers*. There, the strict authoritarian father,

Demea, and the suave and elegant Micio (who has adopted one of Demea's sons) dispute about how to raise Demea's sons. At first Cicero is elegant and urbane, speaking lines that could come from Micio (28). Then, he brings on Appius Claudius Caecus, Clodia's grandfather, in the style and role of the strict authoritarian (33): good thing he's blind and can't see her! But this strategy could be turned against his client, so he brings on Publius Clodius, her brother and his political enemy, in the urbane and polished style (36) of the "helpful friend." Next, Cicero plays stern and severe father from the Roman comic poet Caecilius (37), followed by the elegant and urbane father from Terence's play (38). Thus, ring-composition ends this portion of his speech as we return to the *persona* of Micio.

Cicero's strategy offers entertainment as compensation for jury duty. But, more important, he reconstructs a question of fact as a question of representation and, in so doing, reconstructs a legal case as a comic drama. By critiquing the prosecution's casting and offering several comic defenses, Cicero implies an argument that is never made explicit: the prosecutors are also comic figures – "See their masks?" says Cicero. Behind their perform-ance you'll find Clodia directing the action. They have been giving us words, but it is a bungled production, bungled as a form of entertainment and bungled as a law case. The roles are not so much about the facts of the case as they are about how the production of facts and the construction of the case should be seen. A case of murder and poison is unpacked: out come *personae* no less inventive, predictable or amusing than the trunk-fish. The strategy implicitly casts Cicero as the clever slave: he plays many roles and helps the jury to see both what it may not see in the case (the petty ridiculous motives of the petty prosecutors) and what it cannot see at the *ludi Megalenses* (a comic play). "Don't let them give you words," he says, as he casts about for words and another mask, the last one being the broken father: "Save the son for his father – and the father for the son. Do not let people say you had contempt for an old age whose hopes are already nearly at an end," words more pitiable because they seem to come from the old man himself.

Scene two: M. Tulli, quid agis? *(Cicero,* Against Catiline *1.27.8)*

The strategic use of *personae* is easy to illustrate. But Cicero's shortest, and yet in some ways most brilliant, speech adopts varied postures which serve a much more slavish purpose. The first Catilinarian also plays with percep-tions. In his opening sentences Cicero turns to Catiline: "Don't you see that your conspiracy is already trapped and limited by the knowledge of all of these men?" (1.1). The words mark Catiline's audacity just as they presage

Cicero's confidence and suggest his omniscience. He repeats this claim: "No matter where you turn, you are trapped. For us, all your plans are clearer than daylight" (1.6). But later, when he needs to explain his own inability to take decisive action, he says, "And yet there are some in this order who either do not see what hangs over their heads or pretend not to see what they see" (1.30). Confidence and knowledge has been replaced by uncertainty: do these clever senators not see what he sees or are they dissembling. Cicero does not know, but this uncertainty points to the need for a versatile response and shows Cicero's awareness of depth of the problem: I won't act now because there is a larger problem at hand; I am waiting to eliminate the root and branch of this disease, he says.

These contradictions go to the heart of the problem of interpreting the first Catilinarian: What is its purpose? It cannot be assimilated to deliberative or forensic discourse, although it deals with both fact and policy. It never asks for anything from its audience. But it does display some wily self-recreations. Cicero announces a crisis and makes Catiline responsible: "How much longer will you abuse our patience, Catiline?" (1.1). He claims the senate and the consul are responsible: "Oh the times! O the morals! The senate understands this; the consul sees it. But he still lives" (1.2). He claims the senate is not responsible but he is: "It's not that the Republic lacks a plan or the authority of this body: we are lacking, we are, I say it openly" (1.3). Then he says that the world, the city, the senate are unimaginably corrupt and complicit in Catiline's conspiracy: "I see certain men here in the senate who were together with you. O the immortal gods! Where in the world are we? What kind of state do we have? In what kind of city do we live?" (1.8–9). He condemns himself for worthless inaction (1.4), and then says it is his strategy that Catiline lives and that he lives hemmed in by Ciceronian guards and that Catiline is helpless: "You will live, and you will live a life just like the one you now have, besieged by my many steadfast guards, so you cannot make any move against the state" (1.6). He says he will not allow Catiline to remain in the city and he orders Catiline out (1.10); then, he says that Catiline is already planning to leave (1.10). Finally, he claims that he is not ordering Catiline out but merely advising him to leave (1.13).

The coherence of this apparent improvisation[5] does not lie in its argument, but in its improvisational display. When Cicero first announces a crisis and then calms the fears of his audience, when he speaks for the fatherland in a self-interrogation and then speaks for Jupiter's providence, when he obscures the very function of his speech (to announce the crisis, to isolate Catiline in the city, to drive Catiline into exile, to frighten him into

5 So Craig 1993.

taking action, to tell the senate what Catiline will do anyway), he is not performing a simple or even clear strategic act of persuasion. He is performing the restless, attentive, vigilant and provident, self-sacrificing and self-aggrandizing character of the consul selected by fate to protect Rome. His contradictions are a feature of his capacities. This is wily rhetoric and political theater at its best.

Act three: the rhetorical drama of history

For Sallust, the challenge in writing history was not to be found in the discovery of the truth or the analysis of events. It was twofold: first, actions must be equaled by words (*facta dictis exaequenda sunt*); second, the audience must be convinced that you are not making things up (*The War with Catiline* 3.2). These two basically rhetorical problems pull in opposite directions, since people reject what is, in fact, beyond them. It is Sallust's sense that history is not the record of what happened, but a response to the rhetoric of that record. "Athenian history was rich and magnificent, but not as great as its reputation. Rather, because writers of great (rhetorical) genius were produced there, Athenian deeds are celebrated as the greatest throughout the world" (*The War with Catiline* 8.2). For Sallust, rhetoric and history are inextricable from each other. Although Sallust might not approve of the characterization, history, for him, does "give words" to his audience: it makes them see what they do not see. And, in *The War with Catiline* what they see is the pretense of moralistic rhetoric and the difficulties of finding moral certainty in history. It is, therefore, not surprising that *The War with Catiline* ends with the figure of Catiline speaking and acting in the tradition of the best of Roman generals. As a satiric history, *The War with Catiline* questions the words it gives.

Scene one: quo mihi rectius uidetur
(Sallust, The War with Catiline *1.3)*

The moralistic certainty of the opening to *The War with Catiline*[6] is a rhetoric of illusion that enacts the illusion of rhetoric, the illusion that we have grasped the truth. The mask of this illusion is the moral absolutism of the elder Cato, whose style Sallust also adopts. "All men should strive with all their resources not to pass their lives unnoticed." That sounds good, but it gets us nowhere. Should Catiline use all his resources? He surely passed his life well noticed, if not well regarded, and now, thanks to Sallust, he will enjoy the fame of history as well. Ironic as this may be, it is no different

---

[6] For the logic of the introduction, see Batstone 1990.

from Sallust's proof that mental resources are better than physical resources. This was proved by the first kings and cities to enter history with names: they coveted the possessions of others, their lust for domination justified war, and they measured glory by empire. Later, when Sallust points out that the glory of deeds depends on the rhetorical talent of historians (and their ability to manipulate the skepticism of readers), we may wonder just what one should do. Hire a good historian? Someone to give words to the historical record? The monograph ends, of course, with (Sallust giving) Catiline giving brilliant words to his men and dying in the vanguard on the field.

Scene two: ingens uirtus

The rhetoric of the historian is no less problematic than the rhetoric of his subjects. This problem underwrites Sallust's *sunkrisis*, the comparison of Cato and Caesar.[7] Sallust describes these men as the only men of "extraordinary virtue" in his memory, although their characters were different. And that is part of the problem: virtue is not one thing. It entails the very divisions and tensions that lead to strife and civil chaos. The comparison of Cato and Caesar elaborates tension within *uirtus*, but Sallust complicates the substantive problem with the rhetoric of posturing.

In this comparison, virtues rarely oppose each other. The oppositions are instead rhetorical, only appearing to entail a moral contradiction. Caesar is "beneficent and generous"; Cato has "integrity" (54.2). The problem is that there is no lack of integrity in doing good and generous things. Unless, of course, the implication of "integrity" is that these good and generous deeds are actually self-serving: Caesar's career was marked by bribery, we are told.[8] Now we have an opposition, but we no longer have two sets of virtues; in place of "extraordinary virtue, different characteristics" we have the rhetoric of competition. It is as if Cato sees Caesar's generosity and beneficence as a form of "giving words," the mask of generosity which is really self-serving.

Sallust has composed a rhetorical conflict that plays with *uirtus*. Caesar's virtues appear, like his energies, expansive: beneficence and generosity; kindness and compassion; giving, helping, forgiving. Cato's virtues are simple, singular, repetitious: integrity; moral values; not bribing. "Moral values added dignity to Cato," Sallust says, and Cato takes the very word, dignity, that Caesar used to justify civil war. The word refers to action and

---

[7] For an earlier and more complete discussion of the *sunkrisis*, see Batstone 1988.
[8] See McGushin 1977: 272.

service to the Republic, to offices held and to military successes; not a word that one would give to Cato, a man who never advanced beyond the praetorship. And, "not bribing": how is that a virtue – except as the stern unmasking of Caesar's propensity to give help? Sallust's comparison is becoming a rhetorical contest for who gets to say what Caesar's or Cato's virtues are. As Sallust gives words to these men, trying to make his words equal the facts, we find these men like the clever slaves of Plautus "giving words" to each other, each trying to change the other.

Act four: lyric and the rhetorical drama of self

Who speaks in lyric? The poet talking to himself or nobody (John Stuart Mill)? Catullus, the Roman poet of romantic sincerity, is also a clever *persona*. But Catullus does not always disaggregate mask from self. Just as the actor cannot appear without the mask, so the mask cannot act without the actor. The interrelationship between mask and actor, or self and *persona*, of "who I am" and "what I say," is what makes Catullus' lyric drama of rhetoric more than merely strategic.

I take as my example a poem that I have elsewhere described as the riddle of self and society.[9] In poem 49 Catullus sends thanks to Cicero: "Catullus, the worst of all poets, sends you the greatest thanks, as much the worst of all poets as you are the best of all patrons" (49.4–7). Why does the poet thank the master of rhetoric? The poem never says. Is Catullus merely ironic? Should we reverse the terms and read the poem's praise as insult? Catullus is telling Cicero that he is the worst of all patrons. *Optimus poeta!* Perhaps Catullus is really thanking Cicero for some specific favor. Now we have an occasional poem; perhaps it was never meant to be published. Neither interpretive strategy is particularly satisfactory.

The gracious and ironic readings, however, may not be at odds. In fact, they may inhabit each other both in the poem and in the forum. The poem not only thanks Cicero but offers that thanks as a form of praise, one that recalls his aspirations and achievements: his oratorical style (the superlatives and the tri-colon crescendo: "most eloquent of Romulus' grandsons, as many as are, as many as have been, as many as will be in years to come"), his political achievement (*Marce Tulli* is the address of the senate), his success as lawyer and patron ("best of all patrons"). The praise, however, recalls Cicero's own tendency to self-praise. The words are both imitation and parody: Catullus dons the Ciceronian mask. But as Catullus cannot merely parody or ironize this mask because the cleverness of his trifling

[9] Batstone 1993.

depends upon the fact that those achievements and that forensic style will be identifiable to readers in the future. So, Catullus believes in the very words that parody Cicero's words. Catullan irony depends upon Ciceronian success. Thus, the fame he wishes for wishes for himself ("may my book last through the years for more than one generation" 1.10) reflects the fame he expects for Cicero. If we begin with parody, we arrive at an undeniable sense of Cicero's special greatness: *disertissime Romuli nepotum*, 49.1. If, however, we begin reading the poem as praise, we find parody and a mocking formula of quantitative evaluation.

Once again, the Roman appears as a clever slave, giving words, adopting masks, changing the others in his drama. But, this time we see more clearly how the dramatic rhetoric of self is both self-defining and interactive: Catullus can be a *pessimus poeta* precisely because of Cicero's posturing. In fact, the term *pessimus poeta* comes from Cicero's world; it is what the serious world of the forum would call the trifling neoteric poet.[10] Catullus accepts the distinction, and then gives Cicero back his own words.

Act five: the satiric rhetorical drama of moral pedagogy

After the three diatribes that begin Horace's first book of *Satires*, he turns to self-justification and self-defense. The fourth satire is a clever piece of rhetoric in itself, bobbing and weaving, confusing too much freedom of speech with too much freedom in style and quantity, tracing a history of "satiric discourse" from the manly comedic attacks of Old Comedy to the viciously excessive number of verses written by Lucilius to the pusillanimous reticence of Horace himself. Horace says he is afraid to hold public recitals because some people don't like this kind of writing. "Everyone is afraid of these verses; they hate poets" (33). "Okay," Horace says, "it's time for a defence." But then the Horatian soft shoe: "First of all, this isn't poetry" (39–40); it's more like a conversation (42), like the "ardent father" who criticizes his son. This ain't no Ennian epic, he says (60). Then he backs off: some other time we'll discuss whether this is poetry or not (63–64). But by the end of the poem he has included himself in the band of poets (141). It's an elliptical version of the lawyer's argument: It's not a poem; and if it is a poem, it doesn't do any harm; and if it does do some harm, you deserve it and everyone else is doing it.

---

[10] *pessimus poeta*; the term *pessimus* is regularly associated with the clever slave of comedy. See, e.g., Plautus, *Pseudolus* 1285, and especially Pseudolus' greeting: "Bad man presents himself to best of men," *uir malus uiro optimo obuiam it*, 1293.

But there is another argument going on as well: the important thing is what this verse does for Horace. As the poem moves from political attacks of Old Comedy to the social criticism of Lucilius to New Comedy to Horace's father to Horace alone muttering to himself and occasionally writing down his mutterings, the verse defends and enacts a focus on moral self-pedagogy. By defending this self-pedagogy in terms of a dramatic model, Horace stages self-pedagogy as a gap in consciousness that allows us both to be moral judges of ourselves and to be distant from our capacity to judge at the same time as we exercise that capacity. Let us see how this works in the poem.

Horace asks for indulgence if he happens to speak a bit too freely, joke too broadly. It was his father, he says, who accustomed him to treat the world as moral *exempla* useful for moral pedagogy (103–106). The scene that follows is derived from Terence's *Brothers*: there, Demea explains to the slave Syrus how he has raised his son by using others as moral exempla. In the play, the irony is that Demea mistakenly believes that his moral instruction has been successful. He does not know, as Syrus does, that his son has taken up with a girl and that Syrus has been playing him for a fool. Syrus cannot refrain from mocking Demea further by taking Demea's story of *exempla* as the *exemplum* for his own instructions to the other slaves in the kitchen. Thus, Demea's self-satisfied moral pedagogy becomes a scene of dishwashing and seasoning. Why does Horace reference this scene?

It is a reference to the dangerously self-satisfied nature of moral pedagogy. In other words, Horace simultaneously refers to the healthy (paternalistic) impulse to point out bad examples (this is the satiric impulse) and satirizes that impulse. Thus, Horace's father points out bad examples and in that very act almost becomes a bad example. The grace and sophistication of Horace's satire, however, does not lie in this clever scene of father and (mocking?) son. Horace goes on to say that the impulse to do this has become a part of his own character (105–106), and that it has been largely successful: he is plagued only by the moderate, forgivable vices (129–31), one of which is this very satiric habit (139–40). Thus, like his father, he points out a vice, which is both his own and his father's, a vice which is satire's vice. What is brilliant about the achievement here is Horace's sense that his technique for securing moral health is itself (potentially) a vice, but one that succeeds more or less. This means that moral self-pedagogy and the rhetoric of satire are themselves but masks, the masks in which self-pedagogy appears. So, while Horace asks indulgence for his satiric posture, because that posture is an intermediate vice, it becomes clear that it is this very posture that allows him to overcome his vices. This is not, then, a mask that Horace deploys while maintaining his distance from it, it is the concrete appearance of moral pedagogy.

And if you don't like it, says Horace at the end (140–43), we poets, like the proselytizing Jews, are everywhere. And, of course, they are. We cannot avoid moral discourse, bad examples, and proselytizing. In fact, the Horatian satirist is indistinguishable from the critics who point him out as a bad example, and who should not take their own moral judgments too seriously.

The rhetorical and dramatic contests of the forum that began our discussion with Palaestrio turning Sceledus and Pyrgopolynices into someone else's self ("He's mine," Palaestrio says) play across the field of Latin literature. In Plautus it is ludic and appropriative. In Cicero it creates both the case and the polymorphous capacities of the consul. In Sallust the world's rhetoric swallows up moral absolutism and even virtue, while Catullus plays with how in the forum we are a relationship of masks. Finally, in Horace, moral self-pedagogy becomes a performance that allows us to avoid the vice of taking satire too seriously. The person we are, like the comic actor's mask, is always a performance, always at a distance from the actor, but without it, neither the actor nor the self-conscious subject can appear. In fact, the drama of rhetoric at Rome is what constitutes the Roman subject as the split between mask and actor, the gap where the subject relates to itself and the world by representing itself, by giving words to others and even to itself.

Suggestions for further reading (and writing)

One can find many books and articles about drama as a representative art, as that which is not life but is the art of actors pretending to be something that they are not. In the work done on Roman comedy the tendency has been to treat these plays as either the traces of a foreign culture of slavery and mastery, or as celebrations of authorial cleverness, as "metatheatrical" representations of theater as theater. Similarly, one can find many works on rhetoric as the art of using words to persuade and manipulate, irrespective of the truth, essence, and sincerity. However, putting drama and rhetoric together, as our editor as asked me to do, has allowed me to change the reference of these terms: drama becomes the lawyer's art in comedy's metatheatrical representations of law and in the Roman courtroom itself. In those same metatheatrical representations, the self is represented as a person (*persona*: mask), while in the politico-satirical work of Sallust the history of greatness is refracted in the rhetoric and drama of the historical record and the rhetorical positioning of actors. Even the sincerity of the lyric self dissolves into dramas of self-definition, while the moral pedagogy of satire finds its place in the ironic distance upon oneself that is a staple of comedy. For the most part, this is new territory and there is no easy reading list that will help the curious explore these intersections.

For basic background, however, there are many non-classical works that will be useful. I cite only a few. In the psychological literature, one should begin with and become familiar with the ideas of Jacques Lacan, especially "The Mirror Stage as Formative of the I Function," in *Écrits*, trans. Bruce Fink (New York, 2005) 75–81. The work of Slavoj Žižek has continued to explore Lacanian ideas often in the context of modern popular culture. These explorations are provocative and stimulating. Also useful to me has been Louis Althuser, "Ideology and Ideological State Apparatuses" (available in *Lenin and Philosophy and Other Essays*) and Michael Taussig, *Mimesis and Alterity* (London, 1992). In the literature on comedy and drama, I have benefited from Lionel Abel, *Metatheatre: A New View of Dramatic Form* (New York, 1963), revised and republished with new essays as *Tragedy and Metatheatre* (New York, 2003), and Alenka Zupančič, "The 'Concrete Universal' and What Comedy Can Tell Us about It," in *Lacan: The Silent Partners*, ed. Slavoj Žižek (London, 2006). The field of rhetoric, however, perhaps because it is both more traditional and less contemporary, has produced fewer theoretical texts that are useful to the intersections of self, rhetoric, and drama.

In the field of Classics, there are a few authors and works to whom one can turn. Among the most important and challenging is the work of Erik Gunderson, *Declamation, Paternity, and Roman Identity: Authority and the Rhetorical Self* (Cambridge, 2003). In the field of oratory, one may now begin with John Dugan, *Making a New Man: Ciceronian Self-Fashioning in the Rhetorical Works* (Oxford, 2005). William Fitzgerald, *Catullan Provocations: Lyric Poetry and the Drama of Position* (Berkeley, 1995) may help to introduce readers to Catullan lyric in terms of the Roman rhetoric of social positioning. Work on Roman satire and on the relationship of history and rhetoric has not been much interested in issues that involve the rhetoric and/or drama of self. I hope that my own work in some of these areas, cited in the footnotes, will also be useful. Ultimately, however, the reading that needs to be done is in the classical authors themselves. And then there is the further writing that will explore the intersection of rhetoric and drama as constitutive of the self within and without the forum.

13

SIMON GOLDHILL

Rhetoric and the Second Sophistic

There has been no time in history when the formal study of rhetoric, as inaugurated in the fifth century BCE, has had such a pervasive impact on the education system and the culture of a society as in the so-called Second Sophistic. Rhetoric formed not only an integral and central aspect of the curriculum at all levels of study, but also the horizon of expectation in all aspects of cultural production, from statues of star performers to the language of letters between friends.

The term "Second Sophistic" was coined by the third-century CE writer Philostratus as a way of capturing his sense of how the scholars and orators of his own era looked back to the classical city for a privileged intellectual foundation.[1] It is a useful expression in that it strongly emphasizes two important strands of the history I shall be tracing. First, the writers of the first three centuries CE show an obsessive interest in the past and in the past of the classical city in particular: they are acutely conscious of their own belated status.[2] All the texts I will be discussing are written in the literary Attic Greek of the classical era, although the language of the streets by this period was *koine*, the language of the Christian Gospels.[3] The historical examples that stud the orator's speeches are similarly taken from events of five hundred years earlier. Social performance was calibrated by a knowledge of – and performance in – these borrowed clothes. This willful anachronism is not just a demonstration of technical flair: the imagination was formed by the concerns and figures of an era long passed. Second, the term "sophistic" marks the commitment to a form and style of learning associated with the great sophists of the classical era. This implies not merely a rhetorical training – that is, an ability to follow the strategies of

---

[1] *Lives of the Sophists* 481. See G. Anderson 1993; Swain 1996; Goldhill 2001; Whitmarsh 2001b.

[2] See especially Bowie 1970.

[3] See especially Swain 1996.

the master speakers as performer or as audience – but also a delight in paradox, a reveling in exotic argument, and a polyperverse pleasure in the full range of human knowledge. So Athenaeus imagines a dinner party (that lasts for fourteen books!) where a group of scholars swap quotations on subjects from how to behave at dinner to the great whores of the past; it is called suitably enough "The Sophists at Dinner": *Deipnosophistae*.

The "Second Sophistic" is also a distorting term, however. There is no indication, despite Philostratus, that there ever was a coherent group with a shared agenda (like the Bloomsbury Group or the Pre-Raphaelite Brotherhood) – and certainly not a group who would call themselves "sophists." I will be looking here at orators, politicians, satirists, novelists, essayists, and it would be hard to force them under a single rubric. The chronological boundaries of the Second Sophistic are also far from clear. Even if it were agreed to center the period on the second and third centuries, would Chariton, the novelist, or Plutarch, the polymathic intellectual, be excluded because they are too early – or Heliodorus, the novelist of the fourth century, excluded because too late? Should doctors and philosophers be sidelined because of their opposition to "sophists"? Although this chapter is called "Rhetoric and the Second Sophistic," it would be better to think of its subject more broadly as the burgeoning Greek culture of the Roman Empire.

Horace famously said that fierce Rome conquered Greece but was conquered in turn by Greek civilization, which brought art into rustic Italy (*Graecia capta ferum uictorem cepit et artis intulit agresti Latio ...*; *Epistles* 2.1.156).[4] The Roman *litterateur* may seem a trifle glib in his reckoning of the victims of Roman military and cultural imperialism, but he does reflect the extraordinary role of Greek culture in the Roman Empire. By the first century CE a good proportion of the Roman elite were comfortable speaking and reading Greek, and it was used across the empire especially in a literary or culturally sophisticated environment. Greek provided the models for Roman philosophy (though from Cicero onwards the desire for a Roman philosophy is repeatedly expressed also), and for Roman literature. Vergil's *Aeneid*, a founding text of the empire, parades its Homeric antecedents even as it constructs a myth of Rome's origins. Hadrian, an emperor especially associated with the flourishing of Greek culture in the second century, shaved, had a boyfriend – provocatively Greek gestures – founded the Panhellenion, a league of the truly great Greek cities to which many cities struggled to be admitted, and he promoted Greek studies. The Emperor Marcus Aurelius' *Meditations* are written – of course – in Greek.

---

[4] For the archaeology of the Roman takeover, see Alcock 1993.

This expansive and expanding Greek culture is not centered necessarily on mainland Greece with its great capitals of Athens, Thebes, and Corinth. The Hellenistic kingdoms, which dominated the Eastern Mediterranean after Alexander's conquests, spread Greek institutions, language, and values throughout Northern Africa, Egypt, and Asia Minor. This area is known conventionally as "the Greek East," and many of the writers I will be looking at in this chapter were born in and travelled around these territories between the cities of Ephesus, Smyrna, Halicarnassus, Prusa, Tarsus, and Palmyra. This area lived largely in peace and prosperity – the *pax Romana* – throughout the period I am discussing. Local towns were recognizably Greek: they had fine buildings including the iconic gymnasium, theatre, and *agora* (marketplace) by which a town was recognized as Greek. Local elites continued to rule under the general guidance, military power, and tax farming of the Roman Empire. Local elites also continued to run Greek festivals (and indeed to expand them), to make huge public donations to beautify their own cities, and to travel to and from the other urban centers of the empire, especially Rome and Alexandria.[5] Hadrian may have built Hadrian's Wall, but he spent years of his reign traveling with all the pomp of an emperor's cortege between the cities of the Greek East. From a different perspective, Lucian, the satirist, was born in Samosata in Syria, worked as an orator across the empire, including Rome, and probably took an imperial job in Egypt. Both Hadrian and Lucian, as they travelled the Roman roads protected by Roman soldiers, could expect to find a familiar Greek cultural milieu at each of their stops. Philostratus tells us of the sage Apollonius of Tyana who travelled to the Far East to find the true wisdom of the Orient. When he gets there, his gurus quote Euripides to him. As he puts it, "everything is Greece to the wise man."[6] There was indeed no escaping a Greek cultural perspective for the educated of the Roman Empire.

Greek culture was inculcated in part through the education system, the *enkuklios paideia* (or "cycle of learning") with its standardized curriculum.[7] Children learned first to read and write and progressed into the study of Greek poetry, headed as ever by Homer. Part of studying Homer was already studying the great speeches of the great heroes. The rhetoric training that followed built on these foundations. A child began with *progumnasmata*, "preparatory exercises," which are given a formal description in the rhetorical handbooks, and ninety-six examples are provided by Libanius (from the fourth century CE). These consisted in a series of exercises such as

---

[5] See van Nijf 2001; Wörrle 1988; Veyne 1976.
[6] *The Life of Apollonius of Tyana* 1.35.
[7] See T. Morgan 1998a; Too and Livingstone 1998; Marrou 1956.

an *encomium*, a speech of praise, or a *sunkrisis*, a comparison (of Hector and Achilles, say), or a *thesis*, an argument: "should one marry?" (These led towards the final stages of education, philosophy.) These *progumnasmata* were expanded into writing full speeches, which were practiced, criticized by the teacher, and in the best cases written down and circulated. This was an education in how to speak, how to order argument – how to think, that is – how to persuade (interact), and how to evaluate the presentations of others. As we will see below, it also involved a training in how to stand, how to present oneself, how to walk – how to have a public persona.[8] Rhetoric provided the vocabulary for social scrutiny and social policing. In short, an education in rhetoric was designed to make a citizen.

It is important to emphasize in this way that rhetoric, although it was a formal training, complete with handbooks, institutional practices and sites of specific performances, was not a bounded field. Although Plato was a standard text throughout this era, and, indeed, as Foucault, amongst others, has stressed, philosophy played a major role in the construction of a normative self-awareness in empire culture, nonetheless the familiar, Plato-led opposition of rhetoric to truth, or to sincerity or even to philosophy is not a commonplace of Greek writing in the empire. The most privileged term of literate achievement is *paideia*, which may be translated as education, or culture, or sophistication (the German *Bildung* comes perhaps closest of single-word translations) and the man who achieved this prized attribute is called *pepaideumenos*, "cultured," "educated," "sophisticated."[9] This *paideia* inevitably included a full appreciation of both the *ars rhetorica* and philosophical study. The study of rhetoric influenced all the forms of writing available, as it influenced the public persona of the citizen in all walks of life, not merely in the law court or diplomatic mission. For the educated man, rhetoric was the life-blood of language and self-presentation.

For the Greek elite citizen, living under Rome, rhetoric was crucial to his progress within society. At one level, this was simply that the institutions of local power – assemblies, court-rooms, audiences with the Roman rulers – required skilled verbal performance and brought both prestige and power. As the citizen rose in his own community, he could enter the international world of diplomacy between cities and between his home city and Rome. Dispute resolution, financial policy, political aggrandizement in the *pax Romana* entailed rhetorical authority. As Plutarch noted, there was no

[8] See Gleason 1995; Goldhill 2002: 60–107.
[9] See G. Anderson 1989; Schmitz 1997; Swain 1996: 18–64; Whitmarsh 2001b.

opportunity to emulate the military heroes of the Greek past ("nowadays the affairs of cities no longer include leadership in war, the overthrow of tyrants, grand alliances"; *Moralia* 805a). Success in rhetoric was a requirement of political prestige. At another level, rhetoric also provided a career in and for itself. Rhetoricians traveled between cities, giving performances of their art for money to rapt audiences (much as good lecturers in Victorian Britain and Northern America could garner audiences of over a thousand, and make a career out of lecturing or, in the case of a figure such as Dickens, make a fortune out of a lecture tour).[10] These epideictic performances could be light-hearted or trivial: Lucian's *Encomium of a Fly* or Synesius' *Encomium of Baldness* are designed for the pleasure and amusement of the audience, full of flashy, witty arguments, and clever turns of phrase. (So, paradigmatically, Synesius proves delightfully that Achilles, the greatest of Greek macho-men heroes, was bald in front. Athene, he notes, in the famous opening scene of the *Iliad* went behind Achilles to pull his hair. Why would she do this, if he were not bald in front?) But these speeches could have greater political or cultural import. Rhetoricians appealed to the moral or intellectual life of their audiences with arguments of potentially lasting influence. Dio of Prusa's three speeches *On Kingship*, delivered apparently to the court of Emperor Trajan, articulate a particular ideal of how to rule in the very center of Roman power – and thus perform with vivid intensity the role of a philosopher faced by a king.[11] What is at stake here is far more than the amusement of the audience or a display of a speaker's virtuosity.

Rhetoric, then, is not simply a skill or a field, but a fundamental medium for the circulation of ideas, the circulation of power, the performance of the self in the public life of the empire. From the schoolroom to the grandest political venue, rhetoric is integral to the formation and expression of elite culture for the Greek-speaking society of the Roman Empire.

Lucian, the second-century satirist, wrote a dramatic dialogue set on Mount Olympus, called the *Twice Accused*, in which the gods hear a series of legal cases (complete with very contemporary-sounding moans about administrative backlogs and bureaucratic hassles: Lucian knew his empire institutions from the inside). The final case is an accusation by Rhetoric and Dialogue against a certain Syrian orator. Lucian is Syrian and an orator, but this figure, typically for Lucian's playfulness, remains unnamed even in the court's deposition against him.[12] Rhetoric's accusation is one of abuse

[10] See Bowersock 1969. This work is now supplemented by Puech 2002.
[11] See Whitmarsh 1998.
[12] See Goldhill 2002: 80–107.

and neglect. She – in this world of figural representation, Rhetoric is a woman – begins amusingly with:

> In the first place, men of Athens, I pray to all the gods and goddesses that as much good will as I steadily entertain towards the city and all of you may be shown to me by you in this case, and secondly that the gods may move you to do what is above all the just thing to do – to bid my opponent to hold his tongue and to let me make the complaint in the way that I have preferred and chosen. I cannot come to the same conclusion when I contemplate my own experiences and the speeches that I hear...

At one level, the joke here is that with a jury of gods and goddesses, the standard language of divine support just does not work. But at another, any educated reader will immediately note that the first sentence of this speech is the first sentence of one of the most famous speeches of antiquity, Demosthenes' *On the Crown*. At least the sentence begins with Demosthenes' words, but Rhetoric makes a poor job of adjusting it to her case. Where Demosthenes asks that his opponent should not be allowed to set the agenda for how his case is heard, Rhetoric just wants her opponent to keep quiet so she can make her complaint in the way she wants. Her petulance distorts the celebrated Demosthenic flow. The second sentence of Rhetoric's introduction may not seem to follow elegantly from the first (or indeed to make much sense at all after the first). That is because it is the first sentence of another famous speech, Demosthenes' *Third Olynthiac*, which has been tacked on to *On the Crown*'s opening. Lucian has Rhetoric make a hash of her own principles of training. She knows that Demosthenes writes the paradigmatic *prooemia* (introductions), which were circulated separately as training devices, and she knows that imitating the great masters is good practice; but her attempt to cobble together some Demosthenic material comes out as a parody of a beginning student's exercise.

Rhetoric does get into her flow, however, with the *diēgēsis* ("narrative") which follows: "I found this man, gentleman of the jury, when he was but a youth, a barbarian still in his voice, and all but wearing a caftan in Assyrian style. He was still wandering about Ionia; he didn't know what to do with himself. So I took him up and educated/cultured [*epaideuse*] him." Rhetoric portrays the Syrian as a foreigner at a loose end in the Greek East, marked out by his dodgy accent and weird clothes. He lacks *paideia*, which is what she gives him. Indeed, she marries him, and they travel the empire together gaining fame and wealth. The Syrian agrees "Yes, she did educate me and we travelled abroad together, and she inscribed me in the class of Greeks. For this much at least, I owe her thanks for my marriage." The picture in this story is of a young man from the East who through education and rhetorical performance becomes accepted as a Greek – with all the cultural capital that implies. Rhetoric gives an entry to society, like marrying a rich Greek woman.

It is always difficult to read through the ironic layers of Lucian's highly sophisticated prose. This is a parody, and like all good parodies it fully inhabits its subject: it is a highly rhetorical joke about the claims of rhetoric. But what underlies the humor is the serious cultural observation that rhetoric is essential for acculturation into Greek society, and that it is also a route to power and wealth and fame. Yet this is also a story of the rejection of rhetoric. Rhetoric explains how the Syrian deserted her for another genre, Dialogue: "Instead of saying what he wants in a grand voice, he fits together and spells out short paragraphs, for which he cannot get fulsome praise or huge applause from the audience, but only a smile or a restrained hand gesture or a nod of the head or a groan over his words." The response to genres is fully physicalized. Rhetoric, with great voice, demands the full audience, the applause, the public celebration of praise, that is, the superstar status of the successful rhetorical performer. Dialogue suggests the private and intimate response of the small gesture, quiet nods, a smile rather than a belly laugh, that is, the library or salon rather than the public arenas of the city. The Syrian, interestingly, defends himself by accusing rhetoric of being a whore, reveling in a string of lovers and their raucous parties. The very public nature of rhetoric is turned against itself, with a neat mixture of Platonic disdain and barrack-room sexual innuendo.

Here, then, is our first image of rhetoric in the Second Sophistic. In Lucian's playful and highly self-aware portrayal, rhetoric is on the one hand the cultural training which makes Greek citizens Greek, which leads to wealth and fame, which links the elite of empire; but it is also, on the other hand, the blowzy strumpet which he rejects first in the name of dialogue, the genre he is writing here. Yet to appreciate the jokes of this dialogue one needs an expert awareness of rhetoric: the citations from Demosthenes, the mocking of the use of Demosthenic *prooemia*, the parody of the *diegesis* from a sex'n'scandal case, all point to Lucian's insider dealing. He has his rhetorical cake and mocks it.

The self-consciousness that marks Lucian's parody is a constant aspect of Second Sophistic rhetoric. When everyone has been trained in rhetoric, the audience for any speech is a knowing group. Tropes are shared, like clichés, but need careful working if they are to be persuasive. Few writers manipulate the self-consciousness of the rhetorically sophisticated *pepaideumenos* with as much flair as the second-century novelist Achilles Tatius.[13]

---

[13] On Achilles Tatius see Bartsch 1989; Goldhill 1995: 46–111; and especially Morales 2004.

Every character in the novel, *Leucippe and Cleitophon,* is capable of bursting into a fully trained rhetorical expressiveness. In front of a picture, a character delivers an *ekphrasis*, with all the correct critical vocabulary; at a funeral, a lament with paradoxical and balanced phrases (which inevitably strikes the modern reader as "insincere"); a woman faced by a would-be rapist launches a tirade of defense that verbally batters him into retreat; men on board ship have a formal debate about whether sex is better with a boy or a girl (no decision is reached). But this is all passed through the prism of a first-person narrator, the hero of the novel, Cleitophon, whose love affairs and tribulations we follow. The self-consciousness is heightened for the reader because the narrative is continually expressed as the self-expression of the narrator. The delight in the games of self-awareness is particularly evident in the many scenes of erotic seduction. *Peithō* in Greek means "persuasion" and it is the aim of rhetorical performance (as expressed in handbooks from Aristotle's *Rhetoric* onwards). But *peithō* is also the normal Greek for sexual seduction, and it is a term closely associated with *erōs* in Greek writing from the fifth century BCE onwards.[14] So it should be no surprise that we see the novel's rhetorical *élan* as lover approaches lover.

In the first book, for example, Cleitophon takes the opportunity of a walk in a garden to have a conversation with his servant Satyrus about desire – designed all too consciously to be overheard by Leucippe and her attendant. He has been instructed in erotic matters by his cousin and confidante, and told that he should not say anything direct about sex to a young girl, since such a blunt approach will result in shame, blushes, and rebuttal. So here he wants "to make the girl compliant in the ways of desire" (1.16.1) by more indirect means. As they promenade, they pass a peacock, which had "fanned out his glory and staged a show of his feathers" (*to theatron epideiknunai tōn pterōn*). And this prompts our hero also to make a show of his epideictic rhetorical skills:

> "Not without art," I said, "does the bird act. He is a lover, you see. When he wishes to seduce his beloved, he glorifies himself like this."

Cleitophon, with a lover's eyesight, may be seeing love in the natural world all around him, but he is also delightfully describing his own arrant indirection. As Cleitophon wants to make his beloved compliant (*euagōgon*), so the peacock is depicted as seducing (*epagagesthai*) his beloved. Cleitophon, like the peacock, is displaying his art (*tekhnē* – ever the technical term for rhetoric's training). Like the peacock, he is strutting his stuff and showing

---

[14] See Buxton 1982.

his colors, glorifying (*kallōpizetai*) himself in and through his rhetorical skill. Indeed, Cleitophon, testing his rhetorical virtuosity to the limits, is prepared to find the display of desire anywhere, even in the proverbially unfeeling rock and iron (1.17.2):

> The loadstone loves (*erāi*) the iron. If she sees it and touches it, she drags it towards herself, as though she had some erotic force in it. Is this not a kind of kiss between the desirous stone and her beloved, the iron?

Cleitophon is trying to create a world of heightened erotic sensibility, where love is everywhere, in order to stimulate the girl's erotic feelings. So the magnet's force over the iron is fully personalized: the magnet *sees* the iron, it *touches* the iron, its *attraction* of iron is erotically motivated, and, with a final hyperbolic twist, their touching is described as a *kiss*. (It is clear enough what Cleitophon is angling for here and will achieve shortly afterwards.) Plato in his *Ion* famously used the image of the magnet and iron to express the dangerous emotional disturbance of theatrical performance, where the power of performance lures the shaking and overwhelmed souls of the audience towards itself. In Cleitophon's theater of rhetoric as seduction, the same image is reveled in, as a device to promote the very psychological disturbance which Plato so feared.

Cleitophon shows off his training with some skill. His stylish pose helps us see how certain texts of the Second Sophistic, which are not always discussed under the rubric of rhetoric, become part of rhetorical performance and the training of the *pepaideumenos*. Aelian, for example, wrote his encyclopedic book *On Animals* probably in the first decades of the third century. Aelian appears in Philostratus' *Lives of the Sophists*, where the accuracy of his Attic Greek and the simplicity of his style are celebrated, along with the bizarre fact that he had never left Italy or even been on a boat in his life. (He also never married and had no children – thus living out one side of the standard sophistic debate, whether it is better to marry or not.) Aelian's *On Animals* is a vast collection of short paragraphs collecting paradoxes about the animal kingdom. He tells us for example of the Moray, a sea-snake, which copulates with the viper, a land-snake (1.50), and how desire thus brings together those that seem so far apart. Cleitophon uses exactly the same story as one of his examples of how all nature is full of the erotic (1.18.3). Aelian wrote after Achilles Tatius, of course; but Achilles Tatius lets us see how Aelian might have been used. *On Animals* is read to provide the *pepaideumenos* with an arsenal of paradoxical facts and bizarre stories to parade in conversation. It is a handbook to be raided to cut a dash in conversation. In a similar way, Philostratus' own *Erotic Letters* constructs a series of snapshots of erotic scenarios and in particular the articulate and literary response to such imbroglios. They "provide a manual for self-expression as a Greek lover within the tropology of classical eros,"[15] that is, they teach the readers how to perform the rhetoric of desire in a proper Greek way. The self-expression of the educated Second Sophistic lover depends on its well-learned tropes and forms of articulacy. This is true even when the need for education is being denied: when Cleitophon's cousin tells Cleitophon not to seek advice because "love is a self-taught sophist," not only is this the opening to a long speech of precisely such advice, but also the idea of love teaching eloquence is lifted from Euripides, just as the description of love as a sophist is lifted from Plato and Xenophon.[16] The paradoxical delight of such a learned dismissal of learning is typical of the flair of Achilles Tatius' rhetorical prose.

The novel shows us, then, the young and well-educated man-about-town trying out his rhetorical talents. As readers we enjoy his self-conscious verbal display, while we observe his seductive virtuosity with our own amused distance. Because it is a first-person narrative, however, told through Cleitophon's mouth, we only see the effects of his speech through the eyes of the speaker. As the lovers meet, fall in love, and travel the Mediterranean in their picaresque adventures, the whole story is played out through Cleitophon's rhetorically informed exegesis. There is no vantage point untouched by the wit and self-serving interest of the *pepaideumenos* as narrator. With Achilles Tatius we are immersed in the world of rhetoric in action.

Dio of Prusa, known as Dio Chysostom ("Golden Mouth") because of his eloquence, gives us a quite different way to appreciate the performance of rhetoric in the Second Sophistic. Dio lived from the second half of the first century into the first decades of the second century.[17] While we know next to nothing about the lives of either Lucian or Achilles Tatius, except what can be gleaned from their own writing (a process usually undertaken in an overzealous manner), in Dio's case we also have some external evidence which allows us to see the life of a Greek intellectual in the Roman Empire in more detail. His speeches were delivered, it seems, across the empire, from his home city in the province of Bithynia (the Greek East), to the great sites of the Greek mainland such as Olympia, to Rome itself. He is a figure with strong local ties, who speaks for Greek culture both as a politician and as an orator, and who works in Rome within the power structures of the

---

[15] Goldhill forthcoming.

[16] Cf 5.27 where "Eros teaches eloquence." Euripides, fr. 430 (Nauck); Plato, *Symposium* 203d; Xenophon, *The Education of Cyrus* 6.1.41.

[17] On Dio, see Swain 2000; Gangloff 2006.

imperial system. He was exiled by the Emperor Domitian (because of his association with a disgraced nobleman, he tells us).[18] He was rehabilitated under Trajan, however, and Pliny and Trajan swap letters about a political plot against Dio in 110–11 CE, when Pliny was Governor of the province of Bithynia (Pliny, *Letters* 10.81–82). They both agree to act to support Dio against his enemies. Dio was an orator fully embedded in and engaged with the upper echelons of authority within the Roman Empire.

Dio was a hero of later rhetoricians, including the Christian bishop Synesius, whose *Encomium of Baldness* was written in response to Dio's *jeu d'ésprit*, an *Encomium to Hair*. Philostratus lavishes praise on Dio in the *Lives of the Sophists* and gives two memorable anecdotes, which tell us a good deal about the idealizing image of the orator in this period. In his exile Dio worked at menial tasks and dressed in rags, in which guise he would visit military camps (*Lives of the Sophists* 488). He was at one such camp when the news of the assassination of Domitian arrived. The soldiers were beginning to mutiny, but Dio leapt on to an altar, threw off his rags, and began a stern moralizing speech with the Homeric verse, "Then Odysseus of the many wiles stripped off his rags." He revealed who he was and he encouraged them not to mutiny but to follow the will of the Roman people. "The persuasive charm (*peithō*) of the man," writes Philostratus, "was such as to captivate even those not versed in Greek letters" (*Lives of the Sophists* 488). The soldiers (who may be expected to have had a range of responses to the quotation from a Greek epic poet in such a crisis, not to mention a lecture from a philosophizing Greek intellectual), even though they are not the *pepaideumenoi*, the usual audience for Dio's rhetoric, nonetheless respond positively and the dangerous crowd is quelled by the authority of the great man (as Homer depicts Odysseus controlling the rioting Greeks in the *Iliad*). This is the power of rhetoric, vividly enacted. In the second anecdote we are told that Dio rode in the triumphal chariot of Trajan in Rome, and Trajan remarked, "I do not know what you are saying, but I love you as myself." It is not relevant whether this story is true or not. What it shows us is how the historian of the great orators of the past and present is happy to tell a story of a Greek intellectual having the ear of the most powerful man on earth, even if it is a story which seems precariously double-edged about the success of Dio's advising. In the first anecdote Dio embodies the hero who makes a glorious return out of disguise and humiliation – hence the references to Homer. But where a hero would slaughter

---

[18] Dio's exile has been the source of great debate: see Moles 1978; Sidebottom 1996; Griffin 1996; Whitmarsh 2001a.

his enemies, Dio makes a speech that demonstrates the full power of his oratory. The return from exile is a return to the role of public figure, a moral and political arbiter. In the second anecdote we see Dio back at the centre of power, by the right hand of the emperor, as befits the man who wrote the orations on kingship. Dio lets us see, then, first of all, an image of the rhetorician as man of power, swaying the crowds, influencing authority, advising heads of state.

This role of the orator as adviser to kings and moral authority for the citizens is regularly enacted in the writings of the Second Sophistic. In his speech known as the *Euboicus* (*Oration* 7), Dio tells a story of how he was shipwrecked off the coast of Euboia (hence the name of the speech), and how he fell in with a noble but poor farmer, whose simple life contrasts tellingly with the sins and corruption of the big city. This innocent went to the city, where he became embroiled in a nasty court case. Dio depicts the city's orators with a mixture of satire and scorn: they appear as a fully Aristophanic portrait gallery of charlatans, swindlers, and self-interested politicians.[19] (Even the innocent farmer, as in Aristophanes, gets his share of mockery, as his bumpkin understanding of the city is exposed along with his nobler innocence.) But all of this story (1–80) is a prelude to Dio's own moral fervor. The speech becomes an argument for poverty against wealth, a simple life against the delights of civilized living, which ends up with a ringing attack on prostitution as an institution. This is the first time that an attack on prostitution as such is articulated in the ancient world. Dio sets out to question the standard assumptions of sexual behavior in the city in a far more provocative way than his attack on the life of luxury (which is a time-honored theme of Roman rhetoric in particular). It is no surprise that Dio became a favorite of Christian writers such as Synesius. His advice should be seen within the frame of shifting attitudes towards sexuality (that have been extensively traced in recent years, following the lead of Peter Brown and Michel Foucault). Dio's grand speech, the longest in his corpus, uses both his cleverly attractive story-telling and his strongly provocative arguments to construct a powerful case against the flabby sexual license of the ancient city (as he sees it). This is the orator performing as moral authority for the citizens. This powerful, didactic, argumentative rhetorical performance stands at the opposite end of the spectrum from Achilles Tatius' sly eroticism.

The role of the orator as advisor of princes can also help us see how rhetoric enters the everyday lives of the elite of the empire. Favorinus from

---

[19] See Ma 1996.

Gaul was a superstar performer, who when he spoke in Rome attracted to his audience even people who knew no Greek, since his odd appearance, and his high-pitched and strangely modulated voice apparently made enough of a show in itself.[20] He was born a hermaphrodite and made himself into a celebrity, which he summed up in three paradoxes. He was a Gaul who became Greek, a eunuch who was prosecuted for adultery, and a man who argued with the emperor and lived. We have already seen with Lucian the capacity of *paideia* to make a man, even one from Gaul, into a "Greek" – a member of the cultured elite; the ability of the performer to excite scandal and sexual allure is captured in the second paradox (and the fact that each self-definition is a paradox is in itself typical of the sophistic love of irony and reversal). But the third paradox indicates that more is at stake here than the celebrity of a strange performance artist. Favorinus boasts that he disagreed with the supreme power and yet escaped punishment. The orator's role at court as advisor is always precarious, and it demands a particular rhetorical mastery because of the constant threat involved in such a position.

Indeed, in a hierarchical system where the differences in power are immense, the danger of social exchange is painfully felt. In public life the citizen is judged by his words (and self-presentation), and in the potentially violent, recriminatory political search for success, every word must be weighed. The orator before the emperor is only a limit case of every citizen's scrutiny and risk. Hence, we have essays in the Second Sophistic on "how to praise oneself in passing," or discussions of *eschēmatismenos logos*, "figured speech," speech that conceals any criticism within carefully guarded neutrality.[21] In particular, there is a sequence of texts that worry about true friendship and the dangers of flattery (a theme that builds on Aristotle's classical concerns, but takes them into a new social arena).[22] The danger of a flatterer is that his rhetoric will lead you astray. He "imitates the personal voice of friendship," as Plutarch writes: he mimics "the frankness of speech" which is "the true mark of friendship." Such a man is hard to detect: "flatterers apply a frankness which is not true or helpful but which, as it were, leers from beneath its brow and simply tickles" (*Moralia* 51c). The flatterer's apparent frankness is dangerous because it is neither true nor aimed at helping. Plutarch would love the flatterer to be clearly distinguishable by physiognomics: a distortion of the face, a leer, an itch. But the "as it were" remains to mark the slippage in Plutarch's desire. Plutarch can only

---

[20] See Gleason 1995.
[21] See Ahl 1984.
[22] See Konstan 1996.

declare the flatterer to be "as it were," "as if," "like" the corruption he would have liked to be able to see. The risk is always there of getting it quite wrong, and paying the consequences of one's own rhetorical naivety or misprision.

Hence the need for an education in rhetoric, in the techniques and devices of self-representation. From an early training in listening to poetry, right through to the performance of set speeches in a courtroom, every citizen walks the tightrope between being the victim rather than the master of words. In this way, rhetoric conditions all aspects of empire culture, as a necessary but also an ambivalent force. The theory of rhetoric (and here Plutarch stands in for a broad and extensive tradition) is not merely a question of textbooks for children or handbooks for lawyers. The theoretical discussion of language in action affects all aspects of social discourse and lets us see the anxiety of self-presentation in the hierarchies of empire culture.

The images and practices of rhetoric pervade all realms of self-presentation and linguistic expression in the Second Sophistic. This is one reason why Victorian scholars with their post-Romantic privileging of sincerity and spontaneity regarded the Greek writing of the Roman Empire as second-rate as well as "late." It is, however, why contemporary scholarship with its fascination with the cultural history of self-fashioning has rediscovered the excitement and importance of this period's writing.

Suggestions for further reading

Most books and articles on the Second Sophistic have something to say on rhetoric, although surprisingly there is no book dedicated to this topic. Whitmarsh 2001b is a rhetorically sophisticated discussion of the literature of the period, as is Schmitz 1997. Goldhill 2001 contains a range of articles which introduce some of these problems. Bowersock 1969 remains the most useful guide to the characters of the period, and the epigraphical evidence is collected in Puech 2002. Swain 1996 is the best introduction to the issue of the use of Attic Greek and its impact on rhetoric. The nicest introduction to the anxiety of performance is Gleason 1995; and specifically on Lucian, see Goldhill 2002.

PART IV

Epilogues

14

TODD PENNER AND CAROLINE VANDER STICHELE

Rhetorical practice and performance in early Christianity

According to the Gospel of Luke (4:16–20), Jesus of Nazareth inaugurates his mission in his hometown by entering the synagogue on the Sabbath and reading a passage from the prophet Isaiah (Isaiah 61:1–2). In this story Jesus not only reads from the scroll of Isaiah, declaring that this particular prophecy has now been fulfilled, but also goes on to offer an interpretation of the meaning of that text (Luke 4:23–30). In Luke's second book, the Acts of the Apostles, Paul similarly visits a synagogue on the Sabbath (Acts 13:14–43). He is asked to deliver an exhortation or "word of encouragement" (*logos paraklēseōs*) after the reading from the "law and the prophets." Here, in Pisidian Antioch, Paul proceeds to offer one of the more extensive examples of early Christian "missionary preaching," designed to win his primarily Jewish audience over to the "gospel of Christ." These two narratives provide intriguing glimpses, if not so much into the actual preaching of Jesus or Paul, at the very least into the character of the preaching that ostensibly predominated in early Christian practice, identity construction, and historical remembrance. Even more so, these two narratives indicate the complexity of early Christian rhetoric insofar as the performance of oratory appears already to have been bound up with both Jewish Scripture/tradition and the development of Christian narrative.

The "character" of early Christian oratorical discourse

One of the formative perceptions, in large part generated by images offered up by early Christian literature itself, is that missionary preaching and community teaching grounded the burgeoning first- and second-century Christian movement. A significant part of this picture comes from reading the Acts of the Apostles in conjunction with the letters of the New Testament. The question looms large, however, whether these bodies of literature allow us to reconstruct *actual* early Christian practices or if they should rather be interpreted as ideal and secondary representations of these practices.

An even more critical issue is the degree to which our later perceptions of the genre of homily and sermon shape the manner in which we read and group these earlier performances. Since a technical term for "sermon" does not appear in Greek before the third century CE, we are left with a seemingly insoluble problem of definition, highlighted, most of all perhaps, by the Latin term *sermo*, which, most closely translating the Greek *logos*, has such a wide, varied, and general range of meaning as to make classification of any sort impossible. Yet, in one form or another, discourses related to preaching are abundant throughout both the New Testament and other early Christian texts of the first and second centuries CE: from the fiery preaching of John the Baptist (forming quite literally the "beginning of the gospel" in Mark 1), to the exhortations of Jesus in the gospel traditions (e.g. Mark 4; Sermon on the Mount in Matthew 5–7), to the more extended discourses offered by Jesus in the Gospel of John, to the public oration that Paul is depicted as delivering before a primarily Greek audience on the Areopagus in Athens (Acts 17), to the wisdom paraenesis of the Epistle of James, to the pastoral (sometimes soothing, oftentimes chastising) rhetoric of Paul, to the longer homilies of *sunkrisis* found in the letter to the Hebrews, to the impassioned pleas of John the Seer to the seven churches of Asia Minor in the book of Revelation (chs. 2–3). The diversity of and in this material, however, makes it difficult to identify a particular (or unified) sermonic form in early Christian literature. For that reason, we opt to focus on the broader rhetorical practices and the diverse range of expression found in early Christian oratorical discourses.

Overall, diverse linguistic expressions are used to denote oratorical discourse in the early Christian literary corpus. For example, one finds occurrences of the Greek words *kērussō* (to proclaim, to preach) and *homileō* (to converse, to talk), the latter of which formed the root for the noun *homily*. Other terms are used as well (e.g. *homolegeō*, "to confess, to declare"; *euangelizō*, "to preach the good news"; *paraineō*, "to advise, to exhort"). Naturally, this is not technical vocabulary per se, but rather general descriptions of basic communicative practices, denoting a relative lack of precision in early Christian perception and articulation. One might be tempted to push for a more implicit but sophisticated appreciation of *homileō*, which, although used rarely in the New Testament, in its two primary occurrences, in the Gospel of Luke and the Acts of the Apostles (both written by the same author), is found in contexts that bear marked Eucharistic overtones (Luke 24:15; Acts 20:11). Those associations are clearer in the second instance, where Paul "converses" *after* "breaking bread and eating it." Yet it is difficult to assess with any certainty whether the author, let alone the early readers/hearers, of these texts actually intended/perceived those same links. Herein we observe one of the marked differences between early Christian rhetoric and the classical exemplars: there is much more fluidity and ambiguity in the Christian use of terminology. This lack of precision also points to a broader feature of early Christian rhetorical practice, which is the hybridity in and flexibility of the appropriation and application of Greek and Roman conventions of rhetoric.[1] Attempts to define early Christian rhetoric as "radical" spirit-inspired discourse[2] that cannot easily be interpreted in light of classical rhetorical categories thus misses this sociocultural blending that the rhetoric itself reflects. This phenomenon no doubt bears a marked correlation to the formation of Christianity as a diverse and variegated movement in the ancient world, itself a syncretistic and hybrid entity.

Notwithstanding the flexibility and ambiguity of early Christian terminology, the language that coalesces together does assume the presence of an "audience" (real or imagined) related to the activity of preaching. In this light, then, the *performative* side of early Christian oratorical practice comes into fuller view. Such a performance is already evident in Jesus' Sermon on the Mount, the *locus classicus* for thinking about the sermon in early Christianity, which obtained its name from Augustine (in the second half of the fourth century CE). Despite some important differences in terms of content and rhetorical function, the Sermon on the Mount (Matthew 5–7) and the Sermon on the Plain (Luke 6:17–49) share a basic overall pattern: they are exhortative discourses (combining primarily deliberative and epideictic themes) that aim to foster a particular mode of (primarily ethical) identity among the hearers. As with oratory in general, one of the key emphases is on its *oral* character. Leaving aside the long-debated historical issues related to the presence of *actual words* (if any) of Jesus in this "sermon," a more critical matter to our discussion here is its nature as oral discourse, now only accessible in a secondary narrative setting created for Jesus' speech. Our sources are all literary and are frequently embedded in secondary forms of hortative discourse. As a result, it is difficult to reconstruct the prehistory of the sermon in early Christianity. Still, it appears that, as some scholars have argued, we are dealing with a unique blending of oral and literary textualities in the development of early Christian preaching, a kind of "oral-scribal" culture of composition wherein models attuned to either oral or written dynamics are inadequate to assess fully the complex nature of early Christian discourse.[3]

[1] Robbins 1996.
[2] Kennedy 1980.
[3] Robbins 1996.

In the end, a variety of factors can be distinguished that complicate an overall assessment and account of the origin of the "sermon" in early Christianity. Not only is the language vague and the form rather amorphous, but the social location is also difficult to determine.[4] While we have, at the very least, imaginative settings for early Christian forms of preaching – the Areopagus, synagogues, the Jewish temple in Jerusalem, a mountain, a boat, a house – these are frequently secondary sites, and many of these speeches seem to have been created for these particular narrative contexts. To appreciate the diversity of this material, one needs to pay attention to its multiple roots and cultural backgrounds, examining the kinds of rhetorical features that were used by early Christians to create (the beginnings of) a distinctive discursive performance and form in the ancient world. In what follows, then, we will focus on the rhetorical nature of the material in question, examining those forms of public speech in which the developing belief system of predominantly male Christians takes centre stage. This approach thus envisions a broader sociocultural and rhetorical process, configured and manifested in diverse ways by divergent Christian groups in different parts of the Roman Empire.[5] This process, in our assessment, was firmly rooted in the existing rhetorical practices in Jewish and Greco-Roman cultures that helped to shape a particular and peculiar form of Christian preaching and teaching.

Tracing the Jewish roots of early Christian rhetoric

Returning to the two examples mentioned in the opening of this essay, Jesus in the synagogue of Nazareth and Paul in the synagogue in Pisidian Antioch, several noteworthy features arise. First, although early Christian discourse can in fact draw on a variety of different reservoirs for argumentation, one of the primary and dominant resources is the Hebrew Bible, which is used extensively in early Christian exhortation. The manner in which Scripture is invoked differs widely; yet, either overtly or more subtly, it plays a

[4] Form-criticism, which associates forms of literature with particular "settings-in-life," tended to locate the "sermon" in the *actual* speaking contexts of missionary preaching (to outsiders) and community instruction (to insiders). For instance, Dibelius 1965, one of the premier early form-critics, argued that early Christian sermons consisted more specifically of an elaboration of the *kerugma* (confessional material related to Jesus' suffering, death, and resurrection) with Scripture acting as the proof in the argument. Within this framework the prehistory of the sermon is understood to proceed from an oral form to a literary recording (Stewart-Sykes 2001). It is not clear, however, that such a trajectory works well for depicting the complex interrelation of orality and narrativity in early Christian circles.
[5] Cameron 1991: 29–43.

formative role in the development of the preaching discourses abundant throughout early Christian texts. In Luke 4, for instance, Jesus relies on Isaiah (as well as two stories related to the prophets Elijah and Elisha in 1 Kings). In Acts 13 Paul is indebted to a broader and more general scriptural narrative pattern infused at the end with explicit citations from the Psalms (here given a uniquely Messianic twist in meaning). Even Paul's speech on the Areopagus (Acts 17:22–31), perhaps the least "Jewish" speech in the book of Acts, still resonates with intertextual allusions and interplays with the Jewish scriptural tradition (here the creation accounts in Genesis 1–2). In this speech, however, Paul cites a Greek source as well (Acts 17:28; the quotation appears to be derived from Aratus, *Phaenomena* 5), a feature considered appropriate to this particular rhetorical situation (i.e. a deliberative address to the Greeks in Athens). Herein one perceives the ready overlap between the *exemplum* (the proofs used to support the basis of the argument/case in oratory, often historical in nature) from Scripture and the *auctoritas* (general proverb used as a proof in argumentation) from poetry. In fact, an analysis of early Christian oratorical discourse from the vantage point of the Greek and Roman rhetorical handbooks would suggest that, with respect to the deployment of the Hebrew Bible, it is difficult to draw a firm line between *exemplum* and *auctoritas* in so far as both scriptural citations and broader narrative references provide "proof-texts" for the argument being developed. Such argumentation presumes the weight of the scriptural texts thus used and secures, in turn, the authority of the material that is cited. This particular pattern also reflects back on the orator, who is portrayed as an ideal model adept in using such interpretive strategies, an emphasis that naturally gives way to the importance of *parrhēsia* in ancient civic identity, a motif that early Christians employed in a unique way. The fact that the various speeches are specifically (and appropriately) tailored both to their narrative audience as well as to the particular theme unfolding in the broader context also makes clear that the author of the narrative in which the speeches occur has played a vital role in shaping (if not, more likely, creating) them. Moreover, Christian scriptural tradition further develops in interaction with these speeches and, as a result, the use of *exempla* expands to include early Christian examples (and sayings of Jesus). Thus, in the Acts of the Apostles, for instance, the *experience* of various characters in the narrative, as well as the quintessential *experience* of Jesus in terms of his earlier suffering, death, and resurrection (reflected in the gospel traditions), become proofs for particular arguments *as well as* the goal of argumentation in certain cases. In the process, the form of this discourse becomes intertwined with the birth of Christian Scripture itself, a phenomenon that pointedly reveals the character of early Christian ideology. Preaching thus appears not only as a performance for an audience but also as constitutive for the development of early Christian tradition itself, demonstrating the symbiotic relationship between the two.

This larger process of interpretation can best be understood through an appreciation of the long tradition, already established in the Hebrew biblical material, of discourses of exhortation given to the Israelites, which provide indispensable paradigms for later Jewish tradition but are constitutive for early Christian conceptions and compositions as well. The book of Deuteronomy, for instance, is filled with various hortatory speeches delivered by Moses, which culminate in his departing address in chapters 29–30. This so-called "deuteronomic tradition" is critical for the development of both Jewish and early Christian discourse in which Moses and the Law/Torah play a prominent role. In a similar vein, Ezra's address in Nehemiah 9 is prototypical for later literature: the recitation of authoritative narrative is used in a speech that mixes both explicit epideictic, in this case overt praise for God's saving actions, and implicit deliberative modes of argumentation, in the form of warnings for "present" hearers based on past negative examples of those forefathers who rejected God's ways. This type of discourse became predominant in many strands of post-biblical Judaism, such as the *Targums*, which offer Aramaic translations alongside interpretations of the Hebrew biblical text. Philo of Alexandria (first century CE) similarly used the commentary format to present ideal images of Jewish traditions and culture, while the well-known Dead Sea Scrolls (often associated with the "Qumran community") offer examples of interpretation and sermonic exhortation in which the two are frequently (and intricately) interwoven, with commentary on scriptural passages energizing implied deliberative aims. The elaboration of this practice can also be seen in Jewish testamentary literature, which adopts the "testimony" format to embody exhortation to ethical living within the fictional final testament of a biblical patriarch or hero (in a similar vein, see Jesus' farewell address in the Gospel of John 13–17 and Paul's in Acts 20, which are modeled on such testamentary literature). The strong exhortative style arises from within this trajectory, as does the persistent appeal to *exempla* as the primary mode of persuasion. Even later rabbinic traditions reflected in the Mishnah and Talmud are much indebted to these earlier practices. Thus, preaching and the process of scripturization itself cannot easily be separated. Not surprisingly, then, when Jesus ascends the mountain in Matthew to deliver his famous "Sermon on the Mount," he does so in the *habitus* of a "new Moses." The fundamental argumentative force of the sermon thus comes from Jesus' embodiment as a new lawgiver offering a set of new commandments, modeled after the figure of Moses (fulfilling, not coincidentally, the Mosaic prediction of "one like Moses" arising in the future; Deuteronomy 18:15). In this way Christianity's own scripturizing and preaching processes are linked to the patterns already evident in Jewish tradition.

Alongside this scriptural influence that proved highly influential for the form, function, and argumentative substructure of early Christian oratory, one also needs to highlight the major influence that the prophetic tradition of the Hebrew Bible had on the development and deployment (as well as the consumption) of early Christian discourse. Overall, the prophets served as a model of oratorical exhibition and execution for the early Christians. As a result, the performative side of the prophets also formed an essential component of early Christian identity. In the Gospel of Luke and the Acts of the Apostles the prophets are portrayed as marginalized figures, who are raised up by God but rejected by the people (Luke 4:24; 13:34; Acts 7:52). Early Christians often picked up on these themes of inversion and were able to use them effectively in terms of creating and sustaining their own identities over against the dominant cultural ones (Jewish, Greek, Roman). Moreover, biblical prophets perform from this marginalized position, thus emulating *parrhēsia*, one of the critical virtues of male citizens in the Greek assembly and one of the backbones of oratorical display in the Greco-Roman world. From John the Baptist to Jesus to Peter and Paul, these figures are framed as prophets in their speeches, which draw heavily on that strand of biblical tradition in terms of the particular themes that are appropriated and exploited for rhetorical elaboration. In the letters attributed to him, Paul constructs his own identity in this same vein, as someone who speaks the truth in power, boldly proclaiming his gospel (Romans 1:16). In a predictable move, moreover, early Christians also began to shape their own identities even more explicitly in this prophetic direction, insofar as they portrayed themselves as receiving exhortations for the community directly from God (1 Corinthians 14:1–5). This development represents a further entrenchment of the biblical prophetic paradigm, one that shifts towards the *charisma* that early Christians claimed was manifested in their communities and expressed by both men and women (Acts 2:17 and 1 Corinthians 11: 2–16). In both the Acts of the Apostles and the New Testament letters, then, prophetic speech is often presented as being indebted thematically and functionally to the Hebrew prophetic tradition, while at the same time also being "inspired" by the "spirit of God" that imparts to Christian speech both its argumentative potency and an authority based on divine revelation. Indeed, early Christians claimed that the spirit inspired both speech and community values (Luke 4:16; Mark 13:11; John 14:26), and the charismatic nature of their speech became a trope of early Christian identity.

Moreover, this reconfiguration of *parrhēsia* was easily linked with other forms of rhetorical display in the ancient world, such as the ready correlation with the Cynic tradition, with its emphasis on offering rhetorical disruptions of everyday life through bold proclamations. It is therefore evident that various facets of Christian oratorical discourse could be readily reconfigured within other contexts, evoking multiple associations in the minds of ancient authors and audiences. In this way, early Christian rhetoric showed itself to be highly malleable in adaptation and interpretation, which probably accounts in part for the varied (and often loose) deployment of rhetorical forms in early Christianity.

Aside from the more general background delineated above, other scholars argue for more systemic patterns of Jewish rhetorical influence in early Christian materials. One such identifiable sermonic form is the rabbinic *proem* homily, in which an opening scriptural text from the Torah is cited followed by an interpretation, which also includes a group of other biblical texts that highlight, either overtly or more subtly, the lectionary text from the Prophets for that Sabbath.[6] While the New Testament texts do not contain any of the formalistic features of the *proem* homily, the two examples from Jesus and Paul in the synagogue do follow the basic outlines found in the rabbinic *proem* form. As such, they reflect, even if only indirectly, Jewish practices that (may) have been formative in the development of early Christian discourse. Still, how we assess the influence of Jewish traditions on early Christian rhetorical practices depends on how we situate the broadly diversified Christian movement itself. The relationship of early Christians to the Jewish synagogue in the first century is much in dispute, as is, for that matter, the social status of early Christians in empire. Defining influence and determining the direction in which influence is understood to flow largely depends on the geographical, historical, and social locations of the communities under consideration. This element is further complicated by the fact that it is difficult to determine the various locales and time periods in which particular early Christian texts emerged. We cannot pinpoint early Christian writers in the first century as easily as we can a Cicero or a Dio Chrysostom, because we often do not even know who these early Christian writers were. Hence, our ability to assess with more precision some of the more complex interrelations with Jewish tradition is limited. Finally, one should keep in view that this early Christian movement was diverse and complex in its formation. It is clear that different streams of early Christianity drew on different reservoirs, and a full account

---

[6] Bowker 1967.

of early Christian rhetorical practice and performance would need to engage a wider range of evidence.

In addition to the above consideration, one also needs to consider the general practice evolving in Palestine and the Hellenistic Diaspora, whereby the Hebrew Bible was no longer read in the original Hebrew but in Greek translation. This latter practice became dominant in the early Christian communities, who wrote the majority of their texts in the Greek language. Another tendency taking place in the Diaspora, which affected Christian practice, was the use of categories and concepts from Greek language as well as the employment of rhetorical tools in the interpretation following the reading of the scriptural text. Already evidenced in these various shifts is the impulse towards literacy and reading in the formative stages of early Christianity, as well as the important role of written texts more generally.[7] It thus becomes readily apparent that early Christians were deeply indebted also to the literary and rhetorical world of the Greeks and Romans.

The Greek and Roman cultural sphere

If Moses is the model for Jesus in the Sermon on the Mount in Matthew, it is not difficult to imagine that Socrates might function as a similar model with respect to Paul's performance on the "hill" in Athens in Acts 17. Indeed, this paradigm works exceedingly well in terms of capturing the profound influence of Greek and Roman rhetoric on early Christian oratorical discourse. Speeches in the New Testament, such as Paul's sermon in Pisidian Antioch, are more easily correlated with the "rules" of rhetoric from the rhetorical handbooks than more complex constructions such as the Sermon on the Mount or Paul's missives to his various congregations.[8] As a result, the problem of how to understand the influence of rhetoric in early Christianity has to a large extent beset modern scholarly analysis. Some scholars have sought to analyze classical rhetorical elaboration in the New Testament,[9] while others, in contrast, have tended to focus on the influence of more general forms of persuasion.[10] As we have already detailed above, oratorical discourse is embedded in diverse ways throughout the corpus of early

[7] M. M. Mitchell 2006.

[8] There has been a tendency in recent research, in part as a reaction to early rhetorical critics such as Hans Dieter Betz who saw numerous correlations between letters like Galatians and the Greco-Roman rhetorical handbooks, to downplay and complicate the usefulness of classical rhetorical analysis for New Testament letters (R. D. Anderson 1999).

[9] Mack and Robbins 1989.

[10] Kennedy 1984.

Christian literature, interweaving oral and scribal cultures in the production of early Christian textuality (and identity), a feature that aids in uncovering more fully the rhetorical dimensions of this first-century movement.

This discussion naturally leads, then, to a consideration of the primary rhetorical education of elite male citizens in the Roman Empire. Aelius Theon's *Progymnasmata*, for instance, one of the chief extant examples of rhetorical training (for younger students), comes from around the same time period as the earliest Christian writers (first century CE), providing evidence of the kinds of exercises in which male students preparing for a full range of oratorical composition and performance would have engaged. The progymnastic exercises not only prepared a young student in basic oratorical skill but also infused all other aspects of composition – oral and literary – with a deeply embedded rhetorical ethos that permeated all communicative practices.[11] We do not have extant early Christian educational exercises, or at least any that we can explicitly identify as such (although the complex evolution of the Jesus tradition, the energetic expansion of apostolic narratives, and the extensive early Christian practice of writing "speech-in-character" and pseudepigraphy could all have some connection to or associations with rhetorical training). We should be fully aware, however, that some writers who authored the existing Christian writings were in fact trained in a classical rhetorical mode. Not only did they write in Greek, but their texts reflect rhetorical conventions as well. Thus, in thinking about oratorical discourse in early Christianity, one has to keep in mind the relationship that likely existed between broader Greco-Roman rhetorical educational practices and the kind of influence those would presumably have had on the evolution of Christian oral performative traditions and the textual inscription of the same. Moreover, one also has to be cognizant of the male-centered nature of this enterprise, and the profound stamp that that had on the evolution of early Christian discourse. Although female characters occasionally appear in prominent roles in early Christian texts, particularly in non-canonical narratives such as the *Acts of Paul and Thecla*, they rarely engage in public speech. Herein we catch a glimpse of the gendered nature of this discourse. Still, unlike the elite males of empire who propagated the Greco-Roman traditions of rhetoric, the earliest Christians used these techniques in the course of seeking wider appeal.[12] Evidently, then, elite culture was appropriated by some early Christians but in many respects also popularized and diffused, not unlike the kinds

---

[11] Penner 2003.
[12] Cameron 1991: 85–86, 111–12, 147–48.

of shifts we see in the second century. Indeed, we might observe already in the early Christian movement the burgeoning of the Second Sophistic (however amorphous that movement may have been).[13] It is, moreover, apparent that early Christian missionaries found themselves in conflict with other speakers who were vying for community loyalty and patronage. Paul tackles alleged "rhetorical sophists" in the opening chapters of 1 Corinthians, individuals he characterizes as "strong" in word and deed. But here we see how adeptly Paul the rhetor inscribes weakness (as the imitation of the suffering of Christ) as a potent symbol of superior rhetorical display and thus character.[14] At the very least, the general shifts in culture and social life taking place in the Second Sophistic contributed to creating an environment in which Christian rhetoric could easily take root and spread. Both the shifts to a spectator culture in the Greek East[15] and the more general insinuation of rhetoric into the fabric of the sociocultural life of the period as well as the ensuing rhetorical saturation of all forms of its social discourse (see Goldhill in this volume) might help to explain how Christian rhetoric could, with seeming ease, gain a hearing and a following.

The emergence of both particular forms of Christian reasoning and modes of argumentation can thus be connected to broader social configurations. The blending involved in early Christian rhetoric may attest to broader social and cultural changes as well, in reconfiguring public and private space, lower and upper social status, civic and barbarian identities, male and female roles, going as far as redeploying unsavory Greco-Roman *topoi* to new and potent ends (e.g. the use of culturally shameful forms of suffering and death as heroic means of attaining divine status and reward). There are thus complex social crossings that become mapped onto the rhetoric of the early Christians.[16] Moreover, in the process, the figural dimensions of early Christian rhetoric readily leant itself to remapping social space, so that not only were new networks of knowledge initiated by Christian rhetorical practice, but new social configurations were generated too.

---

[13] Winter 2002.

[14] Given 2001.

[15] Cameron 1991: 76–79, 83–84.

[16] Cameron 1991: 38–39. One thinks here also of the numerous associations between the image of Paul in early Christian texts (including his own letters) as an itinerant preacher and, for example, the tradition of Dio Chrysostom as a wandering Cynic (Downing 1998). Further, in the book of Romans we find examples of the Cynic-Stoic diatribe placed in service of protreptic rhetorical aims. That is not necessarily to suggest that Paul was a self-styled Cynic, but it does help us see how rhetoric and life become intermingled in and through these unique Christian blendings.

TODD PENNER AND CAROLINE VANDER STICHELE

On the one hand, then, early Christian literature bears many of the marks of the variant forms and conventions of broad rhetorical preparation as well as oratorical training more specifically.[17] On the other, we would be hard pressed to find a complete oration in the New Testament, at least one comparable to what we have in Dio Chrysostom or Cicero.[18] Rather, the early Christian materials tend to mix and match various rhetorical features in creative and enterprising ways. Moreover, despite the ongoing separation of orality and literary production in much of contemporary scholarly analysis, from Christianity's inception these two media appear to have interacted, leading to the adoption, adaptation, and reconfiguration of formal Greco-Roman oratorical structures. For instance, one of the features of the speeches in the gospel traditions, which is different from the discourses offered by the Apostles in the Acts of the Apostles, is that the gospel authors utilize what appear to be evolving complexes of sayings traditions attributed to Jesus. While it can be debated whether these were necessarily oral in their earlier stage, it is clear that the existing speeches of Jesus are composed of composite collations of pre-existent sayings material, often grouped together thematically. The sometimes difficult to comprehend compilation of sayings in Mark 4, for example, owes a great deal to a rather sophisticated elaboration of *khreia* involving Jesus.[19] That is, from the beginning, didactic material appeared to be integrated within short narrative settings that created the context for, initially at least, short pointed responses (*khreia*). The role of these *khreia* in early Christian composition is important for understanding the relationship of these *logia* to their narrative context, as the Jesus tradition appears to have developed along *khreia*-lines. Moreover, the character of the teacher/preacher is intertwined with the teachings and proclamations that are uttered, which helps to explain how (and perhaps why) stories about Jesus set in conjunction with his speeches evolved into larger narrative complexes. The acts of writing and narrative composition in early Christianity are thus deeply influenced by rhetorical convention[20] and so much so that it becomes difficult to divide neatly between oratory and narrative invention.

In line with this emphasis on educational practices, one must also draw out further the role that pedagogy plays in identity formation. It has recently been argued that the Hebrew biblical tradition takes fullest shape in the Hellenistic period precisely through the Jewish adaptation of Greek educational curricula, which ironically then employs Jewish texts and traditions

---

[17] C. C. Black 1988.
[18] But see Wills 1984.
[19] Mack and Robbins 1989: 143–60.
[20] Robbins 1991.

in an anti-Hellenistic stance to preserve traditional Jewish culture from perceived Hellenistic assault.[21] Early Christian rhetorical practices also take shape as a result of this refocusing from the synagogue to the school, since, it would seem, early Christians, at least in some regions of the Roman Empire, initially drew their following from adult converts with a Jewish background. This is not to suggest that the early Christian communities abandoned the "synagogal" context altogether, as there is plenty of (literary) evidence to suggest the presence of "house-churches" throughout the empire, involving a loose network of interaction among at least some of them. Still, the recent shift towards viewing these formations as *collegia*,[22] with activities modeled along the lines of the symposia-like adult gatherings evident elsewhere in the Greco-Roman world, would also, presumably, shape the way in which we conceptualize the social setting of early Christian instructional discourses. The educational context, of course, never completely disappears, and it is likely that already by the late first century Christians (second generation, possibly even third) were also teaching their children through the use of scriptural *exempla* set alongside more classical exemplars for imitation, repetition, and reconfiguration. Thus, we probably need to have more sophisticated social models in order to appreciate more fully the dynamic features that went into shaping the process, products, and performances of burgeoning early Christian oratorical discourses.

Perhaps, in all of this, the emphasis in Greco-Roman culture and education on imitation deserves special emphasis. The mimetic spirit infuses almost all early Christian examples of oratorical discourse, whether Jesus appears in the guise of a new Moses, or Paul as a new Socrates. With this emphasis also comes a strong pull towards the public sphere of interaction – the very place in which broader oratorical training assumed its students would eventually be located. The public nature of oratory thus seems to have provided a model for early Christians. From the beginning, the descriptions and reinscriptions of oratorical material take centre stage as oral performance in the *polis*. This was not, as Paul claims at the end of Acts, "done in a corner," a statement that attests to the critical role enacted by the missionary impulse of the early Christian movement.[23] Both the canonical and apocryphal Acts, for instance, portray the Apostles as operating in the public forum, whether in the court house, the temple, the market place, houses of prominent citizens, to name just a few locations.[24] Oratorical

---

[21] Carr 2005.
[22] Ascough 2003.
[23] Schnabel 2004.
[24] L. Alexander 2002.

discourse thus takes on a uniquely identifying function as a result, but it is also transformed in the process as it is crafted according to the rhetorical "rules of the game," in which it becomes paramount to construct the ethos of the Apostles as skilled and adept performers whose rhetorical mastery of speech parallels their virtue as male citizens of the empire and their authority as leaders of the Christian communities. Moreover, this presentation also reflects back on the Christian movement as one that is constructed as being fully compatible with the larger Greco-Roman culture. Herein early Christian males developed a form of discourse that put them front and center in the *polis*. Of course, this is the image that the Acts of the Apostles *projects* (as do the apocryphal Acts as well) and it does seem that in other texts a more community-centered character frames oratorical discourse. Still, private and public are always interacting and intersecting in the ancient world, and early Christians seem to have known how to exploit (in reality and/or in the imaginary) that interaction rather adeptly.

Concluding observations: oratorical discourse and early Christian identity

One should not lose sight of the profoundly hybrid nature of early Christian oratorical discourse, ultimately reflecting a similar amalgam in Christianity itself, as it was shaped by both its Jewish and Greco-Roman heritages. It is exactly this combination of elements that, structurally speaking, creates the unique blend of rhetorical features we find operative in both the early Christian material and the later Church homilies. In this latter context, the great homileticians and commentators of the later periods naturally come to mind – Origen, Augustine, Cyril of Jerusalem, Basil, John Chrysostom, Gregory Nazianzen, Jerome – and the earlier paschal homilies of Hippolytus and Melito of Sardis. In these works abound examples of lengthy meditations on the Old and New Testament texts, expounding matters relevant to Christian life, practice, and belief. Still earlier, the *First and Second Letters of Clement*, written in the first part of the second century, already structurally bear the marks of the longer homily forms that would soon become prominent.

If we have focused primarily on canonical texts in this discussion, one could just as easily turn to other early Christian materials, looking at the complex and varied oratorical discourses reflected in everything from the apocryphal Acts of the Apostles to the Gnostic texts, to the Pseudo-Clementine Homilies, to the second century Greek apologists, to the (possibly first-century) *Gospel of Thomas*. Further, as oratorical practice and performance mutate and transform across differing boundaries of early Christian groups, it similarly aids the growth and expansion of Christian teaching and preaching. In this way the Jewish process of scripturization continues in early Christianity, which eventually lays claim to the Jewish Scriptures in the very same movement that generates its own Scripture. And this scripturization process is subject to the rhetorical rules of performance and delivery that created it in the first place. One also has to consider, in this light, the deeply ingrained rhetorical character and structure of early Christian *pistis* (faith/belief) itself, which may owe more to rhetorical practice than to theological reflection.[25] In other words, rhetorical influence is deeply ingrained in the very practice and fabric of scriptural, community, and ideological formation among the early Christians.

Finally, one cannot overlook the formative role that rhetorical ideology played in the shaping of early Christian identity. The unrelenting focus of oratorical discourse is on the public forum or, at the very least, public performance. Regardless of whether the earliest material reflects historical reality or not, the recollection of these bold acts of speech, manifesting *parrhēsia*, in turn emboldened those hearers of these words and spectators of these images to recreate these remembrances in their present. In this act, then, oratorical discourse transitions ancient readers towards the rhetorical end embedded therein. It is rather intriguing in this light to query further regarding the effects of oratorical discourse in the development of early Christianity. For instance, one has to wonder to what degree this male form of discourse reinforced the firm lines of male authority in the various Christian communities of the pre-Constantinian era. Indeed, the form may have been so popular (and popularized) in Christian circles precisely because of these (prior) gendered associations. Further, this interlacing of form and function continued to create communities in the image that this discourse projects. And here, finally, we may now need to reverse the traditional lines of inquiry: rather than seeking the setting in life that formed the genesis of early Christian rhetorical and oratorical practices, we may do better to consider the setting in life to which these elements themselves gave birth.

Suggested further reading

A significant amount of literature explores the influence of ancient rhetorical theory on the composition of particular early Christian texts. Much less attention, however, has been given to the sociocultural context of the

---

[25] Kinneavy 1987.

appropriation and performance of ancient rhetorical practice in early Christian communities. Kennedy 1984 demonstrated the relevance of ancient rhetorical theory for the analysis of New Testament literature, and his work is a major point of reference for most subsequent studies. B. L. Mack 1990 followed suit, providing a short but substantive alignment of diverse aspects of the Greek and Roman rhetorical handbooks with the formation of New Testament literature. Focusing more explicitly on the development of the homily, Stewart-Sykes 2001 assesses the origin of Christian "preaching" discourse in the context of early Christian communities. Two recent engagements of Paul's rhetoric are supplied by Given 2001 and Winter 2002, who connect emergent Christian rhetorical practice with the social and cultural worlds of early Christianity. A sophisticated and nuanced treatment of the unique discursive character and influence of early Christian rhetoric in the context of empire is offered by Cameron 1991, who details numerous and broad interconnections with Greek and Roman sociocultural contexts. Combining social-scientific and literary-critical approaches, Robbins 1996 delineates a socio-rhetorical methodology, which elucidates patterns of emergent Christian rhetorical discourses in texts as they are connected to broader sociocultural and literary contexts and traditions.

15

PETER MACK

Rediscoveries of classical rhetoric

The renaissance of classical rhetoric can be characterized in three words: recovery, addition, and change. First it was necessary to copy and circulate the texts (after 1460 by printing them). The order in which the texts were recovered and the traditions of teaching established around the earliest known texts constrained the ways in which rhetoric could be thought about. Then rhetorical doctrine had to be adapted to changed social circumstances both by the way in which selected classical texts were grouped into syllabi and interpreted, and through the composition, especially in northern Europe, of new rhetoric textbooks. For most medieval and renaissance teachers rhetoric was about writing rather than speaking and the three classical genres, with their built-in assumptions about audience and context, did not really suit the newly important occasions of letter-writing and preaching. Some of the ways in which renaissance authors developed classical rhetoric resemble the approaches and techniques of classical adapters, though sometimes extending the approach to the point where the product becomes rather different. Some of what looks mechanical in renaissance rhetoric will generate writing which is surprisingly playful and creative.

The rhetorical legacy of the ancient world has proved particularly imposing.[1] In antiquity Quintilian's *Institutes* selected and organized the ideas of Greek and earlier Roman rhetoricians as a sort of classic canon. Even today the fourth edition of Edward Cobbett's successful university textbook *Classical Rhetoric for the Modern Student* assumes that the precepts of classical rhetoric (suitably selected, packaged, and adapted) can still teach the principles of good writing. The post-antique success of classical rhetoric is owed partly to the weight of what survives, partly to the perceived importance of instruction in the use of language (paired with the conceptual difficulty of

---

[1] On post-classical rhetoric more generally see Conley 1990; Fumaroli 1999; Monfasani 1988; Vickers 1988.

making a new start on it), and partly to the circumstances in which learning and education were reborn.

Within the history of scholarship (in some versions of which it is presented as foundational) the idea of renaissance has been strenuously contested. The texts that were found, copied, and (sometimes) taught in the ninth century were never completely lost again. And yet the Twelfth-Century Renaissance and the Italian Renaissance of the fourteenth and fifteenth centuries both added significantly to what was known of ancient rhetoric and changed the way in which it was understood and taught. The texts which were widely known in complete form prior to the fourteenth century were Cicero's *On Invention*, the anonymous *Rhetoric to Herennius*, Boethius' *De Differentiis Topicis* and Horace's *Art of Poetry*. Partial manuscripts of Cicero's *On the Orator* and Quintilian's *Institutes* were available to some medieval scholars but they were not widely known. A tradition of commentary on *On Invention* and *Rhetoric to Herennius* developed in the eleventh and twelfth centuries.[2] William of Moerbeke's Latin translation of Aristotle's *Rhetoric* was available in Paris from 1270. In the thirteenth century we find new developments in the study of rhetoric, spreading from France and England to Italy: a more logical approach connected with the study of the topics, especially in Boethius' version; the composition of new manuals of poetry composition, focusing on the doctrine of amplification, such as Geoffrey de Vinsauf's *Poetria Nova*, so called to distinguish it from Horace's work; the production of rhetorics adapted to preaching; and the growth of letter-writing manuals (*artes dictaminis*). It was among the letter-writing teachers of northern Italian universities that we find the origins of renaissance humanism, in composing Latin tragedy and in imitation of Cicero's style.[3]

The Italian Renaissance added to the rhetorical heritage both an important group of newly rediscovered texts and a renewal of the study of Greek in the West. Poggio in 1416 discovered the complete text of Quintilian's *Institutes* and in 1422 Landriani discovered complete texts of Cicero's *On the Orator, Orator,* and *Brutus*.[4] George of Trebizond's Latin translation of Aristotle's *Rhetoric* was made around 1443–6 and first printed in 1476–7. Eight more Latin and four Italian translations were made in the sixteenth century. Many of the principal Greek texts on rhetoric, including Aristotle's *Rhetoric* and Aphthonius' *Progymnasmata*, were printed by Aldus Manutius in 1509. But the *Rhetoric to Herennius* and *On Invention* were already

[2] Ward 1995, with ample bibliography, see especially the works mentioned by Camargo, Copeland, Fredborg, Kelly, Murphy, and Woods.
[3] Kristeller 1979: 85–105.
[4] Reynolds and Wilson 1991: 134–39.

established as, and remained, the most widely used textbooks, with a combined total of 183 editions.[5] Students of rhetoric found it relatively easy to absorb Quintilian as an advanced rhetoric text because it follows essentially the same structure as the *Rhetoric to Herennius*. *On the Orator* (93 editions) could be understood as a supplement to these established manuals, discussing and questioning assumptions which underlie their approach. Aphthonius' *Progymnasmata*, which was immensely successful in heavily commented Latin editions, provided exercises which were fully compatible with established teaching, but it was much harder for sixteenth-century people to understand and absorb Aristotle's *Rhetoric*. Some scholars tried to concentrate on the second half of the work, which is more concerned with rhetorical technique, while others tried to understand its teaching through ancient or modern ideas about the soul.[6] Nevertheless it became one of the most important rhetoric texts of the Renaissance with 106 Greek, Latin, or Italian editions before 1600.

Beside the intensive use of classical texts we find many new textbooks of all or part of rhetoric. In the highly selective account which follows I shall try to describe some of the innovations in the renaissance rhetoric textbooks I know, inevitably only a small proportion of the 3,842 works by 1,717 authors listed in the *Renaissance Rhetoric Short-Title Catalogue*.

One sixteenth-century approach to the syllabus of classical rhetoric was to criticize its fundamental assumptions. Juan Luis Vives found that the five skills of the orator (invention, disposition, style, memory, and delivery) were cast too widely, since, for example, invention and disposition were parts of logic which were required in all subjects, proposing that the true province of rhetoric was style. He found the three genres of oratory out of date and restrictive, insisting correctly that there were many other kinds of speaking and writing and argued that there were far more levels of style than three.[7] These criticisms drew attention to the over-simplicity and arbitrariness of some of the founding doctrines of classical rhetoric but they also made it hard for teachers to use Vives' books because such structuring features as the three genres and the five skills had become the expected way of organizing a course on rhetoric.[8]

---

[5] This does not include editions of Cicero's works more generally. There were 108 editions of the *Rhetoric to Herennius* and *On Invention* together, 54 of the *Rhetoric to Herennius* alone and in combination with other works, and 21 of *On Invention*. All comments on publication and numbers of editions in this chapter rely on Green and Murphy 2006.

[6] Green 1994; Green 1998.

[7] Vives 1882b: 159–62.

[8] See the essays by Heath and Steel in this volume.

Since the expectations from schools and universities about what would be taught under the heading of rhetoric were strongly established, those who wanted to reform the syllabus were obliged to repackage the existing contents in more or less the existing order (as Caesarius did, for example), or to make their innovations broadly within the established syllabus (Melanchthon), or to conduct a vigorous publicity campaign for changes in those expectations (Ramus). Ramus' changes to the syllabus of both rhetoric and dialectic presuppose first that both subjects will be taught together (so that even though invention and disposition are removed from rhetoric, pupils study topical invention and the organization of arguments in dialectic alongside their rhetoric studies) and second that the simplification of the syllabus, which ensures that pupils will know the whole of both subjects relatively quickly, will be compensated for by the careful analysis of the way in which the precepts are employed in classical Latin speeches and poems.[9]

Several of the most important innovations in renaissance rhetoric resulted from making connections between rhetoric and dialectic. This combination can be seen to reflect both Cicero's view that orators should study dialectic and the centrality of logic in the medieval university, but the Renaissance gave this a new twist in the way it used logical techniques to understand texts and applied rhetorical principles to the analysis of logic and argument. The starting point for many of these ideas was the work of Rudolph Agricola, on whom I will focus as an example of several kinds of renaissance innovation in rhetoric. Most of the other northern humanists whom I shall discuss (for example Erasmus, Vives, Melanchthon, and Ramus) explicitly presented themselves as admirers of Agricola and continuers of his work.

In *De Inventione Dialectica* (1479) Rudolph Agricola composed a version of the topics of invention which can serve the purposes of all types of argumentative writing. Like other writers on the topics he regards definition as an important source of arguments, but he recognizes that writers will often need to compose definitions and provides a step-by-step worked definition of law. In order to understand definition better he approaches it as a writing task, which is also a process of exploratory thinking.

> It is not at all easy to pass on instructions for finding a definition. This much is certain, it will be very useful for anyone who wishes to define some given thing to have a knowledge of the nature of the thing and to have surveyed it carefully. In this case he should easily find, first, something general in that thing in which it agrees with others of similar nature. Let us take the example of defining law. We find first that law has in it a certain force of compelling

---

[9] Mack 1998b.

and ordering (*iussum*), from which it seems to have taken its name. So law will be either something we have agreed or some sort of decree. However, not every decree will be a law. For we do not call the decrees which masters give slaves, which fathers give children and which philosophers give disciples, laws. So let us think of something by which we shall exclude these cases. We see that they have some sort of power, but that it is smaller than what laws can make; so let us add "pleasing to a higher power," that is, of the people or of those to whom the people have transferred their power, such as a senate or a prince. Well then, will whatever a prince orders be a law? Will it be a law when he orders his slaves to spread out a bed or to set a table? I do not think so. But what is ordered by a city, and what belongs to preserving its state will be. But it will not be a law either if it weighs more heavily upon some part of the city, or if it harms neighboring people against the custom of nature or of nations. Therefore it ought also to be equitable. Let us inspect the matter and see whether anything can be embraced by the definition which does not come under the name of the thing defined. Conversely, as well, is anything included in the thing defined which the definition does not admit? If it does not seem so, let us recapitulate and say: a law is a decree of a higher power, for the sake of preserving the state of the city, formulated in agreement with equity and goodness.[10]

Agricola approaches definition as a practical writing task which requires him to think around a subject and question and refine the formulation he has reached. His example of writing in progress suggests a method which can be applied to other definitions. He follows this careful account of the process of making a definition with some rules which a successful definition must satisfy (e.g. neither too wide nor too broad, conveying the essence of the thing, avoiding ambiguous, obscure, or metaphorical language) and some advice on practicing making definitions. Finally he suggests that someone who can make good definitions will acquire authority before an audience because he exhibits knowledge and discrimination (28–29). He gives no discussion of arguments derived from definition, as Cicero, Quintilian, and Boethius had because he believes that the person who understands something well enough to make a definition of it will also be able to work out how to argue effectively using it. Later in the list of topics he provides a careful analysis of the different and interconnected ways in which things can be regarded as causes and effects of other things, showing, for example, how to the shipowner the ship is an efficient cause enabling him to make money, whereas to its constructor it is a final cause and to his laborer an effect.

---

[10] Agricola and Alardus 1967: 27–28, page numbers in text hereafter. This work was printed forty-four times in full and thirty-two times in epitome. P. Mack 1993: 136–67, 259–79.

He discusses the different argumentative uses of comparison and similitude:

> Comparison is a crowded topic and one of great use to orators. It is usually ready and to hand. And because it does draw from things which do not have to be pulled up from the depths, but which are usually known and conspicuous, it also consequently possesses a ready strength for convincing the minds of ordinary people (132) ... Of all the topics from which arguments are drawn almost none has less strength against a resistant hearer than similitude; on the other hand there is none more suitable for the hearer who follows willingly and shows himself apt to be taught. For if it is correctly applied it opens up a thing and places a sort of picture of it before the mind so that although it does not bring with it the necessity of agreeing, it does cause an implicit reluctance to disagree. Therefore it is not so frequently used for proving things, but it is often used by orators for exploring and illuminating things and is even more often used by poets. In spite of this, similitude very often has an appearance of proving by the very fact that it shows how something is. Thus when you read that similitude of Quintilian: "just as a vase with a narrow mouth rejects an excess of liquid but is filled by flowing or pouring gradually" [*Institutes* 1.2.28], it does not therefore follow that on account of this the delicate wits of boys must be taught according to their own strengths, but nonetheless, once someone has conceived the matter in his mind according to this image, he persuades himself that it cannot be otherwise. (142)

Prompted by the topics of invention, Agricola reflects on examples to suggest new and subtle perceptions about the effect of comparisons on the way a reader thinks. Rhetoric provides a framework; logic, tools of analysis which yield new insights when applied to texts.

Working from rhetoric's traditional division between narration and argument, the two central elements of the four-part oration,[11] Agricola finds that all persuasive language can be considered as either exposition or argumentation. A speaker uses exposition when the audience follows willingly and when the main need is to explain one's ideas clearly. Argumentation is employed when the audience is more resistant. It aims to persuade them of the truth of something and almost to force their assent. The difference between the two is a matter of one's attitude to the audience and of the linguistic texture one employs. In exposition we concentrate on clarity of statement and on order; in argumentation we make connections between propositions, we add reasons and justifications (1–2, 258). Agricola illustrates the difference by analyzing two passages from the *Aeneid*, showing how one could rewrite the first of them, identified as exposition, in order

---

[11] See Heath and Steel above.

to make it into argumentation (258–59). This distinction leads Agricola to make a series of rich comments on the persuasive force of exposition. He analyzes the speech from *Aeneid* 2 in which Sinon explains the value of the wooden horse to the Trojans and in effect persuades them to take it within their walls. Sinon sets out a series of propositions (some of them true, some of them parallel to true ones and some of them not unlikely) which the Trojans then connect together to persuade themselves that it will benefit them to take possession of the horse (262–63).[12] Agricola finds that people are more likely to believe connections which they have discovered for themselves. This suggests that speakers aiming to write convincing expositions should themselves know the connections between their statements but should not state them overtly. Argumentation, by contrast, involves setting out the connections, though even here it may be rhetorically more forceful not to state all forms of argumentation in full.

Analyzing the distinction between exposition and argumentation helped Agricola see how narrative could serve argument. This leads on to one of Agricola's most successful innovations. In the course of his highly practical chapters on the use of the topics, Agricola outlines the method of dialectical reading. Dialectical reading involves comparison of each proposition as one reads it with the question which the writer is addressing at a particular moment (which may be a question derived from or related to the main question of the oration). By connecting these questions and propositions together one can recover the dialectical structure of the text. Agricola exemplifies this technique in his commentary on Cicero's oration *Pro Lege Manilia*, which provides first a rhetorical commentary on the text and then a dialectical analysis of the structure of the arguments (354–60, 464–68). This became the model for a whole series of dialectical analyses of texts by Latomus, Melanchthon, and Ramus.[13] This style of commentary is very different from Asconius Paedianus' mainly historical commentary. The first important renaissance commentaries on Cicero's orations (Antonio Loschi's *Inquisitio super XI Orationes Ciceronis*, composed in the 1390s) preceded the rediscovery of Asconius, to which it is superior.

In arguing for the usefulness of the topics of invention Agricola analyzed a section of Dido's lament from the *Aeneid* to show that a moving speech can be created by identifying linked propositions suitable for proving something and repeating them in different words (199). The contribution of logic

---

[12] Quintilian had referred to the same speech, citing it as an example of rhetorical question (*Institutes* 9.2.9).

[13] van der Poel 1997; Meerhoff 2001: 25–99.

to the creation of emotion at the local level is matched by its importance in determining strategy: "Two things are necessary in order to induce pity: something which has happened to someone, which should seem harsh and the person who undergoes it who should seem not to deserve it" (199).

Agricola analyzes the successive moves of Cicero's peroration to *Pro Milone* uncovering the arguments which Cicero devises to establish in the minds of the audience the idea that Milo does not deserve to be found guilty and punished (199–201). Quintilian had examined this passage both as an example of speaking in another's voice (*Institutes* 6.1.24–27) and to describe Cicero's delivery (*Institutes* 11.3.172–73), but Agricola's logical analysis of the emotional effect is entirely different. Agricola devotes several chapters of his third book to a more general theory of using ideas from the topics to arouse emotions. He distinguishes three different ways in which a speaker deals with emotion, providing practical advice and analysis of existing examples for each type (378–84). His treatment of emotion is very different from that we find in Cicero and Quintilian, where the emphasis is on feeling the emotion oneself and the talent required to communicate that feeling to others. Rather Agricola's ideas look like an intelligent generalization and simplification of Aristotle's comments on arousing pity and indignation in *Rhetoric* 1385b11–1387b21. Agricola directly refers his readers to the treatment of a range of emotions in Aristotle's *Rhetoric*, a text which was neglected at the time he wrote.[14]

Renaissance writers attempted different reforms of disposition, the second of the tasks of the orator. Since textbooks such as the *Rhetoric to Herennius* and Quintilian's *Institutes* organize their account of invention according to the four traditional sections of the oration (introduction, narration, arguments in favor and against, conclusion), disposition tends to have been pre-empted and is often restricted to discussions of when to omit one of the parts or when to vary their usual order. By contrast Agricola insists that disposition is something which has to be thought about for each individual composition rather than assuming that all compositions are variants on the four-part oration. Following Cicero he defines disposition as "the ordering and distribution of things which shows what belongs and should be placed in which places." In order to establish principles for his discussion he distinguishes three kinds of order adopted by writers (natural, arbitrary, and artificial) and four senses of the word prior (time, genus, place, dignity) (413–15). Different things may be prior in different ways and writers may choose different approaches to priority in writing works of

[14] P. Mack 1998a.

different kinds or for particular audiences. With these principles in mind Agricola analyzes different genres of writing, showing how poems, plays, and histories treat temporal priority differently. A poem may begin in the middle of events but a history should not. A play will always have to begin near the end of the action, filling in the back-story as it proceeds. Within expositions of subjects, on the other hand, one should begin by sifting truth from error in received opinions in order to establish general principles, then one should discuss those principles and later by means of definition and division describe the various levels of genus and species derived from them. In describing particular things one should provide definitions, discuss their parts and nature and consider, using the topics of invention, their adjacents, force, actions, subjects, and other "topics around the substance" (418–20).

Then Agricola turns to examples, demonstrating the immense variety of ways in which works can be organized: Pliny describing the visible creation starting from the heavens and moving down to the earth and its inhabitants; Valerius Maximus organizing his exemplary biographies according to the virtues; Ovid moving from one myth to the next by means of shared or comparable details which seem quite arbitrary; and the organization of Tacitus' *Germania* (422–23). He treats the four-part oration as one form among many. He uses a similar combination of analyzed examples and general principles to discuss the different ways in which one might order sequences of arguments or organize the points one planned to make in a disputation. His account of disposition ends with a wide-ranging summary. The key is to consider everything which has been found through topical invention (including lines for emotional persuasion as well as arguments), and to compare this with what one wants to achieve in the mind of the audience.

> The first requirement for anyone who wishes to do well at disposition is that he should lay out in front of him the whole raw material of his invention, that is everything he is thinking of saying. Then he should decide carefully what he wants to bring about in the mind of the hearer. Then he should compare carefully the things themselves, the parts of the things, the force and nature of them singly and together, first among themselves and then all together with the precepts. Then he will see without difficulty when the order of time should be followed, when things should be separated into their species and single things should be distinguished as if by certain boundaries; when one should be derived from another, depending on whichever is nearest or most suitable. Then he should determine how to please the audience, how to make his point and win it, and what order of questions, argumentations, and propositions to observe. (449–50)

Agricola contributed to the translation of Aphthonius' *Progymnasmata*, which with the commentary of Lorichius was one of the best-sellers of sixteenth-century Europe, with over two hundred editions, almost all from northern Europe. The instructions which Aphthonius gives for preparing fourteen different composition exercises themselves break down the monopoly of the oration (as well as providing practice in invention), while Lorichius' commentaries and additional examples show how examples of these genres have been built into longer compositions.[15] Like the Middle Ages, the Renaissance also produced specialized rhetorics for a number of important "modern" genres: letter-writing, preaching, giving advice. There were also specialized rhetorics designed for lawyers. Many of these works begin by acknowledging the three classical genres of rhetoric but later discuss forms more suited to contemporary needs.

In theory Ramus takes a more direct approach to disposition, which he places in dialectic and excludes from rhetoric, proposing that all texts should move from first principles to individual examples by definition and division, using the earlier figures of the syllogism to ensure the coherence of the argument. But in his commentaries on speeches and poems he proves to be rather more flexible in reconstructing argumentative structures while acknowledging the expectations of different genres of writing.

Erasmus' very successful letter-writing manual, *De Conscribendis Epistolis*, with more than ninety sixteenth-century editions, first proposes that the main types of letter should correspond to the three types of oration identified in the rhetoric manuals, but he then subverts this structure, first by adding a fourth main type, the familiar letter, and then by expanding the number of sub-types while reducing the deliberative genre to a page and the nine sub-genres of the judicial letter to a couple of pages each. The crude criterion of the number of pages given to each sub-type suggests five principal motives for writing letters (encouragement, persuasion, consolation, request, and advice) and six next most significant types (recommendation, providing information, giving thanks, lamenting sorrows, congratulation, and offering assistance) out of a total of twenty-seven sub-types.[16] By providing patterns, phrases, and suggestions for lines of thought for these sub-genres Erasmus absorbs the very different sixteenth-century situation of intimate written communication within the traditional rhetorical framework. In his hands the letter-writing manual serves as a training laboratory for aspects of rhetoric connected with self-presentation

---

[15] The 1575 London edition (STC 700.3) is available on microfilm and online through EEBO.
[16] Erasmus 1971b; P. Mack 2002: 24–26 and 41; Chomarat 1981.

and audience, as students are instructed about ways to think about the person they are addressing and adapting the arguments they might make on a particular topic to their sense of their own person and of their relationship to the person being addressed. Vives goes further than this, both in insisting in his letter-writing manual on the essentially free content of the letter (while giving examples of a few types entirely unrelated to the three genres of oratory) and, in *De Ratione Dicendi*, by providing definitions, divisions, and instructions for ten contemporary forms of writing: description, history, probable narration, fables, poetic fictions, precepts of an art, paraphrase, epitome, commentary, and translation.[17]

Moving beyond the traditional three genres encouraged renaissance rhetoricians to think differently about invention and style. The most important figure here is Erasmus (1466/7–1536), the most famous of the northern renaissance humanists, who made important contributions in editing Seneca, the Bible, and St. Jerome, as well as writing celebrated letters, creative works, and rhetoric books.[18] His *De Copia*, the most successful of all rhetoric works composed in the Renaissance with around 180 editions, describes a technique which combines logical and stylistic procedures.[19] Copia of words involves varying a sentence which has already been written by applying different rhetorical figures to the individual words. Thus (to use an example) which he subjects to two hundred variations, "your letter pleased me greatly" could be rendered as "your epistle delighted me extremely" or "from your letter an unaccustomed happiness swept over my spirit" or even, "I cannot find the words to relate how your letter entranced me." The essentially mechanical act of making one of twenty proposed kinds of substitution for each word (which in different instantiations and combinations produces a much larger number of ways of varying a complete sentence) leads first to putting one in the position to choose the most suitable of a huge range of alternative formulae and then to a virtuosic pride in the ability to generate ever more extravagant substitutions. What starts as a directed, relatively mechanical exercise ends up as a celebration of the creativity and richness of language.

The second type of copia, copia of things, involves looking for and describing material related to an initial idea which will enable it to be expressed more fully. So instead of writing "Holbein delivered the painting" we might choose to describe the events which led up to this moment or the

---

[17] Vives 1882a: 89–237; P. Mack 2005.

[18] Augustijn 1991. See also the ongoing editions of his *Opera Omnia* (Amsterdam) and of the translated *Collected Works of Erasmus* (University of Toronto Press).

[19] Erasmus 1971a and references in note 16 above.

attendant circumstances of the ceremony of presentation or the sequence of causes which enabled the painting to be executed. Further material could be sought in comparisons or in lively descriptions, in the addition of strings of adjectives or in collecting numerous logical propositions in support of the statement. Copia of things encourages a writer to think around a subject, to look in different directions for material which may enable it to be presented more effectively for a particular audience. But the awareness of copia of things prompts a reader to ask what effect the writer intended to achieve by elaborating a particular part of a text and what might be implied by the decision to amplify one section rather than another.

Erasmus explained that the acquisition of copia of expression would be of use to readers of classical texts and to translators, to people searching for the best way to express something and to those who wanted to evaluate the meaning and impact of one expression by comparing it with others that could have been chosen. But it also gives resources and techniques for composing a dense, full style of writing, "surging along like a golden river, with thoughts and words pouring out in rich abundance," whose impact may be discerned in the writings of Montaigne and Rabelais.[20] *De Copia* shows writers how to compose descriptions, how to use examples, and how to collect, store, and reuse sententiae and proverbs. A few of Erasmus' techniques are borrowed from Quintilian's account of amplification; others come from Agricola's chapter on copia, and others may owe something to the techniques described in Geoffrey de Vinsauf's *Poetria Nova*.

Under the heading of style renaissance authors devoted considerable efforts to trying to understand and exploit the system of discriminations available in the classical Latin vocabulary but which had been lost in medieval Latin. The classic text here is Lorenzo Valla's *Elegantiae*, which exploits its author's very wide reading in Greek and Latin to investigate the usages of particular words and the implications of some choices between parallel expressions.[21] Inspired by Valla, Agostino Dati composed his *Elegantiolae*, a short guide to writing classical Latin for beginners, which went through 144 editions. Erasmus gives over much of *De Conscribendis Epistolis* and *De Copia* to lists of useful but elegant phrases, both taken from his reading and of his own devising.

Juan Luis Vives began his treatment of style, *De Ratione Dicendi*, with discussions of words, sounds, and sentence structures, into which he embedded descriptions of selected figures. His entirely reasonable point was that

---

[20] Cave 1979.

[21] Valla 1962; Regoliosi 1993. A modern edition is a great desideratum for students of renaissance humanism.

style is a product of every linguistic choice made in the composition of a paragraph, not simply a matter of adding a few figures to sentences which were otherwise envisaged as plain. In order to substantiate his claim that it was impoverishing and inaccurate to divide style into three levels of style he wrote descriptions of some forty different kinds of style and the forms of language which characterize each. On the whole he provides too many types and he does too little to relate them to the vocabulary Quintilian and Hermogenes had developed for describing style. His description of the serious style is the more effective because earlier writers had provided him with starting points and because of his use of examples from Ovid and Cicero:

> Serious discourse arises from *sententiae* of great weight and deep intelligence, from arguments that are solid and firm rather then witty or contorted, with emotions moved moderately. The periodic sentences should be freer as long as they are not entirely disconnected and over-loose. The clauses should be longer, the metaphors safer and more sparing, the figures and tropes infrequent, the vowels long, the sound firm and strong. Occasional harshness and hesitation in the flow of words, even a halting, give the discourse more weight, just as in the movement of a body.[22]

Within classical rhetoric the list of tropes and figures with its subdivisions, examples, and suggestions for usage, as exemplified by the *Rhetoric to Herennius* book 4 or by Quintilian's *Institutes* books 8 and 9, was always regarded as one of the most practically useful sections. Just as in antiquity and the Middle Ages attempts had been made to organize the rather diverse and miscellaneous list of linguistic techniques, so the figures and tropes were subjected to different types of reform in the Renaissance. Melanchthon attempted to establish a new and more logical classification of the figures and tropes, adding a new category of figures associated with amplification. Mosellanus (Peter Schade) produced a highly successful (80 editions) *Tabulae de Schematibus et Tropis*, which was often published with summaries of Erasmus' *De Copia* and Melanchthon's rhetoric. After distinguishing figures and tropes, Mosellanus follows the classical division between figures of meaning and figures of words. Figures of words are again subdivided into figures of diction, which includes the figures usually taught in grammar texts, of locution, including most of the traditional figures, and of construction (prolepsis, zeugma, syllepsis, evocatio, appositio).[23] It is not obvious that these new subdivisions help much. The virtue of the book was that it

---

[22] Vives 1882a: 152.
[23] Mosellanus 1573.

defined and exemplified a large number of figures in a very short space. Probably pupils learnt it by heart. Omer Talon's rhetoric (114 editions), inspired by his collaboration with Ramus, reduced the tropes to four (metonymy, irony, metaphor, and synecdoche) and the figures to twenty, organizing them into categories and tree diagrams and analyzing literary examples to illustrate and explain the use of each figure.[24] Some of Ramus' commentaries on classical texts indicate the figures and tropes employed by superscript letters and numbers.

The renaissance effort to write Latin as eloquently and flexibly as the ancients required scholars and teachers to engage with the issue of imitation, another topic which had interested Cicero and Quintilian. While everyone agreed that Cicero's letters, treatises, and orations offered models of Latin style, controversies developed about whether he should be the exclusive model in prose and about how exactly ancient works should be imitated in the modern world. These controversies are typified by the exchanges of letters between Poliziano and Cortesi (around 1490), and between Gianfrancesco Pico and Bembo (1512–13), as well as by Erasmus' *Ciceronianus* (1528).[25] At the same time a rather slavish imitation of Cicero was made easier by the publication of dictionaries of the words used by Cicero such as Mario Nizolio's *Thesaurus Ciceronianus*, first published in 1535 and printed forty-four times before 1626, mainly in Venice and Basel. The admiration for Cicero encouraged fashions for very elaborate styles also in the vernacular (for example the vogue for Euphuism in England) and then to a backlash in which the preferred stylistic model in Latin and in the vernaculars was the clipped sententious Latin of Tacitus and Seneca.[26]

From one small subdivision of style, the use of proverbs, Erasmus built a highly successful and increasingly large reference book. His *Adagia*, which draws both on classical collections (like those by Plutarch and Valerius Maximus) and on his own extensive reading in Greek and Latin literature, aims to list and explain the most important proverbs in Greek and Latin so as to make them available for writers in persuasion, as decoration, in order "to make the language as a whole glitter with sparkles from antiquity ... gleam with jewel-like words of wisdom" (16), to help in understanding the use other authors have made of proverbs, and as valuable and memorable moral guidance in their own right. He develops a capacious definition of the proverb ("a saying, in popular use, remarkable for some shrewd and novel turn") in response to the variety of its forms and sources. For each proverb

[24] Talon 1548.
[25] Sabbadini 1885.
[26] G. K. Hunter 1962: 257–89; Croll 1966.

(there were 4,151 in the last edition Erasmus oversaw) he provides an explanation, which often involves considerable historical or literary scholarship, some examples from authors often organized into types and some advice on usage. Some of the explanations develop into essays in their own right, especially when he becomes involved in expounding, exemplifying, and amplifying the moral lesson encapsulated in the proverb. The reference book turns into a record of his responses to his times and a model of copious writing in its own right.[27]

I began this tour of new developments in renaissance rhetoric by emphasizing the strong role of syllabus expectations in determining which manuals would be printed and taught widely. I should like to end by qualifying the institutional implication of that claim. The Tudor grammar school was set up and its syllabus was determined by people who knew what they expected from rhetoric,[28] yet the founders and early teachers seem to have accepted that, apart from very special occasions which probably required extra preparation by the teacher, pupils would not be expected to make speeches and that accordingly study of a full manual of rhetoric and of Cicero's speeches could be deferred until the university. The main role of the grammar school was to teach Latin reading, writing, and speaking as a step towards virtue. Nevertheless the syllabus, which also included a good selection of Latin authors (as a minimum, Terence, Cicero, selected letters and *On Duties*, Vergil, Sallust, or Caesar, Ovid and/or Horace) and a range of composition exercises can fairly be termed rhetorical. But it features a specialized kind of rhetoric, with rather little of the traditional syllabus (apart from the tropes and figures) and that little taught through the rather different medium of letter-writing, itself begun through imitation of Cicero's simpler letters. Their main writing exercises were letters, *progumnasmata*, and moral themes. The books they read, the way they read them and the writing exercises they performed tended to reinforce a body of knowledge and skill which is in some respects independent of that overtly promoted by Quintilian: moral sententiae, proverbs, moral stories, narratives, histories, letter-writing, *progumnasmata*, thinking about an audience, amplification, commonplace-books, and figures of rhetoric.[29]

---

[27] Phillips 1964; Barker 2001.

[28] The Tudor grammar school was so directly inspired by continental theorists and the works taught correspond so closely to the list of most printed books across Europe that it is tempting to assume that other northern European grammar schools used the same texts. Baldwin 1944. On schooling in Italy see Grendler 1989; R. Black 2001.

[29] P. Mack 2002: 11–47 and *passim*.

The continuing use and adaptation of the precepts and texts of classical rhetoric across Europe in the fifteenth and sixteenth centuries reflects the perceived usefulness and prestige of competence in the Latin language and understanding of classical culture even for people whose primary everyday business would be conducted in the vernaculars. This training promoted norms for what would be recognized as persuasive discourse. It encouraged people to incorporate proverbs, maxims, and certain types of classical, historical, or ethical narratives in their letters, speeches, and published compositions. It showed writers what effects their stylistic choices and their use of figures or amplification could be expected to have. It encouraged readers to read as potential writers, assessing, storing up for reuse or simply enjoying the ways in which particular words or metaphors were employed. Knowing something of their readers' expectations gave writers further resources for creative play.

Suggestions for further reading

Introductions to rhetoric in the Middle Ages: E. R. Curtius, *European Literature and the Latin Middle Ages* (Princeton, 1953); J. O. Ward, *Ciceronian Rhetoric in Treatise, Scholion and Commentary* (Turnhout, 1995). Essential bibliographical foundation for the study of renaissance rhetoric: L. D. Green and J. J. Murphy, eds., *Renaissance Rhetoric Short-Title Catalogue, 1460–1700* (Aldershot, 2006). Useful general histories of renaissance and post-renaissance rhetoric: T. Conley, *Rhetoric in the European Tradition* (New York, 1990); M. Fumaroli, *L'âge de l'éloquence* (Geneva, 1980); M. Fumaroli, ed., *Histoire de la rhétorique dans l'Europe moderne: 1450–1950* (Paris, 1999); P. O. Kristeller, *Renaissance Thought and its Sources* (New York, 1979); J. Monfasani, "Humanism and Rhetoric," in A. Rabil jr., ed., *Renaissance Humanism: Foundations, Forms and Legacy*, 3 vols. (Philadelphia, 1988), vol. III, 171–235; J. J. Murphy, ed., *Renaissance Eloquence* (Berkeley, 1983). Useful on the connection between rhetoric and dialectic: P. Mack, *Renaissance Argument: Valla and Agricola in the Traditions of Rhetoric and Dialectic* (Leiden, 1993); K. Meerhoff, *Entre logique et littérature* (Orléans, 2001); C. Vasoli, *La dialettica e la retorica dell'Umanesimo* (Milan, 1968). On Erasmus: J. Chomarat, *Grammaire et rhétorique chez Erasme*, 2 vols. (Paris, 1981). Useful on the neo-Latin sentence and on issues of style: M. Baxandall, *Giotto and the Orators* (Oxford, 1971); M. W. Croll, *Style, Rhetoric and Rhythm* (Princeton, 1966). Studies on a central text whose contribution to the rhetorical tradition is still not fully understood: G. Dahan and I. Rosier-Catach, eds., *La rhétorique d'Aristote: traditions et commentaires* (Paris, 1998). Helpful on the place of rhetoric in education and its relation to poetics and literature: T. Cave, *The Cornucopian Text* (Oxford, 1979); V. Kahn, *Rhetoric, Prudence and Scepticism in the Renaissance* (Ithaca, 1985); P. Mack, *Elizabethan Rhetoric* (Cambridge, 2002); P. Mack, ed., *Renaissance Rhetoric* (Basingstoke, 1994); K. Meerhoff, *Rhétorique et poétique au XVI siècle en France* (Leiden, 1986).

16

JOHN HENDERSON

The runaround: a volume retrospect
on ancient rhetorics

It's too bad that the people
who know how to ruin the country
are busy teaching school.
(Naff bumper sticker)

Performance

Accustomed to public speaking as all our companions are, they have none of
them told us if they trained and how, pebbles in Demosthenic cheeks above
the roar of the surf, or mantras intoned at some imaginary Archias' feet.
They have indeed regaled us with precious little of the mythology surrounding the star speakers of antiquity (with the necessary exception of Penner
and Vander Stichele's Jesus, Paul, and co.). And they have suppressed detail
on their own investment in rhetoric, ancient or modern (with the exception
of Heath's adversion to his own hands-on teaching of ancient rhetoric in
school). But in performative terms, the rest of these scholar essays practiced
house-style exegetics even while preaching the intrication of rhetoric with
form–content fusion and fission – whereas Batstone dared enter into the
spirit of things, casting his dramas of genre-indifferent rhetorical performa-
tivity in the outward shell of *a scriptwriter's formatting*, as he cooks up a
narrative leading us from staged scenes of worlds talked into existence and
on to settings for world-shattering debate in and as historiography, then out
towards a finale vista of entire cultures manned by selves realized as roles;
and Gunderson was (acting out) toying with his reanimation of Quintilian's
project as the realization of its own training by mounting his account as a
fresh *realisation of Quintilian's training* – with the didactic difference that
the essay runs us lap after lap through explicitation of his quasi-oration's
ticking the grand manual's boxes.

Several arguments are built with *exemplary feature passages* from Greek
and Latin texts (esp. Rosenbloom and Goldhill, more than illustrative,
symptomatic), and other, lower-profile, figured approaches abound. But in
general, the volume has rolled out sundry mixes of standard takes on

278

academic responsibility secured on the page, well away from lush and austere.[1] At any rate, I registered no fantasia purring and whirring of roared rhodomontade from the diaphragm, a-tickling and a-tinkling the ebonies and ivories of the laptop dancing keyboard; nor read terse what's what. (So) We drew a blank by way of "*poetic*" stunt (lyricism in Porter's account of uplift, but mercifully disciplined lyricism) – whereas Wardy's presentation of the "*philosophical*" mode does the job he's ~~hired~~ for, menacingly un/ wrapping diversionary anfractuosities that serve to import at every way-marked fold the tortuous inwardness of (self-)critical thought that has held the citadel of pre-Socratic radicalism ever since the crusade began; while recruiting from "Rhetoric Class 101," Sage Difficulty holds at bay the variously anti-intellectualizing publics in our heads. When it comes to splitting hairs, allusions to ancient encomia on hair and on hair loss (Hesk and Goldhill) rather make the bald point that *humor* is a scarce ingredient in this *microcosmographia academica* – and just about all tracks of *odium philologicum* are covered, too.[2] If politeness is to square with decorum, then *obscenity* will be at a premium – and it is, with the protatic scene of a mouthful facial of ordure from Homer (Worman) warning us off further muck-raking until rumbustious Aristophanic carnival comes and buggers up the pleasantries … so we can enjoy a spurt of filth, and farce can foul the public interface, while doing its worst to deplore anything that moves (Rosenbloom). When Steel took up the onus of informing us on the run-around-of-the-mill "rhetoric manual" of antiquity, she nobly stood in for the idiom – but spared us anything like the reams of mind-rot awaiting the unwary there.

The sole mention of the topos/strategy of the *disclaimer of training in oratory* we ran into during Connolly's insistence on the real dangers and high stakes represented by investment in public debate, whether seen as delivering "deliberative democracy" or as vested in repression: with Worman's immediate focus on interplay and equivalence/displacement between public speaking and non-verbal violence (cf. Habinek), these two essays most *strikingly* cue the tangle of subjects that we can, with the editor's "Introduction," loosely call "anti-rhetoric." There's no rude party-pooper crashing the party to upset anybody. Not yet.

[1] Companion pieces are commissioned *ad hoc*; seldom, if ever, tested before a live audience. A thoroughly "written" genre, then.
[2] Contrast the roasting *onomasti kōmōdein* polemic from Vitanza 1993. None of that from us and ours (as the song sings): "All I get from you is your runaround."

Politesse

Nose-in-the-air aristocrats in the mould of Scipio Nasica could decoct the art of rhetoric into the act of anti-rhetoric, with an "I know best, guys/rabble, leave it to me to sort" (Dugan). And we could indeed cram, maybe re-stock, the *Companion*'s contents with a training/detention camp full of autarchic insurgent cells and loners where rhetoric was (not) just a name for nothing left to lose – and *they* would non- or para-verbally denounce/renounce ancient culture as words backed by swords, and pens mightier than both. For tyrants from Herodotus' to Damocles', and Caesars treating senators as horsemeat or crushing conspiracy by mail, had not much more use for *speech* than proper Spartans, Celtic hordes, dumbshow Aesopian slaves, or defiant women lifting their skirts in opprobrium. Suicide senators and other mute martyrs existed – lived and died – to shout liberty and faith in silence.

But, as the editor argues in the "Introduction," (that is why) *interstitial* out-groups make more productive guides to the empire-framing role of rhetorical protocols than frankly othered folk-devils: in particular, when the time came, we engaged with originary Christians seeking separate identity by fashioning clout for their marginal but organization-promoting "rebellion," as they found themselves (by) trading in hybridized discursive forms after, but at an emphatic distance from, the universalized trademarks of dominant (Roman/subaltern Greek-Judaic) power: Penner and Vander Stichele work out the need to achieve and occult re-branding of the (Hellenizing) forms of persuasion which held valency in their target audiences to the point where they could be imagined to have transpired naturally – so Christ never needed to learn in school to bespeak Christian sermonizing (but Jewish media would never have come up with those riffs).

For the rest, the scenarios our sights have been trained on were always insider-dealing – from the founding Homeric fantasies of chieftain-warriors gathered for pasting in as place-holders for the classical order of rhetorical strategies, through the Second Sophistic gang of players bidding and trumping in the currency of moves and cons they all learned from the same schooling, effortlessly blanking Rome from their conceptual radar, when (not) competing to cadge a superior deal (Worman through Goldhill). Our swift excursion round the Renaissance with Mack traced out a subsequently emerging elite intelligentsia's drive to find this order in this order, and re-launch its (re-fashioned and re-styled) currency as a system for ordaining a new improved civility in line with its own determinations of historical reference and conjuring with discursive technologies.[3]

---

[3] Now you're fired up for the grand tour, see Conley 1990.

Now the writtenness of approved cultural performance in Greco-Roman epistolarity and novelistic fiction which was brought to our attention for Greece under Rome by Goldhill marked for sure the supersession of the always already depleted primacy of the axiomatic "orality" of face-to-face congregation in the city-wide community; and a barrage of further such shifts in media culture hugely transformed the apparatus of the culture machine as the first-world's communication systems outworked the post-classical carapace, eventually re-founding modernity on eventfully (news)printed, shipped, now cabled, beamed cctelevised, and net-wwworked technologies of globality.[4] To the point where we might have felt the want or an urge for either one thing or the other to join the assembled company – either a concluding chapter on ancient rhetoric in the third millennium, or a recursive theme of ancient-through-contemporary/contemporary-through-ancient interfacing woven through the chapters.[5] Instead, we got this post-amble running around tearing its hair out trying to say so.

Procrustes

To run this past more concretely, the explosion of rhetoric as its own discipline, especially across the United States since 1900 or 1950 (which depends on what you mean),[6] has assumed what is for a historian of classics the characteristic trajectory of overeager unilateral declaration of independence from the all-embracing mantle of first-world civilization (i.e. classics), succeeded by phases of technical and institutional self-accreditation, and issuing into an outcome of (more, or less, intelligible) capitalization on success in the imperialist form of expansion to the status of all-embracing arbiter of education and administration.[7] Or so the tale tells. Continuing: in governing modernity, rhetoric did a deal with democracy, proposed itself as master discourse of discourses.

Along the way, "classical rhetoric" was polemically exposed, eschewed, expunged, and defended to death, as instrument and standard-bearer for the hagiographic mystification of oligarchic superiority as populace-control – on the model of Vergil's imperious similitude inaugurating his national myth

---

[4] See Welch 1999.

[5] E.g. Welch 1990.

[6] Rhetoric as breaking away towards expressive literacy from wonder at literariness or rhetoric as the omni-disciplinary guide to power through language: see Andrews 1992, Valesio 1980; and cf. Porter in this volume.

[7] Esp. Burke 1969, etc. and Booth 1974, etc. Cf. Simons 2004.

naturalizing Augustan Rome as cosmographic silencing of the mob (see Dugan).[8] It was very often presumed and sometimes argued that classical rhetoric's day was done because it presupposed cool enough culture for the consecration of staticity as stability to prevail as dominant mode and matrix for persuasion – and that's long gone.[9]

Even in the supposed hotbed that produced the original of democratic oratory, late-fifth-century BCE Athens, the contrast drawn by Thucydides' history between the masterful performance of the born aristocratic word-master Pericles and the revolutionary "extremism" of his well-worded ideological commitment to citizenship as parity clinched its historian's thesis that the elite's self-identification with top-down command through ruses of persuasion courted collective doom (Hesk, Wohl): bracketing out the bunch of specifics, we make out a – the – classic montage of mob and demagogue (obscenely) tonguing and licking their reciprocal way through rounds of irresponsibility to degradation and disaster (Rosenbloom). Behold the cult of flash talk and customized spin brought to Athens via organized induction into rhetoric, Cleon to Alcibiades. A typological smear that tied unmoderated democracy to unreason was planted by Plato in the representation of Socrates' condemnation by a people's court at that very particular time and place when the Athens dreamscape collapsed into internecine nightmare. So it was that the founding ethical-intellectual pros-ecution of sordid rhetoric by sublime philosophy was eternalized as the pandemic struggle for the hearts and minds of civilized and civilizing culture ([but] see Wardy). And there we go, forever stuck, torn, fudging, going round and round, between principle and pragmatism.

But as modern, or "new," rhetorics progressively incorporated more and more of the territory of all discourses in the twentieth-century "linguistic turn", philosophy was ready-installed, to be fought over off-stage and in-study by cohorts in the shade, but rhetoric was re-conceived as embracing and accessing the power coursing through all semiotic events, high or low – always already now texts.[10] Classical sermonizing could now be defended,

---

[8] Displaced: e.g. Perelman 1979; defended: esp. Vickers 1988, with Dugan 2007: 12–13.

[9] For this argument and a rebuttal, see Hesse 1992: 22–24.

[10] In Europe, investment in formal rhetoric unremarkably permitted seamless transferability between even the most jejune "classical" manual (vindicated as vector of incisive intelligence in the re-creation by Barthes 1988) and the scariest prosecution of "the rhetoric of contemporary criticism" (De Man 1971). Booth particularly enjoys recommending Derrida among "major rescuers" of rhetoric (Booth 2004: 77–79, citing the profession from Derrida 1990: "The fact I've been trained in and that I am at some level true to this classical teaching in rhetoric is essential … whether in the sense of the art of persuasion or in the sense of logical demonstration").

because de-throned; and in turn, the rhetoric of rhetoric[11] could be recognized as now "democratized" to the point where listening, critiquing, demystifying rhetorical analysis has on the one hand valorized every performance as a resourced and powered bid to prevail, but on the other delivered the public straight into the hands of technicians of spin, whose dissimulative power to create winning oratory through down-home tonality and celebrity glitz have finessed and outflanked the reasoned argument and intelligent formulation as elitist modes of extinct oligarchy. Something of the sort, boiling up so you couldn't miss the passion of controversy giving us all the runaround.[12]

Pinpoint

But then there is what the invention of the autocue has enabled us to see. This *Companion* does not operate in ignorance of or by ignoring the wider debates over the fun, function, and functioning of rhetoric in the armature of contemporary culture, for all that the widely celebrated take-over launched by Burke[13] makes hardly a mark on the page. What is happening, instead, is that re-examination of theory and practice from Aristotle to Quintilian and Demosthenes to Cicero from within post-modernity permits/ obliges and shapes/opens revaluation of ancient rhetoric to the point where its afterlife in the form of garbled a-historical and anti-historical typologies unmoored from historical specifics is opened for inspection, along with its unwarranted manual of bogus lessons.

The sequence of essays was planned from the start to cohere, and the plan is so coherently set out in the "Introduction" that it mocks re-statement.[14] They resist treating presentations of rhetoric in and of antiquity, including their own stories, as accounting for rhetoric this side of or beyond their status as themselves bids to persuade – as *arguments* (sc. in an argument).[15] Thus the "descriptive" chapters that set out the praxis of classical rhetoric

---

[11] See Booth 2004: 23–34, "A condensed history of rhetorical studies," reporting just 19 of over 600 titles of publications in the form *"The Rhetoric of ..."* as pre-1950, and listing a choice selection in an "Appendix" (34–38).

[12] This schism marks our era – as Nine Inch Nails' "Beginning of the End."

[13] 1969.

[14] Underrepresentation of epideixis after Gorgias and Isocrates (see Wardy and Connolly) may stem from overcompensation after the success of Gunderson 2003 on imperial declamation: the elder Seneca's twelve-book rhetorical induction and weaning of his sons in and off the debating game interposes a telling lesson on "the system" before the Second Sophistic (Goldhill; cf. Henderson forthcoming).

[15] See White 1989.

all address not a settled body of itemic knowledge, but phases in the writing of loaded and committed attempts to process the shaping of vocal power. Its heartbeat as productive regulator of cultural values/delivery of political formation is monitored so we couldn't miss it: society configured through its rhetoric (esp. Connolly, Batstone).

Education, education, education, in the classroom of culture, busy running/ ruining the country, as we get our acts together, and make like the movies. Campaigning for office as auditioning for the part – histrionics – does not merely afflict debased public service; this performative regime is the in-built condition of possibility for political credibility, short of dictation. By attending to their own patch, to the re-presentation of public speech in antiquity, as our companions have been showing ways to see and to say it, they have run around, through, and past the given accounts, and the upshot for their various appropriations in contemporary doctrine. I move.[16] Not that this retrospect was ever going to be "the last word," or even mine, on any of these, or its, subjects. We roam around around around.

Pickwickian

I'm like writing this and you're like "oh, no" and "what is that" and like I'm thinking "whatever, it's like, yeah, I'm like 'or we're all (.) oral-fixated.' " What we'd all like *really* like to know is whether the swish orators actually did put it over on the people, and if they did what did that have to do with any training programme – when? (Cf. Hesk, Steel.) It's not that we are short of Greco-Roman materials to get our heads around. Rather that they come to us through a hail of promotional publicity and pre-packaging noise.

If every version of any "public school" curriculum has faithfully stepped that kid up to the plate groomed to look the part, get the hand-signals fluently right and corroborate the belief in elocution delivering coherent material, then how should we apportion the power as between livery, deportment, conformist clubbism, and verbal-conceptual techniques (Habinek),[17] and/or technical strategies adapted to strengthen improvisatory dexterity into self-realizing personalized profile? And is the dilemma thus put already to downplay, in confronting education with launch into

---

[16] When Gunderson recognized "There is so much out there ... There are so many *Companions to Ancient Rhetoric* already in print," he well knew Jost and Olmsted 2004, with its significant classical quotient, but was anticipating in particular the appearance of Worthington 2007 and Dominik and Hall 2007, both featuring one or two of "our" companions, though sadly lacking a volume retrospect.

[17] And see his classic chapter "Rhetoric as acculturation" (Habinek 2005a: 60–78).

assembly, court, or debating society, the "kairotic" challenge for any speaker to seize the moment, boss crisis, imprint jury, gild lily, by transferentially incarnating audience satisfaction – the rapprochement between what's wanted and how far that allows/dictates the terms for success in persuasion?[18]

When an Athenian expert came up with the right script for a defendant client to go tell the people's court, how far did the sophist mask his own gift of the gab in order to ventriloquate "in character"? Collaterally, when Plato writes a defense for Socrates to deliver, does he mean it to sound like Plato's Socrates, out of kilter with defendant, occasion, and forensic short-termism? In the Assembly, did the Pericles myth *arise* as gilded memory for spanking "demagogue" successors as yardstick for loser Athens? Could Thucydides or any other narrator from Homer and Hesiod onwards *both* acclaim resounding performances showcased in their texts *and* produce versions that actually deliver on the billing? (Worman. Remember Vergil's sidestep into paraphrase when Anchises some-undisclosed-how "fired his son's mind with love of fame to come, proceeding to premember the wars that hero must wage subsequently," *Aeneid* 6.889–90.) What in any of our repertoire of texts of and about oratory was the outcome of study – and (again) how much in study has ever been down to the teachings in the manual, rather than to trial and practice, and up to the coaching staff? (Heath).

When we press the Roman Republic for its answers, hero-cult blocks the way: the great exception Cicero writes himself up as the rule. Fixation on him as the culture-hero of deliberative oligarchy tooled the most spectacular "text book" of rhetorical education in Quintilian's dream of a virtuous novitiate (Gunderson, Heath) and prevailed for real in the Roman archive, to the point, way beyond the wildest dreams of star and sacristan, where we have no corpora for him to compare with and bow to or beggar. The only towering Roman word wizard we *are* in a position to emulate himself writes down and writes up his performances to serve as the designed self-promotion campaign of the least typical senatorial success-story, and he crowns this by narrating his own career into the role of supervenient *telos* of the entire tradition of Roman eloquence (in *On the Orator* and *Orator*; Heath, Dugan). Starring in his own theorizing dramas of politically effective eloquence, Cicero makes sure to cut loose of his teachers' writings as well as their teaching/s, but all the while graphically documents his bid to ride

---

[18] See Poulakos 1993: 63–65 on *kairos* in rhetoric (63), "a contradiction in terms, now asking us to attend to the opportune moment, now to knowledge about it."

court, council, and sparring partners to the top of the tree. There, shaping events as chief executive first left him with the price to pay of popular exile for tyrannical abuse of power, then relegated him to the sidelines while the legions ousted debate, before he was finally extirpated along with the aristocracy club system he had infiltrated and installed himself as spokesman and quasi metaphor. Even as we learn Roman success through Cicero, hi/story should make it clear that no protégé of any Quintilian could ever succeed the master and martyr of the Republic, and nothing to do with technical empowerment, either. If we cannot forget the Orator's end as the sadistic trophy that inaugurated autocracy – his lopped head and orator's right hand pinned to the rostra from where he had worked the people to his will[19] – it proves no more tractable to try to isolate from history the dynamics of the rest of his atypical *floruit*.

This very counsel who majestically affirms the thoroughgoing dependence of his persuasive powers on his training in Greek rhetoric, attributing every scalp to one teacher's influence, through inculcation of the doctrine of the indivisible nucleation of all the liberal-humanist arts within "rhetoric," underlines in the very act of enunciation that that's why he's talking and sounding uniquely weird in court "today"; that is to say, you will detect Greek rhetorical training speaking through Cicero's mouth before a Roman court *only* when it suits him to parade it – under the unique circumstance that for this runaround suit he is defending said Greek teacher (of "Greek" rhetoric; see the famed *Pro Archia* proem). We can of course play at impersonating Ciceronian delivery of the speeches (including this odd-man-out, the proem made strange by the brief). And we can juggle with his own account/s of Roman oratory culminating with his own, taunting us with his exceptionality. But we can dig, too, the bank of expertise which lifts his contributions to Roman worship of word-power way above anything resembling the "practical" manuals of rhetoric where he started (and with which he started).

In much the same way, we can get around, get around, get around *to* rereading Aristotle's *Rhetoric* for *its* rhetoric, feeling our way with him towards uncovering the forces at work that govern public speech, and (preferably)[20] those that should, and confirm that his preoccupation is with reasoning out the prospects of reason in interplay and competition with the other dimensions of persuasive communication – feelings and traits (Heath). The *Companion* brings out how extraordinarily Aristotle brings pioneering

---

[19] See Richlin 1999, head; S. Butler 2002, hand.

[20] For the idealism of rhetorical "virtue theory" from Aristotle through Quintilian, see Connolly and Gunderson.

intelligence and analytic innovation to the mundanities of Greek rhetorico-didaxis, long before his work became first an advantageous idiom and in time the amazingly predominant mainstream of Roman, imperial Greek, and all "classical" teaching, advocacy, critique, and theory-in-practice.

The flipside of this is that, while we are given rousing revaluations of both paragons of rhetoric/oratory, Aristotle and Cicero, the ordinariness of the training manual/s has not figured in the running. What I would give for a run down on ordinary speakers like "learning to learn" with their manual/s (cf. Gunderson).

Procul Harum

Some ancient rhetoricians knew how to complexify categories till the cows would never come home; there was a collective drive to mystify, raise the tariff for participation, wear down all precocity; but even the most cowing of homework assignments in the characteristic pseudo-scientific form of listed divisions up jargon trees and down bullshit burrows was part of an ongoing contest in know-how, with knock-on effects for actual performance (Heath, Steel). I think, though, we should ac-knowledge that a lot of it comes through minds running on empty. For instance, the mapping of the basic triad of assembly, court, and display scenario onto temporality, with "counseling" future-oriented, "advocacy" working on what transpired, and "encomium/invective" wowing now, *can* help to open up the whole inexhaustibility of implication through nuance of tense, aspect, syntax (Hesk); but, equally, this sort of stipulative maneuvering *will* lapse into formalist sterility, into mind-numbing enumeration frenzy.[21]

It should not be *so* hard to notice that all the effort going into blueprinting positive speechifying envisages uninterrupted once-through-and-done participation, whether self-standing or in combination with a tag team or series of rival declaimers on the same theme: but the question-and-answer interrogation style of Thucydides" sick "debate" on Melos, sick not least for its deliberately paraded formal structuring *as* a "dialogue," serves notice to us that reality threw up many a challenge less amenable to representation in wish-fulfillment pages than that uninterruptible monologue, the "classical oration" (Hesk).

Moreover, when ancient speakers were supplied with full instructions on how to turn theory into successful application, this turned on the taps of "invention," suggesting a myriad lines of approach, it coached "argument"

---

[21] I'd admit it takes a vivid historical imagination to share (post-)Renaissance relish even for Cicero's *On Invention* (Mack).

into affording a panoply of realizable storylines, and it helped interminably with the creative work of "expression." What did not happen – the task-topic of "memorization" bred the undying alchemy of retrieval systems and its legendary feats of memorious heroics (Steel) – was effectual exploration of "delivery," of performance (Heath). Not, that is, all that business of turning up as suit-ably stylish hombre, but the crucial bit, the actual bid to close out the verbal deal with an audience *on location*, the *hic et nunc et nos et illud*.

The way philology tackles this is to reanimate written oration, extra-polating from internal clues, consonance with rhetorical prescription, and (for embedded speeches) situational information. Whereas contemporary sociolinguistics is forging ahead with "discourse analysis" attempts to catch the electricity in speech-events, not excluding famed moments of truth where oratory rang clear. One outcome is ever-deepening awareness of the decisive weight of "situation," in the sense of both the issue and the audience (cf. Dugan on 63 BCE Rome). Such oralist phenomena as duetting and harmonizing with favorably disposed fans are attested for antiquity, deplored both for cheerleader Cleon (Wohl on Thucydides' Mytilene debate), and – by Cicero, in the classic letter, *Letters to Quintus* 2.3.2 – for the demagogic, disclaiming aristocrat, Clodius, making mayhem with his gang, football-chant style). But never in today's multi-track rich text format. Here's a snippet of where you can get to. It's Nye Bevan hamming it up with a little help from his friends plus a spate of idiolectally ponderous olde world/hyper-Welsh intonation tricks, at Eden's "suez" expense:[22]

                     ou   ə
24 ... and there is only <u>one</u> <u>way</u> in <u>which</u> they can (.) even be<u>gin</u> to
re<u>store</u> their
                a: u ei
<<harsh>> <u>tar</u>nished repu<u>ta</u>tion [audience: *get out*]
                                        əʊ   əʊ   əʊ
25 and that is to <<high pitch>> get <u>out</u> (.) get <u>out</u> get <u>out</u>
                                              [
                                        ((loud cheers)).[23]

So what *made* this demolition work (it did)? For reasons that take into full account decades of image-delivery building, plus pre-microphone-formed political-rally style, plus socialist plebeianism, plus tide-gates opened wide to government humiliation, all pumping up the momentum of momentous-ness. Not much that you could plausibly think would make it work, say, *here and now*. And/So how much traces back to "study"? Our style of

[22] Coupland 2007: 156–63.
[23] Coupland 2007: 160.

recording technology, we can understand now we have it, was not around in antiquity, but classical rhetoric is ... after something else. Including running rings round the lot of us.

Procatalepsis

The companions prepare no one for creative writing and composition class; nor do they see their way to taking sample compositions or purple passages to pieces, colon by colon, period by period, proem through narration to ... peroration, so as to expose the resources of verbal power that are being harnessed by Attic orators or Cicero (but see *cursim* especially Wohl on Lysias 10 and 24, Dugan on the *First Catilinarian*). Instead, their work applies and pursues critical consciousness to a robustly *problematic* conception of persuasion.

Words are not just words. In the utterance come together the ever-recessive whatever it is that switches words on: there is the materiality and musicality behind their "voicing," the surge that sets off good vibrations, uplift, the ring of rightness (Porter). Then there is the rationale and grava-men behind their "logos," the conceptualization that pushes mental buttons, conviction, the ordinance of truth (Wardy). And there is the axiomatic chiming with experience and outlook behind their congruence with the pool of local "enthymemes," common sense, the confirmation of obviousness (Gunderson, Heath). In a key argument designed to align "the rhetoric of Aristotle with Bakhtin's rhetoric" as "complementary," Bialostosky maintains that the latter is "functionally prior" to the former:[24]

> There can be persuasion without argument, grounded in shared evaluation expressed through intonation, and the selection and disposition of arguments in rhetorical utterances must be ruled by their provocations and their antici-pations of response, not by their availability alone. Rhetors possessed of a storehouse of available means of persuasion like the one Aristotle compiles will lack means of choosing and ordering them unless they can respond to the questions posed to them and select among those means with knowledge of what their auditors already know, believe, and hold dear. They cannot decide what to say just by knowing what might be said; they must also know what has just been said by others and what goes without saying for their audience ... Entechnic argument is no substitute for enthymematic utterance ...

The *Companion* would argue to the contrary that the philosophy of Aristotelian – "classical" – rhetoric is pledged to gear the enthymeme to "logos," without wishing away sound-track pathologies and aesthetics.

---

[24] 2004: 406.

(Remember, the "Introduction" began from Kant and Nietszche.) Ancient orators plied their craft, but the teaching kept plugging the ethical in and into the performative. Bound to its stake in the debate about the nature of (the) debate.

One way and other, we all want to runaround, and get behind the words. Thanks for your company.

Appendix 1

Rhetorical terms

The following explication of technical terms and taxonomies is meant to be a useful overview, not a definitive account or even an especially authoritative adumbration. Only some of the major headings are on offer as well as a sample of subheadings. These divisions and definitions should only be taken as starting points: there are many available modifications of them in our technical literature. This *Companion* regularly flags disputes that circulated around such terms in antiquity. Readers who only consulted this appendix without reading those discussions in the body of the text would be in possession of an impoverished and somewhat distorted appreciation of these issues. Nevertheless, an outline of a relatively canonical version of some of the chief areas of concern will be of service if one is going to follow detailed discussions about such issues and to appreciate the eventual emergence of areas of broad agreement.

I. The major categories of oration

deliberative (*sumbouleutikon, deliberatiuum*) The oratory of public persuasion and speeches that argue before a duly assembled and authorized body either in favor of or against some course of action to be taken in the future.

judicial (*dikanikon, iudicale*) The oratory of prosecution and defense in a court convened to make a ruling on a matter of law relative to some past event.

demonstrative (*epideiktikon, demonstratiuum*) The oratory of display. A gathering hears the praise or blame of a person, place, or even thing.

Potential complications of this schema:

A judicial speech might advocate, for example, the release of a guilty man who is nevertheless a great general owing to an immanent military threat. See Cicero, *Against Verres* 2.5.2–4 for an outline of this sort of strategy and how orators use it when making their cases. Gambits like this ask jurors to conceive of themselves as a deliberative assembly who have put to them a question of public policy that affects the future of the state. We can also observe a confusion of genres in *controuersiae*. These were fictional judicial speeches that were not delivered in a court. Instead they might be performed for a gathering of friends. Such a speech is judicial in form, but set within a demonstrative performative context.

II. The basic divisions of an oration

introduction   (*prooimion, exordium*) Here the orator is told to secure his audience's attention, favor, and willingness to learn. These ends are to be borne in mind throughout a speech, but they are felt as most pressing in the introduction, and they accordingly govern the handling of highly variable issues such length, contents, and directness of approach.

narration   (*diēgēsis, narratio*) This is a selective telling of the facts of the case. This narrative looks forward to the proofs that will be furnished in the segment of the speech given over to formal argumentation. Narratives are supposed to evince the virtues of clarity, brevity, and plausibility.

proofs   (*pistis, probatio*) Though often translated as "proofs," the English word "proof" can suggest undue logical rigor or access to concrete evidence. At issue is confirmation and refutation so as to effect persuasion. This is generally the most substantial portion of a speech. If the orator is expected to teach, move, and delight his audience, here the overt emphasis is on "teaching." Theorists explore highly elaborate taxonomies of argumentation. See also the discussion below of "rhetorical proofs."

peroration   (*epilogos, peroratio*) This is the conclusion of the speech. A brief recapitulation of the chief points of the speech is usual. Also usual are vigorous efforts to move the passions of the audience by stirring up anger or pity.

Potential complications of this schema:

There are several competing versions of this overall taxonomy and of the terminology to be used within the taxonomy itself. This template is ideally suited for judicial speeches. Within any given speech elements might be expanded, contracted, rearranged, or even omitted. Strategic considerations will always trump formal ones.

III. The basic divisions of the orator's craft

invention   (*heuresis, inuentio*) This is the discovery of ideas and techniques to be used in the course of the speech that will be conducive to demonstrating one's position. The colloquial English term "brainstorming" could be invoked. But the ancient version of discovering has been highly codified and is offered as an actual art of researching the formal details of one's case. Invention is the most theoretically elaborated of the divisions of the orator's art. Invention is used to explore each of the divisions of an actual speech. For example, how one will handle the narration is a matter for invention, as is the exploration of the arguments to be employed when making one's proofs.

arrangement (*taxis, dispositio*) What invention has found, arrangement sets in order. The raw mass of ideas provided by the former will be ineffectual without the force and clarity afforded by the latter. One's arrangement affects both the large-scale economy of the whole speech and the ordering of small-scale phenomena such as the details of a narrative episode or the ordering of a string of arguments.

style (*lexis, elocutio*) This is the second most elaborated of the divisions. If invention discovers ideas, then style gives them concrete expression. Style is regularly subdivided into the examination of individual word-choice and the treatment of collocations of words. Arrangement interacts with questions of style when it comes to building phrases. In contradistinction to the often broad and vague use of the word "style" in English, ancient discussions of style tend to be highly technical and focused on evaluating very small-scale phenomena by means of a vast albeit rather heterogeneous aesthetic vocabulary.

memory (*mnēmē, memoria*) In antiquity there is a strong expectation that the orator will speak without recourse to notes. Accordingly major portions of a speech are learned by heart in advance. Those who cannot commit everything to memory will memorize the remaining material of the case while improvising the specific words. Thus the products of invention receive priority while style is allowed to take a second place. Exercises train natural powers of memory. One learns associative techniques that can facilitate the recollection of vast quantities of material.

delivery (*hupokrisis, actio*) The performance of a speech is itself theorized. The theory of delivery analyzes both the voice and the body. One is expected to attend to every aspect of self-presentation from dress, pitch of voice, movement of the eyebrows, regulation of breathing, and complex hand gestures. Effective self-staging is viewed as essential to rhetorical success. Performance is likewise profoundly implicated with questions of audience's attention, favor, and willingness to learn.

Potential complications of this schema:

Despite the eventual canonization of the above list, not every theorist recognized all five of these divisions. The terminology in Greek and Latin was not fixed. The perceived relationships among the elements varies. See the chapters by Heath and Steel in this volume.

*IV. Some ways of analyzing the chief issue at stake
in a case* (stasis, status)

Issue-theory offers a way to produce taxonomies of cases. It will be invoked, then, at a very early stage of the process of invention. The elaboration of the theory of *stasis* postdates the initial period of the formulation of rhetorical theory, and it offered new ways of exploring cases. Its integration into the mainstream of rhetorical theory was, though, uneven. Nevertheless its effects are long-standing. Below are some of the basic categories.

conjecture   (*stokhasmos, coniectura*) At issue are the facts themselves. The case will turn around the question, "Did he do it?"
definition   (*horos, finitio*) At issue is the proper (legally binding) term to apply to the facts. The case will turn around the question, "What was it he did?"
quality   (*poiotēs, qualitas*) At issue is the legality or propriety of the act itself. Thus one concedes who did the act and the name to give it, and the case instead turns around the question, "Did he act appropriately?"

Potential complications of this schema:

As a reading of Quintilian, *Institutes* 3.6 reveals, there was extreme variation in the number of categories and their names from theorist to theorist. Both the major headings and the subheadings were open to highly varied interpretations. Quintilian complains that some try to make a name for themselves as the inventor of a new category or taxonomy of categories. What ideally might be a useful tool becomes instead a tangled site of scholarly debates (3.6.22).

V. Types of rhetorical proof (entekhnoi pisteis,
probationes artificiales)

This is a subheading of invention. The arguments thus found, when duly arranged, are naturally going to cluster in the segment of the speech specifically dedicated to arguments. The inherited translations of these terms can be confusing. The valence of the term "proof" itself is probably too strong and overly closed. "Means of persuasion" or "demonstration" probably captures the situation somewhat better: we are examining that which is conducive to establishing a specific conclusion. One could thus also describe the category of *entekhnoi pisteis/probationes artificiales* as "demonstrations that are informed by the art of rhetoric." Such rhetorical demonstrations are also commonly known by the potentially misleading name of "artificial proofs." Artificial proofs are distinguished from proofs to which rhetorical art has not been applied. Such "inartificial proofs" (*atekhnoi pisteis*) include testimony derived from the torture of slaves, documentary evidence, rumor, and prior verdicts in similar cases. These are materials that precede the case and the orator's efforts. In practice, however, all of this "inartificial" material is itself subjected to rhetorical elaboration. That is, "proofs" that come to the case from outside the zone of "art" when subsumed within the economy of the case become the object of new demonstrations that are derived from reflection on the case as a whole and are informed by the art of rhetoric. The orator routinely confirms or refutes the soundness of evidence gained under torture, the validity of documents, the trustworthiness of rumors, and the applicability of precedents.

signs   (*tekmēria/sēmeia, signa*) These are non-verbal tokens that stand in need of rhetorical elaboration. Some signs are certain, others are doubtful. Breathing is a certain sign of life. Blood on a man's hands is a doubtful sign. The man may be a murderer, someone who just had a bloody nose, or someone who recently sacrificed an animal. Rhetorical elaboration is needed to bring out the meaning of such signs for the audience.

arguments   (*enthumēmata/epikheirēmata/apodeixeis, argumenta*) Arguments operate according to a process by which one thing is concluded from another and by which something which is not in doubt confirms a second thing which is. There is a rich variety of types of argument available to orators. And the finding of arguments is a special subheading of the art of oratory. See below.

examples   (*paradeigmata, exempla*) These are demonstrations drawn from outside the case. The orator highlights the similarity or dissimilarity of the matter at hand to some other act. The example is often more than a mere example. There is a pronounced tendency to invoke culturally central moments and figures. It is possible, however, for a speaker to invoke or even compose a fable to which he will compare the current case. This last tactic is, though, rare and considered to be "low" from a stylistic as well as a sociological standpoint.

Potential complications of this schema:

The terminology and taxonomy can become cumbersome and misleading. Meanwhile the majority of the theorization on this topic concerns itself only with arguments and not with either inartificial proofs more generally or with signs and examples. There is a complex and somewhat uncomfortable relationship between the formal rules and vocabulary of logic and the description of rhetorical argumentation. This problem emerges in Aristotle and never quite goes away.

VI. Some "places" where one can look for arguments
(topoi, loci)

Invention seeks arguments. The process of seeking is guided by a mastery of "topics." The Greek term evokes physical location, and this is brought out even further when Quintilian describes *loci* as the dwelling places of arguments whence they may be sought and drawn forth (Quintilian, *Institutes* 5.10.20). The set of "places" is extensive, and what follows is a mere sample. A study of topics can allow one to appreciate a whole "topography" of the preferred categories of analysis and frames of reference within the world of ancient oratory. The speakers on both sides of a case can be imagined as having arrived at the same game preserve – that is, the case itself – and then they set themselves to hunting out useful classes of arguments from their various lairs (cf. the imagery of Quintilian, *Institutes* 5.10.21).

character   (*prosōpon, persona*) This is seen as the first place to look. It is also immediately broken down into subdivisions such as family, national origin, sex, age, educational background, bodily comportment, wealth, social standing, inner character, favorite pursuits, aspirations, prior sayings and doings. These subheadings are themselves productive of further opportunities for exploration.

the matter at hand   (*pragma, res*) This is a broad heading under which a vast array of subdivisions can be made. A set of questions will guide you through issues such as motive, time, place, opportunity, and instrument: "why? where? when? how? by means of what?" Each subdivision itself admits of extensive expansion: from "place" you can move to "what sort of place?" and run through categories such as public and private, land and sea, spacious and confined. These themselves can be further divided. For example, an urban mansion is not a country retreat.

Potential complications of this schema:

Once again the taxonomy itself can seem a bit forced. Different authors will have different portraits of the *loci*. An alternative way of exploring the topic of the matter at hand (*res*) is to run through aspects that pertain to the matter itself (*in re*), those that are potentially compared to it (*circa rem*), and those that arise from it (*post rem*). Quintilian declares that there is a terminological confusion between the above version of *loci* and a kindred one, *loci communes* or "common places." If you just said the word *loci* at Rome, it might not be clear which you meant (*Institutes* 5.10.20). "Common places" are general topics that are pressed into service on the present occasion. Indictments of the depravity of the age, attacks on luxury, and praise of the countryside are some of the most familiar commonplaces. In Julius Victor the general discussion of "places to look for arguments" occurs within the framework of what he labels as a discussion of *loci communes*. That is, Quintilian's *loci* are Julius Victor's *loci communes*.[1] Even the most attentive student will have every cause to feel confused: the same technical vocabulary does not always designate the same object of inquiry. Similarly the argument about the "circumstances" (*peristasis*) of an undertaking at [Hermogenes], *On Invention* 3.5 gives a long list of subheadings to this category including "character"(*prosōpon*) and "the matter at hand" (*pragma*) as well as "place" (*topos*). The vocabulary that elsewhere furnishes major conceptual headings is invoked in a discussion of a subheading, and these items serve as a collection of species falling under that subheading.

VII. Some "turns" of phrase (tropos, tropus)

Tropes are one of the elements of style. Related topics that also fall under the heading of style are figures, adornment, amplification and diminution, and pithy phrases. Tropes "turn" language away from its expected course. A trope substitues an "improper" word for the proper one in any given situation. Theorists offer a technical analysis of the different kinds of substitution. As ever, there are many divisions and subdivisions on offer. The propriety of many specific tropes is frequently at issue: poets have much more license here than do pleaders, and examples are frequently drawn from the domain of poetry.

metaphor   (*metaphora, translatio*) A metaphor takes a word from one
    context and inserts it into another context in a manner that, owing
    to some underlying similarity, leaves the impression that a fitting sub-
    stitution has been made. An example: "He is a lion." The explicit
    comparative form of this is "He is like a lion." Metaphors are recom-
    mended for a variety of uses. For example, they can offer vividness or
    brevity. They can amplify. They can allow one to avoid obscenity.
metonymy   (*metōnumia, metonymia*) One word is again substituted for
    another. This time the substituted word is in a real relationship to
    the original word, not in a comparative one. The various sorts of "real

---

[1] Julius Victor, *Ars Rhetorica* 395H.

relationships" are enumerated and analyzed. Examples of relationships are persons and objects, containers and contents, causes and effects. Thus one can substitute "Mars" for war or "the theater" for the audience. Similarly one speaks of "miserable old age."

synecdoche   (*sunekdokhē, synecdoche*) This can be described as a metonymy governed by a specific kind of real relationship. This time the substitution occurs along the axis of quantity: parts and wholes, genera and species, plurals and singulars. Thus one substitutes "roof" for house, "iron" for sword, and "The Roman" for "The Romans."

antonomasia   (*antonomasia, antonomasia*) This is a substitution that pertains to a specific proper name. "The first citizen of Roman eloquence" can be used in the place of the name Cicero.

hyperbole   (*huperbolē, hyperbole*) This is an extreme version of metaphor that overshoots any plausible literal similarity. It is usually regarded as a poeticism and only to be deployed sparingly by orators: "Speech flowed forth from his mouth sweeter than honey." Quintilian approves of Cicero's hyperbolic descriptions of Antonius in the *Second Philippic*.

Potential complications of this schema:

The original term for the general phenomenon of altering language (*metaphora*) invites confusion with the more specialized use of this word for the narrower phenomenon of metaphor. The precise terminology used for specific figures in different authors is not necessarily identical especially when it comes to Latin versions of Greek terms. The ancient theory of tropes usually distinguishes them from "figures," but it does not always do so. Tropes involve the alteration of an individual word. Figures concern multiple words. Figures entail the addition, subtraction, or displacement of words away from "standard" use.[2] However there is clearly a strong affinity between the four activities spread between the two categories. Quintilian feels a need to clarify the situation as the ninth book of his *Institutes* opens, but his own preferred definitions contain key equivocations. The ancient distinction separating tropes from figures is utterly jumbled in the standard English definition of the noun trope: "A figure of speech which consists in the use of a word or phrase in a sense other than that which is proper to it; also, in casual use, a figure of speech; figurative language."[3]

---

[2] Figures are themselves also subdivided into figures of speech and figures of thought. The former involve alterations of actual phrasing, the latter shifts at a conceptual level.

[3] *OED*, 2nd edn., s. v. "Trope (n.)."

Appendix 2
Authors and prominent individuals

These biographies are intended to offer a quick and handy reference for readers of this volume. The information on offer is, then, minimal and highly selective. It seldom goes much beyond an author's name, era, and basic intellectual affiliations or achievements. Parentheses after a name indicate optional information that is often used to disambiguate men of similar or identical names.

Achilles Tatius (second century CE) Achilles Tatius was from Alexandria, and he wrote the romance *Leucippe and Cleitophon*. The plot is conventional, but the form and the contents of the text evince erudite preoccupations characteristic of the Second Sophistic. Literary criticism of this "ancient novel" should not be undertaken independently of an appreciation of the rhetorical culture whence it arose.

Aelian (*c.* 170–235 CE) Aelian was from Praeneste in Italy. He taught rhetoric in Rome and is the author of a *Miscellaneous History* and *On Animals*. Philostratus praises his Atticism and unadorned style.

Aelius Theon (*c.* first? century CE) Aelius was from Alexandria. He was a teacher of rhetoric and the author of a collection of *Progymnasmata* or *Preliminary Rhetorical Exercises*.

Aeschines (*c.* 396 – *c.* 322 BCE) Aeschines was an Athenian and one of the ten canonical orators. His style was singled out for its clarity and lofty tone. He is very much remembered for his high-profile clashes with the orator Demosthenes. A devastating loss at the hands of Demosthenes results in Aeschines' exile from Athens. He is said to have founded a school of rhetoric at Rhodes during his exile. Only three of his speeches remain.

Alcidamas (fourth century BCE) Alcidamus was born in Elaea. He was a rhetorician and sophist who was a follower of Gorgias. He wrote an *On the Sophists*. His rhetorical theories attract the attention of both Plato and Aristotle.

Anaximenes (of Lampsacus)   (c. 380–320 BCE) A historian and rhetorician.
He is likely to have been the author of the so-called *Rhetoric to
Alexander* which was preserved among the works of Aristotle and
erroneously attributed to him. This, then, is probably our only surviving
pre-Aristotelian rhetorical handbook.

Andocides   (c. 440–c. 390 BCE) He was an Athenian and one of the ten
canonical orators. His style was subjected in antiquity to some harsh
criticism for being unclear and rambling. He is most remembered for
becoming implicated in the twin scandals of the mutilation of the Herms
on the eve of the Sicilian expedition and the profanation of the Eleusinian
Mysteries. Four speeches under his name survive; one is spurious.

Antiphon   (c. 480–411 BCE) Antiphon was the earliest of the ten canonical
orators of Athens. He was tried, condemned and executed as a leader of
an oligarchic coup in 411. He is a seminal figure in the history of
oratory and of Attic prose. He is said to have been the first to write
speeches for others to deliver. His works include the *Tetralogies* which
are imaginary speeches with a theoretical and didactic thrust. Three
actual speeches are also preserved. Some believe that the author of the
speeches and the author of the *Tetralogies* were two different men.

(Marcus) Antonius   (consul 99 BCE) Antonius was an important figure in
the early history of rhetoric at Rome. He is said to have been the second
Roman to write a technical work on rhetoric. He is one of the central
characters of Cicero's idealizing *De Oratore*. This Antonius should not
be confused with his grandson Antonius. That Antonius was a triumvir,
the object of Cicero's attack in the *Philippics*, and the man who secured
Cicero's murder.

(Aelius) Aristides   (117–81 CE) Aristides was born in Asia Minor. He
studied rhetoric in a number of cultural centers under a series of leading
intellectual figures. He lectured throughout the Greek-speaking world.
A Second Sophistic author famed for his (old) Attic Greek, he wrote
numerous orations and treatises on rhetorical subjects including a
To Plato in Defense of Oratory.

Aristophanes   (450s–c. 384 BCE) Aristophanes was the most famous of the
Athenian poets of Old Comedy. His social and political satire includes
numerous attacks on the speakers and intellectual figures of his day.
Socrates appears in the *Clouds*, rhetoric and the court system are
lampooned in the *Wasps*, and a demagogic Cleon makes more than
one appearance.

Aristotle   (384–322 BCE) Aristotle was one of the most famous Greek
philosophers. He was a student of Plato, the tutor of Alexander the
Great, and founder of his own philosophical school. His extensive body

of writings include scientific treatises, logical works, political and ethical writings, and works on rhetoric and poetry. His *Rhetoric* and *Poetics* will be of particular interest to readers of this volume.

Aristoxenus (b. 375–360 BCE) Aristoxenus was a philosopher and musical theorist who was born in Tarentum, a Greek colony in Southern Italy. He studied under Aristotle at Athens.

Athenaeus (flourishes *c.* 200 CE) He was born in Egypt, and is the author of *The Sophists at Dinner,* a massive work depicting a many-day symposium of learned men and their discussions of various erudite topics. The text is a veritable encyclopedia of ancient culture and contains innumerable citations from a variety of earlier authors and works.

Augustine (354–430 CE) Augustine was born in Northern Africa. He taught rhetoric at Carthage, Rome, and Milan. He was centrally positioned in the classical pagan cultural milieu when he converted to Christianity. He subsequently became a famous preacher and a bishop. His life and works put him squarely at the crossroads of pagan and Christian culture.

(Gaius Julius) Caesar (100–44 BCE) Caesar was a Roman politician from a distinguished family. He is most famous for his military and political exploits, but he was also considered to be easily one of the best orators of his era. He was a leading proponent of a clear and direct Latin style. In addition to his memoirs about his military campaigns he wrote an *Anticato* in reply to Cicero's laudatory and politically charged *Cato* and a theoretical work about Latin entitled *On Analogy.*

Cato (the Elder) (234–149 BCE) Cato was an arch-conservative Roman politician. He was an important innovator in early Latin literature and a key figure in the shift from Greek to Latin as the literary language used at Rome. He was the author of sayings, histories, and a work on agriculture. He wrote a large number of speeches that were read and praised by later Romans but now exist only in fragmentary form. Cato the Elder is also known as Cato the Censor or just Cato. One needs to avoid confusing this Cato with his great-grandson who lived 95–46 CE and who is often called Cato Unicensis or Cato the Younger.

Catullus (84?–54? BCE) Catullus was a Roman poet of the late Republican period. His poems vary significantly in tone and scale. Some are learned Alexandrian meditations, others are occasional pieces. His corpus includes love poems, lyric poetry, satire, and invective. His contemporaries Cicero and Caesar both appear in his verse.

Cicero (106–43 BCE) Born in the Italian city of Arpinum into an equestrian family, Cicero pursued a political career in Rome that won him the consulship, exile, return, and eventual assassination. He was considered

Rome's leading orator in his own time, and he was acclaimed the greatest Roman speaker of all time by succeeding generations. His works have been abundantly preserved and include speeches, theoretical works on oratory, philosophical and political treatises, and private correspondence. Cicero plays a major role in the subsequent history of each of these genres at Rome.

Cleon   (d. 422 BCE) Cleon was an Athenian politician. He was a vocal critic of Pericles and positioned himself as a champion of the democracy. Aristophanes and Thucydides both offer vivid and unflattering portraits of Cleon. They have shaped his reception as a figure who exemplifies the dangers of mass oratory in a democratic society.

Corax (and Tisias)   (fifth century BCE) Both were from Syracuse. One is remembered as the first teacher of rhetoric. The other was his pupil. Who taught whom is not always agreed upon in our sources. They are a semi-mythical pair positioned at the birth of the art of oratory.

Crassus   (140–91 BCE) Crassus was a Roman orator and statesman. He was consul in 95 BCE and censor in 92 BCE. The teachers of rhetoric at Rome were censured in that year. Nevertheless Crassus was himself a leading orator and teacher of other aristocratic speakers and is praised as such by Cicero in his *On the Orator*, where there are strong connections between the portrait of Crassus and Cicero himself. This Crassus (Lucius Licinius) should not be confused with Marcus Licinius Crassus, who was a member of the first triumvirate along with Julius Caesar and Pompey.

Crates (of Mallos)   (alive in 168 BCE) Crates was an important scholar at Pergamum who came to Rome on an embassy in 168 BCE. He slipped, seriously injured himself, and remained in Rome to convalesce. Meanwhile he offered a series of highly influential state-of-the-art lectures on scholarly topics. This was a seminal moment for the emergence of indigenous Roman scholarship, especially research into the Latin language itself.

Demetrius (of Phalerum)   (*c.* 350 – *c.* 280 BCE) Demetrius was an Athenian statesman who was made absolute governor of Athens by the Macedonians in 318. He was a student of the peripatetic Theophrastus and also himself an influential intellectual figure. He wrote philosophical works, orations, and rhetorical theory. The extant work *On Style* was formerly attributed to him in error.

Democritus   (*c.* 460 – *c.* 370 BCE) Democritus was born in Thrace. He was a pre-Socratic philosopher and one of the founding fathers of the theory of atomism. His works include texts on ethics, physics, mathematics, and music. The last also contain philological and literary discussions. His writings survive only in fragmentary form.

Demosthenes (384–322 BCE) Demosthenes was one of the ten canonical orators of Athens. He is usually considered to be the greatest Greek orator of antiquity. He was a master of a variety of styles and rhetorical effects which he could combine with great versatility. His work was held up as a model for students. He was the author both of speeches for others and of ones he himself delivered. His extant corpus includes private law-court speeches, public deliberative orations, a funeral oration, and prologues to lost speeches. Several of the preserved speeches, including the funeral oration and the "erotic discourse," are no longer considered to be authentic works of Demosthenes.

Dinarchus (c. 361 – c. 290 BCE) Dinarchus was the last of the ten canonical orators. He was born in Corinth and not an Athenian citizen. Accordingly his career was confined to writing speeches for others. Praise of him tends to be faint: he is ranked as both last and least of the great orators. Only three of his speeches survive.

Dio (Chrysostom) (c. 40 – c. 110 CE) He is also known as Dio(n) of Prusa after his birthplace in Bithynia. Dio rises to local prominence through his rhetorical efforts. He moves to Rome during the reign of Vespasian, is banished by Domitian, and restored under Nerva after an episode wherein he purportedly persuaded wavering imperial troops to side with Nerva after Domitian's death. Dio was a prominent intellectual figure and much admired by critics. His orations are written in a direct style, and they have an essay-like quality. They regularly address themselves to political, moral, and philosophical topics. A number are learned disquisitions on frivolous topics such as the *In Praise of Hair*. His works in both form and content offer a relatively early example of the sort of path followed by Lucian, Philostratus, and Synesius.

Diogenes Laertius (third? century CE) Nothing is known of Diogenes' life. Diogenes is the author of *The Lives and Opinions of Eminent Philosophers*. The work compiles details about the lives and teachings of the earliest philosophers up through Epicurus. Most of the information is at second or third hand. The work is a valuable source of citations of material that would otherwise be lost, but his interests and methods should be borne in mind when making use of his work.

Dionysius (of Halicarnassus) (c. 60 – post 7 BCE) A Greek rhetorical teacher and historian, Dionysius lived and taught at Rome for decades. He is the author of a massive account of early Roman history entitled *Roman Antiquities*. He also wrote a number of works on rhetoric and composition as well as a stylistic analyses of several old Attic orators and Thucydides.

Dionysius Thrax   (*c.* 170 – *c.* 90 BCE) Apparently an Alexandrian by birth, Dionysius taught grammar and literature at Rhodes. He is the author of the earliest extant Greek work on grammar. This *Art of Grammar* had a lasting influence on the shape of similar works, especially in Latin. He focuses squarely on the individual word, its letters and their qualities, accentuation, morphology, part of speech, etc. Syntax is omitted.

Euripides   (*c.* 485 – *c.* 406 BCE) Euripides was an Athenian dramatist. He was immediately canonized as one of the greatest authors of tragedy as is clear from Aristophanes' *Frogs* and Aristotle's *Poetics*. A major element of his often striking innovation within the genre is his engagement with contemporary developments in rhetoric and philosophy.

Favorinus   (*c.* 80 – *c.* 160 CE) Born and educated in Gaul, Favorinus was a leading intellectual figure at both Rome and Athens. His intimates included Plutarch, Herodes Atticus, Fronto, and Aulus Gellius, as well as the emperor Hadrian who banished him to Chios in 130 CE. Antoninus Pius restored him in 138 CE. Favorinus' career exemplifies the significant social and political dimensions that intellectual pursuits could have during the Second Sophistic.

Fronto   (*c.* 100 – *c.* 166 CE) Born in Northern Africa, Fronto was the leading orator of his day and his reputation for a while equalled that of the greatest Roman speakers of all time. He was the rhetoric tutor of the future emperors Marcus Aurelius and Lucius Verus and remained on close terms with them throughout his life. He was a leading figure in the contemporary archaizing movement at Rome and kept company with major figures of the Greek Second Sophistic. A portion of his correspondence and some trifles such as a *Praise of Negligence* have been recovered from a badly damaged manuscript. His full-scale orations have been lost.

Gorgias (of Leontini)   (*c.* 480 – *c.* 380 BCE) Gorgias was a Greek from Sicily. He was a traveling celebrity performer and the most (in)famous of the sophists. His arrival in Athens in 427 BCE was a watershed moment in the history of rhetoric there. He promised to speak extemporaneously for or against any topic. His measured clauses, rhymes, and ostentatiously paradoxical theses attracted a great deal of attention, often highly negative. Plato uses him to establish the boundaries between rhetoric and philosophy. His most famous pupil was the orator Isocrates.

(Gaius) Gracchus   (154–121 BCE) Gracchus was a Roman aristocrat who was principally remembered by his countrymen for his radical populist reforms. These led to his death amid political violence after being labeled an enemy of the state by the senate. He is also remembered by subsequent generations as an important luminary from the early history of oratory at Rome.

Heliodorus (third? or fourth? century CE) Nothing certain is known about Heliodorus himself. He perhaps lived in Thessaly. His era is inferred from the style and contents of his lengthy romance, the *Aethiopica* or *Ethiopian Story*. Much of the spirit of the enterprise is characteristic of the Second Sophistic even if the author's date seems to fall outside the traditional boundaries of that movement.

Heraclitus (*c.* 535–475 BCE) Heraclitus was born in Ephesus on the coast of Asia Minor. He was a pre-Socratic Greek philosopher. His philosophy is famously obscure even within antiquity. His maxims bear a paradoxical sense on the surface. He is also a philosopher of *logos*. These last features of Heraclitus' work are themselves in a profound dialogue.

Hermagoras (of Temnos) (flourishes *c.* 140–130 BCE) Hermagoras was from Asia Minor. He was a major rhetorical theorist from the Hellenistic period. His work significantly shapes the reception of rhetorical theory at Rome given that Hermagoras' system is effectively state of the art when Romans begin to develop their own version of rhetorical theory. His chief contributions lay in invention and in *stasis*-theory (also known as issue-theory). For more on these terms, see Appendix 1.

Hermogenes (of Tarsus) (*c.* 160–*c.* 230 CE) Hermagoras was from Asia Minor. He was a prominent speaker and theoretician in the age of Marcus Aurelius. He writes on issue-theory and types of style. In both cases one can see the further development of existing theoretical discourses. Hermogenes' works become standard texts for later students.

Herodian (*c.* 180–250 CE) Herodian was from Alexandria and active as a grammarian at Rome. He was a prominent and prolific writer on technical questions pertaining to the Greek language, especially accentuation. This sort of research was a central element of the revivification of old Attic Greek as a literary language during the Second Sophistic.

Hesiod (born *c.* 750–720 BCE) Hesiod was an archaic Greek poet from Cyme, a town on the northwest coast of Asia Minor. He composed hexameter poems within a tradition of wisdom literature. The colorful invention of a "Contest between Homer and Hesiod" in antiquity speaks to his stature as an early author of Greek literature. His two main works were the *Theogony* and the *Works and Days*. Other minor poems survive in fragmentary form. He left a lasting mark on the tradition of didactic poetry in antiquity, but his direct influence on the rhetorical tradition proper is slight.

Hippias (of Elis) (*c.* 485–415 BCE) Hippias was born in southern Greece. He was a traveling intellectual professing competence in a great variety of subjects including mathematics, poetry, and the history of the heroic age. This public performance of knowledge marks him out as a "sophist." He appears in two eponymous Platonic dialogues as an interlocutor of Socrates.

Homer (ninth–eighth century BCE?) Today Homer is commonly regarded as the authorial name attached to two great oral poems that arose during the archaic era of Greece. The name Homer and the assignation of authorship have themselves been handed down from antiquity, but the poems appear to be the products of a rich oral tradition that coalesced in the form in which we now read them. This probably occurred in the seventh century BCE. Exploring and taking a position on "The Homer Question," though, can itself occupy a whole scholarly career. For an ancient Greek or Roman of the historical period, Homer was a discrete individual with his own colorful biography. He was the superlative poet of the *Iliad* and the *Odyssey* as well as other lesser works. His poems provided the undisputed cornerstone of Greek literature in general, and they cast a long shadow over Latin literature as well.

Horace (65–8 BCE) Born in southern Italy to a freedman father, Horace studied philosophy in Athens, served as a military tribune, worked as a treasury clerk, and eventually was recognized for his poetry around 38 BCE. Horace thereupon became one of the leading intellectual figures of Augustus' Rome. His varied poetic output includes invectives, lyric poems, satires, and verse epistles. Horace's long verse epistle known as the *Ars Poetica* or *The Art of Poetry* is a major and influential work on aesthetics. Throughout his corpus one can observe an elaborate staging of the persona of the narrator. This is an element of a self-aware meditation on the relationship between language and power.

Hortensius (114–50 BCE) Hortensius was the leading Roman orator of his day. He is an older contemporary of Cicero. The arrival of Cicero on the scene displaced Hortensius from the summit of eloquence. His style was florid and exuberant. The death of Hortensius is the ostensible occasion of Cicero's *Brutus*, but that text turns into a meditation on the death of Republican oratory more generally. Hortensius' own orations have been lost.

Hyperides (390–322 BCE) Hyperides was one of the ten canonical orators of Athens. He was a student of Isocrates, although his own style is far less ornate. Hyperides both wrote speeches for others and was himself an active politician. His reputation as a stylist was very high owing to his great breadth, and he regularly ranks as second only to Demosthenes.

Six of his orations remain, although five of these have suffered significant losses.

Isaeus   (c. 415–340 BCE) Isaeus was one of the ten canonical orators. His biography becomes obscure as early as the first century CE. It is possible that he was not a citizen of Athens. He is said to have been a student of Isocrates and a teacher of Demosthenes. He took no part in public life, and his speeches were all written for others. Eleven of them remain. These concern highly technical issues of inheritance law.

Isocrates   (436–338 BCE) Isocrates was an Athenian and one of the ten canonical orators. He positions himself as an educator and philosopher, not as an orator. He is said to have been unable to deliver speeches effectively owing to problems of body and of temperament. Nevertheless he is one of the dominant rhetorical figures from the era. He taught other leading speakers. His general theories of moral pedagogy also had a lasting impact. His political pamphlets promulgated the idea of a broader Greek identity as against the rivalry of individual city-states. Isocrates expands upon the style of his teacher Gorgias. Isocrates' own style is elaborate and architectural, and he is very attentive to rhythm. His ornate prose left a lasting legacy.

(Gaius) Julius Victor   (fourth century CE) Julius Victor is an obscure figure who wrote an *Art of Rhetoric* in Latin. The work ends with the first extant theorization of the art of letter-writing. The main body of the text contains a relatively brief and direct discussion of rhetorical theory. It has a declarative framework that recalls the *Rhetoric to Herennius*. Julius Victor read and reflected upon Cicero and Quintilian; he also may have read Hermagoras at first hand. Though not an especially innovative author, his synthesis and adaptation of earlier works reveal that he was no mere copyist.

Libanius   (314–93 CE) Born in Antioch, Libanius studied in Athens and taught rhetoric at Constantinople, Nicomedia, and Antioch. He was one of the most important rhetorical figures of his era. He taught a number of prominent pagan and Christian authors. He corresponded with the emperor Julian. His substantial surviving corpus includes letters, orations, declamations, and rhetorical exercises for students. His outlook is pagan and classicizing. Nevertheless, he serves as a model in the Byzantine period.

[Longinus]   The unknown author of *On the Sublime*. Longinus (c. 210–73 CE) was a rhetorician and philosopher who taught at Athens. The work *On the Sublime* was erroneously attributed to him. This is likely a first-century CE work. *On the Sublime* is a major contribution to the theory of aesthetics, and it regularly breaks free from the more familiar body of rhetorical theory in order to establish a distinctive vision of literary merit.

Lucian   (b. *c.* 120–d. post 180 CE) Lucian was from Samosata, a city in modern Turkey. He was a traveling intellectual who was active across the Greek-speaking world, including in his native Syria, Greece, Italy, and Gaul. His biography is derived from his own works. These survive as eighty-six pamphlet-sized pieces on a variety of topics. There are dialogues, display pieces, satires, and prose fiction. His Greek is Attic and learned, but the subjects he treats are often highly contemporary. His caustic wit assails various cultural pretenders in his own era, and he not infrequently engages with rhetoric specifically or the world of *paideia* more generally.

Lycurgus   (*c.* 390–324 BCE) Lycurgus was an Athenian and one of the ten canonical orators. The details of his life are obscure although it is clear that he was a leading Athenian statesman. He was also responsible for the preservation of Athenian tragedy. Lycurgus was noted for his prosecutions. His style is forceful and elevated, but it failed to win the admiration of all critics. Only one of his speeches survives intact.

Lysias   (*c.* 445–380 BCE) Lysias was one of the ten canonical orators and lived in Athens, but he was not a citizen: his father was a Syracusan by birth. As a resident alien, Lysias was not allowed speak in court himself, and his speeches are written for others except for his *Against Eratosthenes*, which either reflects a brief change in legal status or is a pamphlet in the form of a speech. He was a master of plain and direct language as well as characterization. His art regularly conceals itself. His style was long admired and was just the sort of thing later critics had in mind when they praised "Atticism."

Menander Rhetor   (third century CE) Menander was born in southwestern Turkey. He was a rhetorical theorist who worked in the era of the Second Sophistic. His researches, though, reveal a practical side and continuity and engagement with prior teachings. Such contrasts with the showier version of oratory for which the period is generally known. This Menander should not be confused with the substantially more famous Menander who was a poet and author of Greek New Comedies.

Parmenides   (flourishes early–mid fifth century BCE) Parmenides was a Greek from southern Italy. He wrote philosophy in hexameter verse. Fragments of his *On Nature* survive and they include discussions of ontology, the universe, and epistemology. The central speaker is a goddess who addresses the poet. Other pre-Socratic philosophers, Plato, Aristotle, and the Epicureans all engage with Parmenides' ideas.

Pericles (*c.* 495–429 BCE) Pericles was an Athenian statesman. He is remembered as the dominant political figure during the cultural and political acme of democratic Athens. He was said to be both a student of philosophy and a supreme orator. None of his own work survives, but he was much commented upon by his contemporaries, and his oratory is portrayed in Thucydides' history. The Roman tradition also reproduces an image of Pericles as a master politician and master orator.

Philodemus (*c.* 110–*c.* 40/35 BCE) Philodemus was born at Gadara in modern Jordan. He studied Epicureanism in Athens and came to Rome in the 70s BCE and became the teacher to a number of prominent Romans. He worked both as a poet and as a philosopher. His theoretical works, which include treatises on poetry, rhetoric, and music, have only recently emerged in editions of fragments. A collection of texts that were largely destroyed by the eruption of Vesuvius in 79 CE required modern technological advances before they could become legible. What emerges is a direct look at a scholar and lines of research that were otherwise known only indirectly or not at all.

(Flavius) Philostratus (*c.* 170–*c.* 247 CE) Philostratus was born to a distinguished Athenian family, studied at Athens, and became a prominent speaker and teacher. The emperor Septimius Severus and his wife Julia Domna patronized his circle. He wrote *The Life of Apollonius of Tyana* about a mystic from the first century CE. His *Lives of the Sophists* provides us with portraits of contemporary speakers, and it is a key text in our appreciation of the Second Sophistic.

Plato (428/7–348/7 BCE) He was an Athenian born into an eminent family. He founded a philosophical school at Athens known as the Academy. His numerous philosophical dialogues have been enormously influential in the history of philosophy and its various branches. Though himself one of the most brilliant prose stylists in the history of the Greek language and a master of literary technique in his dialogues, he nevertheless repeatedly offers highly critical explorations of rhetoric specifically or language more generally in their relationship to philosophy.

Plato Comicus (flourishes late 400s BCE) He was an Athenian comic poet and contemporary of Aristophanes. Only fragments of his plays remain. As with Aristophanes, his work also seems to have been highly political. He also wrote a *Sophists*. The label "Comicus" is designed to distinguish the poet from the philosopher.

Plautus (*c.* 254–184 BCE) Plautus was a major Roman comic playwright who lived during the time of Cato. His biography is unclear and filled with seeming inventions. Plautus adapts scripts from Greek New Comedy for a Roman stage which had a strong tradition of farce and improvisation. His language and meter are exuberant, and both he and his characters love to toy self-consciously with stock situations. Subordinate social figures frequently play central and guiding roles in his dramas.

Pliny (the Younger) (*c.* 61–*c.* 112 CE) Pliny was a prominent Roman speaker, politician, and author. He was the adoptive son of Pliny the Elder who wrote a monumental *Natural History*. Pliny's own writings include one book of official letters to the emperor Trajan and a more substantial collection of literary letters on varied gentlemanly topics. The latter serve as little essays both on and revelatory of taste and manners. A number are addressed to or mention leading literary figures. Pliny's sole surviving oration is a panegyric to Trajan. The speech offers a study on how one speaks to and about power in the imperial age.

Plutarch (*c.* 45–after 120 CE) Plutarch was an intellectual from Chaeronea in central Greece. He visited Athens, Rome, and Egypt. He was the author of a large number of works. His *Parallel Lives* compares the biography of a famous Greek with that of a prominent Roman. His *Moralia* offers a broad array of works including rhetorical display pieces, dialogues on scholarly topics, antiquarian investigations, moral essays, and technical philosophical treatises.

Prodicus (flourished fifth century BCE) Prodicus was born on the Greek island of Chios. Prodicus was a sophist and rhetorician. He moved from Chios to Athens, where he opened a lucrative school of rhetoric. He was interested in questions of language and ethics as well as natural philosophy. A variety of leading Athenian intellectual figures took note of his teaching including Aristophanes, Socrates, and Xenophon.

Pythagoras (*c.* 570–*c.* 480 BCE) Pythagoras was born on the island of Samos in the eastern Aegean sea. His interests combined in a rigorous fashion the spheres of mathematics, religion, and philosophy. He founded a politico-religious society in southern Italy. He becomes an obscure figure early on in the Greek tradition, and details of his life and teaching become the objects of speculation for later generations.

Quintilian (*c.* 35–*c.* 100 CE) Quintilian was a Spaniard who studied in Rome, returned to Spain, and then came back to Rome to teach rhetoric. Though he had practiced as a pleader, Quintilian was particularly known for being a teacher. He was probably the first teacher of rhetoric to be paid by the state. He was a tutor to the emperor Domitian's nephews and heirs. His pupils included Pliny the Younger. His *Institutio Oratoria* is a massive survey of the whole of the craft of rhetoric that champions Ciceronian theory and practice as essential points of orientation for orators of the imperial age.

Rhetoric to Herennius (80s? BCE; 50s? BCE) This is a treatise on rhetoric dedicated to Gaius Herennius. It was assigned to Cicero in the manuscript tradition, but it is not by him. It is perhaps the earliest extant work on oratory in Latin. It may, though, be a hybrid of older and newer material. The presentation is pointedly clear and direct. The work makes available and distills Greek teaching for a Roman audience. This work seems not to affect rhetorical theory in Latin until the Middle Ages and beyond, whereupon it becomes a canonical textbook.

Scipio Africanus (236–183 BCE) Scipio was a Roman general and statesman. He came from a distinguished family and swiftly added his own luster to it with a variety of military exploits. His victories earned him the name Africanus as a memorial of his exploits. He was censor and head of the senate in 199 BCE. But his career ended on a dark note: accusations of accepting bribes from Antiochus circled around him. Scipio played a major role in the later Roman imagination of the Roman Republic and one of its most storied eras.

Scipio Nasica (*c.* 183 – *c.* 132 BCE) Scipio Nasica was the grandson of Scipio Africanus. He was a conservative politician who is most remembered for his opposition to Tiberius Gracchus. The political disputes of 133 BCE grew violent, and Gracchus was clubbed to death. Scipio himself died under suspicious circumstances in the next year. He played a leading role in a drama that was controversial in its day and one that had a long afterlife in the Roman imagination.

Seneca the Elder (*c.* 55 BCE – *c.* 40 CE) Seneca the Elder was an equestrian from Spain who moved to Rome at a relatively young age. He was a devotee of the rhetoric of his day. He wrote for his sons a collection of reminiscences of highlights from various declamatory speakers whom he heard over the course of his very long life. His text provides a vivid portrait of rhetorical practice in the period just after Cicero's death. The compressed and selective nature of his excerpts can, though, produce a misleading impression as to what the norm might have looked like.

Seneca (the Younger) (*c.* 4 BCE–65 CE) The younger Seneca was born in Spain. He was the son of Seneca the Elder. He studied rhetoric early on but turned to Stoic philosophy later. He was already a major literary figure when Caligula came to power in 39 CE. Seneca went into exile under Claudius in 41 CE and did not return until 49 CE under the influence of Nero's mother, Agrippina. Seneca became the young emperor's tutor and political advisor. He was accordingly one of the most important men of his era in both the political and cultural spheres. His style was distinctive, influential, and criticized for its innovations.

His surviving works include tragedies, a work of natural philosophy, moral essays, and moral letters. His speeches have been lost.

Sextus Empiricus   (flourishes second century CE) The life of Sextus Empiricus is very uncertain. He is important for his philosophical works *Outlines of Pyrronism* and *Against the Mathematicians*. The former text advocates philosophical skepticism. In the latter text Sextus offers a critique of different major intellectual and philosophical enterprises including grammarians, rhetoricians, geometers, natural philosophers, and ethical philosophers. The work is not original, but it offers an invaluable collection of ideas and arguments that shed light on earlier philosophy.

Socrates   (469–399 BCE) Socrates was an Athenian thinker of note in his own day. His philosophical enquiries attracted prominent students who themselves became important thinkers in their own right. He was lampooned by Aristophanes, who associated him with the sophists. Socrates was tried, convicted, and executed by the Athenians for "corrupting the youth" and "introducing new gods." His lasting fame rests on the central role given to him in the works of Plato and, to a lesser extent, his portrait in the writings of Xenophon. Socrates himself wrote nothing.

Synesius   (*c.* 370 – *c.* 413 CE) Synesius was born in Northern Africa, studied in Alexandria, and visited Constantinople and Athens. He was a student of Neoplatonist philosophy as well as being a Christian bishop. He straddles pagan and Christian culture. His non-religious works include a treatise on dreams, a speech on ruling delivered before the emperor Arcadius, as well as a *Praise of Baldness*.

Tacitus   (*c.* 55 – *c.* 120 CE) Tacitus was a Roman statesman and historian who might have been born in Northern Italy or Gaul. He perhaps studied under Quintilian. Pliny writes letters to him as a friend. His historical works examine the institution of the principate in the years following the death of Augustus. They are dark, cynical, and written in a striking and innovative style. Among his shorter works is the *Dialogue on Orators*, a treatise written in Ciceronean Latin on the reason why stellar orators such as Cicero have passed from the world. The work is unusual in that it offers a sociological and historical analysis of oratory whereas ethics and esthetics tend to predominate in other authors.

Thrasymachus   (*c.* 459 – *c.* 400 BCE) Thrasymachus was born in Chalcedon near modern Constantinople. He traveled to Athens and was active there as a teacher and an intellectual who took an interest in rhetoric and emotions, especially as produced by gesture and prose rhythm. Aristotle, Dionysius of Halicarnassus, and Quintilian mention him in rhetorical contexts. He is most famous, though, for his appearance in Plato's *Republic*, where he maintains that justice is "the advantage of the more powerful."

Thucydides   (c. 460–c. 395 BCE) Thucydides was an Athenian historian who wrote an incomplete account of the war between Athens and Sparta that took place during his own life. His methods are to modern eyes much more careful and documentary than those of most other ancient historians. His style is rough and bold and was commented upon in antiquity itself. One of the highlights of the work is the speeches of prominent figures that he sets into his history at key junctures.

Vergil   (70–19 BCE) A Roman poet born in Mantua but active in Rome, Vergil emerged as a significant literary figure during his own life. He was also connected to leading political figures of his age including the emperor Augustus. Vergil wrote learned poetry on the bucolic life and agriculture, but his chief work was the epic tale of Rome's own foundation, the *Aeneid*. This poem establishes Vergil as a Roman Homer, and it casts a long shadow for all subsequent verse authors. As a standard author read, memorized, and commented upon in school, Vergil naturally affects the evolution of Latin prose as well. Citations from Vergil in Quintilian's *Institutes* are nearly as numerous as his evocations of works of Cicero.

REFERENCES

Achard, G. (1989) *Rhétorique à Herennius*. Paris, Les Belles Lettres.

(1994) *Cicéron. De l'invention*. Paris, Les Belles Lettres.

Adams, J. N. (2003) "*Romanitas* and the Latin Language." *Classical Quarterly* 53, 184–205.

Agamben, G. (1993) *The Coming Community*. Minneapolis, University of Minnesota Press.

Agricola, R. and A. Alardus (1967) *De Inventione Dialectica Lucubrationes*. Reprint of the Cologne, 1539 edn., Nieuwkoop, B. de Graaf.

Ahl, F. (1984) "The Art of Safe Criticism in Greece and Rome." *American Journal of Philology* 105, 174–208.

Alcock, S. E. (1993) *Graecia Capta: The Landscapes of Roman Greece*. Cambridge University Press.

(2002) *Archaeologies of the Greek Past: Landscape, Monuments, and Memories*. Cambridge University Press.

Aldrete, G. S. (1999) *Gestures and Acclamations in Ancient Rome*. Baltimore, Johns Hopkins University Press.

Alexander, L. (2002) "'Foolishness to the Greeks': Jews and Christians in the Public Life of the Empire," in Griffin, M. T., G. Clark, and T. Rajak (eds.), *Philosophy and Power in the Graeco-Roman World: Essays in Honour of Miriam Griffin*. Oxford University Press, 229–49.

Alexander, M. C. (2002) *The Case for the Prosecution in the Ciceronian Era*. Ann Arbor, The University of Michigan Press.

Allen, D. (2000) *The World of Prometheus: The Politics of Punishing in Democratic Athens*. Princeton University Press.

(2006) "Talking about Revolution: On Political Change in Fourth-Century Athens and Historiographic Method," in Goldhill, S. and R. Osborne (eds.), *Rethinking Revolutions through Ancient Greece*. Cambridge University Press, 183–217.

Anderson, B. (1991) *Imagined Communities: Reflections on the Origin and Spread of Nationalism*. Revised and extended edn., London, Verso.

Anderson, G. (1989) "The Pepaideumenos in Action: Sophists and their Outlook in the Early Empire." *Aufstieg und Niedergang der römischen Welt* II: 33.1, 80–208.

(1993) *The Second Sophistic: A Cultural Phenomenon in the Roman Empire*. London, Routledge.

Anderson, R. D. (1999) *Ancient Rhetorical Theory and Paul*. Revised edn., Leuven, Peeters.

Andrews, R. (1992) "Introduction," *Rebirth of Rhetoric: Essays in Language, Culture, and Education*. London, Routledge, 1–18.

Arrowsmith, W. (1973) "Aristophanes' *Birds*: The Fantasy Politics of Eros." *Arion* 1, 119–67.

Arweiler, A. (2003) *Cicero Rhetor: Die Partitiones Oratoriae und das Konzept des Gelehrten Politikers*. Berlin, De Gruyter.

Ascough, R. S. (2003) *Paul's Macedonian Associations: The Social Context of Philippians and 1 Thessalonians*. Tübingen, Mohr Siebeck.

Asmis, E. (2004) "The State as a Partnership: Cicero's Definition of *Res Publica* in his Work *On the State*." *History of Political Thought* 25, 569–98.

Augustijn, C. (1991) *Erasmus: His Life, Works, and Influence*. University of Toronto Press.

Austin, R. G. (1954) *Quintiliani Institutionis Oratoriae Liber XII*. Oxford University Press.

Ax, W. (1986) *Laut, Stimme und Sprache: Studien zu Drei Grundbegriffen der Antiken Sprachtheorie*. Göttingen, Vandenhoeck & Ruprecht.

Badian, E. (1972) "Tiberius Gracchus and the Beginning of the Roman Revolution." *Aufstieg und Niedergang der römischen Welt* 1.1, 668–731.

Bakker, E. J. and A. Kahane (1997) *Written Voices, Spoken Signs: Tradition, Performance, and the Epic Text*. Cambridge, MA, Harvard University Press.

Baldwin, T. W. (1944) *William Shakspere's Small Latine & Lesse Greeke*. Urbana, University of Illinois Press.

Balot, R. (2004) "Free Speech, Courage, and Democratic Deliberation," in Sluiter and Rosen (eds.), 232–59.

Barber, B. R. (2003) *Strong Democracy: Participatory Politics for a New Age*. Revised edn., Berkeley, University of California Press.

Barker, W. (2001) *The Adages of Erasmus*. University of Toronto Press.

Barthes, R. (1988) "The Old Rhetoric: An Aide-Mémoire," *The Semiotic Challenge*. New York, Hill and Wang, 11–94.

Bartsch, S. (1989) *Decoding the Ancient Novel: The Reader and the Role of Description in Heliodorus and Achilles Tatius*. Princeton University Press.

   (1994) *Actors in the Audience: Theatricality and Doublespeak from Nero to Hadrian*. Cambridge, MA, Harvard University Press.

Bassi, K. (1998) *Acting Like Men: Gender, Drama, and Nostalgia in Ancient Greece*. Ann Arbor, University of Michigan Press.

Batstone, W. (1988) "The Antithesis of Virtue: Sallust's *Synkrisis* and the Crisis of the Late Republic." *Classical Antiquity* 7, 1–29.

   (1990) "Intellectual Conflict and Mimesis in Sallust's *Bellum Catilinae*," in Allison, J. W. (ed.), *Conflict, Antithesis, and the Ancient Historian*. Columbus, Ohio State University Press, 112–32.

   (1993) "Logic, Rhetoric, Poesis." *Helios* 20, 143–72.

   (1994) "Cicero's Construction of Consular Ethos in the First Catilinarian." *Transactions of the American Philological Association* 124, 211–66.

Beard, M. (1993) "Looking (Harder) for Roman Myth: Dumézil, Declamation and the Problems of Definition," in Graf, F. (ed.), *Mythos in Mythenloser Gesellschaft: Das Paradigma Roms*. Stuttgart, B. G. Teubner, 44–64.

Benediktson, D.T. (2000) *Literature and the Visual Arts in Ancient Greece and Rome*. Norman, University of Oklahoma Press.

Berry, D.H. (1996) *Cicero: Pro P. Sulla Oratio*. Cambridge University Press.

Bers, V. (1994) "Tragedy and Rhetoric," in Worthington (ed.), 176–95.

Bialostosky, D. (2004) "Aristotle's *Rhetoric* and Bakhtin's Discourse Theory," in Jost and Olmsted (eds.), 393–408.

Black, C.C. (1988) "The Rhetorical Form of the Hellenistic Jewish and Early Christian Sermon: A Response to Lawrence Wills." *Harvard Theological Review* 81, 1–18.

Black, R. (2001) *Humanism and Education in Medieval and Renaissance Italy: Tradition and Innovation in Latin Schools from the Twelfth to the Fifteenth Century*. Cambridge University Press.

Bollack, J. (1965) *Empédocle*. Paris, Les Éditions de Minuit.

Booth, W.C. (1974) *A Rhetoric of Irony*. University of Chicago Press.

(2004) *The Rhetoric of Rhetoric: The Quest for Effective Communication*. Oxford, Blackwell.

Bourdieu, P. (1977) *Outline of a Theory of Practice*. Cambridge University Press.

(1988) "Social Space and Symbolic Power." *Sociological Theory* 7, 18–26.

(1990) *The Logic of Practice*. Stanford University Press.

(1991) *Language and Symbolic Power*. Cambridge, MA, Harvard University Press.

Bowersock, G.W. (1969) *Greek Sophists in the Roman Empire*. Oxford, Clarendon Press.

Bowie, E. (1970) "The Greeks and their Past in the Second Sophistic." *Past and Present* 46, 3–41.

Bowker, J. (1967) "Speeches in Acts: A Study in *Proem* and *Yelammedenu* Form." *New Testament Studies* 14, 96–111.

Brennan, T.C. (2004) "Power and Process under the Republican 'Constitution,'" in Flower, H.I. (ed.), *The Cambridge Companion to the Roman Republic*. Cambridge University Press, 31–65.

Brittain, C. (2001) *Philo of Larissa: The Last of the Academic Sceptics*. Oxford University Press.

Buchheim, T. (1989) *Gorgias von Leontinoi: Reden, Fragmente und Testimonien*. Hamburg, Felix Meiner.

Burian, P. (1985) "*Logos* and *Pathos*: The Politics of the *Suppliant Women*," in Burian, P. (ed.), *Directions in Euripidean Criticism: A Collection of Essays*. Durham, Duke University Press, 129–55.

Burke, K. (1945) *A Grammar of Motives*. New York, Prentice-Hall.

(1969) *A Rhetoric of Motives*. Berkeley, University of California Press.

Burkert, W. (1975) "Aristoteles im Theater: zur Datierung des 3. Buchs der 'Rhetorik' und der 'Poetik.'" *Museum Helveticum* 32.2, 67–72.

Butler, J. (1990) *Gender Trouble: Feminism and the Subversion of Identity*. New York, Routledge.

(1995) "Conscience Doth Make Subjects of us All." *Yale French Studies* 88, 6–26.

Butler, J., E. Laclau, and S. Žižek (2000) *Contingency, Hegemony, Universality: Contemporary Dialogues on the Left*. London, Verso.

Butler, S. (2002) *The Hand of Cicero*. London, Routledge.

Buxton, R.G.A. (1982) *Persuasion in Greek Tragedy: A Study of Peitho*. Cambridge University Press.

Cameron, A. (1991) *Christianity and the Rhetoric of Empire: The Development of Christian Discourse*. Berkeley, University of California Press.

Cape, R. (1995) "The Rhetoric of Politics in Cicero's Fourth Catilinarian." *American Journal of Philology* 116.2, 255–77.

(2002) "Cicero's Consular Speeches," in May, J. M. (ed.), *Brill's Companion to Cicero: Oratory and Rhetoric*. Leiden, Brill, 113–58.

Carey, C. (1994a) "Comic Ridicule and Democracy," in Lewis, D. M., R. Osborne, and S. Hornblower (eds.), *Ritual, Finance, Politics: Athenian Democratic Accounts Presented to David Lewis*. Oxford, Clarendon Press, 68–83.

(1994b) "Rhetorical Means of Persuasion," in Worthington (ed.), 26–45.

(2000) *Aeschines*. Austin, University of Texas Press.

Carr, D. M. (2005) *Writing on the Tablet of the Heart: Origins of Scripture and Literature*. Oxford University Press.

Carter, L. B. (1986) *The Quiet Athenian*. Oxford University Press.

Casson, L. (2001) *Libraries in the Ancient World*. New Haven, Yale University Press.

Cave, T. (1979) *The Cornucopian Text: Problems of Writing in the French Renaissance*. Oxford University Press.

Chiron, P. (2002) *Pseudo-Aristote: Rhétorique à Alexandre*. Paris, Les Belles Lettres.

Chomarat, J. (1981) *Grammaire et rhétorique chez Erasme*. 2 vols. Paris, Les Belles Lettres.

Christ, M. R. (1998) *The Litigious Athenian*. Baltimore, Johns Hopkins University Press.

Citroni, M. (1998) "Percezioni di classicità nella letteratura Latina," in Cardini, R. and M. Regoliosi (eds.), *Che cos'è il classicismo*. Roma, Bulzoni.

Clarke, M. L. (1996) *Rhetoric at Rome: A Historical Survey*. 3rd edn., London, Routledge.

Cohen, D. (1995) *Law, Violence, and Community in Classical Athens*. Cambridge University Press.

Cole, T. (1991) *The Origins of Rhetoric in Ancient Greece*. Baltimore, Johns Hopkins University Press.

Colson, F. (1924) *M. Fabii Quintiliani Institutionis Oratoriae Liber I*. Cambridge University Press.

Conley, T. M. (1990) *Rhetoric in the European Tradition*. New York, Longman.

Connolly, J. (1998) "Mastering Corruption: Constructions of Identity in Roman Oratory," in Joshel, S. R. and S. Murnaghan (eds.), *Women and Slaves in Greco-Roman Culture: Differential Equations*. London, Routledge, 130–51.

(2001) "Problems of the Past in Imperial Greek Education," in Too, Y. L. (ed.), *Education in Greek and Roman Antiquity*. Leiden, Brill, 339–72.

(2007a) *The State of Speech: Rhetoric and Political Thought in Ancient Rome*. Princeton University Press.

(2007b) "The New World Order: Greek Rhetoric in Rome," in Worthington, I. (ed.). *A Companion to Greek Rhetoric*. Malden, Blackwell, 139–65.

Connor, W. R. (1992) *The New Politicians of Fifth-Century Athens*. Indianapolis, Hackett.

Constantinides, C. N. (2003) "Teachers and Students of Rhetoric in the Late Byzantine Period," in Jeffreys, E. (ed.), *Rhetoric in Byzantium: Papers from the Thirty-Fifth Spring Symposium of Byzantine Studies, Exeter College, University of Oxford, March 2001*. Aldershot, Ashgate, 39–53.

Cooper, J. M. (2004) "Plato, Isocrates, and Cicero on the Independence of Oratory from Philosophy," *Knowledge, Nature, and the Good: Essays on Ancient Philosophy*. Princeton University Press, 43–64.

Cope, E. M. (1867) *An Introduction to Aristotle's Rhetoric, with Analysis, Notes and Appendices*. London, Macmillan.

Corbeill, A. (1996) *Controlling Laughter: Political Humor in the Late Roman Republic*. Princeton University Press.

(2001) "Education in the Roman Republic: Creating Traditions," in Too, Y. L. (ed.), *Education in Greek and Roman Antiquity*. Leiden, Brill, 261–87.

(2002) "Rhetorical Education in Cicero's Youth," in May, J. M. (ed.), *Brill's Companion to Cicero: Oratory and Rhetoric*. Leiden, Brill, 23–49.

Coupland, N. (2007) *Style: Language Variation and Identity*. Cambridge University Press.

Courbaud, E. (1967) *Cicéron. De l'orateur*. Paris, Les Belles Lettres.

Coxon, A. H. (1986) *The Fragments of Parmenides: A Critical Text with Introduction, and Translation, the Ancient Testimonia and a Commentary*. Assen, Netherlands, Van Gorcum.

Craig, C. J. (1993) "Three Simple Questions for Teaching Cicero's First Catilinarian." *Classical Journal* 88, 255–67.

Croll, M. W. (1966) *Style, Rhetoric, and Rhythm; Essays*. Princeton University Press.

Csapo, E. and W. J. Slater (1995) *The Context of Ancient Drama*. Ann Arbor, University of Michigan Press.

De Man, P. (1971) *Blindness & Insight. Essays in the Rhetoric of Contemporary Criticism*. Oxford University Press.

Deleuze, G. and F. Guattari (1994) *What is Philosophy?* New York, Columbia University Press.

Derrida, J. (1981) "Plato's Pharmacy," *Dissemination*. University of Chicago Press, 63–171.

(1990) "Jacques Derrida on Rhetoric and Composition: A Conversation." *Journal of Advanced Composition* 10, 1–21.

Dibelius, M. (1965) *From Tradition to Gospel*. New York, Scribner.

Diels, H. (1886) "Über das 3. Buch der Aristotelischen Rhetorik." *Philosophische und historische Abhandlungen der kgl. Akademie der Wissenschaften zu Berlin* 4, 1–34.

Dolar, M. (1993) "Beyond Interpellation." *Qui Parle* 6, 75–96.

(2006) *A Voice and Nothing More*. Cambridge, MIT Press.

Dominik, W. J. and J. Hall (2007) *A Companion to Roman Rhetoric*. London, Blackwell.

Douglas, A. E. (1956) "Cicero, Quintilian, and the Canon of Ten Attic Orators." *Mnemosyne* 4.1, 30–40.

Dover, K. J. (1974) *Greek Popular Morality in the Time of Plato and Aristotle*. Oxford, Blackwell.

Downing, F. G. (1998) *Cynics, Paul, and the Pauline Churches*. London, Routledge.

Dugan, J. (2005) *Making a New Man: Ciceronian Self-Fashioning in the Rhetorical Works*. Oxford, Oxford University Press.

(2007) "Modern Critical Approaches to Roman Rhetoric," in Dominik and Hall (eds.), 9–22.

Dyck, A. R. (2004a) *A Commentary on Cicero, De Legibus*. Ann Arbor, University of Michigan Press.

(2004b) "Cicero's *devotio*: The Rôles of *Dux* and Scape-Goat in his *Post Reditum* Rhetoric." *Harvard Studies in Classical Philology* 102, 299–314.

Dyer, R. R. (1990) "Rhetoric and Intention in Cicero's *Pro Marcello*." *Journal of Roman Studies* 80, 17–30.

Edmunds, L. and R. Martin (1977) "Thucydides 2.65.8: Ελευθερως." *Harvard Studies in Classical Philology* 81, 187–93.

Edwards, M. and S. Usher (1985) *Greek Orators*, volume I, *Antiphon and Lysias*. Warminster, Aris & Phillips.

Egbert, J. (1969) "Die Gestalt des Thersites in der *Ilias*." *Philologus* 115, 159–75.

Enos, R. L. (1993) *Greek Rhetoric before Aristotle*. Prospect Heights, Waveland Press.

Erasmus (1971a) *Opera Omnia: I–6*. Amsterdam, North Holland.

    (1971b) *Opera Omnia: I–2*. Amsterdam, North Holland.

Fantham, E. (2002) "Orator and/et Actor," in Easterling, P. E. and E. Hall (eds.), *Greek and Roman Actors: Aspects of an Ancient Profession*. Cambridge University Press, 362–71.

    (2004) *The Roman World of Cicero's De Oratore*. Oxford University Press.

Farrell, J. (2001) *Latin Language and Latin Culture: From Ancient to Modern Times*. Cambridge University Press.

Ferrari, G. R. F. (1987) *Listening to the Cicadas: A Study of Plato's* Phaedrus. Cambridge University Press.

Finley, M. I. (1988) "Athenian Demagogues," *Democracy Ancient and Modern*. 2nd paperback edn., New Brunswick, Rutgers University Press, 38–75.

Fisher, N. R. E. (2001) *Aeschines: Against Timarchos*. Oxford University Press.

Flower, H. I. (1996) *Ancestor Masks and Aristocratic Power in Roman Culture*. Oxford University Press.

Ford, A. (2001) "Sophists without Rhetoric: The Arts of Speech in Fifth-Century Athens," in Too, Y. L. (ed.), *Education in Greek and Roman Antiquity*. Leiden, Brill, 85–109.

Fortenbaugh, W. W. (1985) "Theophrastus on Delivery," in Fortenbaugh, W. W., P. M. Huby, and A. A. Long (eds.), *Theophrastus of Eresus: On his Life and Work*. New Brunswick, Transaction Books, 269–87.

    (1988) "*Benevolentiam Conciliare* and *Animos Permovere*: Some Remarks on Cicero *de Oratore* 2.178–216." *Rhetorica* 6, 259–73.

    (2005) "Cicero as a Reporter of Aristotelian and Theophrastean Rhetorical Doctrine." *Rhetorica* 23, 37–64.

Fortenbaugh, W. W. and P. Steinmetz (1989) *Cicero's Knowledge of the Peripatos*. New Brunswick, N. J., Transaction Publishers.

Fotheringham, L. S. (2004) "Repetition and Unity in the *Pro Caecina*," in Powell, J. G. F. and J. Paterson (eds.), *Cicero the Advocate*. Oxford University Press, 253–76.

    (2006) "Gliding Transitions and the Analysis of Structure: Cicero's *Pro Archia*," in Deroux, C. (ed.), *Studies in Latin Literature and Roman History XIII*. Brussels, Latomus, 32–52.

    (2007) "The Numbers in the Margins and the Structure of Cicero's *Pro Murena*." *Greece and Rome* 54.1, 40–60.

Foucault, M. (1997) "Theatrum Philosophicum," in Faubion, J. D. (ed.), *The Essential Works of Foucault, 1954–1984*, volume II: *Aesthetics, Method, and Epistemology*. New York, New Press, 343–68.

(2001) *Fearless Speech*, ed. Pearson, J., Los Angeles, Semiotext(e).

Fraenkel, E. (2007) *Plautine Elements in Plautus*, trans. Drevikovsky, T. and F. Muecke, Oxford University Press.

Fuhrmann, M. (1960) *Das Systematische Lehrbuch; ein Beitrag zur Geschichte der Wissenschaften in der Antike*. Göttingen, Vandenhoeck & Ruprecht.

Fumaroli, M. (ed.) (1999) *Histoire de la rhétorique dans l'Europe moderne: 1450–1950*. Paris, Presses universitaires de France.

Gagarin, M. (2002) *Antiphon the Athenian: Oratory, Law, and Justice in the Age of the Sophists*. Austin, University of Texas Press.

Gangloff, A. (2006) *Dion Chrysostome et Les Mythes: Hellénisme, communication et philosophie politique*. Grenoble, J. Millon.

Geuss, R. (2005) "Liberalism and its Discontents," *Outside Ethics*. Princeton University Press, 11–28.

Given, M. D. (2001) *Paul's True Rhetoric: Ambiguity, Cunning, and Deception in Greece and Rome*. Harrisburg, Trinity Press International.

Gleason, M. W. (1995) *Making Men: Sophists and Self-Presentation in Ancient Rome*. Princeton University Press.

Glucker, J. (1984) "Chapter and Verse in Cicero." *Grazer Beiträge* 11, 103–12.

Goldhill, S. (1991) *The Poet's Voice: Essays on Poetics and Greek Literature*. Cambridge University Press.

(1994) "Representing Democracy: Woman at the Great Dionysia," in Lewis, D. M., R. Osborne, and S. Hornblower (eds.), *Ritual, Finance, Politics: Athenian Democratic Accounts Presented to David Lewis*. Oxford University Press, 347–69.

(1995) *Foucault's Virginity: Ancient Erotic Fiction and the History of Sexuality*. Cambridge University Press.

(ed.) (2001) *Being Greek under Rome: Cultural Identity, the Second Sophistic and the Development of Empire*. Cambridge University Press.

(2002) *Who Needs Greek?: Contests in the Cultural History of Hellenism*. Cambridge University Press.

(2006) "Rethinking Religious Revolution", in Goldhill, S. and R. Osborne (eds.), *Rethinking Revolutions through Ancient Greece*. Cambridge University Press, 141–63.

(forthcoming) "'Drink to Me Only with Thine Eyes': Philostratus' Letters," in Bowie, E. and J. Elsner (eds.), *Philostratus*. Cambridge University Press.

Goldhill, S. and R. Osborne (eds.) (1999) *Performance Culture and Athenian Democracy*. Cambridge University Press.

Graf, F. (1992) "Gestures and Conventions: The Gestures of Roman Actors and Orators," in Bremmer, J. N. and H. Roodenburg (eds.), *A Cultural History of Gesture*. Ithaca, Cornell University Press, 36–58.

Green, L. D. (1994) "The Reception of Aristotle's Rhetoric in the Renaissance," in Fortenbaugh, W. W. and D. C. Mirhady (eds.), *Peripatetic Rhetoric after Aristotle*. New Brunswick, Transaction Publishers, 320–48.

(1998) "Aristotle's *Rhetoric* and Renaissance Conceptions of the Soul," in Dahan, G. and I. Rosier-Catach (eds.), *La* Rhétorique *d'Aristote: traditions et commentaires de l'antiquité au XVIIe siècle*. Paris, J. Vrin, 282–97.

Green, L. D. and J. J. Murphy (eds.) (2006) *Renaissance Rhetoric Short-Title Catalogue, 1460–1700*. 2nd edn., Aldershot, Ashgate.

Greenwood, E. (2006) *Thucydides and the Shaping of History*. London, Duckworth.

Grendler, P. F. (1989) *Schooling in Renaissance Italy: Literacy and Learning, 1300–1600*. Baltimore, Johns Hopkins University Press.

Griffin, M. (1996) "Cynicism and the Romans: Attraction and Repulsion," in Branham, R. B. and M.-O. Goulet-Cazé (eds.), *The Cynics: The Cynic Movement in Antiquity and its Legacy*. Berkeley, University of California Press, 190–204.

Gunderson, E. (2000) *Staging Masculinity: The Rhetoric of Performance in the Roman World*. Ann Arbor, University of Michigan Press.

(2003) *Declamation, Paternity, and Roman Identity: Authority and the Rhetorical Self*. Cambridge University Press.

Habicht, C. (1990) *Cicero the Politician*. Baltimore, Johns Hopkins University Press.

Habinek, T. N. (1998) *The Politics of Latin Literature: Writing, Identity, and Empire in Ancient Rome*. Princeton University Press.

(2005a) *Ancient Rhetoric and Oratory*. Malden, Blackwell.

(2005b) *The World of Roman Song: From Ritualized Speech to Social Order*. Baltimore, Johns Hopkins University Press.

Hall, E. (1995) "Lawcourt Dramas: The Power of Performance in Greek Forensic Oratory." *Bulletin of the Institute of Classical Studies* 40, 39–58.

Halliwell, S. (1991a) "Comic Satire and Freedom of Speech in Athens." *Journal of Hellenic Studies* 111, 48–70.

(1991b) "The Uses of Laughter in Greek Culture." *Classical Quarterly* 41.2, 279–96.

(1994) "Philosophy and Rhetoric," in Worthington (ed.), 222–43.

(1997) "Between Public and Private: Tragedy and Athenian Experience of Rhetoric," in Pelling, C. B. R. (ed.), *Greek Tragedy and the Historian*. Oxford University Press, 121–41.

Halperin, D. M. (1990) "The Democratic Body: Prostitution and Citizenship in Classical Athens," *One Hundred Years of Homosexuality: And Other Essays on Greek Love*. New York, Routledge, 88–112.

Hanson, A. E. (1990) "The Medical Writer's Woman," in Halperin, D. M., J. J. Winkler, and F. I. Zeitlin (eds.), *Before Sexuality: The Construction of Erotic Experience in the Ancient Greek World*. Princeton University Press, 309–38.

Harrison, A. R. W. (1971) *The Law of Athens,* volume II: *Procedure*. Oxford, Clarendon Press.

Haskins, E. V. (2004) *Logos and Power in Isocrates and Aristotle*. Columbia, University of South Carolina Press.

Havelock, E. A. (1963) *Preface to Plato*. Cambridge, MA, Harvard University Press.

Heath, M. (1994) "The Substructure of Stasis-Theory from Hermagoras to Hermogenes." *Classical Quarterly* 44, 114–29.

(1995) *Hermogenes on Issues: Strategies of Argument in Later Greek Rhetoric*. Oxford University Press.

(1997a) "Aristophanes and the Discourse of Politics," in Dobrov, G. W. (ed.), *The City as Comedy: Society and Representation in Athenian Drama*. Chapel Hill, NC, University of North Carolina Press, 230–49.

(1997b) "Invention," in Porter, S. E. (ed.), *A Handbook of Classical Rhetoric in the Hellenistic Period, 330 BC – AD 400*. Leiden, Brill, 89–119.

(2002) "Hermagoras: Transmission and Attribution." *Philologus* 146, 287–98.

(2004a) *Menander: A Rhetor in Context*. Oxford University Press.

(2004b) "Practical Advocacy in Roman Egypt," in Edwards, M. and C. Reid (eds.), *Oratory in Action*. Manchester University Press, 62–82.

(2007) "Teaching Rhetorical Argument Today," in Powell, J. G. F. and L. Rubenstein (eds.), *Logos: Rational Argument in Classical Rhetoric*, 105–22.

(forthcoming) "Platonists and the Teaching of Rhetoric in Late Antiquity," in Clark, S. R., L. Vassilopoulou, and P. Vassilopoulou (eds.), *Epistemology in Late Antique Philosophy*.

Heath, S. (1981) "On Suture," in Heath, S. (ed.), *Questions of Cinema*. London, Macmillan, 76–112.

Hellegouarc'h, J. (1963) *Le vocabulaire latin des relations et des partis politiques sous la République*. Paris, Les Belles Lettres.

Henderson, J. (forthcoming) "Tales of the Unexpurgated (*Cert PG*): Seneca's Audionasties (*Controversiae* 2.5, 10.4)," in Gale, M. and D. Scourfield (eds.), *Texts and Violence in the Roman World*. Cambridge University Press.

Herzfeld, M. (1985) *The Poetics of Manhood: Contest and Identity in a Cretan Mountain Village*. Princeton University Press.

Hesk, J. (1999) "The Rhetoric of Anti-Rhetoric in Athenian Oratory," in Goldhill and Osborne (eds.), 201–30.

(2000) *Deception and Democracy in Classical Athens*. Cambridge University Press.

(2006) "Homeric Flyting and How to Read It: Performance and Intratext in *Iliad* 20.83–109 and 20.178–258." *Ramus* 35, 4–28.

Hesse, D. D. (1992) "Aristotle's *Poetics* and *Rhetoric*: Narrative as Rhetoric's Fourth Mode," in Andrews, R. (ed.), *Rebirth of Rhetoric: Essays in Language, Culture, and Education*. London, Routledge, 19–38.

Hubbard, T. K. (1991) *The Mask of Comedy: Aristophanes and the Intertextual Parabasis*. Ithaca, Cornell University Press.

(1997) "Utopianism and the Sophistic City in Aristophanes," in Dobrov, G. W. (ed.), *The City as Comedy: Society and Representation in Athenian Drama*. Chapel Hill, University of North Carolina Press, 23–49.

Hunter, G. K. (1962) *John Lyly, the Humanist as Courtier*. London, Routledge & Kegan Paul.

Hunter, V. (1990) "Gossip and the Politics of Reputation in Classical Athens." *Phoenix* 44.4, 299–325.

Jakobson, R. and M. Halle (1956) *Fundamentals of Language*. The Hague, Mouton.

Janko, R. (2000) *Philodemus: On Poems, Book 1. Introduction, Translation, and Commentary*. Oxford University Press.

Jex-Blake, K., E. Sellers, and H. L. Urlichs (1896) *The Elder Pliny's Chapters on the History of Art*. Rpt. Chicago: Ares., 1976 edn., London, Macmillan.

Johnstone, S. (1999) *Disputes and Democracy: The Consequences of Litigation in Ancient Athens*. Austin, University of Texas Press.

Jost, W. and W. Olmsted (2004) *A Companion to Rhetoric and Rhetorical Criticism*. London, Blackwell.

Kahn, C. H. (1979) *The Art and Thought of Heraclitus: An Edition of the Fragments with Translation and Commentary*. Cambridge University Press.

Kant, I. (1951) *Critique of Judgement*. New York, Hafner.

Karp, A. J. (1977) "Homeric Origins of Ancient Rhetoric." *Arethusa* 10, 237–58.

Kaster, R. A. (1988) *Guardians of Language: The Grammarian and Society in Late Antiquity*. Berkeley, University of California Press.

(1998) "Becoming 'Cicero,'" in Knox, P. E., C. Foss, and W. V. Clausen (eds.), *Style and Tradition: Studies in Honor of Wendell Clausen*. Stuttgart, Teubner, 248–63.

(2001) "Controlling Reason: Declamation in Rhetorical Education," in Too, Y. L. (ed.), *Education in Greek and Roman Antiquity*. Leiden, Brill, 317–37.

Kennedy, G. A. (1957) "The Ancient Dispute over Rhetoric in Homer." *American Journal of Philology* 78, 23–35.

(1963) *The Art of Persuasion in Greece*. Princeton University Press.

(1968) "The Rhetoric of Advocacy in Greece and Rome." *American Journal of Philology* 89, 419–36.

(1969) *Quintilian*. New York, Twayne Publishers.

(1972) *The Art of Rhetoric in the Roman World, 300 BC–AD 300*. Princeton University Press.

(1980) *Classical Rhetoric and its Christian and Secular Tradition from Ancient to Modern Times*. Chapel Hill, University of North Carolina Press.

(1983) *Greek Rhetoric under Christian Emperors*. Princeton University Press.

(1984) *New Testament Interpretation through Rhetorical Criticism*. Chapel Hill, University of North Carolina Press.

(1994) *A New History of Classical Rhetoric*. Princeton University Press.

(2007) *Aristotle. On Rhetoric: A Theory of Civic Discourse*. 2nd edn., New York, Oxford University Press.

Kinneavy, J. L. (1987) *Greek Rhetorical Origins of Christian Faith: An Inquiry*. New York, Oxford University Press.

Kirk, G. S., J. E. Raven, and M. Schofield (1983) *The Presocratic Philosophers: A Critical History with a Selection of Texts*. 2nd edn., Cambridge University Press.

Konstan, D. (1996) "Friendship, Frankness and Flattery," in Fitzgerald, J. T. (ed.), *Friendship, Flattery, and Frankness of Speech: Studies on Friendship in the New Testament World*. Leiden, Brill, 7–19.

(2001) *Pity Transformed*. London, Duckworth.

Kristeller, P. O. (1979) *Renaissance Thought and its Sources*. New York, Columbia University Press.

Krostenko, B. (2004) "Binary Phrases and the Middle Style as Social Code: *Rhetorica ad Herennium*." *Harvard Studies in Classical Philology* 102, 236–74.

Kurke, L. (1991) *The Traffic in Praise: Pindar and the Poetics of Social Economy*. Ithaca, Cornell University Press.

(1999) *Coins, Bodies, Games, and Gold: The Politics of Meaning in Archaic Greece*. Princeton University Press.

Kustas, G. L. (1973) *Studies in Byzantine Rhetoric*. Thessalonike, Patriarchikon Hidryma Paterikon.

Lacan, J. (2006) *The Other Side of Psychoanalysis*. New York, Norton.

Laclau, E. (1988) "Metaphor and Social Antagonisms," in Nelson, C. and L. Grossberg (eds.), *Marxism and the Interpretation of Culture*. Urbana, University of Illinois Press, 249–57.

Laclau, E. and C. Mouffe (1985) *Hegemony and Socialist Strategy: Towards a Radical Democratic Politics*. London, Verso.

Lausberg, H. (1998) *Handbook of Literary Rhetoric: A Foundation for Literary Study*. Leiden, Brill.

Leeman, A. D. (1963) *Orationis Ratio: The Stylistic Theories and Practice of the Roman Orators, Historians and Philosophers.* Amsterdam, Hakkert.

(1982) "The Technique of Persuasion in Cicero's *Pro Murena,*" in Ludwig, W. (ed.), *Éloquence et rhétorique chez Cicéron.* Geneva, Fondation Hardt, 193–228.

Levene, D. S. (1997) "God and Man in the Classical Latin Panegyric." *Proceedings of the Cambridge Philological Society* 43, 66–103.

Lintott, A. W. (1999) *The Constitution of the Roman Republic.* Oxford, Clarendon Press.

Livingstone, N. (1998) "The Voice of Isocrates and the Dissemination of Cultural Power," in Too and Livingstone (eds.), 263–81.

(2007) "Writing Politics: Isocrates' Rhetoric of Philosophy." *Rhetorica* 25.1, 15–34.

Lloyd, M. (1992) *The Agon in Euripides.* Oxford University Press.

Long, A. A. and D. N. Sedley (1987) *The Hellenistic Philosophers.* Cambridge University Press.

Loraux, N. (1986a) *The Invention of Athens: The Funeral Oration in the Classical City,* trans. A. Sheridan. Cambridge, MA, Harvard University Press.

(1986b) "Thucydide a écrit la Guerre du Péloponnèse." *Métis* 1, 139–61.

Ma, J. (1996) "Public Speech and Community in the Euboicus," in Swain (ed.), 108–24.

MacDowell, D. M. (1990) *Demosthenes: Against Meidias.* Oxford, Clarendon Press.

Mack, B. L. (1990) *Rhetoric and the New Testament.* Minneapolis, Fortress Press.

Mack, B. L. and V. K. Robbins (1989) *Patterns of Persuasion in the Gospels.* Sonoma, Polebridge Press.

Mack, P. (1993) *Renaissance Argument: Valla and Agricola in the Traditions of Rhetoric and Dialectic.* Leiden, Brill.

(1998a) "Aristotle's Rhetoric and Northern Humanist Textbooks," in Dahan, G. and I. Rosier-Catach (eds.), *La Rhétorique d'Aristote: traditions et commentaires de l'antiquité au XVIIe siècle.* Paris, J. Vrin, 299–313.

(1998b) "Ramus Reading." *Journal of the Warburg and Courtauld Institutes* 61, 111–41.

(2002) *Elizabethan Rhetoric: Theory and Practice.* Cambridge University Press.

(2005) "Vives's *de Ratione Dicendi*: Structure, Innovations, Problems." *Rhetorica* 23, 65–92.

Mackie, C. J. (2004) *Oral Performance and its Context.* Leiden, Brill.

Marks, J. (2005) "The Ongoing *Neikos*: Thersites, Odysseus, and Achilles." *American Journal of Philology* 126, 1–31.

Marrou, H. I. (1956) *A History of Education in Antiquity.* New York, Sheed and Ward.

Martin, R. (1984) "Hesiod, Odysseus, and the Instruction of Princes." *Transactions of the American Philological Association* 114, 29–48.

(1989) *The Language of Heroes: Speech and Performance in the Iliad.* Ithaca, Cornell University Press.

Mastronarde, D. (1986) "The Optimistic Rationalist in Euripides: Theseus, Jocasta, Teiresias," in Cropp, M., E. Fantham, and S. E. Scully (eds.), *Greek Tragedy and its Legacy: Essays Presented to D. J. Conacher.* University of Calgary Press, 201–11.

May, J. (1988) *Trials of Character: The Eloquence of Ciceronian Ethos.* Chapel Hill, University of North Carolina Press.

May, J. and J. Wisse (2001) *Cicero: On the Ideal Orator.* New York, Oxford University Press.

McGlew, J. F. (2002) *Citizens on Stage: Comedy and Political Culture in the Athenian Democracy.* Ann Arbor, University of Michigan Press.

McGushin, P. (1977) *C. Sallustius Crispus, Bellum Catilinae: A Commentary.* Lugduni Batavorum, Brill.

Meerhoff, K. (2001) *Entre logique et littérature: autour de Philippe Melanchthon.* Paris, J. Vrin.

Miller, J. -A. (1977) "Suture (Elements of the Logic of the Signifier)." *Screen* 18.4, 24–34.

Mirhady, D. C. (1994) "Aristotle, the *Rhetorica ad Alexandrum* and the *Tria Genera Causarum*," in Fortenbaugh, W. W. and D. C. Mirhady (eds.), *Peripatetic Rhetoric after Aristotle.* New Brunswick, Transaction Publishers, 54–65.

Mitchell, M. M. (2006) "The Emergence of the Written Record," in Mitchell, M. M., F. M. Young, and K. S. Bowie (eds.), *Cambridge History of Christianity*, volume I: *Origins to Constantine.* Cambridge University Press, 177–94.

Mitchell, T. N. (1979) *Cicero, the Ascending Years.* New Haven, Yale University Press.
  (1991) *Cicero, the Senior Statesman.* New Haven, Yale University Press.

Moles, J. (1978) "The Career and Conversion of Dio Chrysostom." *Journal of Hellenic Studies* 98, 79–100.

Monfasani, J. (1988) "Humanism and Rhetoric," in Rabil, A. (ed.), *Renaissance Humanism: Foundations, Forms, and Legacy.* 3 vols. Philadelphia, University of Pennsylvania Press, volume III: 171–235.

Monoson, S. (1994) "Frank Speech, Democracy, and Philosophy: Plato's Debt to a Democratic Strategy of Civic Discourse," in Euben, J. P., J. R. Wallach, and J. Ober (eds.), *Athenian Political Thought and the Reconstruction of American Democracy.* Ithaca, Cornell University Press, 172–97.

Morales, H. (2004) *Vision and Narrative in Achilles Tatius'* Leucippe and Clitophon. New York, Cambridge University Press.

Morgan, K. (2004) "The Education of Athens: Politics and Rhetoric in Isocrates and Plato," in Poulakos, T. and D. J. Depew (eds.), *Isocrates and Civic Education.* Austin, University of Texas Press, 126–54.

Morgan, T. (1998a) *Literate Education in the Hellenistic and Roman Worlds.* Cambridge University Press.
  (1998b) "A Good Man Skilled in Politics: Quintilian's Political Theory," in Too and Livingstone (eds.), 245–62.

Morris, I. (1996) "The Strong Principle of Equality and the Archaic Origins of Greek Democracy," in Ober, J. and C. W. Hedrick (eds.), *Dēmokratia: A Conversation on Democracies, Ancient and Modern.* Princeton University Press.

Morstein-Marx, R. (2004) *Mass Oratory and Political Power in the Late Roman Republic.* Cambridge University Press.

Mosellanus (1573) *Tabulae de Schematibus et Tropis.* London, John Kingston.

Nagy, G. (1979) *The Best of the Achaeans: Concepts of the Hero in Archaic Greek Poetry.* Baltimore, Johns Hopkins University Press.

Nietzsche, F. W. (1989) "Ancient Rhetoric," in Gilman, S. L., C. Blair, and D. J. Parent (eds.), *Friedrich Nietzsche on Rhetoric and Language.* New York, Oxford University Press, 2–193.

Nightingale, A.W. (1995) *Genres in Dialogue: Plato and the Construct of Philosophy*. Cambridge University Press.

Nippel, W. (1995) *Public Order in Ancient Rome*. Cambridge University Press.

Norden, E. (1915) *Die Antike Kunstprosa vom VI Jahrhundert v. Chr. Bis in die Zeit der Renaissance*. Leipzig, Teubner.

Ober, J. (1989a) *Mass and Elite in Democratic Athens: Rhetoric, Ideology, and the Power of the People*. Princeton University Press.

(1989b) "The Nature of Athenian Democracy." *Classical Philology* 84, 322–34.

(1998) *Political Dissent in Democratic Athens: Intellectual Critics of Popular Rule*. Princeton University Press.

(2001) "The Debate over Civic Education in Classical Athens," in Too, Y. L. (ed.), *Education in Greek and Roman Antiquity*. Leiden, Brill, 175–207.

Ober, J. and B. Strauss (1990) "Drama, Political Rhetoric, and the Discourse of Athenian Democracy," in Winkler, J. J. and F. I. Zeitlin (eds.), *Nothing to Do with Dionysos?: Athenian Drama in its Social Context*. Princeton University Press, 237–70.

Ong, W. J. (1982) *Orality and Literacy: The Technologizing of the Word*. London, Methuen.

Ostwald, M. (1986) *From Popular Sovereignty to the Sovereignty of Law: Law, Society, and Politics in Fifth-Century Athens*. Berkeley, University of California Press.

Overbeck, J. A. (1868) *Die Antiken Schriftquellen zur Geschichte der Bildenden Künste bei den Griechen*. Leipzig, W. Engelmann.

Parks, W. (1990) *Verbal Dueling in Heroic Narrative: The Homeric and Old English Traditions*. Princeton University Press.

Parry, A. (1964) "The Language of Achilles," in Kirk, G. S. (ed.), *The Language and Background of Homer; Some Recent Studies and Controversies*. Cambridge, W. Heffer, 49–54.

Paterson, J. (2004) "Self-Reference in Cicero's Forensic Speeches," in Powell, J. G. F. and J. Paterson (eds.), *Cicero the Advocate*. Oxford University Press, 79–95.

Pelling, C. (2005) "Tragedy, Rhetoric, and Performance Culture," in Gregory, J. (ed.), *A Companion to Greek Tragedy*. Malden, Blackwell, 83–102.

Penner, T. (2003) "Reconfiguring the Rhetorical Study of Acts: Reflections on the Method in and Learning of a Progymnastic Poetics." *Perspectives in Religious Studies* 30, 425–39.

Perelman, C. (1979) *The New Rhetoric and the Humanities: Essays on Rhetoric and its Applications*. Dordrecht, D. Reidel.

Phillips, M. M. (1964) *The Adages of Erasmus*. Cambridge University Press.

Pickard-Cambridge, A. W. (1968) *The Dramatic Festivals of Athens*. 2nd edn., London, Oxford University Press.

Pollitt, J. J. (1974) *The Ancient View of Greek Art: Criticism, History, and Terminology*. New Haven, Yale University Press.

Porter, J. I. (1993) "The Seductions of Gorgias." *Classical Quarterly* 12.2, 267–99.

(2001) "Des sons qu'on ne peut entendre: Cicéron, les 'Kritikoi' et la tradition du sublime dans la critique littéraire," in Auvray-Assayas, C. and D. Delattre (eds.), *Cicéron et Philodème: la polémique en philosophie*. Paris, Rue d'Ulm, 315–41.

(2006) "Feeling Classical: Classicism and Ancient Literary Criticism," in Porter, J. I. (ed.), *Classical Pasts: The Classical Traditions of Greece and Rome*. Princeton University Press, 301–52.

(forthcoming) *The Origins of Aesthetic Inquiry in Antiquity: Matter, Experience and the Sublime*. Cambridge, Cambridge University Press.

Porter, S. E. (1997) *Handbook of Classical Rhetoric in the Hellenistic Period, 330 BC–AD 400*. Leiden, Brill.

Poulakos, T. (1993) "Terms for Sophistical Rhetoric," in Poulakos, T. (ed.), *Rethinking the History of Rhetoric: Multidisciplinary Essays on the Rhetorical Tradition*. Boulder, Westview Press, 53–74.

(1997) *Speaking for the Polis: Isocrates Rhetorical Education*. Columbia, University of South Carolina Press.

(2004) "Isocrates' Civic Education and the Question of *Doxa*," in Poulakos, T. and D. J. Depew (eds.), *Isocrates and Civic Education*. Austin, University of Texas Press, 44–68.

Pratt, L. H. (1993) *Lying and Poetry from Homer to Pindar: Falsehood and Deception in Archaic Greek Poetics*. Ann Arbor, University of Michigan Press.

Pucci, P. (1987) *Odysseus Polutropos: Intertextual Readings in the Odyssey and the Iliad*. Ithaca, Cornell University Press.

(1998) *The Song of the Sirens*. Lanham, Rowman & Littlefield.

Puech, B. (2002) *Orateurs et sophistes grecs dans les inscriptions d'époque impériale*. Paris, Librairie philosophique J. Vrin.

Raaflaub, K. A. (2004) *The Discovery of Freedom in Ancient Greece*. 1st English edn., rev. and updated from the German edn., University of Chicago Press.

Radermacher, L. (1951) *Artium Scriptores (Reste der Voraristotelischen Rhetorik)*. Vienna, In Kommission bei R. M. Rohrer.

Rapp, C. (2002) "Aristotle's *Rhetoric*," in Zalta, E. N. (ed.), *The Stanford Encyclopedia of Philosophy*. Summer 2002 edn., Stanford, Center for the Study of Language and Information, http://plato.stanford.edu/archives/sum2002/entries/aristotle-rhetoric/.

Rees, R. D. (2001) "To Be and Not To Be; Pliny's Paradoxical Trajan." *Bulletin of the Institute of Classical Studies* 45, 149–68.

(2007) "Latin Panegyric," in Dominik, W. and J. Hall (eds.), 136–48.

Regoliosi, M. (1993) *Nel cantiere del valla: elaborazione e montaggio delle "Elegantie."* Roma, Bulzoni.

Reinhardt, T. (2000) "Rhetoric in the Fourth Academy." *Classical Quarterly* 50, 531–47.

(2003) *Marcus Tullius Cicero: Topica*. Oxford University Press.

Reynolds, L. D. and N. G. Wilson (1991) *Scribes and Scholars: A Guide to the Transmission of Greek and Latin Literature*. 3rd edn., Oxford University Press.

Richlin, A. (1997) "Gender and Rhetoric: Producing Manhood in the Schools," in Dominik, W. J. (ed.), *Roman Eloquence: Rhetoric in Society and Literature*. London, Routledge, 90–110.

(1999) "Cicero's Head," in Porter, J. I. (ed.), *Constructions of the Classical Body*. Ann Arbor, University of Michigan Press, 190–211.

Riedweg, C. (2005) *Pythagoras: His Life, Teaching, and Influence*. Ithaca, Cornell University Press.

Riggsby, A. M. (1999) *Crime and Community in Ciceronian Rome*. Austin, University of Texas Press.

(2004) "The Rhetoric of Character in the Roman Courts," in Powell, J. G. F. and J. Paterson (eds.), *Cicero the Advocate*. Oxford University Press, 165–85.

Robbins, V. K. (1991) "Writing as a Rhetorical Act in Plutarch and the Gospels," in Watson, D. F. (ed.), *Persuasive Artistry: Studies in New Testament Rhetoric in Honor of George A. Kennedy*. Sheffield Academic Press, 142–68.

(1996) *The Tapestry of Early Christian Discourse: Rhetoric, Society, and Ideology.* London, Routledge.

Roisman, J. (2005) *The Rhetoric of Manhood: Masculinity in the Attic Orators.* Berkeley, University of California Press.

Rose, P. (1988) "Thersites and the Plural Voices of Homer." *Arethusa* 21.1, 5–25.

(1992) *Sons of the Gods, Children of Earth: Ideology and Literary Form in Ancient Greece.* Ithaca, Cornell University Press.

(1995) "Cicero and the Rhetoric of Imperialism: Putting the Politics back into Political Rhetoric." *Rhetorica* 13, 359–99.

Rosenbloom, D. (1993) "Shouting 'Fire' in a Crowded Theater: Phrynichos's *Capture of Miletos* and the Politics of Fear in Early Attic Tragedy." *Philologus* 137, 159–96.

(2002) "From *Ponēros* to *Pharmakos*: Theater, Social Drama, and Revolution in Athens, 428–404 BCE." *Classical Antiquity* 21, 283–346.

(2004a) "*Ponēroi* vs. *Chrēstoi*: The Ostracism of Hyperbolos and the Struggle for Hegemony in Athens after the Death of Perikles, Part I." *Transactions of the American Philological Association* 134, 55–105.

(2004b) "*Ponēroi* vs. *Chrēstoi*: The Ostracism of Hyperbolos and the Struggle for Hegemony in Athens after the Death of Perikles, Part II." *Transactions of the American Philological Association* 134, 323–58.

Rubinstein, L. (2005) "Differentiated Rhetorical Strategies in Athenian Courts," in Gagarin, M. and D. Cohen (eds.), *The Cambridge Companion to Ancient Greek Law.* Cambridge University Press, 129–45.

Ryan, M. (1989) *Politics and Culture: Working Hypotheses for a Post-Revolutionary Society.* Baltimore, Johns Hopkins University Press.

Sabbadini, R. (1885) *Storia del Ciceronianismo e di altre questioni letterarie nell' età della Rinascenza.* Torino, E. Loescher.

Saxonhouse, A. W. (2006) *Free Speech and Democracy in Ancient Athens.* Cambridge University Press.

Schechner, R. (1985) *Between Theater and Anthropology.* Philadelphia, University of Pennsylvania Press.

Schiappa, E. (1999) *The Beginnings of Rhetorical Theory in Classical Greece.* New Haven, Yale University Press.

Schmitz, T. (1997) *Bildung und Macht: Zur sozialen und politischen Funktion der Zweiten Sophistik in der griechischen Welt der Kaiserzeit.* Munich, Verlag C. H. Beck.

Schnabel, E. J. (2004) *Early Christian Mission.* Downers Grove, InterVarsity Press.

Schofield, M. (1995) "Cicero's Definition of Res Publica," in Powell, J. G. F. (ed.), *Cicero the Philosopher: Twelve Papers.* Oxford, Clarendon Press, 63–83.

Schütrumpf, E. (1988) "Platonic Elements in the Structure of Cicero *de Oratore* Book I." *Rhetorica* 6, 237–58.

(1994) "Non-Logical Means of Persuasion in Aristotle's *Rhetoric* and Cicero's *de Oratore*," in Fortenbaugh, W. W. and D. C. Mirhady (eds.), *Peripatetic Rhetoric after Aristotle.* New Brunswick, Transaction Publishers.

Seel, O. (1977) *Quintilian: Oder, die Kunst des Redens und Schweigens.* Stuttgart, Klett-Cotta.

Seibel, A. (1995) "Widerstreit und Ergänzung: Thersites und Odysseus als rivalisierende Demagogen in der Ilias (B 190–264)." *Hermes* 123, 385–97.

Sidebottom, H. (1996) "Dio of Prusa and the Flavian Dynasty." *Classical Quarterly* 46, 447–56.

Silverman, K. (1983) *The Subject of Semiotics.* New York, Oxford University Press.

Simons, H. W. (2004) "The Rhetorical Legacy of Kenneth Burke," in Jost and Olmsted (eds.), 152–67.

Sinclair, R. K. (1988) *Democracy and Participation in Athens.* Cambridge University Press.

Sluiter, I. and R. M. Rosen (eds.) (2004) *Free Speech in Classical Antiquity.* Leiden, Brill.

Small, J. P. (1997) *Wax Tablets of the Mind: Cognitive Studies of Memory and Literacy in Classical Antiquity.* London, Routledge.

Solmsen, F. (1941) "The Aristotelian Tradition in Ancient Rhetoric." *American Journal of Philology* 62, 35–50.

  (1954) "The 'Gift' of Speech in Homer and Hesiod." *Transactions of the American Philological Association* 85, 1–15.

Sommerstein, A. (1996) "How to Avoid Being a *Komodoumenos.*" *Classical Quarterly* 46, 327–56.

Spivak, G. (1994) "Can the Subaltern Speak?," in Williams, P. and L. Chrisman (eds.), *Colonial Discourse and Post-Colonial Theory: A Reader.* New York, Columbia University Press, 66–111.

Stangl, T. (1964) *Ciceronis Orationum Scholiastae.* Hildesheim, G. Olms.

Steel, C. (2005) *Reading Cicero: Genre and Performance in Late Republican Rome.* London, Duckworth.

  (2006) *Roman Oratory.* Cambridge University Press.

Steiner, D. (2001) "Slander's Bite: *Nemean* 7.102–5 and the Language of Invective." *Journal of Hellenic Studies* 120, 154–58.

Stewart, S. (2005) *The Open Studio: Essays on Art and Aesthetics.* University of Chicago Press.

Stewart-Sykes, A. (2001) *From Prophecy to Preaching: A Search for the Origins of the Christian Homily.* Leiden, Brill.

Strasburger, H. (1956) *Concordia Ordinum: Eine Untersuchung zur Politik Ciceros.* Amsterdam, A. M. Hakkert.

Svenbro, J. (1976) *La parole et le marbre: aux origines de la poétique grecque.* Lund, [s. n.].

Swain, S. (1996) *Hellenism and Empire: Language, Classicism, and Power in the Greek World,* AD *50–250.* Oxford University Press.

  (ed.) (2000) *Dio Chrysostom: Politics, Letters, and Philosophy.* Oxford University Press.

Talon, O. (1548) *Rhetorica.* Paris, M. David.

Tatum, W. J. (1999) *The Patrician Tribune: Publius Clodius Pulcher.* Chapel Hill, The University of North Carolina Press.

Thalmann, W. G. (1988) "Thersites: Comedy, Scapegoats, and Heroic Ideology in the *Iliad.*" *Transactions of the American Philological Association* 118, 1–28.

Todd, S. C. (1993) *The Shape of Athenian Law.* Oxford, Clarendon Press.

Too, Y.L. (1995) *The Rhetoric of Identity in Isocrates: Text, Power, Pedagogy.* Cambridge University Press.

Too, Y.L. and N. Livingstone (eds.) (1998) *Pedagogy and Power: Rhetorics of Classical Learning.* Cambridge University Press.

Toohey, P. (1994) "Epic and Rhetoric," in Worthington (ed.), 153–75.

Usher, S. (1999) *Greek Oratory: Tradition and Originality.* New York, Oxford University Press.

Valesio, P. (1980) *Novantiqua: Rhetorics as a Contemporary Theory.* Bloomington, Indiana University Press.

Valla, L. (1962) *Opera Omnia*, ed. Garin, E., reprint of the Basel 1540 edn., Torino, Bottega d'Erasmo.

van der Poel, M. (1997) "The Scholia in Orationem Pro Lege Manilia of Rudolph Agricola." *Lias* 24, 1–35.

van Nijf, O. (2001) "Local Heroes: Athletics, Festivals and Elite Self-Fashioning in the Roman East," in Goldhill (ed.), 306–34.

van Ophuijsen, J.M. (1994) "Where Have the Topics Gone?," in Fortenbaugh, W.W. and D.C. Mirhady (eds.), *Peripatetic Rhetoric after Aristotle.* New Brunswick, Transaction Publishers, 130–73.

Vasaly, A. (1993) *Representations: Images of the World in Ciceronian Oratory.* Berkeley, University of California Press.

Veyne, P. (1976) *Le pain et le cirque: sociologie historique d'un pluralisme politique.* Paris, Seuil.

Vickers, B. (1988) *In Defence of Rhetoric.* Oxford University Press.

Vitanza, V. (1993) "Some Rudiments of Histories of Rhetorics and Rhetorics of Histories," in Poulakos, T. (ed.), *Rethinking the History of Rhetoric: Multidisciplinary Essays on the Rhetorical Tradition.* Boulder, Westview Press, 193–239.

Vives, J.L. (1882a) *Opera Omnia*, volume II. Valencia, B. Monfort.

(1882b) *Opera Omnia*, volume 6. Valencia, B. Monfort.

Von Reden, S. and S. Goldhill (1999) "Plato and the Performance of Dialogue," in Goldhill and Osborne (eds.), 257–92.

Wallace, R.W. (1997) "Poet, Public, and 'Theatrocracy': Audience Performance in Classical Athens," in Edmunds, L. and R.W. Wallace (eds.), *Poet, Public, and Performance in Ancient Greece.* Baltimore, Johns Hopkins University Press, 97–111.

(2004) "The Power to Speak – and Not to Listen – in Ancient Athens," in Sluiter and Rosen (eds.), 221–32.

Walsh, G.B. (1984) *The Varieties of Enchantment: Early Greek Views of the Nature and Function of Poetry.* Chapel Hill, University of North Carolina Press.

Ward, J.O. (1995) *Ciceronian Rhetoric in Treatise, Scholion, and Commentary.* Turnhout, Belgium, Brepols.

Wardy, R. (1996) *The Birth of Rhetoric: Gorgias, Plato, and their Successors.* London, Routledge.

Webb, R. (2001) "The Progymnasmata as Practice," in Too, Y.L. (ed.), *Education in Greek and Roman Antiquity.* Leiden, Brill, 289–316.

Welch, K.E. (1990) *The Contemporary Reception of Classical Rhetoric: Appropriations of Ancient Discourse.* Hillsdale, L. Erlbaum.

(1999) *Electric Rhetoric: Classical Rhetoric, Oralism, and a New Literacy.* Cambridge, MIT Press.

West, M. L. (1966) *Hesiod: Theogony.* Oxford, Clarendon Press.

White, H. V. (1973) *Metahistory: The Historical Imagination in Nineteenth-Century Europe.* Baltimore, Johns Hopkins University Press.

(1989) "The Rhetoric of Interpretation," in Hernadi, P. (ed.), *The Rhetoric of Interpretation and the Interpretation of Rhetoric.* Durham, Duke University Press, 1–22.

Whitman, C. H. (1964) *Aristophanes and the Comic Hero.* Cambridge, MA, Harvard University Press.

Whitmarsh, T. (1998) "Reading Power in Roman Greece: The *Paideia* of Dio Chrysostom," in Too and Livingstone (eds.), 192–213.

(2001a) "'Greece is the World': Exile and Identity in the Second Sophistic," in Goldhill (ed.), 269–305.

(2001b) *Greek Literature and the Roman Empire: The Politics of Imitation.* Oxford University Press.

(2006) "Quickening the Classics: The Politics of Prose in Roman Greece," in Porter, J. I. (ed.), *Classical Pasts: The Classical Traditions of Greece and Rome.* Princeton University Press, 353–74.

Williams, G. D. (2003) *Seneca: De Otio. De Brevitate Vitae.* Cambridge University Press.

Wills, L. M. (1984) "The Form of the Sermon in Hellenistic Judaism and Early Christianity." *Harvard Theological Review* 77, 277–99.

Wilson, P. (1991) "Demosthenes 21 (*Against Meidias*): Democratic Abuse." *Proceedings of the Cambridge Philological Society* 37, 164–95.

Wingrove, E. (1999) "Interpellating Sex." *Signs* 24, 869–93.

Winkler, J. J. (1990) "Laying Down the Law: The Oversight of Men's Sexual Behavior in Classical Athens," in Halperin, D. M., J. J. Winkler, and F. I. Zeitlin (eds.), *Before Sexuality: The Construction of Erotic Experience in the Ancient Greek World.* Princeton University Press, 171–209.

Winter, B. W. (2002) *Philo and Paul among the Sophists: Alexandrian and Corinthian Responses to a Julio-Claudian Movement.* 2nd edn., Grand Rapids, W. B. Eerdmans.

Winterbottom, M. (1995) "On Impulse," in Innes, D., H. M. Hine, and C. B. R. Pelling (eds.), *Ethics and Rhetoric: Classical Essays for Donald Russell on his Seventy-Fifth Birthday.* Oxford, Clarendon Press, 313–22.

(2002) "Believing the *Pro Marcello*," in Damon, C. *et al.* (eds.), *Vertis in Usum: Studies in Honor of Edward Courtney.* Munich, Saur, 24–38.

Wirszubski, C. (1960) *Libertas as a Political Idea at Rome during the Late Republic and Early Principate.* Cambridge University Press.

Wiseman, T. P. (1995) *Remus: A Roman Myth.* Cambridge University Press.

Wisse, J. (1989) *Ethos and Pathos: From Aristotle to Cicero.* Amsterdam, Hakkert.

Wohl, V. (2002) *Love among the Ruins: The Erotics of Democracy in Classical Athens.* Princeton University Press.

Wood, N. (1988) *Cicero's Social and Political Thought.* Berkeley, University of California Press.

Woolf, G. (1994) "Becoming Roman, Staying Greek: Culture, Identity and the Civilizing Process in the Roman East." *Proceedings of the Cambridge Philological Society* 40, 116–43.

Wooten, C. W. (1983) *Cicero's* Philippics *and their Demosthenic Model: The Rhetoric of Crisis*. Chapel Hill, University of North Carolina Press.

Worman, N. (1999) "Odysseus Panourgos: The Liar's Style in Oratory and Tragedy." *Helios* 26.1, 35–68.

(2002) *The Cast of Character: Style in Greek Literature*. Austin, University of Texas Press.

(2004) "Insult and Oral Excess in the Disputes between Aeschines and Demosthenes." *American Journal of Philology* 125, 1–25.

(2008) *Abusive Mouths in Classical Athens*. Cambridge University Press.

Wörrle, M. (1988) *Stadt und Fest im Kaiserzeitlichen Kleinasien: Studien zu einer Agonistischen Stiftung aus Oinoanda*. Munich, C. H. Beck.

Worthington, I. (ed.) (1994) *Persuasion: Greek Rhetoric in Action*. London, Routledge.

(1996) *Voice into Text: Orality and Literacy in Ancient Greece*. Leiden, E. J. Brill.

(2007) *A Companion to Greek Rhetoric*. Malden, Blackwell.

Worthington, I. and J. M. Foley (eds.) (2002) *Epea and Grammata: Oral and Written Communication in Ancient Greece*. Leiden, Brill.

Young, I. M. (2000) *Inclusion and Democracy*. Oxford University Press.

Yunis, H. (1996) *Taming Democracy: Models of Political Rhetoric in Classical Athens*. Ithaca, Cornell University Press.

Zanker, G. (1981) "Enargeia in the Ancient Criticism of Poetry." *Rheinisches Museum* 124, 297–311.

Zeitlin, F. I. (2001) "Visions and Revisions of Homer," in Goldhill (ed.), 195–266.

Zundel, E. (1981) *Lehrstil und Rhetorischer Stil in Quintilians Institutio Oratoria: Untersuchungen zur Form eines Lehrbuchs*. Frankfurt/Main, Haag & Herchen.

INDEX OF PASSAGES

1.56 137
1.87 136
1.108 137, 138
1.118–21 137
1.138–45 65
1.145f. 66, 71
1.157 118
1.164 103
1.203 21
1.218 137
1.223 137
1.231 136
2.5 124
2.16–20 118
2.39 117
2.43 64
2.43–71 146
2.63 103
2.77–83 118
2.77–84 66, 67, 138
2.123–24 138
2.130–41 138
2.132 68
2.133 66, 138
2.133–42 66
2.162 66
2.182 148
2.182–83 112
2.307–308 84
2.311f. 67
3.40–41 100
3.41 120
3.41–45 106
3.55 134
3.100 67, 136
3.141 149
3.171 103
3.175 103
3.202–208 88
3.209 89
3.213 86
3.214 137
3.221–23 137
3.222 94
3.337 137
On the Republic 1.39 129
2.56 185
Orator 45 66
55 94
59 135, 136
69 30, 89
77–78 103
78 136

85 185
97 185
149 103
220 103
224 103
Philippics 2.1 191
3.3 191
3.5 191
5.43 191
Topics 85 82
93–95 68
Tusculan Disputations 2.9 67
[Cicero]
Rhetoric to Herennius 1.2 117
1.2f. 65
1.3 117
1.4 83
1.7f. 67
2.47 67
3.16–18 65, 83
3.19 86
3.19–27 65
3.20–22 94
3.20–24 87
3.24–25 87
3.25 87
3.27 87
3.28–40 65
4.1–10 117
4.11–16 182
Cratinus
Fragments 327 201

Demosthenes
Olynthiac 1 1.19–20 149
On the Liberty of the Rhodians
15.35 107
On the Crown 18.28 165
18.122 40
18.139 40
18.170 164
18.173 164
18.180 164
18.197 164
18.219 164
18.259 100
18.276–77 155
18.277–81 164
18.285 99
18.306–13 164
18.313 100
On the False Embassy 19.126 99
19.199 100

INDEX OF SUBJECTS